The ORDEAL of ASSIMILATION:

A Documentary History of the White Working Class

STANLEY FELDSTEIN holds B.S., M.A., and Ph.D. degrees from New York University. He is the author of *Once a Slave: The Slave's View of Slavery* and *The Poisoned Tongue: A Documentary History of American Racism and Prejudice.*

LAWRENCE COSTELLO teaches at Nassau Community College. He received M.A. and Ph.D. degrees from Columbia University, where he did his doctoral dissertation on New York City labor history.

The ORDEAL of ASSIMILATION:

A Documentary History of the White Working Class

Edited by

STANLEY FELDSTEIN

and

LAWRENCE COSTELLO

ANCHOR BOOKS

Anchor Press/Doubleday
Garden City, New York
1974

The Anchor Books edition is the first publication of *The Ordeal of Assimilation: A Documentary History of the White Working Class.*

Library of Congress Cataloging in Publication Data
Feldstein, Stanley, 1937–   comp.
    The ordeal of assimilation: a documentary history of the white working class.
    1. Alien labor—United States—Addresses, essays, lectures. 2. United States—Foreign population—Addresses, essays, lectures. I. Costello, Lawrence, joint comp. II. Title.
HD8081.A5F43   331.6'2
ISBN: 0-385-04876-9
Library of Congress Catalog Card Number 73–16504

Anchor Books edition: 1974
First Edition

5/7/74

Grateful acknowledgment is made for the use of the following material:
    Portions of *The Promised Land* by Mary Antin. Reprinted by permission of the Houghton Mifflin Company.
    "Who Speaks for Ethnic America?" by Barbara Mikulski, from the New York *Times.* Copyright © 1970 by The New York Times Company. Reprinted by permission.
    "The Ethnic Neighborhood: Leave Room for a Boccie Ball" from *Pieces of a Dream: The Ethnic Worker's Crisis with America,* edited by Michael Wenk, S. M. Tomasi and Gene Baroni. Copyright © 1972 by the Center for Migration Studies. Reprinted by permission.
    "Last Stop on the D Train: In the Land of the New Racists" by Leonard Kriegel. Copyright © 1970 by Leonard Kriegel and reprinted by permission of the author.
    "Ozone Park Revisited" by Giulio E. Miranda. Printed by permission of the author.
    Material prepared by The American Jewish Committee, National Project on Ethnic America, and reprinted by permission.
    Material prepared by Nancy Seifer, Director of Community Relations, National Project on Ethnic America, and reprinted by permission.

ACKNOWLEDGMENTS

In the course of researching and editing this collection, we incurred numerous debts and obligations. Librarians, colleagues and friends were most generous with their time, advice and encouragement. Chiefly, our indebtedness to Professor Leonard Kriegel of the City College of New York is great. His unique understanding and familiarity with the material in this book and his suggestions on its organization were essential to the study.

We would also like to thank Irving Levine, Judith Herman and Nancy Seifer of the National Project on Ethnic America for contributing so much time, insight and material. Hopefully, the manuscript will further the work they are doing in the areas of ethnic awareness and ethnic studies. We are also grateful to Loretta Barrett and Mary Ellen Travis of Doubleday & Company for the confidence they have shown in us and for their excellent editorial assistance. And to James Reisman, our appreciation for the lessons he gave us in copyright law.

Lastly, we wish to pay tribute to several people who have made our task so much easier: Joe and Bertha Kutner who gave so much of their time while describing the life-style and aspirations of the ethnic working-class family; Virginia Caridi and Ruth Fried for typing and proofreading the book; and a special thanks to Mr. Leonard Leibowitz, who shared with us his experiences as a labor attorney and his insights into the workings of the American labor movement.

The research for this study was facilitated by many libraries. We are particularly grateful to the staffs of the Columbia University Library, the New York Public Library, the Brooklyn Public Library, the Library of Congress, the New York University Library, the New York Historical Society, the Chicago Public Library, the Chicago Historical Society and the Nassau County Community College Library.

August 1973   Stanley Feldstein
                                                       Lawrence Costello

*In memory of
Moe Feldstein
and Morris Rahinsky
and for Evelyn Costello*

Contents

Introduction

Oscar Handlin, one of the nation's foremost social interpreters, observed pointedly that "immigrants *were* American history." The story of immigrants and their children has been a constantly growing area of research and writing. The way in which these European newcomers, especially in the latter nineteenth and early twentieth century, have affected and been affected by their new environment has comprised an integral part of the nation's history.

Today there is a renewed interest in the story of the immigrant and his succeeding generations of offspring. Many white ethnics are particularly sensitive to what they see as their changing status resulting from the nation's current "social revolution." They hold that the changes taking place have been mainly at their expense. Consequently, in response to the recent proliferation of literature related to the experiences of racial minorities (which has been long overdue), these people insist that their stories be given new emphasis. Mainly from America's white working class, the ethnics seek to have their children and others recognize that the early experiences of their ancestors also were painful; that the life-style of *El Barrio* in New York City's Spanish Harlem had its counterpart in the lives of the European ghetto occupants on Manhattan's Lower East Side in the late nineteenth and early twentieth century.

For many years, immigrant historians concentrated on the contributions that the newcomers made to American life. More recently, they have found inquiry into the ways in which these aliens have been affected by their new environment especially fruitful in understanding the foreign-born's plight in America. The primary objective of this collection is to present material relative to the immigrants' experiences in "uprooting" themselves from their native lands, making the arduous journey to America, trying to establish roots here, facing discrimination and privation, and attempting to adjust to a culture which was totally alien from the one they had left. The results of these experiences had far-reaching effects upon these families and their children.

The newcomers' earliest experiences in America often were traumatic. With memories of their Old World suffering as well as the ordeal of the crossing still fresh in their minds, they faced the threat and difficulty of detention or rejection at the port of debarkation, entrapment by unscrupulous shipping and boardinghouse agents, finding decent lodgings and employment, and adjusting to a very unfamiliar life-style. Further, virulent nativism, sometimes supported by outlandish racial theories, periodically threatened the foreigners, who found they had to keep redefining to themselves the true meaning of Americanism. Nineteenth- and early-twentieth-century immigrants also settled in some of the worst slums in the Western world. They lived in the midst of crime and street gangs and suffered the exploitation that has been the lot of most poverty groups living in large urban areas.

Entering a rapidly expanding but unregulated industrial society with very few means of protecting themselves, these families were among the most abused of the working classes. The exploitation of women and child labor were most prevalent among the foreign-born, and the newcomers suffered severely from the threats of economic insecurity and industrial hazards. Though some skilled immigrant workingmen entered the rising American trade union movement, the larger number of those who were unskilled and semi-skilled were unwelcomed in the craft-union-oriented labor movement well into the twentieth century. Moreover, in many of the nation's bloodiest industrial struggles, such as the Ludlow Massacre of 1914, many of the victims were immigrant workingmen.

The aliens also were constantly under pressure to strip themselves of all aspects of their Old World backgrounds. Furthermore, the advocates of Americanization sought to divest them of their ethnic characteristics and have these new citizens of the republic adopt the customs and language of the predominant culture. While being discriminated against, the foreign-born found themselves in the paradoxical position of being forced to become part of the homogenized mass which was victimizing them. Likewise, the movement for speedy assimilation resulted in severe differences between the immigrants and their American-born children. The older generation sought to retain elements of their native culture while their children, reacting to the Americanization campaigns, often were ashamed of their parents' backgrounds.

As the social revolution of the 1960s unfolded, present-day ethnics envisioned themselves threatened by other minorities—and began to seek reidentification with their own origins. These second- and third-generation hyphenated Americans began to reinvoke the code they had been taught: that through hard work, thrift, respect for authority and patriotism, they would "make it in America." To them, the revolution of the '60s and '70s had changed the "rules of the game" and the change was largely to be at their expense.

Foremost, today's white working-class ethnic wants it known that his ancestors' early experience was not an easy one; that the streets were not paved with gold (as he had been told); and that his story contained striking parallels, of varying degrees, with those of today's oppressed minorities. The newcomers generally lived in the city's worst tenements and were exposed to the ravages of periodic epidemics. They were exploited by absentee slumlords and ruthless employers. The immigrant workingmen often toiled long hours and at very low wages, and many, through no fault of their own, were the victims of serious industrial accidents. The ethnics were one of the first groups to join the unemployed ranks during economic depressions and constantly faced the threat of seasonal layoffs. Their daughters were preyed upon by white slavers, and they saw in the courts a dual system of justice. In addition, these new Americans were the targets of the pseudo-scientific racial theories which became fashionable in intellectual circles at the turn of the twentieth century. Considering all of their trials, it has been apparent that the message of the second- and third-generation offspring has been: whatever progress or success they have achieved, it was due to hard work, struggle and self-sacrifice of both their forebears and themselves.

Nevertheless, *it is very important to note that this study is neither an attempt to justify the attitudes of white working-class ethnics toward today's "third world" Americans, nor an attempt to minimize the problems faced by these groups.* Rather, the anthology is an attempt to explore the historical backgrounds of these particular people in order to discern why they are fast becoming the most alienated group in present-day America. Moreover, the work seeks to appreciate fully what their forebears had to endure and thereby also, hopefully, to understand the parallel plight of today's ghetto peoples.

The book follows both a chronological and topical order with particular regard given to the time sequence. Each part deals with a major topic covering in most cases the entire time period to which the book is devoted. In addition, the parts have subtopics which, in turn, are divided into treatments of specific conditions faced by the ethnics. In the latter areas, there is an attempt to deal with those groups which were most affected by the conditions described. Each of the volume's parts begins with an introduction which presents background material relative to the major topic, enabling the reader to place the documents in their proper historical perspective. To highlight the significance of the selections, a brief explanation precedes each passage. However, in order that the reader be given an opportunity for self-analysis of the readings, in most cases, we have not injected interpretation into the introductions.

The documents presented, selected from a wealth of material, are what we consider representative of the broad range of literature dealing with the adjustment of white ethnics to American society. They comprise both the reflections of the more articulate ethnic figures of the past and present, such as Abraham Cahan, editor of the influential *Jewish Daily Forward,* and Leonard Kriegel, noted critic of present-day ethnic America, as well as those of the less articulate. Among the materials included are selections from newspapers, periodicals, speeches, novels, letters, government publications, laws and contemporary oral accounts. Most of these descriptions are either in the first person or are told by contemporary writers who were witness to the situations treated.

Faced with the vast amount of extant material, we used only those sources which we believed to be most significant and representative for the story. Seeking to avoid writings with which many are familiar, e.g., Upton Sinclair's *The Jungle* (1906), we have attempted to present selections which are not readily accessible or well known. Unfortunately, due to the dictates of space, it was impossible to include numerous other informative sources. Nevertheless, the material presented faithfully represents the feelings, aspirations, thoughts and life-styles of the American ethnic.

Obviously, a complete documentary history of ethnic America cannot be told in a single volume. Each part and its subdivisions could warrant a distinct treatment of its own. Hopefully, the book will shed new light for the reader on the white ethnics' experience and present situation and possibly encourage others to explore further the many facets of the ethnic story either treated or alluded to in this work.

PART I
The Immigrant Experience: Arrival and Adjustment, 1840–1924

INTRODUCTION

During the one hundred years (1830–1930) which spanned America's "old" and "new immigration," the world witnessed the largest movement of people in the history of mankind. It has been estimated that within this period, forty million Europeans made the arduous trip across the Atlantic to settle in the United States.

Although the participants in this uprooting emanated from many geographical locations, practiced different religions, adhered to contrasting cultural traditions, and lived under varied political systems, all came to America for similar reasons, and harbored a universal desire for a happier and more secure future. For the most part, the thread which knit the common goals of these people together was woven from a fabric produced from the political oppression, economic distress, social immobility and religious persecution each group experienced in its respective homeland.

While this massive migration was transplanting millions to these shores, the United States itself was undergoing a vast transition. Due to the constant changes in the nature of American society, and the consequential adjustments immigrants were forced to make in that society, historians have traditionally broken down this time span into distinct historical periods. The most common of these divisions were: (1) Colonial Migration; (2) Unrestricted Immigration; (3) State Regulation; and (4) Federal Control.

The Colonial Era was characterized by an almost total absence of immigration regulations. From the termination of the American Revolution in 1783 until the 1830s, the nation had still not legislated any significant means to control the entry of aliens. Consequently, there existed within these five decades an unrestricted flow of European manpower. The first important measures taken to supervise the transmigration of people to the United States were passed in the early 1830s. Thereafter, from 1830–82, the regulation of immigration was undertaken by the various states. Finally, in 1882, due to the growing complexities of the immigrant problem, control and supervision was placed under the authority of the federal government.

Scholars have further classified and subdivided the migration to America into what has been termed the "old immigration," (1830–82) and the "new immigration" (1882–1930), superimposed on these four distinct periods of immigration. This delineation between those who came in the Colonial, Unrestricted, and State-Regulated periods, and those who arrived between the inception of Federal Control and the passage of the restrictive legislation of 1924, was based upon several significant factors. The most important of these were: (1) an American society which was undergoing a constant and rapid transformation of its economic and social environment; (2) the changing ethnic composition of the immigrant groups which arrived; and (3) the substitution of federal for state control.

During the old immigration approximately ten million people arrived in this nation. This migration, chiefly from northern and western Europe, was characterized by large numbers of Irish Catholics and Germans. Moreover, these immigrants arrived in a country which was essentially agricultural and rural, and whose transformation into an industrial and urban society was still decades away.

As the 1880s approached, the tide of immigrants from Ireland, Germany and Scandinavia began to ebb. In their place came their counterparts from eastern and southern Europe. In sharp contrast to the ethnic make-up of the old immigrants, these newcomers were largely composed of Slavs, Jews and Italians.

Furthermore, these rural-based peasants from Austria-Hungary,

Russia, Poland, Italy, Greece and the Balkans arrived at a time when America's industrial growth was in full swing, the free land of the frontier was gone, and urban centers were becoming the place to "make one's future." Consequently, those who arrived after 1882 found themselves in a nation which was quite different from that encountered by their predecessors. In turn, the change in the economic and social structure of the United States had a profound effect on those of this last immigrant wave. No longer needed to build the railroads or settle the virgin land of the western states, the new arrivals were directed to the factories and sweat-shops of America's slum-ridden cities.

The last significant distinction which set the old and new immigrants apart was the adoption of new methods of immigrant control. Compared to the laxity of state regulation, the settlers from southeastern Europe were confronted in their settlement by more rigid federal policies. Prior to the advent of federal control, congressional legislation dealing with immigration was directed at the welfare of the newly arrived aliens—especially in attempts to correct the deplorable steerage conditions of the trip across the ocean. However, shortly after the appearance of federal control, the government instituted rigid policies of exclusion, selection and deportation.

Although the distinctions between the old and new migrations have been made in the past by historians, it is important for the student to note that both groups met with parallel difficulties in their adjustment to American society. In varying degrees, each of these immigrant waves encountered nativist anti-foreign sentiment, occupied low levels on the socioeconomic scale, and shared a similar cultural disorganization in their attempts to adjust to life in their new homeland.

A. THE MAKING OF AN AMERICAN

1. No Hope for the Future: Desertion from the Old World

The Distressed Condition of Ireland: An Irish View

In the vanguard of the immigrant waves to arrive on American shores in the mid-nineteenth century were the Irish. Driven from their homes by the potato famine, their growing numbers soon replaced the English as the chief source of new American settlers.

The blight which spread over the fertile Irish landscape in 1847 left in its wake the smell of rotting potatoes mingled with the stench of decaying human flesh. Those who were fortunate enough to survive the famine "walked like living skeletons, . . . the men stamped with the livid mark of hunger—the children crying with pain—the women too weak to stand." By 1847 500,000 had starved to death; and many who endured foresaw only a life of despair. Thus, faced with the prospect of famine and unbearable living conditions, hundreds of thousands sought refuge in England, Canada and the United States.

In the first selection which follows, Sir Charles Gavan Duffy presented a historical treatment of the deprivation which the Irish faced. Included in his history was an eyewitness account by W. E. Forster, a representative of the British Society of Friends. The second selection contains a letter written to Captain R. B. Forbes, commander of the United States ship of war *Jamestown,* describing the aforementioned conditions. The *Jamestown,* on an "errand of mercy," was laden with a cargo of food sent by concerned American citizens.

SOURCE: Sir Charles Gavan Duffy, **Four Years of Irish History, 1845–1849** (London, 1883), pp. 430–32.

. . . The state of the country grew worse from day to day. It is difficult now to realise the condition of the western population in the autumn of 1847; but a witness of unexceptionable impartiality has painted it in permanent colours. A young Englishman representing the Society of Friends, who in that tragic time did work worthy of the Good Samaritan, reported what he saw in Mayo and Galway in language which for plain vigour rivals the narratives of Defoe. This is what he saw in Westport:—

"The town of Westport was in itself a strange and fearful sight, like what we read of in beleaguered cities; its streets crowded with gaunt wanderers, sauntering to and fro with hopeless air and hunger-struck look—a mob of starved, almost naked, women around the poorhouse clamouring for soup tickets—our inn, the head-quarters of the road engineer and pay clerks, beset by a crowd of beggars for work."

As he approached Galway, the rural population were found to be in a more miserable condition:—

"Some of the women and children that we saw on the road were abject cases of poverty and almost naked. The few rags they had on were with the greatest difficulty held together, and in a few weeks, as they are utterly unable to provide themselves with fresh clothes unless they be given them, they must become absolutely naked."

And in another district:—

"As we went along, our wonder was not that the people died, but that they lived; and I have no doubt whatever that in any other country the mortality would have been far greater: that many lives have been prolonged, perhaps saved, by the long apprenticeship to want in which the Irish peasant has been trained, and by that lovely, touching charity which prompts him to share his scanty meal with his starving neighbour."

The fishermen of the Cladagh, who were induced to send the Whig Attorney-General to Parliament a few months before, had to pledge the implements of their calling for a little daily bread:—

"even the very nets and tackling of these poor fishermen, I heard, were pawned, and, unless they be assisted to redeem them, they will be unable to take advantage of the herring shoals, even when they approach their coast . . . In order to ascertain the truth of this statement, I went into two or three of the largest pawnshops, the owners of which fully confirmed it and said they had in pledge at least a thousand pounds' worth of such property and saw no likelihood of its being redeemed."

In a rural district which he revisited after an interval he paints a scene which can scarcely be matched in the annals of a mediaeval plague:—

"One poor woman whose cabin I had visited said, 'There will be nothing for us but to lie down and die.' I had tried to give her hope of English aid, but, alas! her prophecy has been too true. Out of a population of 240 I found thirteen already dead from want. The survivors were like walking skeletons—the men gaunt and haggard, stamped with the livid mark of hunger—the children crying with pain—

the women in some of the cabins too weak to stand. When there before I had seen cows at almost every cabin, and there were besides many sheep and pigs owned in the village. But now all the sheep were gone—all the cows—all the poultry killed—only one pig left—the very dogs which had barked at me before had disappeared—no potatoes—no oats."

.   .   .

Fever had followed famine, as it commonly does, and in every considerable town the best men in the community, the zealous physician, the benevolent guardian, the pious clergyman, were its prey. In Galway one of the members of the county died of typhus, the same incident happened in Tipperary; in the north a similar fate befell Lord Lurgan, in the south the Mayor of Cork, and in the west the Catholic bishop of Clonfert. Half-a-dozen ministers of the Established Church, more than as many doctors, and three times as many Catholic priests fell victims to it. Under the new system sanctioned by Parliament, 70,000 men were discharged from the public works in a batch, and 100,000 in a second batch. The remainder got notice to leave speedily. Agricultural employment was found only for a handful of this multitude, and deaths increased fearfully. The weekly returns of the dead were like the bulletin of a fierce campaign. As the end of the year approached, villages and rural districts, which had been prosperous and populous a year before, were desolate. In some places the loss amounted to half the resident population. Even the paupers shut up and poor-houses did not escape. More than one in six perished of the unaccustomed food. The people did not everywhere consent to die patiently. In Armagh and Down groups of men went from house to house in the rural districts and insisted on being fed. In Tipperary and Waterford corn-stores and bakers' shops were sacked. In Donegal the people seized upon a flour-mill and pillaged it. In Limerick 5,000 men assembled on Tory Hill, and declared that they would not starve. A local clergyman restrained them by the promise of speedy relief. "If the Government did not act promptly, he himself would show them where food could be had." In a few cases crops were carried away from farms. The offences which spring from suffering and fear were heard of in many districts, but they were encountered with instant resistance. There were 30,000 men in red jackets, carefully fed, clothed, and lodged, ready to maintain the law. Four prisoners were convicted at the Galway assizes of stealing a filly, which they killed and ate to preserve their own lives. In Enniskillen two boys under twelve years of age were convicted of stealing one pint of Indian meal cooked into "stirabout," and Chief Justice Blackburn vindicated the outraged law by transporting them for seven years. Other children committed larcenies that they might be sent to gaol, where there was still daily bread to be had. In Mayo the people were eating carrion wherever it could be procured, and the coroner could not keep pace with the inquests: for the law sometimes spent more to ascertain the cause of a pauper's death than would have sufficed to preserve his life.

The social disorganisation was a spectacle as afflicting as the waste of life; it was the waste of whatever makes life worth possessing. All the institutions which civilise and elevate the people were disappearing one after another. The churches were half empty; the temperance reading-rooms were shut up; the mechanics' institute no longer got support; only the gaols and the poor-houses were crowded. A new generation, born in disease and reared in destitution, pithless and imbecile, threatened to drag down the nation to hopeless slavery. Trade was paralysed; no one bought anything which was not indispensable at the hour. The loss of the farmers in potatoes was estimated at more than twenty millions sterling, and with the potatoes the pigs which fed on them disappeared. The seed procured at a high price in spring again failed; time, money, and labour were lost, and another year of famine was certain. All who depended on the farmer had sunk with him; shopkeepers were beggared, tradesmen were starving, the priests living on voluntary offerings were sometimes in fearful distress when the people had no longer anything to offer.

SOURCE: Robert Bennet Forbes, **The Voyage of the Jamestown on Her Errand of Mercy** (Boston, 1847), pp. cxvi–cxx.

Moor Park, April 20, 1847.

Sir,—The sympathy and generosity of the citizens of the United states, having prompted them to forward a large supply of food, for the use of the starving population of Ireland, and the trust of seeing that this food is given gratuitously to the most needy and destitute, being reposed in you, I am prompted to lay before your notice the sad situation in which the dense population in the Kilworth district, at the Northern extremity of the county of Cork, is at present placed. But before I go into any detail, I must observe, that the greatest amount of distress is confined to a few counties, amongst which, the county Cork, on account of its immense population, stands one of the foremost; and, as a general rule, it will be found that those districts containing a large population, and which are mountainous, are exposed to a greater intensity of privation than any other. The Kilworth district belongs, I regret, to this last and worse class. It comprises a great part of that very extensive range of upland, known as the Kilworth mountains, and the low land attached to it is comparatively of small extent.—This extensive district, (comprising two poor law districts,) contains four parishes, with a population of about 9800 souls. Some of this district belongs to me, but more than three-fourths to others. As a resident I witness the sufferings of all, and feel for the misery they are exposed to. I need not here detail the sacrifices and exertions I have made, to assist the overwhelming mass of pauperism around me, during the last inclement winter. The poor know it, and are grateful; but my resources are at an end, and most of my tenants unable to pay me anything they owe me, so that I can do little more for them, although their situation daily becomes more critical. Out of this population of 9800 souls, according to the most accurate computation made by the clergy of the parishes, there are at this moment over 7000 in the greatest state of misery and distress, out of which 5000 have not, unless given them, a single meal to provide for their wants to-morrow. This has arisen from the total failure of the potatoe, upon which the people solely relied, and also, the unproductive nature of the oat crop last harvest, in these districts. Herewith, I enclose a list of the names of 118 unfortunate beings, who died, either from actual starvation or its effects since the 1st day of January in this place. Some have been found in the fields dead, others have dropped by the side of the roads, but the great majority have expired in their miserable cabins from cold, hunger, and nakedness. The typhus fever, the effect of last winter's sufferings, is now raging with fearful virulence, and hundreds are at this moment struggling here on the brink of eter-

nity. In the town of Kilworth, not to speak of the rural parts, up-
wards of 50 families are lying on beds of straw, attacked by the
contagion. Dysentery has also carried off several heads of families,
leaving the younger branches in a state of complete destitution.
I have only named 118 persons, who have died from famine or
its effects, but let it not be supposed that I have been able to
ascertain anything like the number who have been carried off, or
dropped in the more distant or mountainous parts of this extensive
district. For some time past we have given up the practice of holding Coroners inquests, in consequence of the coroner, (who resides
in this district,) being unable to attend to the numerous calls made
upon him. About three days ago, one inquest was, however, held,
and the case may be considered not unworthy of notice. A poor
man named James Carthy, in the last stage of weakness and exhaustion, having been given a small quantity of meal took it home,
where his unfortunate wife was confined to her bed of straw by
want and fever. Having made a fire, he attempted to cook some
"stir-about," but his strength failed him; he grew giddy, and fell
with his face into the fire. The poor wife perceiving that he could
not extricate himself, in vain attempted to leave her bed to assist
him. She had not the strength to move. She heard the crackling
of the fire, and she saw her husband expire. The effect was too
much for her mind and body to bear, and an hour afterwards she
also was a corpse. The verdict given by the jury was, that both
died from the effects of exhaustion, caused from starvation. It
would be an endless task, as well as a most painful one, to note
down the details of individual suffering. Every day furnishes victims, and the living hear, and endeavour to drive from their minds,
as soon as they can, the horrifying particulars that are related. I
have this day, returning to my house, witnessed more than one
person dying by the road side. I have been informed that there
are dead bodies lying in our district at this moment unburied. I
have known of bodies here remaining in the mountainous parts,
neglected for more than eight days; and I am at this time giving
food to a girl of twelve years old, the only remnant of a family,
consisting of eight persons, her father and mother included, all of
whom were alive one fortnight ago. Need I say more to rouse your
sympathy. Had I the power and the wealth to supply the wants
of so many thousands, I would not apply to you for aid. I have

done, and am doing all I can, yet I can only save a small number. As the citizens of the United States have placed a large amount of food at your disposal, believe me, a portion bestowed on the dying creatures around me, will not be badly employed. Lady Mountcashell has devoted most of her time, during the past winter, in visiting the poor, in giving them food, and in ascertaining their circumstances. No one knows them better, and no one is more beloved by them. Her character is well known both in England and Ireland. I need not then say, that whatever is confided to her charge, will be employed to the best purpose. I think it will be advantageous to intrust to her the distribution of any food, you may *in mercy* grant to these unfortunate creatures, and I am certain, if *their* wishes were consulted, the choice would fall upon her. With many apologies for troubling you with so long a letter, I have the honor to remain, sir,

Your most obliged, and obedient servant,
Mountcashell

Captain Forbes, *U.S. Frigate, Jamestown, Cove of Cork.*

German Emigration

As the migration from Ireland began to ebb, the tide of German emigration to America in the 1850s and '60s mounted. Although the fear of destitution was a motive to emigrate, the principal cause of German emigration during this period was political. Many Germans found themselves stifled by the restrictions enacted by local princes, and they demanded elimination of these oppressive laws.

In 1848 liberal Germans sought reform through the revolution that was sweeping Europe. When they realized that reform was not to be achieved and that they were considered enemies of the state, thousands sought refuge in America. These became the revered forty-eighters.

SOURCE: **"German Emigration,"** *Chamber's Edinburgh Journal,* June 20, 1846, pp. 387–89.

The dread of destitution is a motive to emigrate in Germany, as in England; but not a principal motive. This is clear from the fact that the emigration does not take place in those districts where there is most want, but exists equally where population is dense, and where it is thinly distributed. In Westphalia, for instance, a great number of small proprietors have lately sold their lands, and sailed for America—each of whom, it is reckoned, has taken with him at least thirty pounds' worth of goods and money. The Bavarians emigrate alike from the Rhine country, where population is thickly clustered together, and from the upland districts, where there are not eighty inhabitants to the square mile.

The one great cause of this almost national movement is the desire for absolute, political, and religious freedom; the absence of all restrictions upon the development of society; and the publication of opinions which cannot be realised at home. The great agitation in society, caused first by the French domination, and then by the convulsive rise against it, has never passed away. In that gigantic struggle, when everything rested on the popular soul, the bonds of privilege and class were tacitly abandoned and could never thenceforth be reunited as before. The promises of having constitutional governments at that time, made by the sovereigns to their subjects, have been but partially fulfilled. There is nothing that can be called oppression on the part of the governments; the mass of the people are well satisfied with their rulers—and with reason, for the actual executive has been generally excellent; but there are many restrictions, and the young, the restless, and the imaginative thirst for their ideal freedom, and many of them seek for the realisation of Utopia in America. Complete religious equality is a still more powerful want in a country where Catholics and Protestants are so nearly balanced, and where the state of parties is such, that the minority in faith, though nominally equal in law, must always live under the cold shade of an alien creed. This of itself has urged many across the Atlantic. It is probable that the present schism among the German Catholics will add to the number of the emigrants from religious causes.

Another motive has been the great success of some of the earlier settlers. The Moravians and Shakers, who have emigrated from Germany, have worked wonders in some parts. In 1815, the Separatists, another religious body, sometimes called Rappists, from their head, M. Rapp, sailed from Wurtemburg with a capital of only £1200 and formed a settlement on the Ohio. At the present time, the real property in land belonging to the society is reckoned at £340,000, exclusive of personal property, and a large sum of money in the funds. The success of the colony of Zoar has been equally striking. It was founded twenty years ago by a few families with a scanty capital, and now possesses 40,000 acres of land, a disposable capital of £100,000, and an immense quantity of machinery and stock, foundries, tan-pits, and mills in abundance. This extraordinary affluence is because these two colonies were founded on the principle of a community of property, and have been throughout under a strict religious government. But the present emigrants forget this; and looking only at the prosperity achieved, they think that as the Moravians and Rappists have succeeded, they must succeed to the same extent, without either the same capital or self-denial.

It is not to be expected that the German governments should look with indifference on this constant and increasing defalcation of their subjects. It is not, as we have said, the very poor that emigrate; they cannot, in fact; but it is those who have some little to spare. Every emigrant is reckoned to take with him equal to £25 of English money, which would give an annual subtraction of £1,500,000—a serious loss in a country which has little superfluous capital. And be it remembered that this is all loss. Lord Brougham said, in one of his speeches, with equal truth and force, of the English emigrants, that not an axe falls in America but sets in motion a shuttle at Manchester. But the Germans in America consume English, not German commodities, and remit nothing to Germany in the shape of produce. As it is hopeless to try to stop the tide, the German governments have exerted themselves of late to turn it in a direction nearer home—to Hungary and the countries along the Lower Danube, where there is an immensity of rich virgin soil untouched. Austria, in particular, is naturally very much interested in establishing a German population in Hungary, to balance the Slavonic element; and with this view a number of pamphlets have been drawn up and circulated, with a comparative view of the advantages of emigration to Hungary and the United States, but as yet with little effect.

. . . The most important point connected with the subject, is the influence which such an annual influx of a foreign population, speaking the same language, and nearly all professing the same (the Roman Catholic) faith, cannot fail to exercise upon the future destinies of the United States. At present, as the whole stream is poured into the same country, the annual number of German settlers considerably exceeds those from Great Britain and Ireland. There are of the former resident in America, according to the last census, about four millions. But this is not all. If, like the English and Irish who cross the Atlantic, they were to spread themselves over the continent indiscriminately, wherever there was the greatest chance of success, the whole, in the course of one generation, or two at most, would blend insensibly with the majority. But they carry out with them all the passions, prejudices, and dispositions of the fatherland, and keep them immoveably. The great object of each family that successively arrives, is to fix itself as near as possible to its relatives, if it has any; if not, to its countrymen. Every settlement thus becomes the nucleus of a pure German circle, which is born, marries, and dies within itself, and with the least possible admixture of Anglo-Americans. In the reign of Queen Anne, a numerous colony from the Palatinate settled on the upper waters of the Hudson, where, after a century and a half, their descendants remain to this day a separate people. 'These honest folks,' says one of their countrymen, 'though living amongst Anglo-Americans for the third and fourth generation, can neither read nor write the English language; and adhering to their axiom, never to become Irish (thus they designate the Anglo-Americans, who take their revenge by nicknaming them Dutch), they are contented with their own German idiom'. It is the same with them everywhere. Chance or preference directed the first settlers towards Pennsylvania. To Pennsylvania, accordingly, the stream has steadily set ever since; and the result is, that the German population of that state already balances the Anglo-Saxon; and, in the adjoining state of Ohio, stands as three to seven. Next to these, the greatest number is found in Maryland, Indiana, Illinois, and Missouri, neither going far to the north or south of the same parallel. In most of these states, the debates in the houses of representatives and the laws are printed alike in German and English. If this emigration continues in its present extent and direction, and in the course of time—what is sufficiently probable—a disruption of the great American confederacy should take place, a second Germany will have arisen beyond the Atlantic, and monopolised, along the head waters of the Delaware and Ohio, the possessions of the children of Penn.

Protest Against the Spirit of Medieval Persecution

Foremost among the motivations for the Jewish exodus from Russia (1880–1910) was anti-Semitism, which was sanctioned by Russian officialdom. The Jewish community faced political restrictions, distressing economic conditions, limitations on their ability to earn a livelihood and ever present religious intolerance. In addition, violent anti-Jewish outbreaks called pogroms became part of Jewish life. These riots, incited by government officials, strove to divert the discontent of the Russian people by attributing their plight to the Jews.

Led by Czarist Cossacks, the organized massacres were willingly joined by the civilian population. Stopping at nothing short of looting, arson, rape and murder, these violations caused the Jewish community to live in fear as they waited for the next outbreak of terror. Undoubtedly, the pogrom dictated to the Jewish leaders that emigration from Russia had become a necessity.

After 1881 pogroms increased in intensity. Thus, in anticipation of the continuance of Czarist oppression, the Jewish migration began; and "the cry 'To America'! was taken up by city after city and hamlet after hamlet, till its fascinating echo reached every synagogue in the [Russian] empire."

SOURCE: Abraham Cahan, "The Russian Jew in America," *The Atlantic Monthly*, July 1898, pp. 128–30.

One afternoon in the summer of 1881, when the Jewish quarter of Kieff was filled with groans and its pavements were strewn with the debris of destroyed homes, a group of young men entered one of the synagogues of the ancient city. They were well dressed, and their general appearance bespoke education and refinement. The rabbi had proclaimed a day of fasting and prayer, and the house of God was crowded with sobbing victims of the recent riots, but as the newcomers made their way to the Holy Ark silence fell upon the congregation. The young men were students of the University of St. Vladimir, and although sons of Israel like the others, their presence at a synagogue was an unusual sight.

"Brethren," said the spokesman of the delegation, struggling with his sobs, "we are a committee of the Jewish students of the university, sent to clasp hands with you and to mingle our tears with your tears. We are here to say to you, 'We are your brothers; Jews like yourselves, like our fathers!' We have striven to adopt the language and manners of our Christian fellow countrymen; we have brought ourselves up to an ardent love of their literature, of their culture, of their progress. We have tried to persuade ourselves that we are children of Mother Russia. Alas! we have been in error. The terrible events which have called forth this fast and these tears have aroused us from our dream. The voice of the blood of our outraged brothers and sisters cries unto us that we are only strangers in the land which we have been used to call our home; that we are only stepchildren here, waifs to be trampled upon and dishonored. There is no hope for Israel in Russia. The salvation of the downtrodden people lies in other parts,—in a land beyond the seas, which knows no distinction of race or faith, which is a mother to Jew and Gentile alike. In the great republic is our redemption from the brutalities and ignominies to which we are subjected in this our birthplace. In America we shall find rest; the stars and stripes will wave over the true home of our people. To America, brethren! To America!"

. . . Before 1882 the emigration of Russian Jews to America was restricted to the provinces lying about the Niemen and the Dwina, notably to the government of Souvalki, where economical conditions caused Catholic peasants as well as Jewish tradesmen and artisans to go elsewhere "in search of bread." Some of these Lithuanian and Polish Jews sought their fortune in the southern districts of the empire, where their brethren enjoyed a high average of prosperity, while the more venturesome crossed the frontier to embark for the New World. Among the Jews of the south (Ukraine and New Russia) and of the central provinces (Great Russia) self-expatriation was an unknown thing. But with the breaking out of the epidemic of anti-Jewish riots, which rendered thousands of well-to-do families homeless and penniless, Hebrew immigration to this country underwent an abrupt change in character as well as in volume.

Not only did the government of Alexander III blink at the atrocities and practically encourage them, but it even sent a series of measures in their wake which had the effect of depriving new multitudes of "stepchildren" of their means of livelihood, and of dislodging thousands of families from their long established homes. The cry "To America!" was taken up by city after city and hamlet after hamlet, till its fascinating echo reached every synagogue in the empire. Many left because they had been driven from their homes, and these were joined by many others who, while affected neither by the outbursts of mob violence nor by the new restrictions, . . . succumbed to a general sense of insecurity and of wounded race pride. The efflux which had hitherto been sporadic suddenly became epidemic. The prosperous and the cultivated—an element formerly rare among the Jewish arrivals at New York—came to form a respectable minority in nearly every company of immigrants which, thanks to the assistance of the Hebrew communities of western Europe and of this country, the steamships brought from the domains of the Czar. The Jewish college student, whose faith barred him from the educational institutions of the empire, sought these shores in order to complete his studies, and many a graduated physician, chemist, dentist, architect, and artist came here to take up the profession from which he was interdicted at his birthplace.

The Italian Emigration: Misery, Misery, Misery!

At the turn of the nineteenth century, southern Italy's most abundant "product" was poverty. Being a densely populated nation with insufficient and poorly developed resources, the people of this Mediterranean peninsula were caught in an unbreakable cycle of despair. Refusing to accept a future of indigence, the 12,000 peasants who set sail for America in 1880 grew to 100,000 by 1900. As stories of economic success were sent by mail or brought by those who returned with their "fortunes," thousands more decided to make a new home across the Atlantic. Thus, the lure of economic opportunity in America resulted in one of the greatest migrations in modern times. By the eve of the First World War the number of Italian immigrants swelled to 300,000.

In the article which follows, Antonio Mangano discussed the impact of the migration on Italy and vividly described the destitution which pervaded the southern Italian towns and landscape. Rather than the political and religious motives of the Germans and/or Jews, Mangano concluded that the primary reason for leaving Italy was "the growing desire among the more intelligent peasants to better their condition and rise in the world, to become property-holders and respected citizens, and above all to give their children opportunities for education."

SOURCE: Antonio Mangano, **"The Effect of Emigration upon Italy,"** *Charities and the Commons* (February, 1908), pp. 1475–78, 1484–86.

It would be difficult of course to say in a word just why all Italian emigrants leave their homes, but it cannot be denied that the main cause is poverty. How many times I asked mayors and communal secretaries this question, I cannot tell, but the answer, because of its unvarying repetition, I shall not soon forget— "miseria, miseria, miseria." There certainly is in the southern towns, in all but rare instances, a depth of human wretchedness, want, ignorance, and abject poverty, incredible unless one has seen it with his own eyes. In what used to be the Papal States we frequently saw human beings and domestic animals living together in miserable straw huts strengthened with mud, indescribably dirty. I was told of one long straw shelter which houses twelve families, men, women and children, with only a partition two-thirds the height, to separate the little rooms. Wood is far too expensive to use in building houses, even stone and mortar are more than these wretched people can afford; and lastly, those who are their overlords have cared little how the people are compelled to live, if they only produce a sufficient revenue of grain and flocks. This complete indifference of the landlords to the welfare of the peasantry, strikes even a casual observer. The middle ages have left great class distinctions which persist today. In many remote towns mediaeval customs still prevail, and the manner of living has not improved for centuries.

One of the first towns I visited was Forano, beautifully located on the summit of a long steep hill opposite Horace's favorite snow-capped Soracte. After leaving the train, we rode in a little two-wheeled cart four miles on a winding road climbing up to the town. The one main street is paved with cobblestones. It is narrow and shut in by stone houses crowded close together, but the view from the summit is magnificent. To the east lies the Roman Campagna, green and luxuriant-looking at this distance, marshy and malarial in reality, with the shallow, sluggish Tiber winding through the center. Across the valley rises Mount Soracte, majestic, grand. On all other sides are valleys and vineyard-girdled hills. The town, its fields and vineyards once belonged to the famous Strozzi family of Florence, but the *palazzo* and such fields as still remained to the family have passed into other hands, a bishop's, I believe.

Emigration from this town of 1,600 inhabitants, all crowded into an area not exceeding four of our city blocks, began in 1902. One poor man, ambitious but despairing of ever rising in life at home, went to Brazil and succeeded. In 1902 one hundred and twelve others followed him under contract to work for a coffee company which paid their passage. For two years many more went under similar contracts. Then the coffee crop failed. The company could not pay the new arrivals who were abandoned and left in want. Some who could find no other work wrote home to the government for money to return. This experience checked emigration to South America from this town.

But in 1904 fifteen came to America, twelve on tickets bought with money forwarded from America. Some are now at White Plains, N.Y., engaged in market gardening at $1.50 a day. The news had come back to Forano in a letter that one man had refused a good position at light work and higher wages in New York city, preferring country life. I talked with several men who were to sail in a few days to take up the same occupation. This is interesting, showing as it does that Italians who are accustomed to tilling the soil in their native land, prefer gardening even at less pay, to crowding themselves into cities where they might earn more. If more immigrants could be well started in country life half of our immigration problem would be solved.

The streets and sanitary conditions of this town are in strong contrast with the next village, Stimgliano. The betterment is all due to a generous American lady and her Italian husband. Mrs. Angelini has established a lace-school, to give other employment to the girls of the town than the hard life in the fields. They make beautiful French and Brussels point as well as Venetian, Florentine and other Italian laces. Three of her girls were planning to come to New York to make laces. This is unusual, because Italian girls almost never emigrate except with their families or to meet families already here. The construction of Forano and hundreds of other hill-towns like it, shows the influence of the dark ages when the feudal system existed. The peasant huts are clustered close to one another and to the *palazzo* or palace, on a hilltop, for protection in time of war. The huts are mostly low, one-room hovels with no window or chimney but the door. The very courtyard of the Strozzi palace, a massive three-story castle, plain on the exterior but regally decorated and furnished on the interior, is crowded with these wretched human habitations. Since all houses and buildings in Italy are of stone or concrete, there are no fires, and these houses have lasted for hundreds of years just as they were built, consequently there has been no progress in the manner of living. The accumulation of dirt is enormous. The one room has an earth, sometimes a stone floor, the hearth often no other chimney than the low door. The interior is dark and dreary. The only furniture is a huge bed, and perhaps a chair, a bench or a wooden chest. Potatoes and corn are stored under the bed or in a corner, strings of drying peppers hang from the walls. The accommodating hen lays her daily egg on the bed, or in a basket placed on a shelf for her. In such miserable dwellings live thousands of Italian *contadini* with their families,—man, wife and seven or eight children, if all survive, and it is by no means a rare thing for the family donkey, if they are fortunate enough to possess one, the pig and chickens, to occupy the same hovel, though if possible the pig and donkey have separate little dug-outs or straw lean-tos. As we approached one town, we passed a large sandbank which contained thirty or more caves with barred doors and squealing occupants penned for the night. Further on we met barefoot women with large tubs of swill on their heads, their hands busy knitting, or holding a small distaff spinning flax.

The fields and vineyards of these towns, the *palazzi* and surrounding huts, are often owned by non-resident landlords, who have beautiful villas in Florence or Paris.

The absentee landlord is one of the curses of the country. The owner of large estates—one well-known family is said to possess thirty such towns as Forano, with fields and vineyards—entrusts his property to a financial agent, whose business it is to get as much as possible from the tenants, so that the owner may be maintained in luxury and idleness in the large cities. The property owners care nothing for the welfare of their tenants; the agents care less.

The rental terms differ in different sections, but before emigration had grown to such enormous proportions, the peasant was entirely at the mercy of the land agent, or his padrone. His condition was such that in order to get enough black bread for his family he must accept the most grinding terms, paying in wheat for the little patch of exhausted soil which required the combined labor of man, wife and children to eke out a miserable existence. And if after toiling early and late all summer the crops failed in a bad season, no pity was shown him. The full rent must still be paid; there was no escape; he must submit or starve and even then half starve through the winter. We saw families last winter in a town where there had been no meat for over a month, and if they had their portion of cornmeal *polenta* at noon, it meant they could have no supper at night. The peasant never thinks of moving from one town to another to better his condition. The possibility is too remote, and the moving far too expensive. It is easier to cross the ocean, and this he now does. The third-class government passports for the very poor are free. The steamship agent will gladly lend him money and another sturdy toiler is lost to Italy.

It was most interesting to compare the emigration of certain towns with the report of harvests for the same years. In every instance emigration was small in a year of good crops, and correspondingly large when crops failed. In one part of the province of Bari I was told that emigration would be very light this year (summer of 1907) because the prospects of an abundant almond harvest were excellent. This clearly illustrates the truth of the mayor's answer,—It is absolute misery, the facing of hunger and despair, that compels many a southern Italian to forsake his country, and call it "no good" after he has lived a few months in America. Even when the peasant is a little better off and is able to save a little every year and perhaps owns his own hut worth $60 or $80, he is not able to live much better, and a poor harvest brings him face to face with starvation. So nowadays he sells his hut to buy a ticket which includes his emigration tax to the government, and departs with his family for America.

. . . Mr. Combes denies that lack of work and low wages are causes for emigration. He thinks these people of meagre education are induced to leave home because of the glowing accounts which they see in the newspapers about America, and that the fortunes which they seek here could be found in their own country if they would put forth the same amount of effort. This may be good theory, but in the province of Cosenza near the town of San Demetrio, I came upon an intelligent-looking man digging a large piece of ground with a huge zappa. I said good day and he at once asked me if I were not from America. He said he was preparing the soil for grain and potatoes, but as soon as he finished planting he would leave the rest to his wife and children. "I am going to America," he said.

"But," said I, "why not stay here? Cannot you earn enough to live on here in your own country?"

"Oh, yes, I have managed to live all my life, but I can never get anything ahead. I am always living from hand to mouth and sometimes it seems as if it would be impossible for me to get through the year without debt. I work when I can get anything to do, and the rest of the time cultivate this bit of ground. I get better pay than I used to a few years ago, but everything I buy has become so much dearer that the extra I earn when I work for the padrone, doesn't help me. The government does all it can to keep us down with taxes. In America I hear it is different, and even if it does cost more to live a man can always save something. He only has to work from seven in the morning until six at night. Here I rise before daylight, and start for my field before the sun is seen, and toil until after sunset."

Surely when a man has to slave from early morning till late at night for twenty, thirty or forty cents a day, he cannot reasonably be expected to do so when he hears he can earn a dollar and a half or two dollars a day elsewhere. It is a common notion here in the United States that one lire (20 cents) will go as far in Italy as a dollar in New York. This is not the case. True, many things, as oil, wine, fruit and vegetables are cheaper, but salt, sugar and meat are dearer than in America, and the *contadino* must do without them. Salt is an absolute necessity, especially for flocks.

Now I am well aware that there are men in our Italian colonies in New York and all over the United States, who were not driven here by want and poverty. Many have come in search of greater opportunities than Italy can offer them; many for the spirit of freedom and democracy which is so characteristic of American life. Especially is this true of the student class, numbers of whom have come here during the last five years. Others come to increase their capital. One doctor who has twenty thousand dollars and owns large tracts of land, is coming to make more money. Such emigrants are few, of course, and usually have more difficulty in making their way here if they do not know English than a peasant. Many times when I attempted to advise men of refinement and culture not to come to America unless they were willing to begin with any kind of hard manual work, a thing the Italian of the better class is very loath to do, they answered that hundreds of peasants have made their fortunes here, and they did not see why men of intelligence and learning could not do the same. Somehow nearly everybody, well-informed people as well as the ignorant, believes that all do well in America. They are impressed by the thousands of lire that come to the village post office every month, and fail to notice that not all emigrants send back money. The glowing letters come from the successful ones; the others are silent. While talking with an Italian gentleman of national fame, I told him that I knew hundreds of Italians in New York city and Brooklyn who are dependent upon charity in some form or other. "How can that be," he asked, "when they are all sending back so much money?"

I was quite amused to note the curiosity with which I was regarded by the natives of most towns when I entered the *municipio* and presented my general letter of introduction from the Italian government commissioner of emigration. Little groups of people would gather at the door, and when I was ready to depart, ask anxiously if I were a government official whose purpose it was to check emigration. When I assured them that I was not an official and had no interest in stopping emigration, their relief was evident. Then one would venture the remark that perhaps I was a steamship agent seeking new recruits for America. In every instance I told them that we have enough Italians over here, for the present, and tried to make them understand that the money which most of the emigrants send back to their families is saved at the expense of the workers' health, since they are compelled to do heavy, dangerous work which other laborers refuse, and in order to save money must live on cheap, insufficient food, in crowded quarters, often harshly treated by foremen where hundreds are engaged on a large piece of work. I told them of the disease which was almost unknown in Italy twenty-five years ago, but is making alarming progress among the southern poor, due largely to the returned emigrant. Many go back to their native land to die after they have gathered a little money at the expense of their very life blood, but nothing chills their enthusiasm for America.

As I had visited many towns in Sicily and southern Italy where there were prospects of a good harvest, I believed that emigration would be greatly reduced this year. Such has not been the case. I had been in Brooklyn only a few days when to my great surprise five men came to see me, three of whom I had met in the Basilicata and two in Sicily,—men whom I had emphatically told how difficult it would be for them to get along here since they are not peasants and unaccustomed to hard labor.

Last but not least in the causes of emigration is the growing desire among the more intelligent peasants to better their condition and rise in the world, to become property-holders and respected citizens, and above all to give their children opportunities for education and advancement. The *contadini* represent one half of the population of Italy, fifteen million souls. Angelo Mosso in *Lo Fita Moderna degli Italiani,* puts it well when he says: "He who does not actually see the misery of these poor people, cannot imagine how low and mean existence can become. Their poverty is such that there is scarcely an inundation, a drought, or hailstorm, or a crop failure, but thousands of workingmen suffer hunger, and famine renews itself annually in the winter time."

2. The Great Immigrant Waves: One-Way Traffic Across the Atlantic

The Perils of the Crossing and the Perils of Arrival

Although attempts were made to improve conditions aboard immigrant ferrying vessels, those who traveled the Atlantic during the old immigration (1830–82) were still confronted with a harrowing experience. Taking from six to eight weeks to sail from Europe to North America, passengers were plagued by pestilence and "hunger typhus" which equaled the misery they hopefully had left behind. Described as "ship fever" by physicians, the disease (typhus) which caused the death of many shocked even the most experienced medical officers. Nevertheless, despite the perils of the crossing, the "fever ships" reached their destinations and deposited their cargoes at the several ports of entry.

Following the seagoing venture, many were exposed to vermin-ridden compounds which characterized American immigration facilities. Within these stations, immigrants faced the added hardship of disease, unsanitary and inadequate toilets, lack of medical care and insufficient food.

In the selections which follow, eyewitness descriptions of the sufferings of the passengers are recounted. In the first excerpt, John Francis Maguire related the scene at the docking of the Irish fever ship *Urania* in May 1847. After observing the vessel's interior and the physical condition of those who survived, Maguire reported a sight which was filled with the miserable, the sick and the dead.

The second selection, a report on the fever ship *Leibnitz,* detailed similar conditions on a crossing in 1868. Abroad this vessel, "some families died out entirely." When questioned by officials as to the whereabouts of their parents, some children "pointed to the ocean with sobs and tears, and cried, *'Down there!'* "

The third description appeared in the New York *Herald* in March 1870, and recorded an official investigation of New York City's Ward's Island immigrant station. Examining the causes of a recent riot at the facility, the state legislative committee in charge of the inquiry reported that they were "horrified at the . . . gross neglect of the wretched people committed to the tender mercies of the [station's] superintendent."

SOURCE: John Francis Maguire, **The Irish in America** (London, 1868), pp. 179–83, 134, 139.

On the 8th of May, 1847, the 'Urania,' from Cork, with several hundred immigrants on board, a large proportion of them sick and dying of the ship-fever, was put into quarantine at Grosse Isle. This was the first of the plague-smitten ships from Ireland which that year sailed up the St. Lawrence. But before the first week of June as many as eighty-four ships of various tonnage were driven in by an easterly wind; and of that enormous number of vessels there was not one free from the taint of malignant typhus, the off-spring of famine and of the foul ship-hold. This fleet of vessels literally reeked with pestilence. All sailing vessels,–the merciful speed of the well-appointed steamer being unknown to the emigrant of those days,–a tolerably quick passage occupied from six to eight weeks; while passages of ten or twelve weeks, and even a longer time, were not considered at all extraordinary at a period when craft of every kind, the most unsuited as well as the least sea-worthy, were pressed into the service of human deportation.

Who can imagine the horrors of even the shortest passage in an emigrant ship crowded beyond its utmost capability of stowage with unhappy beings of all ages, with fever raging in their midst? Under the most favourable circumstances it is impossible to maintain perfect purity of atmosphere between decks, even when ports are open, and every device is adopted to secure the greatest amount of ventilation. But a crowded emigrant sailing ship of twenty years since, with fever on board!–the crew sullen or brutal from very desperation, or paralysed with terror of the plague–the miserable passengers unable to help themselves, or afford the least relief to each other; one-fourth, or one-third, or one-half of the entire number in different stages of the disease; many dying, some dead; the fatal poison intensified by the indescribable foulness of the air breathed and rebreathed by the gasping sufferers–the wails of children, the ravings of the delirious, the cries and groans of those in mortal agony! Of the eighty-four emigrant ships that anchored at Grosse Isle in the summer of 1847, there was not a single one to which this description might not rightly apply.

The authorities were taken by surprise, owing to the sudden arrival of this plague-smitten fleet, and, save the sheds that remained since 1832, there was no accommodation of any kind on the island. These sheds were rapidly filled with the miserable people, the sick and the dying, and round their walls lay groups of half-naked men, women, and children, in the same condition—sick or dying. Hundreds were literally flung on the beach, left amid the mud and stones to crawl on the dry land how they could. 'I have seen,' says the priest who was then chaplain of the quarantine, and who had been but one year on the mission, 'I have one day seen thirty-seven people lying on the beach, crawling on the mud, and dying like fish out of water.' Many of these, and many more besides, gasped out their last breath on that fatal shore, not able to drag themselves from the slime in which they lay. Death was doing its work everywhere—in the sheds, around the sheds, where the victims lay in hundreds under the canopy of heaven, and in the poisonous holds of the plague-ships, all of which were declared to be, and treated as, hospitals.

From ship to ship the young Irish priest carried the consolations of religion to the dying. Amidst shrieks, and groans, and wild ravings, and heart-rending lamentations,—over prostrate sufferers in every stage of the sickness—from loathsome berth to loathsome berth, he pursued his holy task. So noxious was the pent-up atmosphere of these floating pest-houses, that he had frequently to rush on deck, to breathe the pure air, or to relieve his overtaxed stomach: then he would again plunge into the foul den, and resume his interrupted labours.

There being, at first, no organisation, no staff, no available resources, it may be imagined why the mortality rose to a prodigious rate, and how at one time as many as 150 bodies most of them in a half-naked state, would be piled up in the dead-house, awaiting such sepulture as a huge pit could afford. Poor creatures would crawl out of the sheds, and being too exhausted to return, would be found lying in the open air, not a few of them rigid in death . . . The deaths were as many as 100, and 150, and even 200 a day, and this for a considerable period during the summer. The masters of the quarantine-bound ships were naturally desirous of getting rid as speedily as possible of their dangerous and unprofitable freight; and the manner in which the helpless people were landed, or thrown, on the island, aggravated their sufferings, and in a vast number of instances precipitated their fate. Then the hunger and thirst from which they suffered in the badly-found ships, between whose crowded and stifling decks they had been so long pent up, had so far destroyed their vital energy that they had but little chance of life when once struck down.

About the middle of June the young chaplain was attacked by the pestilence. For ten days he had not taken off his clothes, and his boots, which he constantly wore for all that time, had to be cut from his feet. A couple of months elapsed before he resumed his duties; but when he returned to his post of danger the mortality was still of fearful magnitude.

It was not until the 1st of November that the quarantine of Grosse Isle was closed. Upon that barren isle as many as 10,000 of the Irish race were consigned to the grave-pit. By some the estimate is made much higher, and 12,000 is considered nearer the actual number. A register was kept, and is still in existence, but it does not commence earlier than June 16th and 30th of June, 487 Irish immigrants 'whose names could not be ascertained.' In July, 941 were thrown into nameless graves; and in August, 918 were entered in the register under the comprehensive description— 'unknown.' There were interred, from the 16th of June to the closing of the quarantine for *that* year, 2,905 of a Christian people, whose names could not be discovered amidst the confusion and carnage of that fatal summer. In the following year, 2,000 additional victims were entered in the same register, without name or trace of any kind, to tell who they were, or whence they had come. Thus 5,000 out of the total number of victims were simply described as 'unknown.'

This deplorable havoc of human life left hundreds of orphans dependent on the compassion of the public . . . Half naked, squalid, covered with vermin generated by hunger, fever, and the foulness of the ship's hold, perhaps with the germs of the plague lurking in their vitiated blood, these helpless innocents of every age—from the infant taken from the bosom of its dead mother to the child that could barely tell the name of its parents—were gathered under the fostering protection of the Church. They were washed, and clad, and fed; and every effort was made by the clergy and nuns who took them into their charge to discover who they were, what their names, and which of them were related the one to the other, so that, if possible, children of the same family might not be separated for ever. A difficult thing it was to learn from mere infants whether, among more than 600 orphans, they had brothers or sisters. But by patiently observing the little creatures when they found strength and courage to play, their watchful protectors were enabled to find out relationships which, without such care, would have been otherwise unknown. If one infant ran to meet another, or caught its hand, or smiled at it, or kissed it, or showed pleasure in its society, here was a clue to be followed; and in many instances children of the same parents were thus preserved to each other. Many more, of course, were separated for ever, as these children were too young to tell their own names, or do anything save cry in piteous accents for 'mammy, mammy!' until soothed to slumber in the arms of a compassionate Sister.

SOURCE: Frederick Kapp, **Immigration and the Commissioners of Emigration** (New York, 1870), pp. 189–92.

To the Board of Commissioners of Emigration:

GENTLEMEN: Although not expressly authorized, yet, because the emergency arose since your last meeting, the undersigned deemed it their duty to go on board the ill-fated ship *Leibnitz,* and to enquire into the condition of her passengers transferred to the hospital-ship *Illinois,* in the Lower Bay.

We were informed that her last trip was her second with emigrants on board. Last summer, she went to Quebec with about seven hundred passengers, of whom she lost only a few on her passage; this time, she left Hamburg, Nov. 2, 1867, Capt. H. F. Bornhold, lay at Cuxhaven, on account of headwinds, until the 11th, whereupon she took the southern course to New York. She went by the way of Madeira, down to the Tropics, 20th degree, and arrived in the Lower Bay on Jan. 11, 1868, after a passage of 61 days, or rather 70 days—at least, as far as the passengers are concerned, who were confined to the densely crowded steerage for that length of time.

The heat, for the period that they were in the lower latitudes, very often reached 24 degrees of Reaumur, or 94 degrees of Fahrenheit. Her passengers 544 in all—of whom 395 were adults, 103 children, and 46 infants—came principally from Mecklenburg, and proposed to settle as farmers and laborers in Illinois and Wisconsin; besides them, there were about 40 Prussians from Pomerania and Posen, and a few Saxons and Thuringians.

It is not proven by any fact, that the cholera (as has been alleged) raged or had raged in or near their homes when or before they left them. This statement appears to have been made by or in behalf of those who have an interest in throwing the origin of the sickness on its poor victims. Of these 544 German passengers, 105 died on the voyage, and three in port, making in all 108 deaths —leaving 436 surviving.

The first death occurred on Nov. 25th. On some days, as for instance on Dec. 1, nine passengers died and on Dec. 17, eight. The sickness did not abate until toward the end of December, and no new cases happened when the ship had again reached the northern latitudes; five children were born; during the voyage some families had died out entirely; of others, the fathers or mothers are gone; here, a husband had left a poor widow, with small children; and there, a husband had lost his wife. We spoke to some little boys and girls, who, when asked where were their parents, pointed to the ocean with sobs and tears, and cried, *"Down there!"*

Prior to our arrival on board, the ship had been cleansed and fumigated several times, but not sufficiently so to remove the dirt, which, in some places, covered the walls. Mr. Frederick Kassner, our able and experienced Boarding Officer, reports that he found the ship and the passengers in a most filthy condition, and that when boarding the *Leibnitz* he hardly discovered a clean spot on the ladder, or on the ropes, where he could put his hands and feet. He does not remember to have seen anything like it within the last five years. Captain True, who likewise boarded the ship immediately after her arrival, corroborates the statement of Mr. Kassner.

As to the interior of the vessel, the upper steerage is high and wide. All the spars, beams, and planks which were used for the construction of temporary berths had been removed. Except through two hatchways and two very small ventilators, it had no ventilation, and not a single window or bull's-eye was open during the voyage. In general, however, it was not worse than the average of the steerages of other emigrant ships; but the lower steerage, the so-called orlop-deck, is a perfect pest-hole, calculated to kill the healthiest man. It had been made a temporary room for the voyage by laying a tier of planks over the lower beams of the vessel, and they were so little supported that they shook when walking on them. The little light this orlop-deck received came through one of the hatchways of the upper-deck. Although the latter was open when we were on board, and although the ship was lying in the open sea, free from all sides, it was impossible to see anything at a distance of two or three feet. On our enquiring how this hole had been lighted during the voyage, we were told that some lanterns had been up there, but that on account of the foulness of the air, they could scarcely burn . . . It had of course, much less than the upper-deck draft or ventilation, and was immediately over the keel, where the bilge-water collects, and adjoining part of the cargo, which consisted of wool and hides. And in this place about 120 passengers were crowded for 70 days, and for a greater part of the voyage in a tropical heat, with scanty rations and a very inadequate supply of water, and worse than all, suffering from the miasma below, above, and beside them, which of itself must create fever and pestilence!

The captain himself stated to us that the passengers refused to carry the excrements on deck, and that "the urine and ordure of the upper-steerage flowed down to the lower." As the main-deck was very difficult of access from the orlop-deck, the inmates of the latter often failed to go on deck even to attend to the calls of nature. There were only six water-closets for the accommodation of all the passengers. They have been cleansed, of course; but the smell that emanated from them was still very intense, and corroborates the statement of the above named officers—that they must have been in an extraordinary frightful condition.

When the ship *Lord Brougham,* belonging to the same line, arrived on the 6th of December last, from Hamburg, and had lost 75 out of 383 passengers, we personally examined the majority of the survivors, and found them not only healthy and in good spirits, but, at the same time, in every respect satisfied with the treatment they had received on board.

The present case, however, is different. There was not a single emigrant who did not complain of the captain, as well as of the short allowance of provisions and water on board. As we know, from a long experience, that the passengers of emigrant ships, with a very few exceptions, are in the habit of claiming more than they are entitled to, we are far from putting implicit faith in all their statements. There is as much falsehood and exaggeration among this class of people as among any other body of uneducated men. We have, therefore, taken their complaints with due allowance, and report only so much thereof as we believe to be well founded.

All the passengers concur in the complaint that their provisions were short, partly rotten, and that, especially, the supply of water was insufficient, until they were approaching port. We examined the provisions on board, and found that the water was clear and pure. If the whole supply during the voyage was such as the samples handed to us, there was no reason for complaint as to quality. But, in quantity, the complaints of the passengers are too well founded; for they unanimously state, and are not effectually contradicted by the captain, that they never received more than half a pint of drinkable water per day, while by the laws of the United States they were entitled to receive three quarts. Some of the biscuit handed to us were rotten and old, and hardly eatable; other pieces were better. We ordered the steward to open a cask of corn-beef, and found it of ordinary good quality. The butter, however, was rancid. Once a week herrings were cooked instead of meat. The beans and sauerkraut were often badly cooked, and, in spite of hunger, thrown overboard.

The treatment of the passengers was heartless in the extreme. The sick passengers received the same food with the healthy, and high prices were exacted for all extras and comforts. A regular traffic in wine, beer, and liquors was carried on between the passengers on the one side and the steward and crew on the other. A man by the name of Frederick Hildebrand, from Wirsitz, in Posen, who lost two children, paid 35 Prussian thalers extra for beer and wine to sustain himself and his sick wife. A bottle of rum cost him one dollar; a bottle of bad wine even more. "This extortion, at such a time, cannot be too strongly condemned," says Captain True, in his report, which confirms the information received by us from the passengers.

When the first deaths occurred, the corpses were often suffered to remain in the steerage for full twenty-four hours. In some cases the bodies were covered with vermin before they were removed.

There was no physician on board. Although we found a large medicine chest, it was not large enough for the many cases of sickness, and was, in fact, emptied after the first two weeks of the voyage.

The captain seems to have been sadly deficient in energy and authority in matters of moment, while he punished severely small offences; as, for instance, he handcuffed a passenger for the use of insulting words; but he did not enforce the plainest rules for the health and welfare of his passengers. Instead of compelling them, from the first, to come on deck and remove the dirt, he allowed them to remain below, and to perish among their own excrements. Of the whole crew, the cook alone fell sick and died, as he slept in the steerage. Three passenger girls who were employed in the kitchen, and lived on deck, enjoyed excellent health, during the whole voyage.

The physicians above mentioned, to whose report we refer for particulars, most positively declare that it was not the Asiatic cholera, but intestinal and stomach catarrh, more or less severe, and contagious typhus, which killed the passengers. From what we saw and learned from the passengers, we likewise arrive at the conclusion that the shocking mortality on board the *Leibnitz* arose from want of good ventilation, cleanliness, suitable medical care, sufficient water, and wholesome food.

SOURCE: **New York Herald,** March 6, 1870.

The Emigrants' Emeute

How the Wards of the State are Treated on Ward's Island. Investigation by the Legislative Committee-Startling Developments-Vermin, Filth and Insufficient Food the Cause of the Late Riot.

In accordance with the resolution of the House of Assembly adopted on Thursday the Committee on Commerce and Navigation, of which Mr. Lawrence D. Kiernan is chairman, made an official visit to Ward's Island yesterday for the purpose of inquiring into the causes of the late riot there and taking evidence as to the management of the Emigrant Institution. The committee embarked on board the steamer Bellview, at the foot of Twenty-sixth street, East river, at eleven o'clock, and arrived at Ward's Island shortly after. Commissioner Bell, several representatives of the press and a number of gentlemen interested accompanied the committee. Before proceeding to take testimony Mr. Kiernan suggested that the committee should first inspect the different departments of the institution and judge for themselves as to its condition. Accordingly, under the guidance of Mr. Wells, the superintendent, and Dr. John Dwyer, the assistant surgeon, the committee and the other visitors made a thorough inspection as to the cause of the recent riot. To say that they were surprised at what they saw would be putting it too mildly. They were horrified at the many evidences of mismanagement and gross neglect of the wretched people committed to the tender mercies of the superintendent.

Mr. Wells had fair warning that the committee of the Legislature were coming, and, as the sequel proved, availed himself of it to the utmost. While, therefore, the inspection showed disgraceful treatment of the emigrants, it may well be supposed that had the visitors come unannounced a still more shameful condition of affairs would have been discovered. The male inmates had finished their midday meal when the committee arrived on the island, but fortunately the females had not dined. Entering the dining hall just as the women were eating, the committee had a fair opportunity of inspecting the food. A row of tin platters was placed on either side of a long deal table, before which the women were seated on forms. Diminutive, dirty bits of meat, that might be either beef or mutton, flanked by a ladleful of boiled oatmeal, thin, dark and nauseating in appearance, hid the sheen of the tin plates; the cups of white, weak, watery soup, flanked the plates, and a slice of bread of stepmother cut was the *piece de resistance*. Not a knife, fork or spoon was to be seen on the table. The women looked up with cheerful faces as they entered, and while the latter stood by speculating as to how the food was to be disposed of they continued to eat. It was

A MOST DISGUSTING EXHIBITION.

The women sunk (too often dirty) fingers in the mush, grabbed a piece of the meat and ate ravenously. There were some, however, pinched, hungry looking creatures who drank down the swill called soup from their tins, ate the bread and left the meat and mush untasted. Each piece of bread would probably weigh six ounces; the meat on each plate three ounces. The spectacle of the unfortunate women daubing their hands in the slimy food and struggling to get it to their eager mouths was too much for the committee. Several gentlemen left hurriedly—Mr. Kiernan, the chairman, with a sick stomach—and repaired to other parts of the building. A number of men were discovered washing in a room which appeared not ill adapted for the purpose, but entirely too small. It was washing-day, and each man of the six or seven hundred in the Refuge might, if he could, wash his own clothes. The bakery and kitchen were next visited, but everything in these departments seemed to be in good order. Mr. Kiernan, the *Herald* reporter and one or two others paid a visit to the "lock up," where insane and refractory persons are put for safe keeping. Nothing objectionable was to be found in this place, however, which may be accounted for by the fact it is under the control of Dr. Dwyer.

The place of chief interest both for the members of the committee and the visitors was

THE REFUGE DEPARTMENT,

in the central building. This is a long, wide room, bare of furniture, except the stoves, and a row of forms on each side which afforded seats for about 100 persons. The floor was wet and sloppy and an air of utter discomfort pervaded the place. There were from 500 to 600 men in the room, of all nationalities and of all degrees of squalor and wretchedness. A hungry cadaverous look in their inquiring faces told a tale too true. There were several, however, who were hale and hearty, but they were new comers. They moved about on the wet floor listlessly, or stood in groups discussing among themselves the cause of the presence of the prying visitors.

When spoken to they told strange and often conflicting tales of neglect on the part of somebody, but they were unanimous in saying that they did not get enough to eat. It should have been mentioned that there was

A WASHING PLACE

in the room. For the accommodation of 100 men it was not too large; for the use of 600 it was absurd. By dint of squeezing it is possible that five men could wash at it at a time; but then four of them would have to wash in the water that had bathed the face and hands of number one, or the man nearest the faucet. And for polishing off the scum and water the supply of towels must be considered rather inadequate, to say the least. Two of these necessary articles have to bear the rubbing of 600 faces every day for a week; that is 4,200 men have the use of two towels. No fractional part of the 600 being engaged in his ablutions when the committee entered, no opportunity was afforded them to examine the material of those wonderful articles of the toilet; but as three intelligent witnesses who were afterwards selected at random from the crowd of emigrants and examined on oath swore that these towels exist, and that they stink when hung up, there can be no reason to doubt that they could be found about the room if a search were made. The committee talked with a number of the men and then returned to the superintendent's room and organized. Beside the chairman, Mr. L. D. Kiernan, there were present W. G. Bergen, Owen Kavanagh and Martin Nachtman of New York; John Ecker of Richmond, and Hugh M. Clarke, of Kings. William C. Jones, James Husted and Henry Ray, also of the committee, were absent. The committee was accompanied by the sergeant-at-arms, clerk and stenographer.

THE INVESTIGATION

The first person examined was Mr. Wells, the superintendent, who was closely questioned by the chairman as to the cause of the riot, the quantity and quality of the food furnished to the emigrants, &c. As the circumstances attending the riot have been already described the evidence of the witness in that respect need not be repeated. Mr. Wells testified that the emigrants get one quart of coffee and a quarter loaf of bread for breakfast; soup, meat, bread and oatmeal for dinner, and tea and bread for supper; they get plenty of food; there are no rules in respect to labor laid down for the guidance of the emigrants; would rather not say how they eat without spoons, knives or forks; the food is of the very best, and is got by contract. Mr. Wells swore that he derived no perquisites from any source; his salary was $3,000 per annum; he was formerly clerk of the Connecticut State Prison and superintendent of Illinois State Prison.

Dr. John Dwyer, assistant surgeon, being called, swore that he thought idleness to be the chief cause of trouble. In answer to a question put to him by the chairman he said that if books and papers were furnished the men to read when they were not engaged in out-door work the result would be beneficial; they had nothing to read now; in his opinion the men got enough to eat now; it was different, however, when they were working; he had nothing to do with the Refuge department, and could answer only for the surgical hospital; no vegetables are furnished the men in the Refuge; these men seek to get into the hospital that they may be better fed.

Mr. Bernard Casserly, General Agent at Castle Garden, being sworn, said that it may be alleged that want of work and the absence of reading matter is the principal source of trouble; can't state any defect in the management of the institution; the Commissioners were ever ready to respond to all reasonable demands; from 1847 to January 1, 1870, four and a half millions arrived in this port, on account of whom eight and a half millions of dollars were paid to the Commissioners by the owners of the emigrant ships; there is $75,000 now unappropriated; the Commissioners have enough money to take proper care of the emigrants, and would be willing to provide everything necessary for the physical and mental comfort of the men on the island if asked by the officers here; can't say if there is collusion between the contractors and Superintendent Wells; there might be; the Commissioners receive no salaries.

BEDS FULL OF VERMIN

Dr. Rymer, assistant physician; Dr. Ford, the principal physician; the clerk; the steward, policeman 220 and three emigrants were then examined at great length. No new facts were elicited by the testimony of the former; but the evidence of the latter amounted to this:—That the food was insufficient, the washing accommodations wretched, the beds full of vermin, and that the neglect of the superintendent was inhuman and disgraceful. These men said—and their statements were fully borne out by others with whom members of the committee had conversed—that they never had such a good dinner since they came on the island as they had yesterday, and that their best days were those when the Commissioners came round. They gave their evidence reluctantly, and several times expressed a fear that condign punishment would be meted out to them after the committee left. They were assured that they would be fully protected.

The only department of the institution which gave satisfaction to the committee, and against which none of the committee uttered a word of complaint, was the surgical department, over which Dr. Dwyer has charge. It was found to be in perfect order. The committee have not yet completed their investigation.

Steerage Class in the Twentieth Century

For those who arrived with the new immigration (1882–1930), steerage conditions improved slightly. The benefits of steam-powered steel ships reduced traveling time considerably, and the elimination of the fever ship guaranteed that most would arrive at their destination alive. Nevertheless, the physical discomforts and emotional indignities suffered by passengers were still the rule rather than the exception.

In an attempt to alter their plight, the United States Immigration Commission (1908–11) undertook an investigation of conditions under which immigrants were compelled to travel. Seeking an unbiased and eyewitness report, the Commission sent investigators to Europe, disguised them as travelers, and had them experience the return trip in typical steerage class.

In the selection which follows, a female investigator recounts the experiences of her trip. Accordingly, the report she submitted indicated the need to regulate and improve the environment of steerage passengers.

SOURCE: **"Steerage Conditions,"** Reports of United States *Immigration Commission,* XXXVII (1911), pp. 13–23.

"The statements in this report, unless otherwise indicated, are based on actual experiences and observations made during a twelve days' voyage in the steerage of the ——.

"I arrived in —— as a 'single' woman in the disguise of a Bohemian peasant, under an assumed name, and with passage engaged in the steerage on the ——. I called out the name of the agent from whom my ticket was purchased, ——, as directed in the circular sent me, and was approached by a porter, who carried my baggage and led me to —— office.

". . . on the day just prior to sailing all the steerage passengers who were not American citizens, were vaccinated by the physician from the —— and one other. The women bared their arms in one room, the men in another. No excuse was sufficient to escape this requirement. However, the skin was not even pierced in any one of the three spots on my arm, and I later found this to be true in the case of many of the other passengers. The eyes were casually examined by the same physicians. Each 'inspection card' was stamped by the United States consulate and also marked 'vaccinated.'

"July 30 we went by train from —— to ——, where in the waiting room we were classed as 'families,' 'single women'—that is, women traveling alone—and 'single men,' or men traveling alone. Thus subdivided we went on board, each class into a compartment especially assigned to it.

"The compartment provided for single women was in some respects superior to the quarters occupied by the other steerage passengers. It was likewise in the stern of the vessel, but was located on the main deck and had formerly been the second cabin. The others were on the first deck below the main deck.

"All the steerage berths were of iron, the framework forming two tiers and having but a low partition between the individual berths. Each bunk contained a mattress filled with straw and covered with a slip made of coarse white canvas, apparently cleaned for the voyage. There were no pillows. Instead, a life-preserver was placed under the mattress at the head in each berth. A short and light-weight white blanket was the only covering provided. This each passenger might take with him on leaving. It was practically impossible to undress properly for retiring because of insufficient covering and lack of privacy. Many women had pillows from home and used shawls and other clothing for coverings.

". . . our compartment was subdivided into three sections—one for the German women, which was completely boarded off from the rest; one for Hebrews; and one for all other creeds and nationalities together. The partition between these last two was merely a fence, consisting of four horizontal 6-inch boards. This neither kept out odors nor cut off the view.

"The single men had their sleeping quarters directly below ours and adjoining was the compartment for families and partial families—that is women and children. In this last section every one of the 60 beds was occupied and each passenger had only the 100 cubic feet of space required by law. The Hebrews were here likewise separated from the others by the same ineffectual fence, consisting of four horizontal boards and the intervening spaces. During the first six days the entire 60 berths were separated from the rest of the room by a similar fence. Outside the fence was the so-called dining room, getting all the bedroom smells from these 60 crowded berths. Later the spaces in, above, and below the fence were entirely boarded up.

"The floors in all these compartments were of wood. They were swept every morning and the aisles sprinkled lightly with sand. None of them was washed during the twelve days' voyage nor was there any indication that a disinfectant was being used on them. The beds received only such attention as each occupant gave to his own. When the steerage is full, each passenger's space is limited to his berth, which then serves as bed, clothes and towel rack, cupboard, and baggage space. There are no accommodations to encourage the steerage passenger to be clean and orderly. There was no hook on which to hand a garment, no receptacle for refuse, no cuspidor, no cans for use in case of seasickness.

"Two wash rooms were provided for the use of the steerage. The first morning out I took special care to inquire for the women's wash room. One of the crew directed me to a door bearing the sign 'Wash room for men.' Within were both men and women.

Thinking I had been misdirected, I proceeded to the other wash room. This bore no label and was likewise being used by both sexes. Repeating my inquiry another of the crew directed me just as the first had done. Evidently there was no distinction between the men's and the women's wash rooms. These were on the main deck and not convenient to any of the sleeping quarters. To use them one had to cross the open deck, subject to the public gaze. In the case of the families and men, it was necessary to come upstairs and cross the deck to get to both wash rooms and toilets.

"The one wash room, about 7 by 9 feet, contained 10 faucets of cold salt water, 5 along either of its two walls, and as many basins. These resembled in size and shape the usual stationary laundry tub. Ten persons could scarcely have used this room at one time. The basins were seldom used on account of their great inconvenience and because of the various other services to which they must be put. To wash out of a laundry tub with only a little water on the bottom is quite difficult, and where so many persons must use so few basins one can not take the time to draw so large a basin full of water. This same basin served as a dishpan for greasy tins, as a laundry tub for soiled handkerchiefs and clothing, and as a basin for shampoos, and without receiving any special cleaning. It was the only receptacle to be found for use in the case of seasickness.

"The space indicated to me as the 'women's wash room' contained 6 faucets of cold salt water and basins like those already described. The hot-water faucet did not act. The sole arrangement for washing dishes in all the steerage was located in the women's wash room. It was a trough about 4 feet long, with a faucet of warm salt water. This was never hot, and seldom more than luke-warm. Coming up in single file to wash dishes at the trough would have meant very long waiting for those at the end of the line, and to avoid this many preferred cold water and the wash basins. The steerage stewards also brought dishes here to wash. If there was no privacy in our sleeping quarters there certainly was none in the wash rooms.

"Steerage passengers may be filthy, as is often alleged, but considering the total absence of conveniences for keeping clean, this uncleanliness seems but a natural consequence. Some may really be filthy in their habits, but many make heroic efforts to keep clean. No woman with the smallest degree of modesty, and with no other conveniences than a wash room, used jointly with men, and a faucet of cold salt water can keep clean amidst such surroundings for a period of twelve days and more. It was forbidden to bring water for washing purposes into the sleeping compartments, nor was there anything in which to bring it. On different occasions some of the women rose early, brought drinking water in their soup pails, and thus tried to wash themselves effectively, but were driven out when detected by the steward. Others, resorting to extreme measures, used night chambers, which they carry with them for the children, as wash basins. This was done a great deal when preparation was being made for landing. Even hair was washed with these vessels. No soap and no towels were supplied.

"Seeing the sign 'Baths' over a door, I inquired if these were for the steerage. The chief steerage steward informed me that this sign no longer meant anything; that when that section had been used by the second cabin the baths had been there. 'Are there then no baths for the steerage?' I asked. 'Oh, yes; in the hospital,' he assured me. 'Where all the steerage may bathe?' I continued. 'They are really only for those in the hospital, but if you can persuade the stewardess to prepare you a bath, I will permit you to have one,' he replied.

"The toilets for women were six in number—for men about five. They baffle description as much as they did use. Each room or space was exceedingly narrow and short, and instead of a seat there was an open trough, in front of which was an iron step and back of it a sheet of iron slanting forward. On either side wall was an iron handle. The toilets were filthy and difficult of use and were apparently not cleaned at all during the first few days. Later in the voyage they were evidently cleaned every night, but not during the day. The day of landing, when inspection was made by the customs official who came on board, the toilets were clean, the floors in both toilets and wash rooms were dry, and the odor of a disinfectant was noticeable. All these were conditions that did not obtain during the voyage or at any one time.

"Each steerage passenger is to be furnished 'all the eating utensils necessary.' These he finds in his berth, and like the blanket they become his possession and his care. They consist of a fork, a large spoon, and a combination workingman's tin lunch pail. The bottom or pail part is used for soup and frequently as a wash basin; a small tin dish that fits into the top of the pail is used for meat and potatoes; a cylindrical projection on the lid is a dish for vegetables or stewed fruits; a tin cup that fits onto this projection is for drinks. These must serve the passenger throughout the voyage and so are generally hidden away in his berth for safe-keeping, there being no other place provided. Each washed his own dishes, and if he wished to use soap and a towel he must provide his own.

"Dish washing is not easy, as there is only one faucet of warm water, and when there is no chance to use this, he has no other choice than to try to get the grease off of his tins with cold salt water. As the ordinary man doesn't carry soap and dish towels with him, he has not these aids to proper dish washing. He uses his hand towel, if he happens to have one, or his handkerchief, or must let the dishes dry in the sun. The quality of the tin and this method of washing is responsible for the fact that the dishes are soon rusty, and not fit to eat from. Here, as in the toilet and wash-rooms, it would require persons of very superior intelligence, skill, and ingenuity to maintain order with the given accommodations.

"The steamship company clearly complies with the requirement that tables for eating be supplied in the steerage, and in spite of efforts can not make the steerage passengers use these tables. Apparently it is true that the immigrants did not make use of the conveniences provided. But where are these tables, and how convenient is it to eat at them? The main steerage dining room was a part of a compartment on the first deck below the main deck. It contained seven long tables, each with two benches, and seating at most 12 persons. The remainder of the compartment contained 60 berths closely crowded together, the sleeping quarters for families. During the first few days the partition between these crowded sleeping quarters and the dining room was but a fence made of four 6-inch boards running horizontally. Only later was this partition made a solid wall. Most people preferred the open deck to this dining room and its disagreeable odors.

"A table without appointment and service means nothing. The food was brought into the dining room in large galvanized tin cans. The meat and vegetables were placed on the tables in tins resembling smaller sized dishpans. There were no serving plates, knives, or spoons. Each passenger had only his combination dinner pail, which is more convenient away from a table than at it. This he had to bring himself and wash when he had finished. Liquid food could not be easily served at the tables, so each must line up for his soup and coffee. No places at table were assigned and no arrangement made for two sittings, and as all could not be seated at once, the result was disorder, to escape which many left the dining room. Beside these seven tables there were two on the main deck, in the sleeping compartments of the single women. In the other two sleeping compartments there were shelves along the wall and benches by the side of these. Including these, there was barely seating capacity for the small number in the steerage on this trip. On inquiring where the passengers were seated when the steerage was crowded, I was told by the Hebrew cook and several others of the crew that then there was no pretense made to seat them. The attempt at serving us at tables was soon given up.

"If the steerage passengers act like cattle at meals, it is undoubtedly because they are treated as such. The stewards complain that they crowd like swine, but unless each passenger seizes his pail when the bell rings announcing the meal and hurries for his share, he is very likely to be left without food. No time is wasted in the serving. One morning, wishing to see if it were possible for a woman to rise and dress without the presence of men onlookers, I watched and waited my chance. There was none until the breakfast bell rang, when all rushed off to the meal. I arose, dressed quickly, and hurried to the wash room. When I went for my breakfast, it was no longer being served. The steward asked why I hadn't come sooner saying, 'The bell rang at 5 minutes to 7, and now it is 20 after.' I suggested that twenty-five minutes wasn't a long time for serving 160 people, and also explained the real reason of my tardiness. He then said that under the circumstances I could still have some bread. However, he warned me not to use that excuse again. As long as no systematic order is observed in serving food in the steerage, the passengers will resort to the only effective method they know. Each will rush to get his share.

.   .   .

"So simple a thing as coffee was not properly prepared. I carefully watched the process by which it was made. The coffee grounds, sugar, and milk were put in a large galvanized tin can. Hot water, not always boiling, was poured over these ingredients. This was served as coffee.

"The white bread, potatoes, and soup, when hot, were the only foods that were good, and these received the same favorable criticism from passengers of all nationalities. The meats were generally old, tough, and bad smelling. The same was true of the fish, excepting pickled herring. The vegetables were often a queer, unanalyzable mixture, and therefore avoided. The butter was rarely edible. The stewed dried prunes and apples were merely the refuse that is left behind when all the edible fruit is graded out. The prune jam served at breakfast, judging by taste and looks, was made from the lowest possible grade of fruit. Breakfast cereals, a food foreign to most Europeans, were merely boiled and served in an abundance of water. The black bread was soggy and not at all like the good, wholesome, coarse black bread served in the cabin.

"During the twelve days only about six meals were fair and gave satisfaction. More than half of the food was always thrown into the sea. Hot water could be had in the galley, and many of the passengers made tea and lived on this and bread. The last day out we were told on every hand to look pleasant, else we would not be admitted in Baltimore. To help bring about this happy appearance the last meal on board consisted of boiled eggs, bread, and fried potatoes. Those who commented on this meal said it was 'the best yet.' None of this food was thrown into the sea, but all was eagerly eaten. If this simple meal of ordinary food, well prepared, gave such general satisfaction, then it is really not so difficult after all to satisfy the tastes of the various nationalities. A few simple standard dishes of fair quality and properly prepared, even though less generously served, would, I am positive, give satisfaction. The expense certainly would not be greater, than that now caused by the waste of so much inferior food. The interpreter, the chief steerage steward, and one other officer were always in attendance during the meals to prevent any crowding. When all had been served, these three walked about among the passengers asking: 'Does the food taste good?' The almost invariable answer was: 'It has to; we must eat something.'

.   .   .

"The two clean, light, airy hospital rooms on the port side of the main deck, one for women, the other for men, made a good first impression. Each contained 12 berths in two tiers. The iron framework was the same as that of all the steerage berths, but the beds had white sheets and pillows with white slips. By the side of each berth was a frame, holding a glass and a bottle of water, also a sick can. A toilet and bath adjoined each hospital. The steerage stewardess, whose chief duties were distributing milk for little children, and giving out bread at meals, acted as nurse. According to her own statement, she had never had any training in the care of the sick. She spoke German and some English. The interpreter, I was told, interprets for her and the doctor when it is necessary. However, when the doctor learned that I could speak both Slavic languages and German, he called on me to interpret for him in the case of each of his four Slavic patients.

"On one occasion a 6 year-old girl was seized with violent cramps. The doctor ordered a hot bath, but the hot-water faucet gave forth nothing. The stewardess had to bring hot water from the galley across one deck, up the stairs, across another deck, and down other stairs. Later he ordered a cold bath, which could be given only after another delay. The water ran so thick and filthy that it was not fit to use. There were no towels, and a sheet was used instead. Aside from the berths and a washstand, there were no hospital conveniences or apparatus in the room. The most trivial articles had to be sent for to the 'drug store' at some distance.

"At another time I had proof of the difficulty of getting the doctor to respond to a call. A Polish girl was suffering with severe pains in her chest and side. This was reported to a passing officer with the request that the doctor be sent. Later the same request was made of the chief steward, and then of another officer. Finally some one secured the stewardess and she went for the doctor. In all more than two and one-half hours had elapsed between the time when the case was first reported and the doctor's appearance. The doctor never was sympathetic, and when not indifferent was quite rough.

"I remarked to this physician that I and many others were not going to have any vaccination mark to present, and I showed some fear of not being admitted at Baltimore. He assured me, with a smile of self-satisfaction, that the mark on the inspection card was the important matter.

"The daily medical inspection of the steerage was carried on as follows: The second day out we all passed in single file before the doctor as he leisurely conversed with another officer, casting an occasional glance at the passing line. The chief steerage steward punched six holes in each passenger's inspection card, indicating that the inspection for six days was complete. One steward told me this was done to save the passengers from going through this formality every day. The fourth day out we were again reviewed. The doctor stood by. Another officer holding a cablegram blank in his hand compared each passenger's card to some writing on it. There was another inspection on the seventh day, when we were required to bare our arms and show the vaccinations. Again our cards were punched six times and this completed the medical examination. Just before landing we were reviewed by some officer who came on board and checked us off on a counting machine operated by a ship's officer.

"In the women's sleeping compartment, in an inconspicuous place, here hung a small copy of section 7, passenger act for 1882, in German and English. A similar copy hung in the so-called dining room. Few of the women could read either of these languages. From the time we boarded the steamer until we landed, no woman in the steerage had a moment's privacy. One steward was always on duty in our compartment, and others of the crew came and went continually. Nor was this room a passageway to another part of the vessel. The entrance was also the only exit. The men who came may or may not have been sent there on some errand. This I could not ascertain, but I do know that, regularly, during the hour or so preceding the breakfast bell and while we were rising and dressing, several men usually passed through and returned for no ostensible reason. If it were necessary for them to pass so often, another passageway should have been provided or a more opportune time chosen.

"As not nearly all the berths were occupied, we all chose upper ones. To get anything from an upper berth, to deposit anything in it or to arrange it, it was necessary to stand on the framework of the one below. The women often had to stand thus, with their backs to the aisle. The crew in passing a woman in this position never failed to deal her a blow—even the head steward. If a woman were dressing, they always stopped to watch her, and frequently hit and handled her. Even though they were sent there, this was not their errand.

"Two of the stewards were quite strict about driving men out of our quarters. One other steward who had business in our compartment was as annoying a visitor as we had and he began his offenses even before we left port. Some of the women wished to put aside their better dresses immediately after coming on board. As soon as they began to undress he stood about watching and touching them. They tried to walk away, but he followed them. Not one day passed but I saw him annoying some women, especially in the wash rooms. At our second and last inspection this steward was assigned the duty of holding each woman by her bare arm that the doctor might better see the vaccination.

"A small notice stating the distance traveled was posted each day just within the entrance to our compartment. It was the only one posted in the steerage as far as I could learn, and consequently both crew and men passengers came to see it and it served as an excuse for coming at all times. The first day out the bar just within our entrance was used. This brought a large number of men into our compartment, many not entirely sober, but later the bar was transferred.

"One night, when I had retired very early with a severe cold, the chief steerage steward entered our compartment, but not noticing me approached a Polish girl who was apparently the only occupant. She spoke in Polish, saying, 'My head aches—please go on and let me alone.' But he merely stood on and soon was taking unwarranted liberties with her. The girl, weakened by seasickness, defended herself as best she could, but soon was struggling to get out of the man's arms. Just then other passengers entered and he released her. Such was the man who was our highest protector and court of appeal.

"I can not say that any woman lost her virtue on this passage, but in making free with the women the men of the crew went as far as possible without exposing themselves to the danger of punishment. But this limit is no doubt frequently overstepped. Several of the crew told me that many of them marry girls from the steerage. When I insinuated that they could scarcely become well enough acquainted to marry during the passage, the answer was that the acquaintance had already gone so far that marriage was imperative.

"There was an outside main deck and an upper deck on which

the steerage were allowed. These were each about 40 feet wide by 50 feet long, but probably half of this space was occupied by machinery, ventilators, and other apparatus. There was no canvas to keep out the rain, sun, and continual showers of cinders from the smokestack. These fell so thick and fast that two young sailor boys were kept busy sweeping them off the decks. It is impossible to remain in one's berth all the time, and as there were no smoking and sitting rooms we spent most of the day on these decks. No benches nor chairs were provided, so we sat wherever we could find a place on the machinery, exposed to the sun, fog, rain and cinders. These not only filled our hair, but also flew into our eyes, often causing considerable pain.

"These same two outdoor decks were used also by the crew during their leisure. When asked what right they had there, they answered: 'As much as the passengers.' No notices hung anywhere about to refute this. The manner in which the sailors, stewards, firemen, and others mingled with the women passengers was thoroughly revolting. Their language and the topics of their conversation were vile. Their comments about the women, and made in their presence, were coarse. What was far worse and of continual occurrence was their handling the women and girls. Some of the crew were always on deck, and took all manner of liberties with the women, in broad daylight as well as after dark.

"Not one young woman in the steerage escaped attack. The writer herself was no exception. A hard, unexpected blow in the offender's face in the presence of a large crowd of men, an evident acquaintance with the stewardess, doctor, and other officers, general experience, and manner were all required to ward off further attacks. Some few of the women, perhaps, did not find these attentions so disagreeable; some resisted them for a time, then weakened; some fought with all their physical strength, which naturally was powerless against a man's. Others were continually fleeing to escape. Two more refined and very determined Polish girls fought the men with pins and teeth, but even they weakened under this continued warfare and needed some moral support about the ninth day. The atmosphere was one of general lawlessness and total disrespect for women. It naturally demoralized the women themselves after a time. There was no one to whom they might appeal. Besides, most of them did not know the official language on the steamer, nor were they experienced enough to know they were entitled to protection.

"The interpreter, who could and should be a friend of the immigrants, passed through the steerage but twice a day. He positively discouraged every approach. I purposely tried on several occasions to get advice and information from him, but always failed. His usual answer was, 'How in the —— do I know?' The chief steerage steward by his own familiarity with the women made himself impossible as their protector. Once when a man passenger was annoying two Lithuanian girls I undertook to rescue them. The man poured forth a volley of oaths at me in English. Just then the chief steward appeared, and to test him I made complaint. The offender denied having sworn at all, but I insisted that he had, and that I understood. The steward then administered this reproof, 'You let them girls alone or I fix you —— —— easy.'

"The main deck was hosed every night at 10, when we were driven in. The upper deck was washed only about four times during the voyage. At 8 each evening we were driven below. This was to protect the women, one of the crew informed me. What protection they gained on the equally dark and unsupervised deck below isn't at all clear. What worse things could have befallen them there than those to which they were already exposed at the hands of both the crew and the men passengers would have been criminal offenses. Neither of these decks was lighted, because, as one sailor explained, maritime usage does not sanction lights either in the bow or stern of a vessel, the two parts always used by the steerage. The descriptions that I might give of the mingling of the crew and passengers on these outdoor decks would be endless, and all necessarily much the same. A series of snap shots would give a more accurate and impressive account of this evil than can words. I would here suggest that any agent making a similar investigation be supplied with a kodak for this purpose.

"To sum up, let me make some general statements that will give an idea of the awfulness of steerage conditions on the steamer in question. During these twelve days in the steerage I lived in a disorder and in surroundings that offended every sense. Only the fresh breeze from the sea overcame the sickening odors. The vile language of the men, the screams of the women defending themselves, the crying of children, wretched because of their surroundings, and practically every sound that reached the ear, irritated beyond endurance. There was no sight before which the eye did not prefer to close. Everything was dirty, sticky, and disagreeable to the touch. Every impression was offensive. Worse than this was the general air of immorality. For fifteen hours each day I witnessed all around me this improper, indecent, and forced mingling of men and women who were total strangers and often did not understand one word of the same language. People can not live in such surroundings and not be influenced.

"All that has been said of the mingling of the crew with the women of the steerage is also true of the association of the men steerage passengers with the women. Several times, when the sight of what was occurring about me was no longer endurable, I interfered and asked the men if they knew they might be deported were their actions reported on landing. Most of them had been in America before, and the answer generally given me was: 'Immorality is permitted in America if it is anywhere. Everyone can do as he chooses; no one investigates his mode of life, and no account is made or kept of his doings.'"

The "Weeding-Out Process" at Ellis Island

The final step in the arduous journey from the "old country" was the medical "line inspection" at the port of entry. Unlike those traveling in cabins, immigrants from steerage class who entered the United States at the Port of New York were first brought to Ellis Island. The average immigrant remained at the medical station for three hours while he underwent an examination by the Public Health Service to determine whether he was to be admitted. For some, the fear and "intimidation" of these examinations caused "emotional, noisy and boisterous" behavior. Consequently, this loss of self-control became the reason for detention and deportation. For others, the traumatic effect of this experience became a lasting problem in their process of adjusting to the new society.

In the following article, E. H. Mullan, a surgeon who administered the examinations, described the "weeding-out process," and detailed the efforts made to refuse entry to those considered "undesirable." According to Mullan, some officials went as far as to bar entrance because the alien was "elated, talkative or surly."

SOURCE: E. H. Mullan, "**Mental Examination of Immigrants, Administration and Line Inspection at Ellis Island,**" United States *Public Health Reports* (May 18, 1917), pp. 733–39.

Immigrants, not traveling in the cabin, who enter the United States at the port of New York, are first brought to Ellis Island in order to undergo an examination to determine their fitness for admission.

The average immigrant remains at Ellis Island two or three hours, during which time he undergoes an examination by the Public Health Service in order to determine his mental and physical condition, and by the Immigration Service in order to find out whether he is otherwise admissible.

Immigrants are brought from the various steamships throughout New York Harbor to Ellis Island by means of barges. As soon as they land at Ellis Island they undergo the medical inspection and examination which are conducted by the officers of the Public Health Service.

Line Inspection

Upon entering the examination plant of the Public Health Service, the immigrants are guided by an attendant into the different inspection lines. These lines, separated by iron railings, are four in number at their proximal end and two in number at their distal end.

. . .

Four medical officers who carry on the general inspection are stationed each in one of the four proximal lines, and two medical officers stand at the extreme ends of the two distal lines or just where these lines merge into two common exits.

. . .

The alien after passing the scrutiny of the first medical officer passes on to the end of the line, where he is quickly inspected again by the second examiner. This examiner is known in service parlance as "the eye man." He stands at the end of the line with his back to the window and faces the approaching alien. This position affords good light, which is so essential for eye examinations. The approaching alien is scrutinized by the eye man immediately in front of whom the alien comes to a standstill. The officer will frequently ask a question or two so as to ascertain the condition of the immigrant's mentality. He may pick up a symptom, mental or physical, that has been overlooked by the first examiner.

He looks carefully at the eyeball in order to detect signs of defect and disease of that organ and then quickly everts the upper lids in search of conjunctivitis and trachoma. Corneal opacities, nystagmus, squint, bulging eyes, the wearing of eye glasses, clumsiness, and other signs on the part of the alien, will be sufficient cause for him to be chalk-marked with "Vision". He will then be taken out of the line by an attendant and his vision will be carefully examined. If the alien passes through this line without receiving a chalk mark, he has successfully passed the medical inspection and off he goes to the upper hall, there to undergo another examination by officers of the Immigration Service, who take every means to see that he is not an anarchist, bigamist, pauper, criminal, or otherwise unfit.

.   .   .

In the medical inspection which is conducted by the first officer or the one who occupies the proximal position, attention is paid to each passing alien. The alien's manner of entering the line, his conversation, style of dress, any peculiarity or unusual incident in regard to him are all observed. Knowledge of racial characteristics in physique, costume and behavior are important in this primary sifting process.

Every effort is made to detect signs and symptoms of mental disease and defect. Any suggestion, no matter how trivial, that would point to abnormal mentality is sufficient cause to defer the immigrant for a thorough examination.

The following signs and symptoms occurring in immigrants at the line inspection might suggest an active or maniacal psychosis: Striking peculiarities in dress, talkativeness, witticism, facetiousness, detailing, apparent shrewdness, keenness, excitement, impatience in word or manner, impudence, unruliness, flightiness, nervousness, restlessness, egotism, smiling, facial expression of mirth, laughing eroticism, boisterous conduct, meddling with the affairs of others, and uncommon activity.

Psychoses of a depressive nature would be indicated by: Slow speech, low voice, trembling articulation, sad facies, tearful eyes, perplexity, difficulty in thinking, delayed responses, psycho motor retardation.

Alcoholism, paresis, and organic dementias may exhibit any of the following signs: Surliness, apprehensiveness, untidiness, intoxication, apparent intoxication, confusion, aimlessness, dullness, stupidity, expressionless face, tremulousness, tremor and twitching of facial muscles, ataxia, stuttering and tremulous speech, great amount of calmness, jovial air, self-confident smile, talkativeness, fabrications, grandioseness, sullenness, fussiness, excessive friendliness, defective memory, misstatement of age, disorientation, difficulty in computation, pupil symptoms, and other physical signs.

Various kinds of dementia, mental deficiency or epilepsy would be suggested by: Stigmata of degeneration, facial scars, acneiform rashes, stupidity, confusion, inattention, lack of comprehension, facial expression of earnestness or preoccupation, inability to add simple digits, general untidiness, forgetfulness, verbigeration, neologisms, talking to one's self, incoherent talk, impulsive or stereotyped actions, constrained bearing, suspicious attitude, refusing to be examined, objecting to have eyelids turned, nonresponse to questions, evidences of negativism, silly laughing, hallucinating, awkward manner, biting nails, unnatural actions, mannerisms and other eccentricities.

* * *

Experience enables the inspecting officer to tell at a glance the race of an alien. There are, however, exceptions to this rule. It occasionally happens that the inspecting officer thinking that an approaching alien is of a certain race brings him to a standstill and questions him. The alien's facial expression and manner are peculiar and just as the officer is about to decide that this alien is mentally unbalanced, he finds out that the alien in question belongs to an entirely different race. The peculiar attitude of the alien in question is no longer peculiar; it is readily accounted for by racial considerations. Accordingly the officer passes him on as a mentally normal person. Those who have inspected immigrants know that almost every race has its own type of reaction during the line inspection. On the line if an Englishman reacts to questions in the manner of an Irishman, his lack of mental balance would be suspected. The converse is also true. If the Italian responded to questions as the Russian Finn responds, the former would in all probability be suffering with a depressive psychosis.

From 50 to 100 per cent of the immigrants who enter the inspection plant are questioned by the medical examiner in order to elicit signs of mental disease or mental defect. The exact number that are stopped and questioned will depend upon the race, sex, and general appearance of the passengers undergoing inspection as well as upon the total number of immigrants to be inspected.

In some instances an idea of an immigrant's mental state may be obtained by asking him such simple questions as: Where are you going? How old are you? Are you a Greek? What is your name? The majority of immigrants, however, are questioned in simple addition. The kind of addition to be propounded depends upon the age, sex, race, and general appearance of those undergoing the inspection. The art of propounding addition during the medical inspection of immigrants can be gained only by experience.

A northern Italian girl whose appearance indicates that she has had some schooling, an Irish girl, a Scandinavian or a male Greek would, in many instances, be thus questioned:

How many are 14 and 14? 14 and 15? or

How many are 13 and 13? 13 and 14? or

How many are 15 and 15? 15 and 16?

An illiterate male Italian from southern Italy would probably respond more readily to addition sums in a somewhat simpler form; such as,

How many are 8 and 8? or 8 and 9?

How many are 10 and 10? 10 and 12?

A Greek woman or a southern Italian girl on account of illiteracy, lack of experience and emotional state at the time of landing would have to be tested with still simpler sums in order to bring out the same mental phenomena as observed in the above cases.

Hence, such sums as 6+6, 7+7, 8+8 are frequently used in inspecting this class of persons.

To immigrant children under 12, very simple sums should be given at the line of inspection. 3+3, 4+4, 2+4, 5+5 etc., are of sufficient difficulty to bring forth the child's mentation.

When a family of children come along the inspection line it is well to question the oldest child first. For instance a child of 12 could be asked the sum of 6+6. The 10-year-old child could be questioned as to the sum of 4+4, the 8-year-old child the sum of 3+3, while the youngster of 4 or 5 would show his mental alertness by simply responding to the question, "What is your name?"

On account of the emotional disturbance in immigrant children at the time of landing difficulty may be experienced in obtaining responses to the above simple tests. The question, "What is your name?" may have to be resorted to in the case of each child.

As above suggested, in propounding the question, "What is your name?" successively to a group of children it is well to start with the oldest child. The younger children will usually follow the leader and reply promptly. In this way it often happens that a child of 4, with a smile on his face, will tell the examiner his name. On the other hand, if the little ones (4 to 5 years) are questioned first, they may remain mute. In this event it is rather hard to get at their mentality.

In all cases, careful attention is paid to the facial expression of the immigrant as the latter thinks and responds to the examiner's questions.

These brief questions enable the officer to bring to view the attention, alertness, reasoning ability, and emotional reaction of the alien.

Not infrequently positive signs of mental disease (as above enumerated) are obtained by bringing the alien to a standstill and giving him these brief mental tests.

Before leaving this subject, it may be said, that in training for line inspection work, it is thought that a brief study of many insane patients is preferable to a comprehensive study of a small number of such persons. In other words, in training for line inspection, it is more profitable to briefly study 2,000 insane than to carefully study 200.

3. Hopes, Possibilities and Disillusionment: First Contact with the New Homeland

An Infamous Case of Extradition

Uppermost in the minds of those who migrated to the United States was the hope of a brighter future. Nevertheless, the possibility of detention and deportation remained a constant threat to those who sought refuge. For many, the charge of pauperism became the unpardonable sin resulting in their rejection and sad return to the old country.

Representative of many of these actions was the infamous case of extradition of Mary Williams and her infant daughter Bridget. In 1855, the state of Massachusetts classified the couple as paupers and authorized their return to Ireland. Subsequently, the incident gained notoriety as several Boston newspapers told the story of the frightened family. Shortly thereafter, the family was expelled because they were guilty of the crime of poverty—a crime "which Massachusetts punishes as no other crime [was] punished in America, by banishment."

SOURCE: From the **Boston Daily Advertiser,** May 16, 1855; reprinted in the *Citizen,* II (New York City), May 26, 1855, p. 332, and June 9, 1855, p. 361.

Yesterday morning there sailed from this port a splendid packet-ship bearing the noble name of Daniel Webster, which fitly belongs to so fine a vessel. Yet so many fine ships sail out of our harbor that the reader may inquire why we make this departure the occasion for such conspicuous notice.

Among the crowd of human beings on board that proud vessel was one poor woman, with an infant daughter. Her passage and that of her child were paid by the rich and powerful commonwealth of Massachusetts. She left our free and happy shores unwilling and reluctant. She went away against her own free will, constrained by force of the civil authorities of the State. Her cries as she begged not to be thus so cruelly banished, were, we are told, most piteous, and such as to cause the accidental witnesses of the scene to burn with indignation.

The offence of this poor woman, for which she was thus violently and ignominiously expelled from Massachusetts, was the fact that she was born in Ireland and is called a pauper. Her infant daughter, who unconsciously shares her mother's sad fate, is a native of the commonwealth of Massachusetts; but she too partakes of that hard lot of poverty which it has been reserved for Massachusetts to make a crime, and a crime which Massachusetts punishes as no other crime is punished in America, by banishment—banishment from one's native land.

The name of this victim to Know-Nothing intolerance was Mary Williams; and her infant, Bridget, is but a few weeks old. About thirty-five paupers, perhaps more, were sent away at the same time, in the same vessel, at the expense of the State. These facts we learn from eye-witnesses of the scene, and from other certain and authentic sources of information.

Our readers are aware that there exists upon our statute book a law which authorizes any Justice of the Peace upon complaint, by a warrant directed to and to be executed by any constable, or any other person there designed, to cause any pauper to be removed out of the State, to any place beyond the sea where he belongs, if the Justice thinks proper, and he may be conveniently removed, and also that, independently of this provision of law, a practice has arisen by which the Commissioner of Alien Passengers undertakes, even without the warrant of a Justice of Peace, to send back paupers in cases in which he sees fit, and pays the expenses from money in his hands belonging to the State Treasury.

On account of the temporary absence of the Commissioner of Alien Passengers, and none of the gentlemen in his office being possessed of the facts, we are unable to state which of these two methods was employed as the pretext of authority for effecting the rendition of the unfortunate creatures who sailed yesterday in the Daniel Webster; nor can we state by what Justice of the Peace, if any, the warrant was issued. But the facts that they were sent away and that the State paid their passage, and that the piteous cries of this poor woman with her child were such as to attract the attention of the bystanders as she was led on board the vessel—these facts we have certainly ascertained.

Every week brings forth some new disgrace for Massachusetts. The extradition of the Irish girl, Mary Williams, and her infant daughter, is fresh in the memory of our readers, but a recent discovery has brought to light a still more atrocious case. The same vessel that bore off this poor, friendless girl, carried also a helpless lunatic, huddled from his cell in the asylum, on board, alone, among strangers, to be conveyed to his native country, where, perhaps, not a solitary relative remains to cheer the dark remnant of his life.

Hugh Carr, a native of Ireland, long resident in this country, an inchoate citizen, who, up to the period when Heaven mysteriously deprived him of reason, faithfully performed all the duties of a good citizen, and contributed his measure of taxation for the support of the State, was, at the time of his affliction, consigned by his family to the Lunatic Asylum, in the hope of restoration to his senses.

His brother and family are all residents of Massachusetts; capable and willing to support him if the State considered him an unjust burden—which he certainly was not—yet, without consulting them as to his provision, or acquainting them with their intentions, the fanatical officials of this hotbed of bigotry smuggle the unconscious lunatic on board ship, and pack him off to Ireland, utterly indifferent as to his future fate.

The threat of an action at law by the brother of Mr. Carr has brought the managers of the Asylum to their sense, and they now propose to bring the unfortunate man back again. It is too late for the reputation of the State. His restitution may lessen *his* misery, but it will not lessen *her* crime. Subsequent investigation also has put the case of Mary Williams in a worse form than it was at first represented. The Boston *Atlas* has sifted the matter to the bottom, and declares:

"She was not a pauper abroad, and she never had been a pauper. She came here with an aunt who is now living in the State, and is not a pauper. This girl—for she is quite young—had been deceived abroad, and she came here to conceal her shame. When near the time of her confinement, she was sent to the alm-house; and when next we hear of her, she is torn from the only being who loves her, and is sent over the sea. Before she could make her wants known, before she could appeal to benevolent men or women for aid, before she could effect any arrangement for supporting herself by her own labor, she is driven by force out of this hospitable Commonwealth—to want, to loneliness, to irreclaimable infamy. And all this cost the State of Massachusetts just $12 passage money!"

Ah! it cost her more than this. It cost her that which is priceless, her "good name." And unhappily this inequity, together with all the others which she is every day heaping upon her head, will bring the whole Republic and its principles into disrepute, at the very time when the Democratic sentiment most needs encouragement, hope, and the guide-star of a bright example among the re-wakening nationalities of the old world.

If there could be any plea for disunion, the crimes of Massachusetts might furnish it. If the bond were not too sacred to be broken, no honest American would regret much to see this rotten member lopped off the glorious body of the union, which its fanaticism and intolerance disgraces.

How the Family Are Brought Out

Many who arrived in America came in the vanguard of their family. Sent with the hope of returning a portion of their earnings "home," thousands of single men and women would make monthly remittances through banks, Emigrant Aid Societies and clergymen. Others would save until the "passage money" was enough to send for someone who anxiously awaited their "turn to come."

The following article described the activities of young Irish girls, whose most important ambition was to "send 'something' to [their] people . . . as soon as [they had] landed . . ." Accordingly, they regarded everything they earned as belonging to those they had left behind. As time went on, these "agents" from the old country would bring over the remainder of the family. This procedure was practiced by immigrants well into the twentieth century.

SOURCE: John Francis Maguire, **The Irish in America** (London, 1868), pp. 315–16, 319–22.

. . . The great ambition of the Irish girl is to send 'something' to her people as soon as possible after she has landed in America; and in innumerable instances the first tidings of her arrival in the

New World are accompanied with a remittance, the fruits of her first earnings in her first place. Loving a bit of finery dearly, she will resolutely shut her eyes to the attractions of some enticing article of dress, to prove to the loved ones at home that she has not forgotten them; and she will risk the danger of insufficient clothing, or boots not proof against rain or snow, rather than diminish the amount of the little hoard to which she is weekly adding, and which she intends as a delightful surprise to parents who possibly did not altogether approve of her hazardous enterprise. To send money to her people, she will deny herself innocent enjoyments, womanly indulgences, and the gratifications of legitimate vanity; and such is the generous and affectionate nature of these young girls, that they regard the sacrifices they make as the most ordinary matter in the world, for which they merit neither praise nor approval. To assist their relatives, whether parents, or brothers and sisters, is with them a matter of imperative duty, which they do not and cannot think of disobeying, and which, on the contrary, they delight in performing. And the money destined to that purpose is regarded as sacred, and must not be diverted to any object less worthy.

I was told in New York of a young Irish girl, who was only one month in the country, going to the office of the well-known Irish Emigration Society's Bank to send her first earnings to her mother, of course to the care of the parish priest. She brought with her five dollars, which in her simplicity she supposed to be equivalent to the 1 £ she intended to transmit. At that time six dollars and fifty cents were required to make up the British pound, and the poor girl's disappointment was intense when she was made to understand that she was deficient a dollar and a half. The friend who accompanied her, and who had been some time longer in the country, lent her a dollar; the clerk advanced her the balance, and the undiminished pound was sent to her 'poor mother, who wanted it badly.' In a few days after, the money advanced by the clerk was paid by the young girl, whose face was soon known in the office, as she came at regular intervals to send remittances, which were gradually increasing in amount. In a very short time she understood the relative value of American 'greenbacks' and British gold, and made no mistake as to the amount of the money-orders she desired to transmit.

. . .

What wonderful things have not these Irish girls done! Take a single example—and there is not a State in the Union in which the same does not occur:—Resolving to do something to better the circumstances of her family, the young Irish girl leaves her home for America. There she goes into service, or engages in some kind of feminine employment. The object she has in view—the same for which she left her home and ventured to a strange country—protects her from all danger, especially to her character: that object, her dream by day and night, is the welfare of her family, whom she is determined, if possible, to again have with her as of old. From the first moment, she saves every cent she earns—that is, every cent she can spare from what is absolutely necessary to her decent appearance. She regards everything she has or can make as belonging to those to whom she has unconsciously devoted the flower of her youth, and for whom she is willing to sacrifice her woman's dearest hopes. To keep her place, or retain her employment, what will she not endure?—sneers at her nationality, mockery of her peculiarities, even ridicule of her faith, though the hot blood flushes her cheek with fierce indignation. At every hazard the place must be kept, the money earned, the deposit in the savings-bank increased; and though many a night is passed in tears and prayers, her face is calm, and her eye bright, and her voice cheerful. One by one, the brave girl brings the members of her family about her. But who can tell of her anguish if one of the dear ones goes wrong, or strays from the right path!—who could imagine her rapture as success crowns her efforts, and she is rewarded in the steadiness of the brother for whom she feared and hoped, or in the progress of the sister to whom she has been as a mother! One by one, she has brought them all across the ocean, to become members of a new community, citizens of a great country —it may be, the mothers and fathers of a future race; and knowing the perils which surround youth in a country in which licence is too often—with the unthinking and inexperienced—confounded with liberty, and impatience of control with proper independence of spirit, the faithful girl seeks to draw them within the influence of religion, in which, as in her passionate love of her family, she has found her safeguard and her strength. Probably she has grown old before her time, possibly she realises in a happy marriage the reward of her youth, of care and toil; but were the choice to be given her of personal happiness, or all-sacrificing affection, she would choose the hard road rather than the flowery path. Such is the humble Irish girl, who may be homely, who may be deficient in book knowledge, but whose heart is beyond gold in value.

There is no idea of repayment of the money thus expended. Once given, there is an end of it.

.   .   .

An eminent Irish clergyman, who, from his position, has much to do with the affairs of a large and important diocese, remarked to an Irish girl, one of his penitents, who came to consult him as to the best mode of bringing out her mother and father, she having frequently sent them remittances, and also brought out and provided for a brother and sister,—'Why, Ellen, you are leaving yourself nothing. Now your father, as you tell me, can get on well, and there is work enough for him here; and surely he ought to pay you back something of what I know you have been sending him for years.' The girl looked at her old friend and adviser, first in doubt, then in surprise, then in indignation. When she replied, it was with sparkling eye and flushed cheek—'What, sir! take back from my father and mother what I gave them from my heart! I could not rest in my bed if I did anything so mean. Never say the like of that to me again, Father, and God bless you!' and the poor girl's voice quivered with emotion, as her eye softened in wistful appeal. 'Don't mind, Ellen,' said the priest, 'I was wrong; I should have known you better.' 'I really,' as he said to me, 'meant to try what answer she would give; for that same day I was cognisant of a very different mode of arranging matters. Sir, let people say what they please of them, the Irish are a grand race, after all, and the Irish women are an honour to their country and their faith.' This was said with an enthusiasm not usual to a man so self-contained as this somewhat Americanised Irish priest.

What Freedom of Education Meant

While growing up in the 1890s in Russian-controlled Poland, Mary Antin experienced the impact of the oppressive Czarist dictatorship. Thus, when her father wrote that the family was to join him in America, the possibilities of a new and meaningful life became a reality. Moreover, Benjamin Antin had stated that "education was free" in the new homeland, and that this was an opportunity which "no thief could touch, not even misfortune or poverty." Accordingly, when Mary entered the Boston grade school, she was "thrilled with the realization of what freedom of education meant."

In a chapter from her autobiography, *The Promised Land* (1911), Miss Antin described the joy and expectation of her first contact with an American public school.

SOURCE: Mary Antin, **The Promised Land** (New York: Houghton Mifflin Company, 1912), pp. 186, 202, 206–12, 216–18. Reprinted by permission.

A little girl from across the alley came and offered to conduct us to school. My father was out, but we five between us had a few words of English by this time. We knew the word school. We understood. This child, who had never seen us till yesterday, who could not pronounce our names, who was not much better dressed than we, was able to offer us the freedom of the schools of Boston! No application made, no questions asked, no examinations, rulings, exclusions; no machinations, no fees. The doors stood open for every one of us. The smallest child could show us the way.

This incident impressed me more than anything I had heard in advance of the freedom of education in America. It was a concrete proof—almost the thing itself. One had to experience it to understand it.

Father himself conducted us to school. He would not have delegated that mission to the President of the United States.

. . .

It is not worth while to refer to voluminous school statistics to see just how many "green" pupils entered school last September, not knowing the days of the week in English, who next February will be declaiming patriotic verses in honor of George Washington and Abraham Lincoln, with a foreign accent, indeed, but with plenty of enthusiasm. It is enough to know that this hundred-fold miracle is common to the schools in every part of the United States where immigrants are received. And if I was one of Chelsea's hundred in 1894, it was only to be expected, since I was one of the older of the "green" children, and had had a start in my irregular schooling in Russia, and was carried along by a tremendous desire to learn, and had my family to cheer me on.

I was not a bit too large for my little chair and desk in the baby class, but my mind, of course, was too mature by six or seven years for the work. So as soon as I could understand what the teacher said in class, I was advanced to the second grade. This was within a week after Miss Nixon took me in hand. But I do not mean to give my dear teacher all the credit for my rapid progress, nor even half the credit. I shall divide it with her on behalf of my race and my family. I was Jew enough to have an aptitude for language in general, and to bend my mind earnestly to my task; I was Antin enough to read each lesson with my heart, which gave me an inkling of what was coming next, and so carried me along by leaps and bounds. As for the teacher, she could best explain what theory she followed in teaching us foreigners to read. I can only describe the method, which was so simple that I wish holiness could be taught in the same way.

There were about half a dozen of us beginners in English, in age from six to fifteen. Miss Nixon made a special class of us, and aided us so skilfully and earnestly in our endeavors to "see-a-cat," and "hear-a-dog-bark," and "look-at-the-hen," that we turned over page after page of the ravishing history, eager to find out how the common world looked, smelled, and tasted in the strange speech. The teacher knew just when to let us help each other out with a word in our own tongue,—it happened that we were all Jews,—and so, working all together, we actually covered more ground in a lesson than the native classes, composed entirely of the little tots.

But we stuck—stuck fast—at the definite article; and sometimes the lesson resolved itself into a species of lingual gymnastics, in which we all looked as if we meant to bite our tongues off. Miss Nixon was pretty, and she must have looked well with her white teeth showing in the act; but at the time I was too solemnly occupied to admire her looks. I did take great pleasure in her smile of approval, whenever I pronounced well; and her patience and perseverance in struggling with us over that thick little word are becoming to her even now, after fifteen years. It is not her fault if any of us to-day give a buzzing sound to the dreadful English *th*.

I shall never have a better opportunity to make public declaration of my love for the English language. I am glad that American history runs, chapter for chapter, the way it does; for thus America came to be the country I love so dearly. I am glad, most of all, that the Americans began by being Englishmen, for thus did I come to inherit this beautiful language in which I think. It seems to me that in any other language happiness is not so sweet, logic is not so clear. I am not sure that I could believe in my neighbors as I do if I thought about them in un-English words. I could almost say that my conviction of immortality is bound up with the English of its promise. And as I am attached to my prejudices, I must love the English language!

Whenever the teachers did anything special to help me over my private difficulties, my gratitude went out to them, silently. It meant so much to me that they halted the lesson to give me a lift, that I needs must love them for it. Dear Miss Carrol, of the second grade, would be amazed to hear what small things I remember, all because I was so impressed at the time with her readiness and sweetness in taking notice of my difficulties.

Says Miss Carrol, looking straight at me:—

"If Johnnie has three marbles, and Charlie has twice as many, how many marbles has Charlie?"

I raise my hand for permission to speak.

"Teacher, I don't know vhat is tvice."

Teacher beckons me to her, and whispers to me the meaning of the strange word, and I am able to write the sum correctly. It's all in the day's work with her; with me, it is a special act of kindness and efficiency.

She whom I found in the next grade became so dear a friend that I can hardly name her with the rest, though I mention none of them lightly. Her approval was always dear to me, first because she was "Teacher," and afterwards, as long as she lived, because she was my Miss Dillingham. Great was my grief, therefore, when, shortly after my admission to her class, I incurred discipline, the first, and next to the last, time in my school career.

The class was repeating in chorus the Lord's Prayer, heads bowed on desks. I was doing my best to keep up by the sound; my mind could not go beyond the word "hallowed," for which I had not found the meaning. In the middle of the prayer a Jewish boy across the aisle trod on my foot to get my attention. "You must not say that," he admonished in a solemn whisper; "it's Christian." I whispered back that I wasn't, and went on to the "Amen." I did not know but what he was right, but the name of Christ was not in the prayer, and I was bound to do everything that the class did. If I had any Jewish scruples, they were lagging away behind my interest in school affairs. How American this was: two pupils side by side in the schoolroom, each holding to his own opinion, but both submitting to the common law; for the boy at least bowed his head as the teacher ordered.

But all Miss Dillingham knew of it was that two of her pupils whispered during morning prayer, and she must discipline them. So I was degraded from the honor row to the lowest row, and it was many a day before I forgave that young missionary; it was not enough for my vengeance that he suffered punishment with me. Teacher, of course, heard us both defend ourselves, but there was a time and a place for religious arguments, and she meant to help us remember that point.

.   .   .

If I was eager and diligent, my teachers did not sleep. As fast as my knowledge of English allowed, they advanced me from grade to grade, without reference to the usual schedule of promotions. My father was right, when he often said, in discussing my prospects, that ability would be promptly recognized in the public schools. Rapid as was my progress, on account of the advantages with which I started, some of the other "green" pupils were not far behind me; within a grade or two, by the end of the year.

My brother, whose childhood had been one hideous nightmare, what with the stupid rebbe [rabbi], the cruel whip, and the general repression of life in the Pale, surprised my father by the progress he made under intelligent, sympathetic guidance. Indeed, he soon had a reputation in the school that the American boys envied; and all through the school course he more than held his own with pupils of his age. So much for the right and wrong way of doing things.

There is a record of my early progress in English much better than my recollections, however accurate and definite these may be. I have several reasons for introducing it here. First, it shows what the Russian Jew can do with an adopted language; next, it proves that vigilance of our public-school teachers of which I spoke; and last, I am proud of it! That is an unnecessary confession, but I could not be satisfied to insert the record here, with my vanity unavowed.

This is the document, copied from an educational journal, a tattered copy of which lies in my lap as I write—treasured for fifteen years, you see, by my vanity.

EDITOR "PRIMARY EDUCATION":—
This is the uncorrected paper of a Russian child twelve years old, who had studied English only four months. She had never, until September, been to school even in her own country and has heard English spoken *only* at school. I shall be glad if the paper of my pupil and the above explanation may appear in your paper.

                                                              M. S. Dillingham.
Chelsea, Mass.

SNOW

Snow is frozen moisture which comes from the clouds. Now the snow is coming down in feather-flakes, which makes nice snow-balls. But there is still one kind of snow more. This kind of snow is called snow-crystals, for it comes down in little curly balls. These snow-crystals are n't quiet as good for snow-balls as feather-flakes, for they (the snow-crystals) are dry: so they can't keep together as feather-flakes do.

The snow is dear to some children for they like sleighing.

As I said at the top—the snow comes from the clouds.

Now the trees are bare, and no flowers are to see in the fields and gardens, (we all know why) and the whole world seems like asleep without the happy birds songs which left us till spring. But the snow which drove away all these pretty and happy things, try, (as I think) not to make us at all unhappy; they covered up the branches of the trees, the fields, the gardens and houses, and the whole world looks like dressed in a beautiful white—instead of green—dres, with the sky looking down on it with a pale face.

And so the people can find some joy in it, too, without the happy summer.

Mary Antin.

.   .   .

About the middle of the year I was promoted to the grammar school. Then it was that I walked on air. For I said to myself that *I was a student* now, in earnest, not merely a school-girl learning to spell and cipher. I was going to learn out-of-the-way things, things that had nothing to do with ordinary life—things to *know*. When I walked home afternoons, with the great big geography book under my arm, it seemed to me that the earth was conscious of my step. Sometimes I carried home half the books in my desk, not because I should need them, but because I loved to hold them; and also because I loved to be seen carrying books. It was a badge of scholarship, and I was proud of it. I remembered the days in Vitebsk when I used to watch my cousin Hirshel start for school in the morning, every thread of his student's uniform, every worn copybook in his satchel, glorified in my envious eyes. And now I was myself as he: aye, greater than he; for I knew English and I could write poetry.

If my head was not turned at this time it was because I was so busy from morning till night. My father did his best to make me vain and silly. He made much of me to every chance caller, boasting of my progress at school, and of my exalted friends, the teachers. For a school-teacher was no ordinary mortal in his eyes; she was a superior being, set above the common run of men by her erudition and devotion to higher things.

.   .   .

He surely was right in his first appraisal of the teacher. The mean sort of teachers are not teachers at all; they are self-seekers who take up teaching as a business, to support themselves and keep their hands white. These same persons, did they keep store or drive a milk wagon or wash babies for a living, would be respectable. As trespassers on a noble profession, they are worth no more than the books and slates and desks over which they preside; so much furniture, to be had by the gross. They do not love their work. They contribute nothing to the higher development of their pupils. They busy themselves, not with research into the science of teaching, but with organizing political demonstrations to advance the cause of selfish candidates for public office, who promise them rewards. The true teachers are of another strain. Apostles all of an ideal, they go to their work in a spirit of love and inquiry, seeking not comfort, not position, not old-age pensions, but truth that is the soul of wisdom, the joy of big-eyed children, the food of hungry youth.

They were true teachers who used to come to me on Arlington Street, so my father had reason to boast of the distinction brought upon his house. For the school-teacher in her trim, unostentatious dress was an un-common visitor in our neighborhood; and the talk that passed in the bare little "parlor" over the grocery store would not have been entirely comprehensible to our next-door neighbor.

"I Hope You Will Understand What I Mean"

The hope for and possibility of a better way of life were universally accepted by those who migrated to America. A major difference that existed among immigrants was their ability to articulate their feelings. In the selections which follow, the statements of the expectations of two East European settlers are reprinted. They are reproduced without correction, representing, as they do, a stage in their writers' American development.

The first selection, "What America Means to a Russian Jewess," was submitted in a competition organized by the Committee for Immigrants in America in 1916. It acknowledged that for some, America was "a fairy promised land that came out true." The second selection was among numerous letters received by the Massachusetts Commission on Immigration in 1913. This letter illustrated the great sacrifice that some immigrants were prepared to make in order to learn English.

SOURCE: **"What America Means to a Russian Jewess,"** *Immigrants in America Review* (January 1916), pp. 70–71.

What did I myself look forward to when I left my home, my mother and my little sisters? My way was hard, harder then many of those emigrants, because I was all alone, no help from any one could I expect, and I was not very big, never worked before. I had just graduate from high school when decided to go away. What made me take the hardships of the long way? Not the looking forward made me go, but the looking backward made me search a new life and struggle a hard battle.

Yes it was hard it is hard still now to bear the home—sickness, loneliness, among strange people not knowing the language doing hard worke without a minute of joy. But when I look back into my childhood without a single spot of gladness in it, always under a terrible fear-fear of "goim" (gentiles). I think that there is not anything harder than hardships of childhood.

I remember myself in my fear-mood—frightened by stories of massacres, unable to go to sleep for fear that gentiles may come and kill my mother and father, as they killed my aunt and her husband. I could see in my imagination their mishaped bodies, swiming in blood, and I almost screamed of horror, when I saw myself left all alone in the big world and no one to care for me and stand for me before the gentiles. What can be worse a sight than a child with a frightened and hating soul? And that what I was.

Now when I meet italians, russians, jews here in America I see the great meaning of that country for us. We who in Castle Garden were still the same poor, desolate emigrants of Europe after a struggle with life, became winners of the battle, we have new ideas of freedom, we think with pride that in seven years we will be "Americans" and citizens and we are proud of our new country (that) because it is so much better than our old country and that it wellkomed us, and we try to be worth it and go to schools to study civics and all do hard work which makes our country just a little better. America means something to an American it means more to us immigrants for this meaning is new and holly and wonderfully dear to us.

When I meet the American children in white dresses and pink ribbons going to school to teachers whom they love and who love them and and try to make their studies as interesting as possible, I see myself and my chums going to school as to a trial, in gray uniforms, black aprons, coming there to repeat words of a strange catechism which was forced into our heads. While young American learn in school how to love and respect your people and your government, 'so wise, so free,' so practical, we were forced to devine our kings who are so cruel so dull and so unsensible. But triying to force into us seeds of patriotism, they raised hatred in them, for teachers who offend us, calling "zudovka" (dirty jew) such teachers are unfit to stand as tutors of growing minds and certainly mislead more than one of the young generation.

In about five month after I came to America, I entered a hospital to take up training for a nurse. I could not speak English at all for some time, but when in a month I aske questions America opened to me through my patients. There were immigrants unable to speak, even to each other because of the mixture of all different nationalities and languages, Americans of all ranks who were sometimes cross and impatient to the little foreign nurse. America opened to me through the Irishmen and Italians hurt in a saloon fight and others their countrymen who were sick because they worked a whole day at hard labor in factories and outside and then went to school to study civics in night school, for their ambition told them, that they ought know their civil duties to a country in which they worke with a shovel diging sewers and laying tracks.

That what I learned during my short life in America: America means for an Immigrant a fairy promised land that came out true, a land that gives all they need for their work, a land which gives them human rights, a land that gives morality through her churches and education through her free schools and libraries. The longer I live in America the more I think of the question of Americanising the immigrants. At first I thought that there is not such a question as that, for the children of immigrants naturally are Americans and good Americans. America is a land made up of foreigners and the virtues of American life is the best Americaniser. The first generation of American immigrants can't be Americanized much for they were raised in different ways the mod of living is different. And yett how much it is when they love America and are such patriots. I remember I took care of an old russian women, I was the only one who could speak to her in the hospital and we always had great conversations while I was fixing her up. Once she was telling me about her husband. On her face was a half sarcastic, half glad smile when she was criticising the way her husband acts. He was getting childish, she said, why only the other day the school teacher gave the boys a book about Washington and the granfather heard them reading it. He pinned a paper flag on his hat and playing on a 5-cent horn led the march of boys who were singing "Washington, Washington, the father of our country." "Something wrong with him" said my patient, but it seemed to me that it was a righted wrong, for a man that never knew the patriotic feeling before became a purest, patriot now. No one tried to teach him be a patriot he came to it by himself.

How often the children of Americans call the immigrants "pollack" and "Diego" and only torment their Americanising, because they loose their confidence in Americans. Here is a way for Americans to help foreigners become Americans: teach their own children to respect those people that struggle such a hard battle.

There is only one kind of immigrants who need for their Americanising something besides sympathy. Those are anarchists and other political parties who do not realise the greatness and wisdom of American government, because they have no idea of morality. They come from Europe in a state of unbelieve and immorality because the church, administration and schools of Europe by forcing them to have certain false ideas of false virtues killed their best feelings in them. They need to be restorted a fallen building and the first thing they need is to build under themselfs a foundation of moral ideas, believe in God and their country.

SOURCE: **Report of the Massachusetts Commission on Immigration** (Boston, 1914), p. 134.

I'm in this country four months (from 14Mai1913-Antverpen).
I am polish man. I want be american citizen—and took here first paper in 12 June N 625. But my friends are polish people— I must live with them—I work in the shoes-shop with polish people —I stay all the time with them—at home—in the slop—anywhere.

I want live with american people, but I do not know anybody of american. I go 4 times to teacher and must pay $2, I have only $4—$3—and now english board house is too dear for me. Better job to get is very hard for me, because I do not speak well english and I cannot understand what they say to me. The teacher teach me—but when I come home—I must speak polish and in the shop also. In this way I can live in your country many years—like my friends—and never speak—write well english—and never be good american citizen. I know here many persons, they live here 10 or moore years, and they are not citizens, they don't speak well english, they don't know geography and history of this contry, they don't know constitution of America.—nothing. I don't like be like them I wanted they help me in english—they could not—because they knew nothing. I want go from them away. But where? Not in the country, because I want go in the city, free evening schools and lern. I'm looking for help. If somebody could give me another job between american people, help me live with them and lern english—and could tell me the best way how I can fast lern—it would be very, very good for me. Perhaps you have somebody, here he could help me?

If you can help me, I please you.

I wrote this letter by myself and I know no good—but I hope you will understand whate I mean.

Excuse me,
F. N.

I Become Naturalized

After establishing themselves in their new nation, the highest hope of most aliens was the awarding of a Certificate of Naturalization. However, the acquisition of this document was one of the most frustrating experiences of the immigrant's adjustment.

For Constantine Panuzio, author of *The Soul of an Immigrant* (1921), the bestowal of his citizenship represented a personal victory over the "unkind [and] cruel . . . methods sometimes used in [the] . . . Americanization program." In a chapter from his autobiography, "I Become Naturalized," he vividly described the bureaucratic entanglements which kept many from earning their American citizenship.

SOURCE: Constantine M. Panuzio, **The Soul of an Immigrant** (New York, 1921), pp. 194–200.

. . . How unkind, how cruel are the methods sometimes used in connection with our so-called Americanization program. Think of our saying to these foreign peoples, some of whom have been in this country for perhaps a brief period: Forget your native land, forget your mother tongue, do away in a day with your inherited customs, put from you as a cloak all that inheritance and early environment made you and become in a day an American *par excellence.*

This was precisely the talk I used to hear when I first came to this country. There was then as now, I regret to say, a spirit of compulsion in the air. "Either become an American citizen or get out," was in substance the attitude of certain people. But how was I to choose so suddenly? "Give me time for try," Thomas Daly makes an Italian say. I needed as every immigrant does, this "time for try," to see whether I could honestly become an American. To speak frankly, what had there been during the first three or four years of my residence in this country which would have made citizenship at all attractive to me? Had I not been sneered at as an undesirable "foreigner"? Had I not been maltreated, discriminated against, robbed, insulted, dragged to prison, despised? I grant you that I had suffered all this at the hands of the worst and very lowest elements of American society, but how was I to know there was any other? The struggle I went through in those early years in America in regard to my citizenship relation to her can only be understood by one who himself has had a similar experience.

It was during my senior year in preparatory school, however, that on the advice of friends I made a long trip to Portland, Maine, and took out my first papers, what the Italians call "the half citizenship." They have an idea that by taking out these papers they are sure of a certain amount of protection from the United States Government, while at the same time the act does not sever their legal tie with Italy, and puts them under no obligation to the United States. Perhaps something of this attitude led me to take out my first papers; at least I was in the state of mind of "well-it-won't-do-any-harm." By the time I was ready to graduate from preparatory school, I had really begun to have a desire to be a part of America, and gradually I came to feel that I would become a full citizen at the earliest possible moment.

Unfortunately, however, I left Maine and established myself in Connecticut while attending college. By my second year in college, the time had expired, and I was now ready to take out my full citizenship papers. But I soon discovered that to do this in Connecticut, I must have present two witnesses who would swear that they had known me for five years and that I had been in this country continuously for that period of time. This was not so easy a matter as might at first appear. Like every "foreigner" in this country, I was, comparatively speaking, a stranger. The only people I knew were either in Maine or somewhere equally far off; to bring them to Middletown, assuming that two such persons could and would leave their work and take the long journey in order to make me an American citizen, would have been a great expense. Later, when I was informed that I could have depositions made, I learned that these would cost me ten dollars, and ten dollars to a boy struggling to make his way through college was like a mountain of gold. There was no choice left but to let it go. I regretted this greatly, for by my senior year in college I had become deeply interested in American life and I wanted to take part in civic-betterment contests in our community.

The matter was still further complicated by my going from Connecticut to Massachusetts for graduate work. I still needed the two witnesses who had known me continuously for five years. How could this be? The friends I had known in Maine had naturally remained in that state and had no way of knowing whether in the interval of my attending college I had remained in this country continuously. On the other hand, persons I had known in college had known me at most for four years, and aside from one or two classmates whom I knew to be in the vicinity of Boston, I had no way of reaching them. It seemed as if I would finally be compelled to import two witnesses unless I was willing to let the matter rest indefinitely. However, if I did this, I might upon my graduation from Theological School go out of the State of Massachusetts, and the intricate round of difficulties would begin all over again.

In the spring of 1914 I made a desperate effort to get through the barbedwire entanglements which were keeping me from American citizenship. I found a college classmate who was willing to put in the time with me. He had by this time known me for about five years. There was another friend who had known me for five years, except for one month, during which period he could not tell whether or not I was in this country. All was off again; the inspector would not have it so, and in order to fill in the gap in my wandering residence over this country I had to import a third man who would swear that I was I and that during a given month I had been in this country. On that day four of us, all college students, spent almost the entire day in the ante-chambers of a certain office until his honor, the immigrant inspector, himself of Italian birth, would condescend to grant us a hearing. Worst of all, my poor pocketbook had to see a number of precious greenbacks emigrate, for it was necessary to feed my witnessing friends both for luncheon and dinner. But then I was growing accustomed to this exodus, for this was not the first time I had gone to his honor the inspector's office. It was a part of the price of acquiring my citizenship.

The absurdity of the whole process comes over me with full force sometimes and I have a hearty laugh over it. Think of a young man trying his best for several years to become a citizen in order that he may perform his civic duties, and then being hindered in every conceivable way. I recall the many times I had to go to the inspector's office; on most occasions we went on appointment, only to find ourselves still at the end of a long line at the end of an imperfect day. Every time this happened it naturally caused me embarrassment in that I was obliged to ask my friends to spend another day with me, not knowing whether the next would be any more fruitful than the last. The rudeness, the inconsiderateness of the officers was most disgusting; as I faced man after man I wondered how they had been worthy of being placed in such important positions, where they were continually leaving bad impressions in the minds of those seeking the new citizenship. There is no place, it seems to me, where courtesy and consideration should be so constantly manifested as toward those "knocking at the gates" of the highest honor we can confer upon them. As I recall, there was anything but a courteous attitude shown throughout the whole process, from the Chief Examiner to the fat, red-nosed policeman at the door of the Court, who held us in a long line like cattle being led to the slaughter.

The moment I entered the courtroom, however, I felt the dignity of the step I was taking. Judge Morton of the District Court of Boston was presiding. He stood up, and amid the breathless silence of the courtroom, addressed us with that true simplicity, that deep earnestness and natural dignity which characterize a public officer who feels the responsibility of his office. His words were profound and inspiring. He spoke of what the step really signified, of the soul and not the shell of citizenship. As he did so, he gave me a new vision of what America would mean to me, and of what I could mean to America. As I stood before him, my only regret was that the larger majority of my "naturalization class" did not even understand the words he was uttering.

And so at last I was a full-fledged American citizen. I wonder whether my Roman forbears could have felt any more dignified than I did. As I reflect upon it, I am exceedingly grateful that I did not hasten into citizenship in answer to the cry of make-Americans-quick schemes; I am glad that I first became by real choice an American in spirit before taking the legal steps of becoming naturalized. I believe that I am a better American for it. And yet on the other hand, when I consider the endless difficulties I encountered in taking these legal steps, I wonder that more do not give it up as a bad job. If one with a comparatively good knowledge of the law and its methods finds it so difficult to go through the process of getting naturalized, [how much more impossible must it be for those who, aside from having no knowledge of the law, do not even understand the English language?]

4. Where Do Immigrants Go?: Entrapment and Immigrant Aid Societies

Frauds upon Emigrants

At the end of their journey, the newcomers still faced the "welcome" of heartless exploiters whose fraudulent practices led to the aliens' disorientation. As with most massive migrations of people, a class of American "grafters was produced—runners, agents and brokers," who preyed upon the gullible and inexperienced "greenhorns."

In the following document, the totality of immigrant entrapment was observed. In response to pressure from complaining Immigrant Aid Societies, state investigating committees were appointed. They found the evils so widespread that they "had no conception of . . . the extent to which these frauds and outrages had been practiced." The selection, "Emigrant Entrappers," summarized the activities of similar exploiters in the mid-1850s.

SOURCE: **"Emigrant Entrappers,"** *Chamber's Journal* (March 3, 1855), pp. 141–42.

With what may originally have been a well-meant interference, the city authorities license men to take charge of the forlorn bands of strangers, and see them put properly on their way to the interior. Under the appellation of Transportation Agents or Emigrant Runners, these functionaries are either themselves, or through factitious and unlicensed representatives, the cause of incalculable loss and misery. It would be hard to blame all alike; among the body of agents of one kind or other, there are probably some with more conscience than others; but, on the whole, they are a 'bad set,' and we must therefore, refer to their proceedings generally. This 'organised banditti,' as the newspapers call them, have thousands of subordinate agents, by whom the immigrant is handed on from point to point, fleeced at every step, and not left till the last farthing has been remorselessly wrung from him. We shall allow the *Tribune* to describe the iniquitous system which is pursued.

As soon as a ship emerges from the Narrows, the runners prepare for a descent upon their prey, and by the time she has come to anchor off the boarding-station at Staten Island, her passengers are sold out to the highest bidder. There are honourable exceptions to this rule, but in nine cases out of ten the captain of a vessel sells his passengers to the runner who offers him the largest price. If the ship is to remain at quarantine to be cleansed, the runner brings a steamboat alongside, takes out the passengers and their luggage, and conveys them to the city. If they have to be quarantined, he takes them ashore in the same way, and when their term has expired, re-embarks them on a steamboat, and brings them to

New York. This he does at his own or his employer's expense, besides paying the captain a bonus of from 100 to 300 dollars, and sometimes gratuitously furnishing a tow-boat to bring the ship up to her wharf into the bargain.

.   .   .

Here we stop to describe another method of cheating by means of railway-tickets. The runner persuades the immigrant to buy from him a series of tickets, which purport to carry the bearer on one line of railway after another as far as Cincinnati or Chicago. The first in the series is a valid ticket, and carries the holder of it probably as far as Cleveland, in Ohio; and when he arrives at that point, he finds to his dismay that all the other tickets are counterfeits and he is unable to get further without paying afresh. Thousands are swindled in this way every season.

Unfortunately for the humbler class of emigrants, they usually fall into trouble from their own blunder. The chief error they commit, is taking heavy bundles and boxes with them: these things retard them at every step, and get them into all kinds of scrapes. In the first place, they cannot move from the ship without a car or some other vehicle, and they require to seek for assistance in various other ways, by all which they are brought within the sphere of the swindler. If an emigrant knew the consequences, he would prefer going without a change of under-clothing for a month, rather than embarrass himself with baggage. I could not but pity the lot of many who fell in my way on the wharfs and in the railway-stations: there they sat, each on a great box, unable to stir. They could not safely leave this precious encumbrance, and were as good as nailed to the spot, while all about them was bustle, and while they ought to have been off on their journey, or helping themselves in some way. Oh these boxes!

The detentions caused by luggage are favourable to the projects of the runners. Until things are arranged, and all can go comfortably off in a body to the West, they are told it will be necessary to stop a day or so at a boarding-house. Afraid to lose their luggage, and glad to proceed in the company of acquaintances, they assent to the proposal. They are now in the hands of the Philistines! An emigrants' boarding-house is a den out of which no man escapes unplundered. The dropping into such quarters, even without the aid of runners, is another of the blunders usually committed. When it is absolutely indispensable to spend a night in New York, the best plan is to go to a respectable inn, where there is a fixed charge. But many persons who ought to know better, are always contriving how to do things cheaply, and suffer accordingly; for cheap lodgings often turn out ruinously dear. At one of the 'cheap' New York boarding-houses, the cost of living for a day is perhaps said to be under a dollar; but a bill is ordinarily run up to much beyond this amount, although the accommodations are wretched. We see it stated, that in May last, an Englishman was charged by a boarding-house keeper, for the maintenance of himself, his brother, mother, and little daughter, the enormous sum of 184 dollars for two days! The case was brought before the Mayor's Court, and by a rare piece of good-fortune the complainant got redress. 'This case was singular only in the fact that the offender was detected, and made to disgorge the products of his knavery.'

Escaping from the hands of the boarding-house keeper, and still entangled with luggage, the poor immigrant is next swindled in coming to the steam-boat, which he is perhaps persuaded to take in preference to the railway. For his luggage, a charge is made according to weight; but the weighing is usually a juggle, and an extortionate charge is submitted to, as there is no time for dispute. Then a charge is made by the runner for a deck-passage to Albany, the amount of which is perhaps double that of cabin-fare. 'And so,' says the *Tribune,* 'the game goes on—robbery, whole-sale fraud, almost without a possibility of redress. The boat starts—the immigrants are huddled together like sheep or swine on the forward deck, among the cargo. Without seats, beds, or any other accommodation than would be afforded to a herd of cattle, these people nightly leave the docks of New York, and, exposed to all the inclemencies of the weather, spend the long night in sleepless discomfort upon the deck, not daring to move beyond their prescribed limits; while those who have paid less for their passage by one-half, are luxuriating in the comforts of cabin and bed.'

The Beginnings of Self-Help

During the old immigration, organizations were created by immigrants already here to do charitable work among the new arrivals. The Germans had organized their self-help programs as early as 1800, and by the 1850s, Irish agencies were found in every major seaport on the Atlantic coast. In the document which follows, the nature of these self-help programs is discussed.

The following selection, a petition of the German Society of New York City, requested a share of the states' "immigrant head tax." Claiming that German immigrants generally sought the aid of their agency rather than go to the Commissioners of Emigration, the Society felt justified in seeking government funds.

SOURCE: **"Memorial of the Officers of the German Society of the City of New York to the New York Legislature, Demanding a Share of the Head Tax Receipts,"** *Assembly Document* 165, 1848, pp. 3–5.

The German immigrant, on his arrival here, if he requires assistance, does not call on the Commissioners of Emigration, but at the place where his native language is spoken, he calls on the German Society; and the German Society does not send him to the office of the Commissioners, (except in extraordinary cases) because the Commissioners have made it a rule to grant relief only in their own institutions. But ample proof is daily furnished by the visitors of our Society, that it is next to impossible to induce the German immigrant voluntarily to become an inmate of those institutions; he will rather submit to actual suffering, and thus, ignorance of the language of the country, and the dread of the alms-house which the German looks upon as a sort of penitentiary, throw the chief burden of the indigent German immigration on the German Society, and the latter, by the force of circumstances, is compelled to perform a part of the duties, and to defray a portion of the expenses, which, by the act of May 5, 1847, "concerning passengers in vessels coming to the city of New York," are intended to fall on the Commissioners of Emigration.

The enormous immigration at this port from Germany, which during the year of 1847, according to the books kept at the office of the German Society, amounted to 70,735 persons, proves a serious burden to the citizens of German origin. It will be readily admitted that among such a mass of people there must be many having neither friends nor relatives among the resident Germans, but requiring medical as well as pecuniary assistance. As already stated, the suffering and needy will in the first place apply to the German Society, but failing to receive all the aid they require, they will throw themselves, not on the Commissioners of Emigration, but on the sympathy of their countrymen, and these cannot possibly resist the appeal. Hence it is that the indigent and suffering German immigration proves a constant and daily increasing tax upon all the resident Germans, and this explains the circumstance, that out of 10,000 German voters, only about 500 are members of the German Society. It is not an unfriendly feeling towards the society which prevents so many from joining the same, but the consciousness of doing enough without contributing towards its funds. On the other hand, the society feels keenly the absence of that general co-operation which it would enjoy, but for the reasonable objection urged by so many of its well wishers.

There is one channel through which the German Society is constantly endeavoring to extend the sphere of its benevolent action, which you memorialists take leave to notice more particularly. This is an arrangement with the regular German physicians of New York and Brooklyn, now numbering about twenty, by which the latter are represented in the board of officers of the society, and take charge of all the sick German poor, attending them gratuitously, the society paying medicines, nurses, &c. According to the last annual report of the society, its physicians, during the last twelve months, prescribed medicines in 2,808 cases, and had under treatment, for account of the society, 714 patients. Considering that the inmates of the hospitals under control of the Commissioners of Emigration, cost $14.21½ each, it will not be deemed extravagant on the part of your memorialists to say, that the medical department of the German Society has saved the city and the Commissioners of Emigration *many thousand dollars*.

But the extraordinary exertions made by the society during the last twelve months, have exhausted its means and it is now threatened with the prospect of having to suspend its usefulness. Your memorialists therefore, compelled by the embarrassing condition of the society, and in consideration of its being so efficient an auxiliary to the Commissioners of Emigration, venture to ask your honorable body for aid, and they also venture to hope their prayer will be satisfactorily responded to on the ground that the German immigrant, as shown in the beginning of this memorial, has not derived the same amount of benefit from the operation of the act of May 5, 1847, as the emigrant from other countries, having in fact furnished the means by which not his own wants but those of others have been relieved.

Immigrant Aid Societies

The Immigrant Aid Societies of the new immigration conducted a much wider range of activities than their earlier counterparts. Since the new immigrants faced a greater variety of problems than the old immigrants, the Aid Societies of the twentieth century had to undertake a broader program of assistance than those of the nineteenth century.

The selections presented below described the work of several of these organizations. The first selection was from the Massachusetts Commission on Immigration. It surveyed the numerous societies which flourished in every immigrant community.

The second selection detailed the work done by the Immigrants' Protective League of Chicago. The League, established in 1908, dealt with immigrant problems throughout the nation. Among their activities were: (1) the protection against exploitation; (2) employment agencies; (3) articulation with schools in the adjustment of immigrant children; (4) adult education; (5) investigation of "detention" cases; and (6) the promotion of social welfare legislation. The Annual Reports which follow set forth the League's work with immigrant girls.

SOURCE: **Report of the Massachusetts Commission on Immigration** (Boston, 1914), pp. 202–5.

The societies which are organized and maintained by the members of the different nationalities, and which flourish in some form in every community where there are large groups of immigrants, are a factor in helping the immigrant through the trials of immigration and the difficulties of adjustment to new conditions. The chief reason among all nationalities for the formation of these societies is insurance against sickness and death, but most of them combine with this some other objects. Nearly all of them outline an educational and civic program. They may lack the means to carry this out, yet the statement of these purposes has an influence upon the members. Cooperation with these organizations on the part of American agencies would help the immigrant in solving his own problems, and might mean the carrying out of these larger ideals. The organizations of the Swedes, French-Canadians and Germans are familiar to Americans, but very few realize the organized efforts which those who come from Southern and Eastern Europe are making in their own behalf.

.   .   .

The Pan-Hellenic Union is a national organization with headquarters in Boston. In addition to the payment of sick and death benefits the Union has outlined a comprehensive program for bettering the conditions of Greeks in America by creating a spirit of self-help, by protecting the Greek immigrants and laborers, by aiding in the furtherance of the political ambitions of their much-loved mother country and, at the same time, by instilling in the Greeks of the United States veneration and affection for the laws and the institutions of America.

There are several local societies in the large Greek communities whose members are from the same towns in Greece, and whose object is to help each other in time of need and to do something for their town or city in the home land. These societies, however, are rapidly being absorbed into the Pan-Hellenic Union.

Among the Italians the societies are not united, for whatever the object of a society, its membership is usually drawn from those who come from one town or province in Italy. The result is a great number of associations. In Springfield, for example, where the Italian population, according to the census for 1910, is 2,915, there are twelve societies. One society has recently celebrated its twenty-fifth anniversary with great enthusiasm. It reports 400 members, a fund of $3,500 and a record of having paid out, in sick benefits and to destitute families, about $15,000. It is described in its report as a society that "unites us and gives us strength, and will make us more acceptable in the eyes of the American people; that will guide us in all vicissitudes and trouble of life; that will give us work when we are idle; that will succor us with money when we are sick; that will help our families and accompany us with dignified ceremony when we die."

The many Italian mutual benefit societies in Boston are of three slightly different types: first, those which require membership in the Catholic church and are usually named for the patron saint of the vicinity from which the group comes; second, those which do not require membership in the Catholic church and are rather political in their objects; and third, those which have a certain patriotic side and whose members have been soldiers in Italy. All three types have essentially the same benefit features.

The Italian Immigrant Aid Society hardly belongs to this part of the discussion, as it has had much American assistance. Still, since it is subsidized by the Italian government, it is an Italian rather than an American organization. Its objects are to protect the Italian against exploitation and to provide for the return to Italy of those who are sick or discouraged. Its representatives are at the docks to assist those who are entering or leaving the country.

* * * *

The Lithuanians have about sixty mutual benefit societies in Massachusetts and about thirty educational societies arranging lectures and classes. Many of these are very closely connected with the church. Distinctive features of the Lithuanian societies of Massachusetts are their "national homes," or club houses, where their clubs can meet, and where a library of Lithuanian books and papers is maintained. There are homes of this kind in three cities, and three more are being built. The Lithuanian Benevolent Society, which was organized to build the home in Boston, is a well-established mutual benefit society with 350 members. The Lithuanian Roman Catholic Alliance has 17 groups in the different industrial centers in Massachusetts, some of the groups having as many as 160 members.

Among Massachusetts Poles there are many branches of the Polish National Alliance. This is one of the largest single societies among the Slavic people in the United States. While it is primarily a mutual benefit society, it is much more than that, for it has special committees for education, agriculture, industry, charity and recreation. The Polish Industrial Association is associated with another large national organization,—the Polish Catholic Alliance. A Pol-

ish immigration society has recently been organized which maintains a temporary lodging house where Poles who arrive in Boston
and are unable to proceed at once to their destination may stay.
It also has a representative to meet the boats in order to protect
and help the Polish newcomer. The Polish Young Men's Alliance
is a national organization with several branches in Massachusetts;
each local branch has a library and a reading room and holds evening classes in English and civics and in gymnastics. The mutual
benefit features are the best-developed part of the work.

SOURCE: **"Protection of Immigrant Girls on Arrival at Interior
Points,"** from the *First Annual Report of the Immigrants'
Protective League of Chicago,* pp. 13–18.

The Work with Immigrant Girls

During the past year and a half the League has received from
the various ports of arrival the names and addresses of the girls
and women destined for Chicago. All of these newly arrived girls
and women have been visited by representatives of the League able
to speak the language of the immigrant. Four, and part of the time,
five women speaking the Slavic languages, German, French, Italian and Greek have been employed for this work. In these visits
information has been accumulated in regard to the journey to Chicago, the depot situation, the past industrial experience of the girls,
their occupation in Chicago, wages, hours of work, their living
conditions, the price they pay for board, and whether they are
contributing to the support of some one at home. On this basis the
League's work for girls has been planned. Some statement or
analysis of the facts ascertained with regard to these points may
be of interest and value.

The Journey to Chicago

Much improvement in the methods of the inspection, detention, and release of immigrants at the various ports of arrival has
been made in recent years. Because of more efficient organization
of the service immigrants are now treated with humane considera-

tion by government officials; moreover, runners from cheap hotels, expressmen, employment agents, and all those who might profit by their ignorance and dependence are denied access to them. The moral exploitation of the girl is guarded against by a careful examination of the person to whom she is released.

But in contrast to these improvements made at the ports, there is, for the girl destined to Chicago, no corresponding protective machinery. She is carefully guarded by the Federal Authorities until she is placed on the train, but the government then considers that its responsibility is at an end. She may be approached by anyone *en route*. Through her own mistake or intention or the carelessness of railroad officials she may never reach Chicago.

At present it is practically impossible to trace the girls who leave New York, but who never reach their friends in this city. Sometimes we are able to reach some conclusion as to what became of them, but these conclusions only point to the necessity for some safeguarding of the journey. For example, two Polish girls, seventeen and twenty-two years of age, whose experience before they started for America had been bounded by the limits of a small farm in Galicia, were coming to their cousin, who lived back of the Yards in Chicago. Her name and address had been sent to us on one of our regular lists and when one of the visitors of the League called at the house she found the cousin and the entire household much alarmed because the girls had not arrived. Inquiring of others who came on the same boat we found that the girls had become acquainted with a man from Rochester on the way over and he was "looking out for them." The only information the Commissioner at Ellis Island could give was that the girls had left there and that one ticket on that date had been sold to Rochester. The girls had completely disappeared and no one was responsible for their failure to arrive in Chicago.

Usually the girls we find are the ones to whom nothing did happen, although they may have been for a time in an extremely dangerous position. One seventeen year old girl was put off the train at South Chicago by mistake and wandered about for several hours at night. Finally a man offered to take her to her friends. He proved worthy of the confidence she had in his kindly intent and she was conducted safely to the northwest side. Another girl nineteen years old who came in by way of Quebec became separated from her sister and friends at Detroit. She was taken to the Police Station for the night and in the morning continued her journey. She arrived at South Chicago without money or the address of her relatives. She spent a night in the South Chicago Police Station and another at the Annex of the Harrison Street Police Station. The police regarded it as impossible to find the girl's friends so the matron of the Annex found her work in a down town hotel. A visitor for the League returning from South Chicago reported great excitement in one neighborhood over the fact that an immigrant girl had been lost at Detroit.

This report was connected with the story of the matron at the Harrison Street Annex and a visit to the hotel proved the identity of the girl. Except for this she would have been alone in Chicago ignorant of our language and the dangers of the city with no one to turn to in case of sickness or unemployment.

Several girls have told of being approached on the trains and invited by strange men to get off at "some big city and see the town," but they wisely concluded to continue their journey without these gay excursions into the unknown.

National and even international attention has been drawn to the work of the United States District Attorney in prosecuting so-called "white Slavers" in Chicago. Important as this work is it should not be the only remedy attempted. For in prosecutions, we must, of necessity, wait until the girl has been ruined and no fine or penitentiary sentence inflicted upon the man or woman responsible for her downfall can undo for her or for society the damage that has been wrought. Some constructive preventive measures should be undertaken as well. First among these perhaps should be the guarantee to every immigrant girl of a safe arrival at her destination, even if it can be done only by making inland cities like Chicago ports of arrival for immigrants just as they are ports of entry for imported merchandise.

Any woman can understand the nervous apprehension which the immigrant girl must feel as she comes into one of Chicago's bewildering railroad stations, but very few realize how well grounded her fears are. Friends and relatives of those who come find it impossible to meet them because immigrant trains are side-tracked for all other kinds of traffic so that no one can determine just when they will reach Chicago. Most of the immigrants arrive either at the Polk Street or Grand Central Stations and numerous visits have been made to these depots by representatives of the League. When on one occasion I attempted to meet an immigrant train that was to come on the Erie Railroad at the Polk Street Station I understood better the stories the girls tell us. This train was due at 7:30 in the morning, but arrived shortly after four in the afternoon and I had to make three trips to the station, although I telephoned each time before starting.

Several hundred immigrants got off the train. Many of them were very young and one felt their disappointment as they peered eagerly and anxiously about for the father or sister or friend they expected to see. Those who were going north or west came out the main gate already ticketed by a representative of the Parmelee Company and were transferred without any confusion just as other travelers are. But those who were to remain in Chicago were directed into a small immigrant waiting room, which opens on Federal street. Here they were hastily sorted into groups and then pushed out the door into the midst of ten or twelve expressmen, who were crowding and pushing and quarreling over the division of spoils. In a short time the struggle was over and they had all been loaded into the waiting wagons. By this time it was almost dark and I watched them drive away with many misgivings. For I remembered our little Irish girl who started on a wagon with a group of other immigrants for the south side. After going some distance the expressman discovered she had a north side address, so charging her four dollars, he put her off the wagon and left her without any suggestion as to what she should do. And then too I remembered the Polish girl of seventeen who was taken at three o'clock in the morning to the place where her sister was supposed to live. But the address was incorrect and the woman who lived there angrily refused to let her stay until morning. The girl had no money and wept disconsolately, when the expressman told her "nobody could find her sister if nobody knew her address and that he wasn't going to take her back for nothing." The saloonkeeper next door finally offered her a refuge and she lived with his family behind the saloon three days before her sister, who was making daily trips to the depot, was found.

.   .   .

Sometimes the grocery stores, saloons, steamship agents and other neighborhood sources of information fail us. Not long ago a girl was brought to the office who had arrived in the city on Sunday afternoon and because her friends could not be found had been taken to the Annex of the Harrison Street Police Station and so had received her first initiation into Chicago life. She had the name and address of the girl friend who lived in Chicago and had promised to get her work, written in the front of her prayer-book and could not understand its incorrectness. She tearfully insisted on accompanying the visitor on the search for her friend and grew more discouraged as one clue after another was tried and failed. Finally the girl said that her friend worked in a bed spring factory. Starting out on this the visitor found her in the third bed spring factory they visited. The friend explained that her address was not as the prayer-book showed, 110 Canal Street, but 1110 Canal Street.

If the United States Immigration Department would establish a protective bureau under the Department of Information and Distribution this situation might be greatly improved. It is true that the railroad companies could by agreement put the business of delivering immigrants on the same responsible and efficient basis that the transfer business now is. But more than this is needed. There should be a central place in Chicago to which those who are expecting friends or relatives from Europe might go and learn whether they had come and to whom they had been released.

Why the Immigrant Patronizes the Immigrant Bank

The appearance of immigrant banks came with the new immigration; they were not found prior to the 1880s. The fear of bureaucratic agencies and ignorance of American institutions caused the immigrant to doubt the reliability of American banks. Consequently, he trusted someone from his native land, such as a steamship agent, saloonkeeper or grocer, to protect his hard-earned funds.

In the mind of the immigrant, these "agents," who spoke their native language, were the sole connecting links with the homeland. Considering him the established representative within the immigrant community, the alien ascribed to the agent a status and responsibility such as he had no cause to assign to any American institution.

Therefore, nothing was more natural than that the immigrant should take his savings to the agent and ask that monthly remittances be sent to his home in Europe. Having made this start, it was logical that he continued to have his savings placed with the agent for safekeeping. It was not long before many agents had the financial foundation for a banking business, and their assumption of banking functions quickly followed. Shortly thereafter, the transition was complete—the steamship agent, saloonkeeper or grocer had become an immigrant banker.

SOURCE: **"Immigrant Banks,"** *Reports of the United States Immigration Commission,* XXXVII (1911), pp. 289–93.

Some Representative Immigrant Banks

In order to illustrate the various features of the immigrant banking system here discussed, detailed descriptions are given below of several banks of the different classes. Nearly all these banks have been referred to in other connections, and where such is the case the topic in question will be noted and treated briefly.

. . .

The first bank to be considered is located in the State of New York, and owned and conducted by two brothers of the Italian race. The brothers are primarily importers and commission merchants, carrying a stock of liquors and operating also a retail grocery. They established this business in 1901. A year later they began to do a banking business in connection. This bank, as well as a steamship agency, labor agency, and postal substation, is located in the office of the grocery store. One of the brothers is himself a contractor on a small scale, and during the year ending August, 1909, furnished through his labor agency about 1,000 men for other contractors. All these different activities, having their headquarters in the office of the store, help to increase the profits of the grocery business. On the other hand, the laborers which the firm itself employs, as well as those sent out for other contractors, together with the customers of the grocery store, become the patrons of the bank and of the foreign-exchange and steamship agency. It would be difficult to find a better example of the intimate association prevailing in the different lines of business followed by bankers of this class.

The firm is not incorporated, but the proprietors have filed a bond in accordance with the New York state law, and possess to this extent authorization for their banking business. Although the term "banca" is displayed on their windows, and although a banking business is done, there is nothing in the financial organization or composition of the concern to indicate that it is a bank. The bank, as such, has scarcely any identity aside from the grocery in connection with which it is conducted. No capital has been invested in the bank, and there is no fund allowed to accrue as a capital account, surplus, or reserve. This is a general condition among banks of this character, although many of them, as in this case, are solvent, the proprietors being possessed of sufficient real property or other resources to cover deposits and money received for transmission abroad.

.   .   .

The manner in which this firm exercises its hold over the customers of its grocery and labor agency as a means of securing patronage for its bank has already been mentioned. These methods, supplemented by advertising and by the added influence given the concern as a postal substation, constitute its chief means of securing business. In the conduct of their grocery the proprietors employ modern business methods, one feature being a daily record showing the exact amount outstanding in credits. But their system of bank bookkeeping is much less complete. No balances or statements are ever drawn. Deposits are kept in checking or interest-bearing accounts with funds accruing from other business, and while a deposit ledger is kept, it is not balanced at regular intervals. To those who signify that their deposits are to be left for a reasonable period and are likely to be augmented from time to time pass books are issued. To those leaving money for short periods ordinary receipts are given. Deposits are not subject to check, but may be withdrawn in person at any time. In order to determine the extent of the firm's foreign-exchange business it was necessary to sum up its advice sheets, inasmuch as no books are kept for that purpose. One of the brothers gives the bank his personal attention, being assisted by the clerks of the grocery store.

. . .

Somewhat typical of banking concerns . . . is the business done by a Croatian saloon keeper in Missouri. In this case deposits are received largely as an accommodation which the proprietor extends to his customers. He has a safe in the saloon, and those of his countrymen (for he deals with Croatians exclusively) who know him well or have cause to trust him find it convenient from time to time to leave small sums with him for safe-keeping or for transmission abroad. His chief gain from this informal and friendly arrangement, as he himself asserts, lies in the fact that the accommodation extended serves to increase his saloon trade. Accepting only such deposits as are brought in by his customers, he has shown no disposition to extend his banking business so that it might become more directly remunerative to himself. He does not solicit deposits nor money for transmission, and does not advertise himself as a banker. In short, his banking business is merely subordinate and contributory to his saloon business.

The proprietor, who is the sole owner of the business, began to send money abroad for his patrons twelve years ago, although he has been a saloon keeper, and probably receiving deposits, for a much longer period. He has a dry-goods store elsewhere in the city but no branch banking offices. He is not now a steamship agent, although he formerly represented a second-rate company which is now defunct. His business is not incorporated, and his banking business is under no supervision or control. Beyond his stocks of liquors and dry goods, he has no capital invested and nothing behind his bank as security. He has, however, real estate, stock, and cash, approximating $5,000, with no liabilities beyond current bills. His business methods and facilities are of the poorest. At one end of his bar are his safe and desk. These constitute his office and bank. As has been mentioned, the only record he has of the amount of deposits on hand is the duplicates of the slips which he issues to each depositor. These are destroyed as the deposits are withdrawn and others are issued upon a renewal of the account. His only records of money orders sold are the stubs in his money-order books. The business receives his personal attention.

On the day of examination, the proprietor held $1,275 that had been left with him for safe-keeping by 11 depositors. He has sometimes held as much as $6,000 of this kind of deposits. These sums he ostensibly holds intact in his checking account against withdrawal, so that they may be obtained in part or in total at any time. Although these deposits are not used for loans or investments, no distinction is made between the proprietor's personal funds and those of his depositors, and he draws upon either indiscriminately in meeting the obligations of his business. He had $500 on hand in his safe on the day of examination. This amount he claims to keep available at all times to meet any ordinary demands.

During the first six months of 1909, this saloon keeper received $3,607.89 for transmission abroad. He sells the money orders (postal remittances) of an express company in New York City at a rate barely above cost, except on orders for less than 100 kronen, upon which he makes a fair profit.

.   .   .

The third bank to be considered is located in a city of Kansas and is conducted by a Bulgarian, who is the sole owner. The bank was established in August, 1908, seven months after the proprietor's arrival in this country. Besides receiving money for safe-keeping and for transmission abroad the proprietor conducts in the same building—which is of two stories—a hotel of fifteen rooms, in connection with which are a restaurant and a pool hall. The proprietor is also a steamship-ticket and labor agent. The office of the "bank" and ticket agency is in a room above the pool hall. Here are located the safe and desk of the banker and the small cabinet of Bulgarian books and novelties which he maintains, but his operations are by no means necessarily confined to this room. He employs no clerks, but desk room is rented to a notary public and real-estate agent. Bulgarians are the chief patrons of the concern, although business is sometimes done with Croatians, Russians, Roumanians, and Serbians.

The bank has no capital, is unincorporated and without legal authorization, and is subject to no supervision or examination. No branches are maintained. The nature of the business is indicated by signs and posters on the front of the establishment. The pool room is a general loafing place. The proprietor forwards letters and extends other accommodation to men sent out to work. He has some medical knowledge and is of assistance to his patrons in the purchase of drugs and other commodities. To such methods as these the proprietor attributes his success in securing business.

During the first seven months of 1909 this banker handled about 200 men through his labor agency. They were chiefly Bulgarian railroad and rock workers. He had no contract with any company merely collecting a nominal fee from the men as they were sent out, and he had no direct commissary privileges, although provisions were supplied to the men through associates of his who conduct groceries. In furnishing employment he generally deals directly with the "boss" or head of a gang of laborers. These heads, he believes, usually serve as temporary custodians of the laborers' funds. He represents 10 of the leading steamship lines, and from August, 1908, to July, 1909, sold 53 outgoing tickets to Budapest, Bucharest, and Belgrade, and 7 incoming or "prepaid" tickets.

As indicated, his banking operations consist of the receiving of money for safe-keeping and for transmission abroad. He does not do a money-changing business and makes no loans except a few personal advancements toward the purchase of prepaid steamship tickets. On the day of examination he held $2,342 that had been deposited with him for safe-keeping. This sum was owned by 30 depositors, principally Bulgarian laborers in the industrial plants of the city or those for whom he had secured employment elsewhere. The banker stated that these sums were largely accumulated against ultimate transmissions abroad. During the first seven months of 1909 he had handled in all about $20,000 of such accounts. A pass book is issued to each depositor, except where sums are left overnight or for a day or two, in which case no form of receipt is issued. The depositor is also furnished with a secret password, this being done, according to the proprietor to guarantee the payment of money to the right person when demands are made by depositors out of town. Deposits are not subject to check, but may be withdrawn upon written or verbal request. No interest is paid upon them. For his own record the proprietor keeps a deposit ledger.

B. SOCIAL AND CULTURAL PATTERNS

1. Their Culture Transplanted

The Importance of Cultural Heritage

The perpetuation of the immigrant's native language was an issue which spanned both the old and new immigration. Responding to "assimilationists" who charged that the use of German rather than English was un-American, Carl Schurz, noted political figure, wrote numerous essays and editorials. In a selection from his *Reminiscences,* he defended the preservation of his cultural heritage as a necessity which filled "a real and urgent want."

SOURCE: Carl Schurz, **The Reminiscences of Carl Schurz,** III (New York, 1908), pp. 257–62.

. . . It may be in place here to say a word about a prejudice entertained by some well-meaning Americans, that the publication of newspapers, and perhaps even the making of political speeches in this republic in any other language than the English, is an undesirable, if not positively dangerous practice. It is said that it prevents immigrants from learning the language of the country; that it fosters the cultivation of un-American principles, notions and habits, and that it thus stands in the way of the development of a sound American patriotism in those coming from foreign lands to make their home among us, and to take part in the working of our free institutions. I think I may say without undue assumption that from personal contact and large opportunities of observation, I have as much personal experience of the German-born population of the United States, its character, its aspirations, and its American patriotism, as any person now living; and this experience enables me to affirm that the prejudice against the German-American press is groundless. On the contrary, that press does the country a necessary and very important service. In the first place, it fills a real and very urgent want. That want will exist so long as there is a large number of German-born citizens in this republic. There will always be many among them, especially persons of mature years who arrived on American soil without any knowledge of the English language, who may be able to acquire enough of it to serve them in their daily walk, but not enough to enable them to understand newspaper articles on political or similar subjects. Such persons must receive the necessary information about current events, questions to be considered and duties to be performed, from journals published in the language they understand, or they will not have it at all. The suppression of the German-American press would, therefore, be equivalent to the cultivation of political ignorance among a large and highly estimable class of citizens.

It is argued that the existence of the German newspaper is apt to render the German immigrant less sensible of the necessity of learning English. This is the case only to a very limited extent. A large majority of the German immigrants of mature age, being farmers or industrial laborers, do not acquire their knowledge of English in this country through regular linguistic instruction, or by reading books or newspapers, but from conversation or attempts at conversation with their neighbors who do not speak German, and that knowledge will, of necessity, remain very imperfect. Their acquaintance with the English language will always be, to a limited extent, of course, a speaking acquaintance, but not a reading acquaintance. It is not the existence of German newspapers that will keep them from reading English newspapers, but it is their inability to read English. German immigrants of education will read English newspapers, but many of them will read German newspapers too, because they find in them things of interest which the English papers do not give them.

•   •   •

That the existence of the German press tells for the preservation in this country of the German language as a language of social and business intercourse is to a limited extent true. But what harm is there in this? While it is of great use to the older immigrants, it does not keep their children from learning English, even in settlements which are preponderatingly German, for such settlements are no longer isolated as the original German settlements in Pennsylvania were. But it does give the younger generation the advantage of knowing two languages. That kind of American patriotism which takes umbrage at an American citizen's knowledge of a foreign tongue besides the English—a sort of patriotism I have here and there met with—is certainly too narrow-minded, not to say too silly, to be seriously considered. No educated, nay, no sound-minded person, will deny, that the knowledge of more than one language tends to widen our mental horizon, to facilitate the acquisition of useful intelligence, and thus to broaden education.

But the preservation of the German language among us has done and is still doing this country a peculiar and very valuable service. It is said of the Englishman that he takes his pleasures and amusements seriously, even gravely. The native American also is somewhat inclined that way. He possesses little of the faculty of finding great enjoyment in small things and of thus making his daily life sunny and cheerful. The German possesses that faculty in a high degree. It manifests itself pre-eminently in the German love for music and especially in the cultivation of song. It may almost be said that one of the happiest and most amiable features of the German character is the German "Lied." It constitutes one of the great charms of German social life. Its invasion of American soil, stimulating the love and cultivation of music and thus softening the rigors of American social life by popularizing a harmless and refining enjoyment, has been one of the special blessings the German immigration has brought with it. It seems to me very probable, if not certain, that the blessing of this influence would have been greatly curtailed had the German immigrants upon their arrival upon these shores permitted the German language to disappear from among them, for without the preservation of that language the German Glee Club and the German Musical Society would hardly have become soundly rooted in American soil.

People and Puppets: The Ghetto Stage in New York

Every immigrant group made efforts to perpetuate their heritages and pass them on to their children. The foreign press, school and theater all endeavored to transplant and carry on the culture from Europe. Perhaps the most significant of all was the creation of the foreign-language theater.

In this selection, Hutchins Hapgood, an observer with a unique understanding of New York's immigrant ghettos, discussed the "spirit of realism" which characterized the Yiddish stage. Recognizing that this was the finest legitimate theater in the nation, Hapgood concluded that it was refreshing in contrast to the boring and inane productions of Broadway.

SOURCE: Hutchins Hapgood, **"Realism on the Ghetto Stage,"** *Atlantic Monthly* (June 1900), pp. 839–43.

The distinctive thing about the intellectual and artistic life of the Russian Jews of the New York Ghetto is the spirit of realism. Among them are men of learning and talent and of consuming energy. The Ghetto is full of socialists and men of expressive mood who in Russia were persecuted for their race, or at least hampered in the free expression of their opinions. Their energy is now let loose in this city, where there are six Yiddish newspapers and several reviews devoted to the discussion of intellectual and political questions. At the cafes on Grand and Canal streets there gather a band of socialists, poets, journalists, actors, and playwrights,— a Yiddish Bohemia, poor and picturesque.

The intellectual impulse of the Ghetto, no matter what its manifestation, is the spirit animating modern Russian literature, the spirit of Turgeniev and of Tolstoi, a spirit at once of realism in art and of revolt in political opinion.

This serious representation and criticism of life pervading the intellectual circles of the Ghetto is noticeable even on the popular stage. The most interesting plays are those in which the realistic spirit predominates, and the best among the actors and playwrights are the realists. The realistic element, too, is the latest one in the history of the Yiddish stage.

. . .

In almost every play given on the Bowery all the elements are represented. Vaudeville, history, realism, comic opera, are generally mixed together. Even in the plays of Gordin there are clownish and operatic intrusions, inserted as a conscious condition of success. On the other hand, even in the distinctively formless plays, in comic opera and melodrama, there are striking illustrations of the popular feeling for realism,—bits of dialogue, happy strokes of characterization of well-known Ghetto types, sordid scenes faithful to the life of the people.

It is the acting which gives even to the plays having no intrinsic relation to reality a frequent quality of naturalness. The Yiddish players, even the poorer among them, act with remarkable sincerity. Entirely lacking in self-consciousness, they attain almost from the outset to a direct and forcible expressiveness. They, like the audience, rejoice in what they deem the truth. In the general lack of really good plays they yet succeed in introducing the note of realism. To be true to nature is their strongest passion, and even in a conventional melodrama their sincerity, or their characterization in the comic episodes, often redeems the play from utter barrenness. And the little touches of truth to the life of the people are thoroughly appreciated by the audience, much more generally so than in the case of the better plays to be described later, where there is a more or less strict form and intellectual intention, difficult for the untutored crowd to understand. In the "easy" plays, it is the realistic touches which tell most. The audience laughs at the exact reproduction by the actor of a tattered type which they know well. A scene of perfect sordidness will arouse the sympathetic laughter or tears of the people. "It is so natural," they say to one another, "so true." The word "natural" indeed is the favorite term of praise in the Ghetto. What hits home to them, to their sense of humor or of sad fact, is sure to move, although sometimes in a manner surprising to a visitor. To what seems to him very sordid and sad they will frequently respond with laughter.

.   .   .

But although the best actors of the three Yiddish theatres in the Ghetto are realists by instinct and training, the thoroughly frivolous element in the plays has its prominent interpreters. Joseph Latteiner is the most popular playwright in the Bowery, and Boris Thomashevsky perhaps the most popular actor. Latteiner has written over a hundred plays, no one of which has form or ideas. He calls them *Volksstucke* (plays of the people), and naively admits that he writes directly to the demand. They are mainly mixed melodrama, broad burlesque, and comic opera. His heroes are all intended for Boris Thomashevsky, a young man, fat, with curling black hair, languorous eyes, and a rather effeminate voice, who is thought very beautiful by the girls of the Ghetto. Thomashevsky has a face with no mimic capacity, and a temperament absolutely impervious to mood or feeling. But he picturesquely stands in the middle of the stage and declaims phlegmatically the role of the hero, and satisfies the "romantic" demand of the audience. Nothing could show more clearly how much more genuine the feeling of the Ghetto is for fidelity to life than for romantic fancy. How small a part of the grace and charm of life the Yiddish audiences enjoy may be judged by the fact that the romantic appeal of a Thomashevsky is eminently satisfying to them. Girls and men from the sweatshops, a large part of such an audience, are moved by a very crude attempt at beauty. On the other hand they are so familiar with sordid fact, that the theatrical representation of it must be relatively excellent. Therefore the art of the Ghetto, theatrical and other, is deeply and painfully realistic.

When we turn to Jacob Gordin's plays, to other plays of similar character and to the audiences to which they specifically appeal, we have realism worked out consciously in art, the desire to express life as it is, and at the same time the frequent expression of revolt against the reality of things, and particularly against the actual system of society. Consequently the "problem" play has its representation in the Ghetto. It presents the hideous conditions of life in the Ghetto,—the poverty, the sordid constant reference to money, the immediate sensuality, the jocular callousness,—and underlying the mere statement of the facts an intellectual and passionate revolt.

The thinking element of the Ghetto is largely socialistic, and the socialists flock to the theatre the nights when the Gordin type of play is produced. They discuss the meaning and justice of the play between the acts, and after the performance repair to the Canal Street cafes to continue their serious discourse. The unthinking nihilists are also represented, but not so frequently at the best plays as at productions in which are found crude and screaming condemnation of existing conditions. It is the custom for various lodges and societies to buy out the theatre for some particular night, and have a fitting play presented as a benefit performance. The anarchistic propaganda, one night last winter, hired the Windsor Theatre for the establishment of a fund to start the Freie Arbeiter Stimme, an anarchistic newspaper. The Beggar of Odessa was the play selected,—an adaptation of The Ragpicker of Paris, a play by Felix Piot, the anarchistic agitator of the French Commune in 1871. The features of the play particularly interesting to the audience were those emphasizing the clashing of social classes. The old ragpicker, played by Jacob Adler, a model man, clever, brilliant, and good, is a philosopher too, and says many things warmly welcomed by the audience. As he picks up his rags he sings about how even the clothing of the great comes but to dust. His adopted daughter is poor, and consequently noble and sweet. The villains are all rich; all the very poor characters are good. Another play recently produced, Vogele, is partly a satire of the rich Jew by the poor Jew. "The rich Jews," sang the comedian, "toil not, neither do they spin. They work not, they suffer not,—why then do they live on this earth?" This unthinking revolt is the opposite pole to the unthinking vaudeville and melodrama represented by Latteiner and Thomashevsky.

The facts of life in the Ghetto are in themselves unpleasant, and consequently it is natural that a dramatic exaggeration of them results in something poignantly disagreeable. The intense seriousness of the Russian Jew, which accounts for what is excellent in these plays, explains also the rasping falseness of the extreme situations.

Some of the more striking of the realistic plays on the Ghetto stage have been partly described, but realism in the details of character and setting appears in all of them, even in comic opera and melodrama. In many the element of revolt, if not a conscious idea, is expressed in occasional dialogues. Burlesque runs through them all, but burlesque, after all, is a comment on the facts of life. And all these points are emphasized and driven home by sincere and forcible acting.

Crude in form as these plays are, and unpleasant as they often are in subject and in the life portrayed, they are yet refreshing to persons who have been bored by the empty farce and inane cheerfulness of the uptown theatres.

The Importance of the Immigrant Press

The foreign-language press represented one of the most important influences on the immigrant. Through this medium, millions of aliens were reached far more effectively through their own language than through English. Publishing news about the United States, these newspapers enabled the readers quickly to acquire knowledge about the customs and institutions of their new homeland. Thus, in spite of the assertion by some that the foreign press retarded assimilation, it was an unparalleled educational tool within the immigrant community.

SOURCE: **Report of the Massachusetts Commission on Immigration** (Boston, 1914), pp. 201–2.

The influence of the foreign-language newspapers must be considered in any program which requires the co-operation of the immigrant population. The commission has found 58 such papers published in the following languages in Massachusetts: Albanian, Arabian, Armenian, Jewish, French, German, Greek, Italian, Lettish, Lithuanian, Polish, Portuguese, Swedish, Syrian and Yiddish. Six of these are dailies. In addition, many foreign-language papers published in other States have a wide circulation in Massachusetts. Although these papers find it very difficult to hold the second generation as readers, they are the only newspapers read by a large per cent of the adult immigrant population.

The explanation of this is simple. In addition to the language difficulties, which make even those who have learned some English prefer their native language, these papers contain much of peculiar interest to the immigrant. There are accounts of what is happening in Galicia, Finland, Portugal or Greece, and of what the Italians, Poles, Syrians or Lithuanians in other parts of the United States are doing; and all the events of the day are interpreted in terms of the immigrant's own experience and special interests.

The policy and character of these papers differ widely. They represent the various religious and political factions of Europe as well as of the United States. All of them are, as is to be expected, strongly "national" in the advocacy of the cause of their own people in the struggles of rival European races; Russian, Austrian or Hungarian officials often complain that the Polish, Slovak or Lithuanian movement at home is kept alive by the American press.

Many of these papers are small and have not the means to purchase real news service. While some of the editors are public-spirited men of wide culture others have practically no knowledge of American life and institutions. The majority are loyal Americans; the patriotism of some of them, however, like that of many native American editors, does not always dictate the choice of the public good when this conflicts with private gain.

But whatever their faults or limitations, the foreign-language papers cannot be ignored as influential factors in the community life. In all educational campaigns for the protection of public health, for the improvement of social, industrial and political conditions, in advertising schools, libraries and lectures their support is needed and it is believed can be secured. The commission has found these papers ready to co-operate in furthering its investigations and in giving publicity to its hearings.

The American public, as well as the editors themselves, should realize that the foreign-language papers have a rare opportunity to serve the interests of their own people and of their adopted country.

2. Group Life in the Ethnic Ghetto

The German Element in the United States

Hundreds of thousands of Germans arrived in the United States in the period 1840–80. Among them were some of the best-educated and politically enlightened aliens of that era. These emigrants came from every corner of Germany, some in flight from religious persecution; others sought refuge from poverty and political suppression.

In spite of their desertion from their fatherland, few shed the customs and traditions which were so much a part of their past lives. Hence, a source of friction developed between the "fun-loving" German and the "puritanical" American nativist.

The transplanted German enjoyed his beer garden, Sunday picnic, shooting festival, theater and music. Despite the opposition to these activities, shortly after his arrival the "German notion that it [was] a good thing to have a good time [had] found a lodgment in the American mind."

SOURCE: E. V. Smalley, **"The German Element in the United States,"** *Lippincott's Magazine* (April 1883), pp. 359–63.

Upon the social life of the country the Germans have exercised a more important influence than we of English ancestry can readily realize, unless our memories go back to a time before their presence was much felt. Probably we should in the end have got rid without their help of the old Puritanical idea that amusements of all sorts are devices of the devil, and that a sense of physical and mental enjoyment is essentially sinful; culture and progress would have brought us out of that dismal delusion; but the example of their hearty and harmless diversions helped us along rapidly.

. . .

The German notion that it is a good thing to have a good time has found a lodgment in the American mind. Except in isolated rural localities where the Teutonic immigration has not penetrated, there is no longer any such feeling about dancing, social games, and dramatic performances as was almost universal among respectable people thirty years ago.

. . .

Their influence upon our drink has been far greater than upon our food. They have made us a beer-drinking nation. Within the memory of men of middle age, lager-beer was almost unknown in this country; now it is the national beverage. That the beer-drinking habit we have acquired from them is a good thing in itself I will not contend, though something might be said of the beneficial sedative influence of this decoction of hops and malt upon our excitable, over-active American temperament; but it is unquestionably a great improvement on the whiskey-drinking habit it has replaced. If we must drink any stimulating fluid, beer is the best, except light wine;

and we are only beginning to learn how to produce a good, sound, light-bodied wine like claret.

We are greatly indebted to the Germans for the advance we have made in the cultivation and appreciation of music during the past thirty years. They are our music-teachers, our band-masters, our orchestra-directors, and to a great extent our professional musicians. Our American element did not get much beyond simple, old-fashioned English songs, marches, dancing-tunes, and negro-melodies in its musical culture until the Germans spread themselves over the country and organized their orchestras, their "Gesangvereine," their "Liedertafeln," and their "Mannerchore." Opera, which a few years ago was a foreign exotic that could scarcely be kept alive outside of New York, now flourishes in every city, big and little, from Portland, Maine, to Portland, Oregon. Poor indeed in musical resources is now the town which does not possess a fair orchestra, and every village boasts a brass band. The quality of our music has improved as much as the quantity.

. . .

The Germans support two excellent theatres in New York, with larger and better-trained companies than can be seen at most of the other houses. The performances at these theatres embrace in the course of a season a wide variety, ranging from opera-bouffe and jolly little farces up to the plays of Shakespeare and Schiller. Modern comedies are given with a finish, balance of parts, and naturalness of acting very rarely seen on the American stage.

. . .

In art the Germans have not accomplished much in this country; but in the artistic handicrafts, such as wall painting, engraving, designing patterns, gold and silver work, bookbinding, etc., they have done a great deal. Upholstering, cabinet-making, and house-decoration are favorite trades with them, and, while they do not originate much that is graceful and tasteful, they are omnivorous copyists, and draw upon the whole world for their forms and color combinations, imitating a Pompeian wall, a French stuccoed ceiling, or a Flemish carved mantel, with equal facility. There is no trade or occupation in which they are not represented; but there are some vocations which they almost monopolize. Wherever a bakery is found, the chance is about ten to one that a German runs it. Butchers and market-gardeners are pretty sure to betray a German origin. It is the same with tailors and watchmakers,—the latter coming chiefly from the German cantons of Switzerland.

The Associated Life of the Italians

Italian settlements in the urban centers of the United States were known as "Little Italies." Although the community was distinctly Italian, there existed within the area geographical divisions which reflected the village or province from which the particular families had migrated. Thus, it was not uncommon for an entire tenement or street to be inhabited solely by those identified as Napoletano, Calabrese, Veneziano, Abruzzese, or Siciliano. These immigrants brought with them their Old World localisms which they transplanted in their New World enclaves. Consequently a variety of separate and distinct subcultures took root within Italo-American neighborhoods.

Antonio Mangano, an Italian Protestant engaged in missionary work for his church, observed the development of subcultures within Italian communities. In the following article, he described the hostility and marked rivalry which characterized this immigrant neighborhood. On the other hand, he discussed those agencies which sought to promote the unification of the Italian community.

SOURCE: Antonio Mangano, "The Associated Life of the Italians in New York City," *Charities* (May 7, 1904), pp. 476–82.

It is generally supposed by those unfamiliar with actual conditions, that the Italian colony of the Borough of Manhattan is a well-organized and compact body of people, having a common life and being subject to the absolute control and leadership of some one person or group of persons. To the reader of popular articles describing Italian life and customs, in these days so frequently appearing in newspapers and magazines; to the enthusiastic and romantic slum visitor, who walks through Mulberry street, and possibly peeps into the dark and dismal hallway of some dilapidated tenement and feels that he knows just how Italians live and act; to the theoretical sociologist, to whom all Italians look alike and in whose estimation all Italians are alike, think alike, and act alike—to such persons the mere mention of the Italian colony inevitably suggests unity of thought and action as well as of mode of life on the part of all who belong to that colony. And yet nothing is farther from the real truth.

· · ·

The members of the Italian colony have a certain element in their general make-up which has rendered it virtually impossible for them to act unitedly and harmoniously. Each man feels that he is a law unto himself: each small group of men are a law unto themselves. They appreciate most keenly that it is their right and privilege to do as they see fit—providing they do not interfere with other people's rights—but they lose sight of this other great fact equally important, that personal rights and privileges should be modified by consideration for the welfare of the community—the only condition under which men can live together in any proper and mutually helpful relation.

· · ·

The New York colony is composed of persons coming from nearly every nook and corner of the old peninsula. It is by no means strange, then, that they should bring with them local prejudices and narrow sympathies; it is not to be wondered that they feel that highest duty consists in being loyal to the handful who come from their immediate section and in manifesting opposition toward those who come from other localities. Thus it comes to pass that while a man may be known as an Italian, he is far better known as a Napoletano, Calabrese, Veneziano, Abruzzese, or Siciliano. This means that the Italian colony is divided into almost as many groups as there are sections of Italy represented.

There are, however, many signs which unmistakably point to a decided change for the better in the near future. There are certain forces at work which have for their ultimate object the development of a larger spirit of co-operation, which will enable the Italians as a whole to unite for the attainment of specific objects. The main purpose of this article, therefore, is to point out the chief Italian institutions which indicate the lines along which Italian organized effort is directed, and to describe briefly their operations.

Among the agencies which have for their ideal united Italian action, there are none more potent than the Italian Chamber of Commerce. This organization, founded in 1887 with but a few members, to-day embraces in its membership of 201 a majority of the Italian business men in Greater New York.

. . .

That the Neapolitan, the Sicilian, the Roman, can all join this organization and have as the one object the advancement of Italian interests, is a step in the right direction and toward another end which is eminently wholesome and greatly to be desired.

The Columbus Hospital is situated on Twentieth street between Second and Third avenues. Organized in 1892 and incorporated in 1895, it has been from its beginning under the direct supervision of the missionary Sisters of the Sacred Heart. Were it possible for the hospital to secure increased accommodations and better facilities, it would be of far greater service to those in whose interests it is dedicated. The following paragraph is taken from the last annual report: "During the year, 1,098 patients were admitted, and of this number only sixty-three paid full board. When we consider that the hospital is devoid of endowment, annuity, or permanent fund for its maintenance, depending entirely upon the energies of the sisters and the voluntary contributions of those who have its well-being at heart, it becomes a problem which those unacquainted with the management would find difficulty in solving."

Columbus Hospital is generally known as an Italian institution, yet of the twenty-one physicians on its medical and surgical staff not one is an Italian, but the sisters who carry it on are all native Italians, and ninety-five per cent of the patients treated are of that race.

Closely associated with the work of the Society for the Protection of Italian Immigrants is the Italian Benevolent Institute. Within the past two years it has taken on new life. The work was encouraged by gifts from many quarters, the most noteworthy one being from His Majesty the King of Italy, which amounted to 20,000 lire. One of its encouraging features is the fact that it is maintained almost exclusively by Italians.

The institute has its headquarters in a double house, 165-7 West Houston street, which is intended as a place of refuge for the destitute. It often happens that newcomers, bound for interior points, land in New York without a cent in their pockets, expecting to find at the post-office or some bank the sum necessary to carry them to their destination; it also often happens that the money expected does not arrive in time. To such persons as these the Benevolent Institute opens its doors. Then, too, there are immigrants who come with the intention of settling in New York. Such persons may have $8 or $10, but unless they find work at once they too are compelled to seek aid from some source. Further, New York has become, in a sense, a central market for Italian labor, and of those who go to distant points in search of work some fail to find it, and return to the city.

Attention has already been called to the fact that the Italian is lacking in the spirit of unity, and of association in a large sense. The last few years, however, have witnessed a few noteworthy victories in the interest of larger sympathy—mainly through the efforts of a few leading spirits who have been prominent in the affairs of the colony. If one can prophesy, in the light of tendencies already at work, the day is coming when the Italian colony will recognize its responsibilities, and, throwing aside petty jealousies, will launch out upon such a policy as will best enhance the interests of the Italians as a whole.

If we were asked, therefore, whether there is any bond which unites the Italian colony as a whole, we must answer no. Even the Roman Church cannot be considered such a unifying factor in the attitude of indifference taken toward its claims.

It must be observed, however, that the Italian manifests a strong tendency toward organization with small groups for social ends and for the purpose of mutual aid. There are in Manhattan alone over one hundred and fifty Italian societies of one sort or another. "The moral disunity of the old peninsula is transplanted here."

The Italian does not lack the instinct of charity or mutual helpfulness; but at present he lacks the instinct in a broad sense. He would take the bread from his own mouth in order to help his fellow townsman; there is nothing he will not do for his *paesano;* but it must not be expected from this that he will manifest such an attitude toward *all Italians*. Not-withstanding, were it not for this strong feeling, even though limited to small groups, we should have many more calls upon public charity on the part of the Italians than we now do.

.   .   .

Probably the institution which has done more than any other for the Italian colony in an educational way is the school on Leonard street, devoted exclusively to Italians and maintained by the Children's Aid Society. This school, with its faithful body of teachers, has exerted a strong influence upon the Italian colony. The day sessions are conducted precisely along public school lines, mainly for children who do not enter the public schools for a variety of reasons. A night school is conducted in the same building, which aims primarily at giving instruction in the English language. There is an average attendance of men and boys at these classes of about three hundred. Besides this, there is a department of Italian instruction. A teacher who has this work in charge is supported by the Italian government. The building is also used for social purposes, and entertainments are held during the winter every Friday evening.

As an evidence of the esteem felt by Italians who have come under the influence of this school, a movement is now on foot among them to secure funds—$3,000 has already been raised—for the establishment of a similar school for the Italians in "Little Italy."

The Bohemians in Chicago

At the turn of the nineteenth century Chicago was the third largest Bohemian (Czech and Slovak) city in the world. This group, which began its migration to America in the 1850s, established in this Midwestern city a tightly knit community, which was characterized by strong family ties. Although they tenaciously clung to their history, language and traditions, the Chicago colony successfully integrated into the political, economic and social life of that urban center.

In the article which follows, Alice G. Masaryk, a University of Chicago settlement worker, described what was typical and characteristic of Bohemian-American life.

SOURCE: Alice G. Masaryk, "The Bohemians in Chicago," *Charities* (December 3, 1904), pp. 206–10.

Half a century has passed since Bohemians first crossed the ocean, and after a long and dreaded journey and much uncertainty, settled down in Chicago, which was then scarcely more than a large village on the Lake shore in the endless prairie.

To-day, Chicago is the third largest Bohemian city in the world, having about one hundred thousand Bohemians, grouped in several colonies of which "Pilsen" is the largest. Originally, the Bohemians lived on Van Buren and Canal streets where now rushing business life is focused. But these settlers were accustomed to villages and small rustic towns, where they cultivated their fields and lived by their handicraft. Therefore, they soon moved from their first seats near the lake and, when the influx of Jews and Italians into their new quarters began to change the character of the settlement, they moved again. The growth of Pilsen thus began after 1870, and after thirty years shows a certain crystallization of what is typical and characteristic of Bohemian-American life. The other quarters are of more recent date and in many respects bear to Pilsen the relation of colonies to a mother land.

.   .   .

The Bohemians at home have a strong family life. A married son or daughter remains under the same roof with the aged parents, who retire into a quiet nook, where they enjoy their flaxen-haired, brown-eyed grandchildren. This trait, though modified, continues in Chicago. On a Sunday afternoon, the Eighteenth street car is filled with families, scrubbed, brushed and starched-up, bound for some festival hall to have a good time.

The Bohemian housekeepers know how to get great results from small means, which is most valuable for the poorer class and shows in the red and glossy cheeks of the children. On the other hand, the heavy food (pork with dumplings, for instance, is very common, and with it the usual glass of beer) produces those of full forms without corresponding strength, so general among the well-to-do citizens.

The Bohemians are capable of being amalgamated quickly. They learn the language easily, they give work for which even under competition, they can demand decent wages; they take an interest in politics.

. . .

Two pages, large sheets of the daily paper *Svornost* lie before me, covered with small print, giving the names of Bohemian clubs, societies, and lodges in Chicago. The Catholic press gives another long list of Catholic lodges, Catholic clubs. This fever for organization is typical of the Bohemians in Chicago. It was forty years ago that the few Bohemian settlers started their first club, the "Slavic Limetree." This beginning was simple, and almost idyllic. "We ought to have a little church for our grandmothers," one of the members suggested a little later. "A church where they could pray their *pater noster* in peace and then we'll be fixed. If we had a mill on the river I should think that we were in Bohemia."

The grandmothers received their church—no small gift in those times. It cost much enthusiasm and good will. Since that simple beginning, many activities have been at work which have resulted in the social organization—the work of individuals, of masses.

. . .

The emigration consists almost entirely of working people of whom it has been shown a large percentage is skilled handworkers. It must be borne in mind that while within the last fifty years, centralization of capital and subdivision of labor have reached an unparalleled height in America, in Bohemia, the old guild system which prevailed for centuries is slowly dying off through the same process. The old settlers, who came forty years ago and filled their stores with homemade goods (in those times one tailor flourished alongside of another on Nineteenth street) look amazed on the newcomers and shake their heads: "The idea of an eight-hour day." "The idea of strikes." The once independent handworkers become foremen in great establishments, cutters in tailor shops, butchers in stock yards, workers in the lumber yards, and a great many become shop-keepers. The middle class naturally dreads the great industrial revolution and hates with equal zest trusts and trade unions. But in the trade union movement the

Bohemian workman, like all other intelligent working people, takes a part. And in Chicago, the unions with a Bohemian administration (over twenty in number) have a Bohemian central body.

A large factor in the industrial life is the fact that the Bohemians in Chicago practically have a third generation on this soil, though the first generation is still coming in. Therefore, it is natural that with the great thriftiness of the people and their desire to give their children a good education, Bohemians should be found in different branches of business as well as in all professions. In the home country brewing and the making of beet sugar are two of the oldest industries, and three breweries, founded by Bohemian capital, operate in Chicago, influencing the number of saloons not exactly to the benefit of the population.

The Bohemians have a tendency to own houses and so to have permanent homes. This tendency has been very much helped by the Subsidiary Loan Association. The first was started in 1870, and by 1902 there were over thirty Bohemian loan associations of this kind. Six per cent is the highest rate of interest. Of the officers, only the secretary is paid and the books are revised once a year by a state officer. The system of mutual benefit societies has also taken on large dimensions. *Svornost* gives the name of sixteen orders, which in Chicago have 259 lodges. *Denni Hlasatal* gives about thirty Catholic associations and this is far from being a full list. These orders pay sick and death benefits, the business basis of the lodges being combined with a social element.

· · ·

The social life among the Bohemians is very much alive. There are dances, concerts, theatrical performances. Since the Columbian Exposition a company of professional actors has resided in Pilsen, who on Sunday evenings play before a full house in the large hall, Thalia.

Besides the tendency to avail themselves of the unaccustomed freedom, other factors enter into the social life, such as the rivalry between the Catholics and Freethinkers, the rivalry of individuals, and the indirect economic interest. A new settler finds customers in the club or lodge he joins. This can be reduced *ad absurdum,* when, for instance, all the grocers from the district meet in the same club with the same intention. The educational element is of great importance. I was struck by the cleverness and efficiency with which the Bohemian women conduct their meetings. The men gain here a training for political life.

Other than these mutual benefit organizations, you will find all kinds of societies especially among the Freethinkers, such as turner (gymnastic) clubs (35), singing clubs (18), printing clubs (7), bicycle clubs (5), dramatic clubs (4) and many others.

The Bohemians are born musicians. "Where is the Bohemian who does not love music?" is a cadence in Smetana's music which says everything. You will find on the West Side many music schools, many violinists and pianists, amateurs, besides the professional musicians who have three unions.

A large park near Dunning, a beautiful garden, is the Bohemian cemetery. Its beginning belongs to the time of the separation of the Freethinkers from the Catholic Church. A Catholic priest refused to bury in the Catholic cemetery a woman who died without a confession, and the Freethinkers resolved to have a cemetery of their own. Like the Catechism of Freethinking, this cemetery proclaims how deeply the roots of Catholic logic and way of thinking penetrated the Bohemian soul. The great pomp with which the dead are buried by Freethinkers belongs to the middle ages, to the shadows of cathedrals. It is touching to watch the pride with which they love this piece of American soil. All the thoughts and memories of their old home, that are so dear to them, seem to be thought more easily and better in this garden of the dead, for something died within them when they left their homes. The pure memory lives as the memory of those who have left them forever and sleep under that velvety grass, under the brightest autumn leaves and the faithful asters.

A Mixing Bowl for Nations

Numerous ethnic groups made their settlement in the city of Chicago. Attracted by the economic opportunities of this large industrial metropolis, the German and Irish, the Poles and Jews, Bohemians, Slovaks, Italians and Greeks established permanent communities. Attempting to re-create some of the Old World atmosphere, these newcomers transplanted many of their European social institutions, in particular the "coffee shop gathering."

Ernest Poole, the Chicago-based novelist, visited these "little cafes and back rooms of saloons." In an article entitled "A Mixing Bowl for Nations," he described the social life within these "ethnic haunts."

SOURCE: Ernest Poole, **"A Mixing Bowl for Nations,"** *Everybody's Magazine* (October 1910), pp. 554–55, 562–64.

CHICAGO, the greatest industrial city on earth. So say most observers, watching the stock-yards, the steel mills and Pullman, the sweat-shops and factories, foundries, tanneries, harvester works. And they miss the most vital process of all. For if, when the day's roar of work has subsided, you watch the men, women, and children that pour out of factories, shops, and mills; the Germans and Irish and Scotch, the Swedes, Norwegians, Poles and Jews, Bohemians, Slovaks, Italians, Greeks; if you follow the human tides to the great foreign quarters of the city, you may be amazed at the scenes you will suddenly enter; opening scenes in a slow but irresistible process, which has for its raw material all the old peoples of Europe, and for a finished product, when at last these shall all be fused—a new race of men upon the earth. The Tower of Babel's drama reversed. Chicago a mixing-bowl for the nations.

In the Cafe Acropolis the night had just begun. It was six o'clock. Outside the open doors, on Halsted Street, the crowds were coming home; there was a ceaseless shuffling tread of feet, and laughing, shouting, talking in a curious babel of tongues. But in here was only Greece. Not a word of English, but a hum of deep, harsh voices from a dozen groups of men, some playing pool in the rear, but most at little round tables, sipping Turkish coffee in small, thick, white cups; reading the *Chronos* (*Times*), an American newspaper printed in Greek; and smoking cigarettes or long Turkish water pipes. Above in festoons hung gay paper ropes of all colors. On one wall, from a gilded picture frame, the Athenian Acropolis looked down; on another, a print of a classic old Parthenon statue, stately and severe, completely ignored its gay neighbor—a gorgeous chromo of Anna Held displaying a new five-cent cigar.

At four of the tables all eyes were intent on the cards.

"Poker?" I suggested, looking for chips.

"No," said the tall, swarthy waiter disdainfully. "Not like it at all. It is a Greek game. You begin. You never want to go. Some time maybe you play all the night."

Here many come to seek news from home. On the wall at one spot were pinned some score of letters, the addresses in strange Greek scrawl. When the postman came in with the evening mail, a half dozen rose and crowded around him, but came back disgusted; except for one chubby-faced man who took a blue letter—also chubby—back to his corner table, and sat complacently smiling down, lighting a fresh cigarette before beginning to read. Stories cluster thick round this rough, simple post-office, but of these you can get only hints. There was a boy of eighteen who walked in every night for over six months, never asking for letters, but simply glancing up at the place on the wall—for the missive which never came. On the wall are some envelopes dingy with months of waiting for readers, the stories still hidden inside. And here one night an anxious group of big workmen sat breathing hard over a letter to be sent to a mother in Greece, to say that her son had lost his leg in a tunnel explosion, that by passing the hat in the cafe for the past five evenings they had collected enough for his passage, and that he would soon start for home.

At some tables faces drew close together scowling, or were thrown far back laughing—over first adventures in America. For this cafe is a meeting-place for Greeks from all over the land. Here stories are told of far-away camps, of the railroads, the mills, and the mines; but more often of South Water Street, near by, the fruit mart of America. For fruit is the Greek's main business field. Thousands peddle it along the city streets, and a few already own big South Water Street stores.

In one corner, at a table by himself, sat a gray old man, prosperous looking, slowly puffing a Turkish pipe and reading the *Chronos*. From this old business gentleman down to the ragged young railroad hobo, you could see in the different grades of clothes and demeanors the various rungs in the social ladder. For even the Greeks are beginning to climb.

"See those fellers," said a jaunty young Greek clerk who sat at my table. He pointed to the jolliest crowd in the room, the jolliest and the raggedest—grimy, hairy giants with clear, black eyes and flashing smiles. "Hayseeds," he remarked. "Fresh from the mountains in Greece, the poor places. Most Greeks are like them when they come here first. Then they learn."

The real Bohemian cafe, when at last I found it on a dirty tenement street far out in the southwest part of the city, was a large, square room that seemed double its size, so low was the ceiling. I came in to supper at seven o'clock, when the evening had just begun. A few spruce youngsters, probably clerks, were playing billiards in shirt-sleeves at two tables in the rear. Around the walls, at small tables sat men of all ages, from young Czechs in their teens to three white-headed old chums who sat together peacefully smoking their pipes, with looks on their faces that were a disgrace to tense, hard-headed, rushing Chicago. All degrees of prosperity were here. Men with good clothes and assured demeanor sat close to men who, from the looks of their clothes and hands, might have come from the neighboring stock-yards, where thousands of Czechs are employed.

But they are slow to forget Bohemia. Around me I heard not a word of English, but only the low, deep, guttural hum of the Czechish tongue, which they proudly claim is the richest language on earth: in its beauty, its fine shades of meaning, its power and rhythm. And truly it has a strange fascination—this speech that for hundreds of years, outlawed by the Teutons, has had to fight for its very life, and has only lately won back its freedom. As you listen, it is easy to imagine wild gorges, old castles, and desperate struggles for liberty. The castles were there, in dusky pictures on the walls: old, gray, ruined, turreted affairs perched high on rocky cliffs; and there were romantic scenes of patriots round bivouac fires in mountain glens. And close beside these dusky old scenes was a brand-new, flaring American poster, entitled "Hurdle Automobiles in the White City at Night."

An affable young man of business sat at my table. He spoke excellent English and kindly guided me through the bewildering bill of fare. Through his aid, for the sum of thirty-five cents, I explored strange soups and stews and dumplings stuffed with meat— all highly spiced. I ate hugely of "ceskazhitna," delicious coarse rye bread, made of a special flour prepared by American mills for our half million Bohemian countrymen. But the main attraction was the beer, light and cool and undoctored (as nearly as I could tell), fresh from old Pilsen.

The talk turning to music, I asked my companion how they got along here without it. He smiled.

"We don't," he said. He pointed to a piano in one corner. "There are two men who come here, one nearly every night. One is a music teacher, the other runs a small music shop in the Quarter. Neither makes much money, but how happy they are! Both are pianists. No doubt there are men in this city who have more brilliant technique. But the phrasing, the feeling that these men put into it! Wait and you will hear."

I waited. And when I left, four hours later, a big man with heavy black and blue eyes still sat at the piano. He had no sheets of music before him. But the tables were still crowded with listeners. He would go on, I was told, until one or two in the morning. His music was full of Bohemian dreams and longings, disappointments, despair, the old feeling of struggling upward in the dark. And as he played men kept turning round from the cards; laughing groups grew suddenly silent, eyes following smoke wreaths or staring into the memories far away. Because he felt the old country —this big man who was playing.

It was here that Kubelik came one night, fresh from his downtown triumphs. Downtown he won thousands of dollars and much hearty applause. But it was here, in the little Czech theatre close overhead, the Chicago home of Bohemian music and drama, that Kubelik played his best. And late at night, when at last the audience, even standing and kneeling in the aisles, would consent that he put up his fiddle, he came down here. And then this place was packed tight with men and boys standing and sitting on tables and chairs—until three o'clock, when they carried him on their shoulders out to his automobile.

The Czechs are to be our kindred!

.   .   .

In the case of the Poles there seems to be no such question. Just as the Germans and the Irish, coming in huge waves decades ago, have toiled slowly up into the skilled work of our industries and have united by thousands with the American born, so the Poles, coming now into the vast fields of unskilled labor, are slowly pushing up, leaving Italians behind them; and already the upper-most stratum is beginning to fuse with the native stock. In the stock-yards for some two months I watched the lowermost strata, the beginners in the slow climbing process.

One Saturday night on Whisky Row, from a hall up over a Polish saloon cafe, came such shouts and laughter and squeaking of fiddles that I went up the steep stairs and entered.

"Just a weddin'," said the stout Irish policeman, who stood in one corner complacently taking it in. Around the walls stood and sat some two hundred of all ages, from the white-headed old woman across the room to the wee, chubby grandchild that stolidly slept in her lap. On the floor were a dozen couples whirling and stamping, some laughing, others as though their very lives depended on the power of each stamp. From the platform the little orchestra was playing fast and hard, repeating the same short, rhythmic squeak over and over.

The week's long grind in the stock-yards, the worries, the anxious planning to save up for a cottage home—all were forgotten. Each time the fiddles resumed their frenzy, the whirling and stamping and laughing began as though it were eight o'clock instead of twelve. Only the babies were silent and dignified—sound asleep.

It is true that at one end of the room, at the little bar, the bar-keeper was kept hard at work. Couples were continually crowding up before him. But the drink was only light beer.

"Only two drunks," said the cop, "and we fired 'em both down-stairs. These people ain't here for that kind of a time."

Over in one corner stood the bride, a husky young girl of perhaps eighteen, dressed in traditional white with a meager veil cheerfully doing its best to flutter and flow in the breeze from the window. She sat by her mother. Her broad, rather dull face was rosy now and glowing. She breathed deep, smiling to herself, now glancing at the coarse white roses in her lap, now at the dancers, now at her brand-new husband, a tall, thin Pole who stood stiff and awkward, but grinning with delight. When a man came over and seized her hand, she bounced up with a quick laugh. And then came new excitement.

For every male guest is expected to ask the bride to dance; and, to defray wedding expenses, the price of each dance is a dollar. On the floor is a thick white plate, upon which the guest may throw his coin with all his force, and if he breaks it his money is returned. But whether from the generous caution of the guests or the thickness of the plate provided by the bride's discreet mamma, this accident rarely happens. And often, if the bride be a belle and the groom a good fellow, the sum amounts to two or even three-hundred dollars—with enough left over to furnish the new American home which is to begin on the morrow.

New homes, new music and dancing, new energy, new vital hopes are here. For it is the lustiest youth, the very bone and sinew of Poland, that is now crowding in, to help make the new race of the future.

And so it is with the Lithuanians, Hungarians, and Slovaks—huge, healthy peasants, the best of raw material. Scattered over the city far and wide, there are little cafes and back rooms of saloons, there are churches and schools and society rooms, where you may catch glimpses of all these peoples. Bewildering glimpses they are, and you wonder how all are ever to be fused in the common stock.

· · ·

Now it is just beginning. The greatest of all immigration waves has come only in the past twenty years; and its ten millions of immigrants—the Italians, Bohemians, Jews, and Poles, the Swedes, Norwegians, and Greeks—are only beginning to form first blood ties with the peoples who have come here before them.

How few of us are awake to these opening scenes of the drama. How many good preachers go on with their work of to-day without thinking what effect on church and creed this race drama is to have. How many busy physicians go on with their day and night practice without stopping to wonder what the future physique is to be. How many lawyers go on with their law; politicians with their votes; employers with their factories, shops, and mills, little dreaming of what may happen to laws and political systems and even to the economic frame of society through the welding of such widely different habits and customs, religions, convictions of every kind—from the slow work of the Past; such varied hopes, desires, ambitions for self, and social-political theories, dreams, and ideals

—for the quickening work of the Future. All these to clash for survival, the fittest at last to endure—in Chicago, huge mixing-bowl for the nations!

The Bookworms of New York

The greatest number of immigrants who arrived with the new immigration were beyond the age of compulsory school attendance. Nevertheless, within some of these groups, the acquisition of knowledge was an important aspect of their lives. Accordingly, many sought out the facilities of the free public libraries.

In the article which follows, Carl W. Ackerman discussed the New York bookworm whose persistent goal was that of self-education. He concluded that the immigrants' "appetite for knowledge [was] more insatiate than that of the seminary student in the university."

SOURCE: Carl W. Ackerman, "The Book-worms of New York," *The Independent* (January 23, 1913), pp. 199–201.

For the first year or two they live huddled together in tenements on Manhattan. During that time they learn English, read thousands of books on science, philosophy and economics, as well as classical literature, and save enough money to move to the suburbs.

Some weeks ago the librarian of the Seward Park Branch of the New York Public Library, which stands on the business thorofare of the Russian Ghetto, investigated the addresses of fifty readers of three years' standing. The names were picked at random from the card index and only one still lived in that community.

Once on New York soil the most persistent work of the foreigner is self-education. His appetite for knowledge is more insatiate than that of the seminary student in the university. This is shown by the records of eight of the forty branches of the public library. During 1912 approximately fifty-three per cent of all books circulated from these centers were non-fiction, and of the forty-seven per cent of fiction more than half were the works of Dickens, Thackeray, Scott, Dumas, Shaw and Tolstoi. Modern fiction—the "best sellers"—remain dusty on the shelves. And these eight libraries are tucked between fire-escape-facades of the tenements in Poverty's Pocket of the metropolis.

The Bowery, at one time famous as the society street of the city, is now the toboggan down which the derelicts coast from the Tenderloin. Chatham Square is the end or "jumping off" place. Yet last October the library in this community circulated 12,281 books; of these 5860 were fiction. A record of 493 books read daily—and only 196 of them fiction. Of course, it is not the castaways who do the reading, but their neighbors, the aggressive, eager Russians, Rumanians, Greeks, Italians and Hungarians.

A stout, deep-eyed, dark-complexioned Russian came to the librarian of the Seward Park Branch several years ago and asked for books on advanced chemistry. He had read all those available thru the library, but lacked enough money to buy the more expensive and technical volumes. His request was similar to those she had frequently heard and she as often had been compelled to refuse. She knew the young man, however, and in a few days interested a chemist from one of the large manufacturing concerns of the city.

In the spirit of adventure this man climbed the stairs of a narrow Canal Street tenement and knocked at the door of an attic room. When the Russian admitted him the visitor stood at the threshold dumbfounded. He thought he was calling at the "bunk" of an immigrant. Instead he walked into a shabby but fully equipped chemical laboratory, hidden under the rafters of a five-story building.

Here was a young man who had been banished from Odessa because he was a Jew. He had sought political and religious freedom in the United States and did his first work in a sweatshop. From there he went to a clothing store, and in the evening tutored himself with public books. The few dollars he could save he spent for instruments.

Not many days after this meeting he was supplied with the latest books. He then passed the Regents' examinations and now is professor of chemistry in a Brooklyn institute.

Preceding the recent presidential campaign the demand for books on political economy, trust, finance and the tariff could not be supplied by these eight libraries. During the Dickens celebra-

tion five hundred volumes of the author's works were inadequate
in one branch alone. There are times when one hundred copies of
David Copperfield, in another library, do not meet the needs.
Woodrow Wilson's *The State* is in constant demand. So are the
books of William James, Henri Bergson and Professor Taussig.

By far the larger per cent of books read by these foreigners are
printed in English. At the Hamilton Fish Branch, of 25,000 volumes only 1800 are printed in other languages. The 22,740 volumes in the Chatham Square library are divided into 19,541 of
English; 1211, Yiddish; 680, Russian; 444, Italian; 434, German; 199, Chinese; 144, Modern Greek, and 87, French. The
proportions vary in other libraries, the number of each depending
upon the per cent of population in that locality which reads. The
average is about one book in a foreign tongue out of every ten in
English.

Formerly the boundaries between the different nationalities in
Manhattan were as distinct as those dividing European countries.
To-day these lines are gradually being erased. The Russians are
invading all sections. The Italians are moving among the Greeks,
the Germans and Irish. "Little Italy" is still a separate community,
but not so exclusive as it was. Chinatown is really the only survival of bygone days.

Each nationality, however, still has its main business street.
Houston Street, for instance, is packed every day by pushcart
merchants selling their wares among Rumanians and Hungarians.
New York has no Halsted Street like Chicago, where one can walk
for twenty miles and at every sixth or seventh intersection enter a
community of different people, but there are still many streets
where only Italian, Yiddish, or Modern Greek is spoken.

In each of these communities there is a public library—so
placed, not by design, but by accident. Their readers once were
mostly of one nationality. Now various peoples read in all of them.
In the evening the men who work in the stores, the factories, on
the docks, or streets, come to the library for the books. Those who
have families carry home the volumes as paternally as they lug
food or clothing—perhaps more so if they happen to be very poor.

As soon as a new reader comes to the library he is acquainted
with the card catalog and the arrangement of books. There are
separate sections for history, philosophy, science, fiction and other

branches. If the reader wants something on European history, he goes to the shelves in search, unless someone recommends a book to him. Then he consults the card index. As a result all are familiar with the system, and the attendants assist only in emergencies and in stamping their cards, making a record of the day the books must be returned. Even little girls and boys, eight and ten years old, know how to get the books. School teachers always suggest books for the children and Fiske's *History of the United States* is one of the volumes most in demand.

These libraries aid in every way to place good books in the hands of children. Only two days during the week are they permitted to look at picture books or read fairy stories. These days are Friday and Saturday. Perhaps it is the only place in the country where one can see children fight for books. They hasten in after school, scramble for places in a line at one end of the reading room, and wait for the attendant to stack the books on the shelves or dole them out. They count it as much of an accomplishment to get one of these books first as the mischievous lad glories when he succeeds in fooling a passer-by with his fake pocketbook.

A good many of the readers are studying for the Regents' examinations of the College of the City of New York—a university maintained by the city. During the day they follow the occupations of their fathers, but most of them are spurred by a desire for leadership and they are picking education as a path to the goal. This is strikingly shown by the large number of clubs, debating societies and other organizations among the immigrants.

In this phase of the foreigner's life these libraries are also indispensable. All of them have large assembly rooms, where these organizations hold their meetings. Only one restriction is made—that religion be taboo. In this way these public libraries are performing the function of community centers which reformers in Wisconsin and other western States are making of school houses. At various times lectures on hygiene, civics and other topics are given by leaders in these subjects, and all of them are well attended.

The success of the immigrant in New York may be measured by the distance he moves from lower Manhattan after he has been here a few years. If he stays in the tenements it is invariably an indication that he is unable to keep pace with the progress of his neighbors. This is not altogether at the basis of the extreme poverty there, for many of those who are skimping are saving a few hundred dollars and awaiting the time when they can move to a suburb. Many of them cannot withstand privation. Disease handicaps them. This is especially true among the Russians. They have sold their homes in the far north to come to America—their libation for freedom. When they are forced to change from a life out-of-doors to one cooped in a tenement they suffer.

The librarians who meet these immigrants all day long study their characteristics. From their observations they say the United States simply gives an outlet for a further expression of the national aspirations of these people. The Russian who has been persecuted studies our government, and as a rule becomes a radical socialist. It is said that but for the corruption in one of the Congressional districts in New York a Russian socialist would have been elected to Congress at the last election. The Italian who likes to do tasks with his hands reads the more practical books. The Hungarian loves poetry and good literature. While the Russians show a preference for their own authors, such as Tolstoi and Gorki, they as a rule have read most of these books before they emigrate. They, however, reread many of them in English.

No one author stands out alone as the most popular among the immigrants. If a group were picked it would include Dickens, Dumas, Thackeray, Scott, Shaw, Ibsen, Shakespeare, Maeterlinck, Bjornson and Tolstoi.

Altho these people are reading mostly English books, they are doing their own thinking and bringing into this country different ideals and standards. In a measure they all become Americanized, but they are also making the United States, and especially New York, a fusion of the Russian's radicalism, the Italian's practicality, the Hungarian's pleasure, the Greek's industry, with the frugality of the German, the loyalty of the Irish and the ambition of the Scotch. They are being educated in American public libraries, but their national traits are being felt—a very little as yet, but perceptible just the same.

An Italian came into the Hudson Park Branch one day to get some books and gave his name as "Bene."

"That isn't your name," the librarian insisted, but he said he wanted to change it from "Bernardino" because his American friends did not like to call him by such a long name.

He was working in one of the uptown stores and took a book with him on Practical Mechanics.

3. Clash of Interests: Rivalry Among the Newcomers

Hostility and Warfare Between the Ethnics

Although the particular groups which settled in America had little prior experience with each other, upon arrival they were faced with bitter rivalries. Thrown into competition for employment, control over political machines and a voice in the operations of their own church, groups began to unify and partake in "ethnic warfare."

In the first selection, the competition for employment and job status between the Irish and Italians was revealed. The riot which ensued gave the Italians "an opportunity to prosecute their *vendetta*" for past grievances. Similarly, in an incident arising out of Irish-German labor struggles, a group of "young Irish toughs" unsuccessfully attempted to break up an outing of the Cecilia Singing Society of Williamsburgh, Brooklyn.

Lastly, the Chicago newspaper *L'Italia* voiced its suspicion of Irish control of the Democratic political machine. This fear, reinforced by previous conflicts with the Irish, caused the newspaper to support the Republican Party as the choice of the Italian people.

SOURCE: New York *Sun*, August 15, 1870. **The Riot in Mamaroneck**

Irishmen and Italians in a Sanguinary Collision

The Italian Population of Grand Park Driven Out—The Women and Children Sheltered in the Town Hall of Morrisania—Our Home War of Races.

Yesterday afternoon a *Sun* reporter called upon Deputy Sheriff Peter Conners, of Mount Vernon, one of the witnesses of the riot, who had been deterred from attempting to suppress it on account of the rioters' overwhelming numbers. Sheriff Conners says that for some time past the bitterest feelings of hatred have been manifested between the Irish and Italian laborers employed in grading and laying out the Grand Park. The Irishmen at first began to domineer over the Italians, who in time became their superiors in numbers, and retaliated upon their former persecutors at every opportunity. Only a few weeks ago, continued the Sheriff, several officers of the law were rather roughly handled by the Irishmen, when the Italians, availing themselves of an opportunity to prosecute their *vendetta* under the protection of the law, joined the officers with an immense crowd and drove a comparatively small number of Irishmen from the field.

THE BEGINNING OF THE WAR

On Saturday evening, at about 5 o'clock, a throng of Italians, numbering over two hundred, were congregated around the Company's pay office, waiting their turn to receive their wages. In knots of two and three were seen the Irish laborers, evidently displeased because the Italians were first in getting their pay. John McGrath, a young Irishman, made an attempt to force his way through the crowd of Italians to the pay window, when he was struck by the Italian foreman, Manuel Zeriga, and knocked down.

The Italians at once set upon McGrath, and beat him fearfully. John Conners, seeing Zeriga over the prostrate form of his comrade, sprang to his rescue, and felled the Italian to the ground. This was a signal of war to the knife.

Crowds of Irishmen, who had been collecting along the railroad, rushed upon the Italians, and a bloody and desperate conflict ensued. Sticks, stones, bludgeons, knives—indeed every imaginable weapon was used. The Italians, nearly all of whom were armed with knives, fought like tigers. But, the Irishmen being constantly reinforced, the Italians were at last forced to fall back.

IN WITH A YELL AND A BOUND

At the railroad station the Italians made a feeble attempt to gain their best ground, and for a few minutes poured an incessant and telling shower of stones upon their antagonists, but the Irishmen, who were maddened to desperation by the treatment which young McGrath and subsequently Conners had undergone, determined to drive them from the grounds.

With a yell and a bound the Irishmen were among the Italians, and a terrific hand-to-hand fight ensued. The Italians, seeing themselves worsted, turned and fled.

The Sheriff further says that McGrath was frightfully cut, and had five deep gashes in his head. His face was pounded out of shape, and his body was horribly bruised. Conners fared but little better. The Italians carried their wounded with them, consequently the Sheriff is unable to state the extent of their injuries.

One Giuseppe Errani had his life saved by the timely interference of the Sheriff, who dragged him from the clutches of the enraged mob. The Sheriff positively asserts that the Irishmen were not in liquor, as he had ordered all barrooms closed.

The residence of Michael Gallagher was visited, and the man was found to be so seriously injured that his wounds may yet prove fatal. A conversation with Gallagher elicited the following statement respecting

THE CAUSE OF THE RIOT.

About 3 o'clock on Saturday afternoon I visited the office of the Grand Park for the purpose of receiving my pay; I then found that the Italians to the number of about 120 had besieged the office, and would allow no one but themselves to get paid off; I went over and stood among them, and, in attempting to get to the office to be paid off, I hit one of the Italians under the chin with my elbow; he at once hit me back again with a hoe; I bucked him with my head under the nose, and his nose began to bleed; the man having charge of the gang of Italians then hit me on top of the head with a fence rail, felling me to the ground and cutting my head badly; as soon as this was done, some of

THE IRISHMEN CAME TO MY RESCUE

but the Italians had more men than we, and beat several of us with stones and clubs; the fight then became general, and though only thirty Irishmen were present, a stand was made; about six Irishmen were badly hurt, including myself; they were McGrath, Sullivan, Gragon; the names of the others I do not know.

Reporter—Is there any intention of renewing the fight?

Gallagher—I cannot say for others; I know I have got enough.

ONE OF THE INJURED ITALIANS

was next visited, and though he spoke in broken English, his story was substantially as follows: We had not received any money for some weeks from the Grand Park people; the Irishmen were jealous of us because we gained employment where as many Irish were turned away; we worked for less money; we were starving, the storekeepers refusing us credit while they gave it to the Irishmen; we went to the office determined to get some money; an Irishman tried to get in before us, and we began the fight; no one was killed, and many of us are hurt as of the Irish; we are willing to work, but we want our money, and we are going to get it if we can; when men are starving they are desperate.

Several other Irishmen were interviewed, and all agreed that

THE ITALIANS STRUCK THE FIRST SERIOUS BLOW.

There can be little doubt that but for the rain Grand Park would have been the scene of one of the most bloody riots ever witnessed in Westchester county. At the time the quarrel was at its height, news of the disturbance was soon sent to the Irishmen at a distance, and

A GENERAL MASSING HAD BEGUN

which was duly dispersed by the heavy shower. Both Irishmen and Italians say that the real cause of the fight was the extraordinary dilatoriness of the Grand Park officials in paying wages which have been fairly earned. The Irishmen are able to gain credit of the storekeepers for the necessaries of life, but such is not the case with the Italians. These latter, who work for less wages than the Irish, have been kept without pay and in the desperation of half starved men, determined on Saturday to take the first chance for wages at the Grand Park office.

Yesterday a dozen men were walking about in the neighborhood of Mamaroneck bearing evidence of the serious nature of the fight, with bandaged heads, broken noses, and blackened eyes.

THE ITALIAN VERSION OF THE FIGHT

Manuel Cussaba, one of the Italian laborers, says that a number of Irishmen, who had been drinking, attempted to drive them away from the pay office as they went up to get their wages. He adds that Pat Riley, alias Crook-neck Riley, the foreman of the Messrs. Hoyt & Hughes workmen, was the leader of the Irishmen, and that he knocked down their foreman, Manuel Zeriga. The Irishmen, he said, greatly outnumbered the Italians, and after driving them from the office, beating them, and robbing them of their pay tickets, they (the Irishmen) took complete possession of the place. The victors and rioters then appeared at the Italian barracks, and threatened to drive out the women and children and set fire to the houses. Fearing that they would execute their threats, the Italians deserted their homes, and with what few articles of clothing they could hastily gather together, with their wives and little ones, set out to walk to the city.

At three o'clock yesterday morning, after a weary tramp over sixteen miles through the mud and rain, the Italians entered Morrisania. The poor women and children were scantily clad and were soaked to the skin. They sought shelter in the Town Hall, which was readily thrown open to them by Justice Hauptman and the kind hearted keeper, Mr. James Morrison. After the complaints of the men had been heard, they were sent to the city. Mamaroneck is utterly deserted by the Italian laborers.

SOURCE: New York *Sun,* August 15, 1870. **The Riot in Williamsburgh**

German Men, Women, and Children Clubbed and Stoned at one of the Piers.

The Cecilia Singing Society of Williamsburgh went down the bay yesterday with their families and friends. When the boat was about casting off, a crowd of young roughs attempted to get on board without invitation, but were repelled, and the excursion party set out under a volley of harmless imprecations.

On their return last evening, however, at the foot of South Sixth street they were received with several volleys of stones by the same crowd, headed, it is said by Terence O'Neil. The excitement among the women and children as stones and brickbats fell among them was at the highest pitch until the arrival of the police. Then the assailants scattered.

Among those badly injured were John Laubenheimer and Mrs. Koppe. They suffered contusions of the head, and were covered with blood. Mrs. Koppe had an infant in her arms when she was attacked. The names of a large number who were slightly injured could not be ascertained as they hurried to their homes. One little girl, whose left arm was broken by a blow with a stick in the hands of a maddened ruffian, was cared for by a lady in the neighborhood after she had been rescued by a sailor.

Terence O'Neil, who is said to be the leader of the attacking party, was arrested, as was also Mr. Christian Fischer, one of the excursion party.

SOURCE: **"The Two Parties Contrasted,"** *L'Italia,* November 1894 (Chicago Foreign Language Press Survey, WPA Project, 1942).

When American citizens of foreign birth refuse to ally themselves with the Republican Party, they make war upon their own welfare. The Republican Party stands for all that the people fight for in the Old World. It is the champion of freedom, progress, order, and law. It is the steadfast foe of monarchial class rule.

It contains the bulk of the intelligence of the nation. That part of the Republic in which the Republican Party is the strongest is that part of the Republic which is the most prosperous.

The brightest names in American history during the last forty years are those of men who followed the Republican banner—Lincoln, Seward, Sumner, Greeley, Grant, Garfield, Blaine, and a host of others.

Look at the achievements of the Republican Party since it sprang into existence. It saved the Republic from disunion and destruction.

It crushed the mightiest rebellion in modern times.

It wiped out the foul stain of slavery. It brought the nation back to honest money and specie payments. It has persistently defended the national credit. It has cut down the national debt until that burden is no longer felt.

It has removed a multitude of taxes. It has built up American industries. It has opened a thousand new avenues for the employment of labor. It has made every citizen, no matter of what complexion, race, or creed, equal before the law.

Under Republican rule the United States reached its highest degree of civilization, liberty, and prosperity. Under Republican rule the American flag became honored and feared abroad as never before.

The record of the Democratic Party is directly the reverse. That party steadily upheld and defended slavery. The leaders of the Southern rebellion were Democratic leaders. It was the Democratic Party that pronounced the war a "failure." It was that party that attempted to flood the country with worthless and cheap money.

It is the Democratic Party that has assailed repeatedly the national credit. It is the Democratic Party that has robbed the voter of the ballot by shotguns and fraud. It is the Democratic Party that is now bent upon tearing down American industries, beggaring workmen, and covering the land with ruin.

Every traitor to the nation, from Aaron Burr down to Jefferson Davis, has belonged to the Democratic Party. Where the greatest amount of ignorance and lawlessness exists in the United States today, the Democratic Party will be found the strongest.

The adopted citizens of the Republic should not be misled by the noisy promises and falsehoods of Democratic demagogues and bosses. On every great question that has come before the people for the last two generations, the Democratic Party has been on the wrong side.

Every great act of legislation that has gone on the statute books of the nation for the last two generations has been put there through the aid of the Republican Party.

It is because the Democratic Party is undoing the work of the

Republican Party that the country is now in the depths of calamity and want.

Foreign-born citizens should become thoroughly posted in the history of the Republican and the Democratic Party.

These citizens are here to found a home and to rear their children. They cannot afford to support a party which proposes to make such a home impossible and to drive them back to their native land. A party like the Democratic Party, which for half a century was the backbone of slavery, is not a party from which the escaped victims of foreign tyranny need expect sympathy or help.

The School and Church as the Ethnic Battleground

The preservation of cultural heritage was an additional source of friction within the immigrant community. Moreover, in these contests, the schools and churches often became the battlegrounds of ethnic conflict.

SOURCE: **"Bohemian in Public Schools Unrecognized,"** *Svornost,* February 27, 1880 (Chicago Foreign Language Press Survey, WPA Project, 1942).

The petition of 258 parents and guardians of children attending the Throop School, for the inclusion of the Bohemian Language as a study, which was referred to a special committee for consideration some two weeks ago was the cause of considerable debate on the part of the School Board yesterday.

The readers of *Svornost* know who the favorable members of the Board were and who were unfavorable. The way we indicated the last time we mentioned this matter is just the way it happened. Of the committee two members, Stiles and Stone, recommended favorable action by the School Board, where as the obstinate German member, Vocke, who happened to preside over the committee, stood out against the introduction of the teaching of Bohemian in the Throop School.

Mr. Stone said that the petition for the introduction of the study of the Bohemian Language in this school, is signed by more than half of the taxpayers of this school district and that the petitioners have just as much right to request the teaching of Bohemian as have the German citizens to have German taught in the public schools.

In opposition to this, Mr. Vocke claims that there is a great deal of difference between Germans and Bohemians, or in other words they are superior. He does not wish the Germans to be given any privileges before other nationalities, but the Bohemian Language is so unimportant that it must not be compared in the least with German. Use is made of the Bohemian Language in only two of the Educational Centers of the world, that is at Prague and Vienna, while the German Language must be considered as a major basis of culture. The knowledge of German is sufficient for every business man to carry on all transactions with benefit and advantage anywhere.

In this same manner Mr. Richberg spoke, moving, in conclusion, that the Board proceed to vote on Mr. Stone's motion that the teaching of Bohemian be permitted in the Throop School. The vote brought out the following results:

For the introduction of Bohemian: Stone, Brennan, Frake, Curran and Stiles (5). Against:—Vocke, Richberg, Keith, Bartlett, Frankenthal, Delaney and Hayne (7).

Therefore, by a majority of two votes the just petition of Bohemian Citizens was rejected and unrecognized.

How easily could this petition of ours have been acted on favorably had it not been for the old, (still from the old country) German obstinate hatred which, in a contemptible and shameful manner, vented its spite on everything Bohemian even in this land of freedom. If these three Germans, Vocke, Richberg and Frankenthal had voted for the teaching of the Bohemian Language, we could be rejoicing today in the just disposition of our petition.

We seek in this land of freedom, in this city, where the Bohemian element is second in numbers only to the Germans only the recognition of our rights. Whether the Bohemian tongue is used in one or ten world centers does not concern us in the least; we are interested only in the preservation of our language and nationality, in the same manner that it concerned, and still concerns the German people. And since they have been given the privilege, why should they take it upon themselves to prevent us from acquiring a like privilege.

Finally, since impudence, selfishness, obstinacy and insolence is excessively rooted in the minds of all Germans, almost without exception, how then could we expect, even in this land of freedom, to receive any support from them? If, at some time or other, they seem to incline toward friendship, it is only because they want some help in some cause, but if they have an idea that they may be able to accomplish their objective without us, then all we get from them are dirty sneers and scorn and opposition to any effort whatever on our part.

Our attempts, efforts, requests, and hopes for the teaching of the Bohemian Language in the public school where over half of the pupils are of Bohemian parentage, were, since yesterday, destroyed, unrecognized and for the time being, we must submit. Perhaps we shall find other ways and means by which we shall finally receive our just rights.

SOURCE: **"The Use of Polish in the Church,"** *Zgoda,* December 20, 1900 (Chicago Foreign Language Press Survey, WPA Project, 1942).

A few months ago Archbishop Ireland said that the Catholic churches in our country, the United States, should be Americanized. This was an insult to all Polish parishes in Chicago as well as in the United States. Polish priests in Chicago are greatly opposed to the demands of Archbishop Keane and Bishop Eis to have all sermons spoken in the English language.

Polish people are greatly opposed to this form of Catholicism compelling Polish Catholic people to listen to sermons spoken in the English language, when the majority of older people do not understand it.

If this request is fulfilled, the Catholics will demand that the Germans, Italians, and all other nationalities do likewise. This question was raised by Archbishop Keane against the Poles. For what reason? Are the Polish parishes getting too rich? Are they expanding too fast or is it that the Irish want to dominate the Catholic world? Can't the Polish Catholics have as much freedom as the other nationalities? Isn't the United States a land of Freedom? It is, but that is no reason that the Irish should have more preference than any other nationality.

The *Dziennik Chicagoski* was the first newspaper to take up the fight on behalf of us Poles. This newspaper wants to remind us Polish parents that if our children grow up and cannot speak their native tongue, the whole blame will rest on the shoulders of the parents. Therefore, now is the time to stand up and fight for your religious rights. In another article this paper pointed out that according to the rules of the church and the Bible, no one can restrict the use and teaching of any language in Catholic schools and churches. What did Archbishop Keane and Bishop Eis think of this idea?

It is true that Bishop Eis said in one of his speeches that the children in this country speak the English language better and more correctly than their own native tongue, but this is largely due to the fact that they came in contact with children speaking this language either in school or at play, while their native tongue is spoken mostly at home.

We Polish people should not trouble ourselves too much with the affairs of the French, the German, the Irish, or any other nationalities in regard to the church, but take care of our own interest. What are these countries doing to help Poland win back its freedom? Nothing. They want us Poles to be under the rule of other countries so they can do what they wish with us. Do they want to do the same with us Poles in regard to the Catholic religion?

The Polish National Alliance took up the fight here and is doing everything possible in its power to awaken within the Polish people the urge to fight for their rights and their native language.

Polish churches were built with the hard-earned money of us Polish people, who donated wholeheartedly; schools were erected, monuments in memory of Polish noblemen and heroes. Our museum and national treasury is a hundred times dearer to us Poles here than the museum and national treasury in Rappersville.

By this time the *Polish Courier* printed an article: "We haven't any right to fight if we have nothing to fight for, but the Polish people would be blind if they didn't fight to protect their own name and nationality. We know that the existence of the church depends on the support of the people and their donations. We must and should do our utmost to protect and prolong the life of the Polish Catholic churches. It is our life, our backbone; without it we are lost. No other nationality in this city can boast of as many churches, Catholic schools, amusement centers, and Polish clubs and societies as the Poles. Be proud of them; we need your support."

The Polish priests are doing their utmost to make the Polish parents realize the worth of this fight. They do not compel the Polish parents to force the children to attend Polish parochial schools; it is up to them whether their children learn the Polish language or attend Polish schools, but this is a minor factor in comparison with the fight that we are confronted with at the present time. We are fighting to continue the use of the Polish language in our sermons, because it is our solemn duty.

Nevertheless, we feel that Archbishop Keane and Bishop Eis will realize what it means to the Polish people to forbid them to use their native language; we feel that eventually this matter will be dropped.

The Incursion of the Jews

The ethnic rivalries which led to violence were not always precipitated by labor competition or transplanted Old World conflicts. Often, they surfaced over the threat of newcomers "taking over the neighborhood." Refusing to yield to these pressures, earlier settlers stood their ground and conducted interethnic warfare.

An example of this combat occurred on July 30, 1902, when New York's Jewish community held a mass funeral for Chief Rabbi Jacob Joseph. The Irish-led riot which ensued was attributed to their festering resentment at being forced out of their homes by the "Jewish incursion." The official investigation of this riot indicated that the Irish-dominated police force contributed to the bloodshed. Using the investigation as an opportunity to voice their grievances, Jewish community leaders charged that the police not only failed to give them adequate protection at the funeral, but were habitually treating them with contempt and frequent brutality.

The second selection, "The Celt, the Jew and Newspapers," recounted the Irish fear of a "Jewish takeover" of the city's journalism industry.

SOURCE: **"The Report of the Mayor's Committee: Responsibility for the Riot,"** *The American Hebrew* (September 12, 1902), p. 498.

Many complaints have also been laid before us that the police have for a long time past been insulting and brutal in their treatment of the Jews of the lower East Side. It is claimed that a number of cases of this character have been brought before the Police Commissioner upon charges preferred against policemen, but in no case with the result of obtaining the dismissal of any of the accused from the force, although the facts charged were sufficiently established to require such a sentence. We find that instances of uncivil and even rough treatment toward the people of this district by individual policemen are inexcusably common. In certain specified cases which have been selected by witnesses who appeared before us as testing their accusations, it appears that charges of unprovoked and most brutal clubbing have been made against policemen, with the result that they were reprimanded or fined a day's pay and were yet retained upon the force. We are informed by the police authorities on the other hand that in all of these cases the past records of the accused policemen were good and the evidence before the Commissioner so conflicting as to render dismissal unjust, although the policeman on trial was believed to be deserving of some punishment, on the other hand it is most important that policemen should not be discouraged from using sufficient force to prevent the escape when apprehending offenders; and that a reprimand is a very serious punishment, since it forever remains part of the policeman's record, not only jeopardizing his defense if any charge is made against him in the future, but also under the Civil Service System impairing his chances for promotion.

By some of the witnesses who appeared before us the conduct of the police, of which complaint has thus been made, is attributed to a complete lack of sympathy between the policemen involved and the residents of the East Side. There is much color for this opinion. We cannot escape the conclusion that the attitude and demeanor of many policemen who have for a long time been on duty in this district have been such as to become the subject of just criticism, and it is believed that much can be accomplished to avoid a continuance of existing conditions if the Police Department should exercise more discrimination in the selection of the men assigned to duty in this quarter. We understand that the Police Commissioner concurs in this view. This opinion is emphasized by the fact that the residents of the East Side are generally acknowledged to be of a peaceable disposition, who can be readily dealt with when they have confidence in those in whose keeping their lives and liberties are placed.

We have likewise received serious complaint, not only from the residents of the lower East Side, but also from the police, of the attitude of some of the City Magistrates. It is claimed that they seriously impair the efficiency of the police by the contempt with which they treat arrests for assaults such as those which contributed to the recent outbreak. It is asserted that not infrequently when an offender is arrested and brought before a Magistrate for such an offense, he is discharged and the policeman rebuked for having made the arrest; that many minor offenses are punished by one Magistrate and disregarded by another, with such a variety of treatment that it is most difficult for a policeman to determine when he should arrest and when not. It is charged by residents of this district that Magistrates are very arbitrary in their action, often deciding cases against the weight of evidence and frequently even refusing to hear the witnesses produced; that certain Magistrates seem to be more interested in the despatch of business than in the administration of justice; and that certain Magistrates appear to have developed such prejudice against Jewish witnesses that they refuse them a fair hearing, even when of the highest character and fully corroborated. These charges have been made not only by the victims of these alleged abuses, and by the leading Jewish residents of the district, but likewise by impartial non-Jewish observers whose statements, made to us confidentially, confirm us in the belief that the matter is worthy of investigation by the proper authorities; but this is not within the jurisdiction of the Mayor.

SOURCE: **"The Celt, the Jew and Newspapers,"** *Life* (August 1909), p. 618.

Will the Jew drive the Celt out of American journalism? We offer this interesting topic to all the debating societies for their use whenever they have finished with woman suffrage, the tariff, direct primaries, and other matters of pressing contemporary interest.

The Celt, especially the Irishman, has shown extraordinary aptitude for newspaper writing. A remarkable proportion of newspaper writers in this country have been and are Irishmen. There are good reasons for it. The Irish have wit, imagination, a liking for argument, a strong turn for politics, and unusual gift of language. Moreover, in this country, as a rule, they have been poor. The newspaper business has always been a refuge of poverty and talent, and the Irish have had both qualifications in unusual measure.

But the Irishman as a rule is not shrewder than other folks, and not exceptionally bent on material gain. He inclines to be swayed by sentiment, is apt to be a partisan, is liable to quarrel with his own bread and butter. He has more talent than the average of the rest of our population but, probably, less thrift. It has indeed been said to be the mission of the Celt in the world to be an obstacle to the strong drift toward materialism, and a force for sentiment and spirituality.

Comes along the Jew; clever, poor, intensely bent on material acquisition; shrewd, diligent, calculating; only slightly affected by many reluctances and compunctions that restrain the man of occidental standards. He observes the newspaper, a vast power, and one with enormous possibilities of all sorts, but difficult to handle profitably. In twenty or thirty years the observer of current phenomena remarks that the Jew has come to be a great power in American journalism; master in the counting-rooms of great and powerful papers, and arbiter of editorial policies. The Celt still writes, but more commonly than formerly, the Jew hires him.

This phenomenon might be ominous if the Jew had dangerous

political aspirations. But he hasn't. As a newspaper owner he wants nothing more than to make a paper acceptable to readers, and advertisers, and favorable and profitable to Jews, including himself. So the phenomenon—what there is of it—is rather curious than dangerous.

PART II

To War on the Ethnic:
The Nativist Crusade,
1845–1924

INTRODUCTION

Nativism, or distrust of newcomers, had its roots deep in the American past. The two major themes of pre-Civil War nativism, anti-Catholicism and anti-foreignism, appeared early in colonial times. Many of the English settlers brought their anti-papal views with them to the New World, and these beliefs found their way into colonial legislative history. The founding fathers Benjamin Franklin, Thomas Jefferson and Alexander Hamilton anticipated the twentieth-century restrictionists' argument by holding that free immigration would introduce elements that threatened the country's basic institutions. Since the bulk of the early immigrants came from England, the great anti-foreigner crusade did not occur until the nineteenth century.

Starting with the 1820s, the pre-Civil War decades witnessed sharp increases in immigration into the United States, especially from Ireland and Germany. Since the largest proportion of the newcomers in the 1820s and 1830s were Catholics, the major nativist theme of those years was anti-Catholicism. Increased Church membership was met by rising anti-papal sentiment. Nativists charged that two Catholic missionary societies, inspired by the Pope and kings of Europe, were engaged in a plot to seize the

United States. Samuel F. B. Morse, the inventor and painter, was most effective in circulating the conspiracy story in his tract *A Foreign Conspiracy Against the Liberties of the United States.* The work, which was widely reprinted, served to link "immigration and Catholicism . . . making both equally objectionable in American eyes." The additional issues of state aid to parochial schools and Bible-reading in the public schools intensified the hostility between Catholics and nativists.

In the 1840s and 1850s the tide of immigration assumed the proportions of a flood. In 1842 over 100,000 newcomers reached these shores; five years later that figure was doubled; and in 1854 the unprecedented number of 427,000 immigrants, including over 100,000 Irish, arrived in America. The nativist propaganda now emphasized the illiteracy, pauperism, criminality and heavy drinking of the immigrants. In addition, as the newcomers became increasingly important in politics, nativist publicists raised the charges of naturalization frauds and the corrupting influences of immigrants upon American political life. Moreover, they appealed to the working classes by accusing immigrants with unfair labor competition and succeeded in recruiting workers for highly secretive and patriotic native American labor societies such as the Order of United Americans.

Organizations like the Order had a tendency to develop political offshoots. In 1850 a secret party known as the Order of the Star-Spangled Banner, adopting most of the secret ritual of the Order of United Americans, emerged. Gradually it became known as the Know-Nothing Party and had some successes in the 1854 and 1855 elections. It declined in the late 1850s as the result of increased agitation over slavery, impending war and the conversion of many nativists, seeking respectability, to the Republican Party.

During the Civil War and post-war period, overt nativism appeared to have declined. Except for a few incidents such as occasional charges of Irish disloyalty and General Grant's order against Jewish peddlers, the need for national unity overrode the complaints of nativists. Nevertheless, the more subtle forms of social and economic discrimination persisted throughout this period.

The latter 1880s saw the next significant revival of nativism. Memories of the Molly Maguires and the violent strikes of the late 1870s, reinforced by the mass media's reporting of the Haymarket affair in 1886 and the industrial turmoil of the late 1880s, created an atmosphere that was ripe for nativist activity. The popular charge of the day was that America's troubles were largely the work of radical immigrants. In addition, the period saw another re-emergence of bitter anti-Catholic feeling. The creation of new dioceses, the rapid growth of the Catholic school system and the appointment of Cardinal Satolli as the first apostolic delegate to the United States from the Vatican convinced many Americans that the Church was bent upon subverting American institutions. This sentiment led to the formation of numerous anti-Catholic societies, the largest of which was the American Protestant Association.

Nativists, however, now began to see an even greater threat than the Catholic Church—the sudden influx of huge numbers of immigrants from eastern and southern Europe. Stressing the cultural differences of these people, the nativists reinforced their arguments against these newcomers with the pseudo-scientific racial theories that then were coming into vogue. They emphasized their pride in the Anglo-Saxon and Teutonic roots of American institutions. Writers like Richard Mayo-Smith even began to question the economic value of immigration, and in 1894 a group of New England intellectuals, led by Prescott F. Hall and Robert DeCourcy Ward, founded the Immigration Restriction League. The League was to spearhead the immigration restriction movement for the next twenty-five years.

At first the League sought to avoid publicly the use of radical arguments against the new immigrants. Instead their strategy was to seek the curtailment of immigration through the use of a literacy test. For years they pursued an unsuccessful attempt to obtain the enactment of a federal literacy law. Frustrated, by 1908 the leaders were stressing the arguments provided by the new school of eugenics which placed little faith in the influence of environmental factors and saw disaster in the intermixing of the races of eastern and southern Europe with the dominant native stock. Not until 1917, on the eve of the American entry into World War I, did the restrictionists win a victory with the passage of the Immigration Law of 1917 over President Wilson's veto.

Though the 1917 law was not the kind of restrictionist legislation for which nativists had hoped, since it was largely a codification of existing immigration law, it was the product of conditions that were destined eventually to close the immigration gates. About the time of World War I, there was a great emphasis upon Americanization and a rising tide of nationalism. In addition the war caused bitter feeling against German-Americans and hostility toward hyphenated Americans. The war emphasized the differences between the Old and New Worlds, and the Americanization movement was strengthened by the rise of Bolshevism. In the years just after the war, nativism thrived on the violent textile and great steel strikes of 1919, the "Red Scare" and Palmer raids, the collapse of Wilsonian idealism, the economic depression of 1920–21 and the resumption of heavy immigration from Europe. These conditions also permitted many Americans to accept the allegations of anti-Semitic publications such as Henry Ford's notorious *Dearborn Independent* and the revival of the Ku-Klux Klan. Influenced by the work of men like Madison Grant, writers, like the novelist Kenneth Roberts, popularized the concept of Nordic superiority. Under these conditions, Congress passed the provisional measure of 1921 which introduced the principle of numerical restriction based upon nationality. Nativism gained its long-cherished goal three years later in the Johnson-Reed Act. The avowed purpose of the legislation was to maintain the "racial preponderance" of the native strain, and this was achieved through a formula which would keep immigration from southern and eastern Europe to a minimum. The 1924 law was the fulfillment of a century-long dream of the nativist movement—America had almost completely closed her door to immigrants. Emma Lazarus' words at the base of the Statue of Liberty now had a hollow ring.

A. THE AMERICAN NIGHTMARE: NATIVIST RESPONSE TO THE OLD IMMIGRATION, 1845–80

A Nativist Declaration of Principles

Nativist feeling in the United States rose in the early decades of the nineteenth century with the increasing number of immigrants, especially Irish, arriving on these shores. The nativist propaganda of the 1830s, including such influential works as Samuel

F. B. Morse's *A Foreign Conspiracy Against the Liberties of the United States* and Maria Monk's fraudulent *Awful Disclosures,* helped to convince even respectable Protestants of the evils of Catholicism in America. Emotions reached a frenzy in the early 1840s as the result of a bitter fight between Protestants and Catholics over the reading of the King James Version of the Bible in public schools. Inspired by the attempt of Bishop Hughes of New York City to obtain public funds for parochial schools, Bishop Kenrick of Philadelphia complained that the Protestant Bible was being read to Catholic children and that religious instruction was a regular part of the public school's instructional program. Aroused, nativists organized the American Republican Party with an anti-Catholic and anti-foreign platform. Before an election could settle the issue politically, a series of terrible riots between natives and foreigners erupted in the Kensington section of Philadelphia. A year later, on July 4, 1845, delegates to the First National Convention of the Native American Party met to take political action against "the danger of foreign influence." Though this early attempt to form a national nativist party met with little success, the convention and its Declaration of Principles reflected the type of nativist sentiment that was shared by the delegates from the many states represented there.

SOURCE: **Declaration of Principles of the Native American Convention, Assembled at Philadelphia, July 4, 1845,** pp. 4–7.

We, the delegates elect to the first national convention of the Native American people of the United States, assembled at Philadelphia on the fourth day of July, 1845, for the purpose of devising a plan of concerted political action in defence of American institutions against the encroachments of foreign influence, open or concealed, hereby solemnly, and before Almighty God, make known to our fellow-citizens, our country, and the world, the following incontrovertible facts, and the course of conduct consequent thereon, to which, in duty to the cause of human rights and the claims of our beloved country, we mutually pledge our lives, our fortunes, and our sacred honor.

The danger of foreign influence, threatening the gradual destruction of our national institutions, failed not to arrest the attention of the Father of his Country in the very dawn of American liberty. Not only its direct agency in rendering the American system liable to the poisonous influence of European policy—a policy at war with the fundamental principles of the American constitution—but also its still more fatal operation in aggravating the virulence of partisan warfare—has awakened deep alarm in the mind of every intelligent patriot, from the days of Washington to the present time.

The influx of a foreign population, permitted, after little more than a nominal residence, to participate in the legislation of the country and the sacred right of suffrage, produced comparatively little evil during the earlier years of the republic; for that influx was then limited by the expenses of a trans-Atlantic voyage, by the existence of many wholesome restraints upon the acquisition of political prerogatives, by the constant exhaustion of the European population in long and bloody continental wars, and by the slender inducements offered for immigration to a young and sparsely-peopled country, contending for existence with a boundless wilderness, inhabited by savage men. Evils which are only prospective rarely attract the notice of the masses; and, until peculiar changes were effected in the political condition of Europe, the increased facilities for transportation, and the madness of partisan legislation, in removing all effective guards against the open prostitution of the right of citizenship, had converted the slender current of naturalization into a torrent, threatening to overwhelm the influence of the natives of the land; the far-seeing vision of the statesman only, being fixed upon the distant, but steadily-approaching cloud.

But, since the barriers against the improper extension of the right of suffrage were bodily broken down, for a partisan purpose, by the Congress of 1825, the rapidly-increasing numbers, and unblushing insolence of the foreign population of the worst classes, have caused the general agitation of the question: *"How shall the institutions of the country be preserved from the blight of foreign influence, insanely legalized through the conflicts of domestic parties?"* Associations under different names have been formed by our fellow-citizens, in many states of this confederation, from Louisiana to Maine, all designed to check this imminent danger before it becomes irremediable; and at length, a national convention of the great American people, born upon the soil of Washington, has assembled to digest, and announce a plan of operations, by which the grievances of an abused hospitality, and the consequent degradation of political morals, may be redressed, and the tottering columns of the temple of republican liberty secured upon the sure foundation of an enlightened nationality.

In calling for support upon every American who loves his country pre-eminently, and every adopted citizen of moral and intellectual worth, who would secure to his compatriots yet to come among us, the blessings of political protection, the safety of person and property, it is right that we should make known the grievances which we propose to redress, and the manner in which we shall endeavor to effect our object.

It is an incontrovertible truth, that the civil institutions of the United States of America have been seriously affected, and that they now stand in imminent peril from the rapid and enormous increase of the body of residents of foreign birth, imbued with foreign feelings, and of an ignorant and immoral character, who receive, under the present lax and unreasonable laws of naturalization, the elective franchise and the right of eligibility to political office.

The whole body of foreign citizens, invited to our shores under a constitutional provision adapted to other times and other political conditions of the world, and of our country especially, has been endowed by American hospitality with gratuitous privileges, unnecessary to the enjoyment of those inalienable rights of man—*life,* liberty, *and the pursuit of happiness*—privileges wisely reserved to the natives of the soil by the governments of all other civilized nations. But, familiarized by habit with the exercise of these indulgences, and emboldened by increasing numbers, a vast majority of those who constitute this foreign body now claim as an original right that which has been so incautiously granted as a favor; thus attempting to render inevitable the prospective action of laws adopted upon a principle of mere expediency, made variable at the will of Congress by the express terms of the constitution, and heretofore repeatedly revised, to meet the exigencies of the times.

In former years this body was recruited chiefly from the victims of political oppression, of the active and intelligent mercantile ad-

venturers of other lands; and it then constituted a slender representation of the best classes of the foreign population, well fitted
to add strength to the state, and capable of being readily educated
in the peculiarly American science of political self-government.
Moreover, while welcoming the stranger of every condition, our
laws then wisely demanded of every foreign aspirant for political
rights, *a certificate of practical good citizenship*. Such classes of
aliens were followed by no foreign demagogues—they were de-
bauched by no emissaries of kings. A wall of fire separated them
from such a baneful influence; and they were elected by their intelligence, their knowledge, their virtue, and love of freedom. But,
for the last twenty years, the road to civil preferment and participation in the legislative and executive government of the land has
been laid broadly open, alike to the ignorant, the vicious, and the
criminal; and a large proportion of the foreign body of citizens
and voters now constitute a representation of the worst and most
degraded of the European population—victims of social oppression
or personal vices, utterly divested by ignorance or crime of the
moral and intellectual requisites for political self-government.

Thus tempted by the suicidal policy of these United States, and
favored by the facilities resulting from the modern improvements
of navigation, numerous societies and corporate bodies in foreign
countries have found it economical to transport to our shores, at
public and private expense, the feeble, the imbecile, the idle and
intractable; thus relieving the burdens resulting from the vices of
the European social systems, by availing themselves of the generous
errors of our own.

The almshouses of Europe are emptied upon our coast, *and this
by our own invitation*—not casually, or to a trivial extent, but systematically, and upon a constantly-increasing scale. The bedlams
of the old world have contributed their share to the torrent of immigration; and the lives of our citizens have been attempted in
the streets of our capital cities by madmen just liberated from European hospitals, upon the express condition that they should be
transported to America. By the orders of European governments,
the punishment of crimes has been commuted for banishment to
the land of the free; and criminals in irons have crossed the ocean
to be cast loose upon society on their arrival upon our shores.
The United States are rapidly becoming the lazar-house and penal

colony of Europe; nor can we reasonably censure such proceedings. They are legitimate consequences of our own unlimited benevolence; and it is of such material that we profess to manufacture free and enlightened citizens, by a process occupying five short years, at most, but practically, oftentimes embraced in a much shorter period of time.

The mass of immigrants, formerly lost among the natives of the soil, has increased from the ratio of 1 in 40 to that of 1 in 7! A like advance in fifteen years will leave the natives of the soil a minority in their own land! Thirty years ago these strangers came by units and tens—now they swarm by thousands. (It is estimated that 300,000 will arrive within the present year.) Formerly, most of them sought only for an honest livelihood and a provision for their families, and rarely meddled with those institutions of which it was impossible they could comprehend the nature; *now,* each newcomer seeks political preferment, and struggles to fasten on the public purse with an avidity in strict proportion to his ignorance and unworthiness of public trust—having been SENT, as is clearly shown, for the purpose of obtaining political ascendency in the government of the nation—having been SENT to exalt their allies to power—having been SENT to work a revolution from republican freedom to the assumed divine rights of monarchs.

From these unhappy circumstances has arisen an *imperium in imperio*—a body uninformed and vicious—foreign in feeling, prejudice, and manner, yet armed with a vast, and often a controlling influence over the policy of a nation whose benevolence it abuses and whose kindness it habitually insults—a body as dangerous to the rights of the intelligent foreigner and to the prospect of his own immediate progeny, as it is threatening to the liberties of the country, and the hopes of rational freedom throughout the world— a body ever ready to complicate our foreign relations, by embroiling us with the hereditary hates and feuds of other lands, and to disturb our domestic peace by its crude ideas; mistaking license for liberty, and the overthrow of individual rights for republican political equality—a body ever the ready tool of foreign and domestic demagogues, and steadily endeavoring by misrule to establish popular tyranny under a cloak of false democracy.

Americans, false to their country, and led on to moral crime by the desire of dishonest gain, have scattered their agents over

Europe, inducing the malcontent and unthrifty to exchange a life of compulsory labor in foreign lands for relative comfort, to be maintained by the tax-paying industry of our overburdened and deeply-indebted community. Not content with the usual and less objectionable licenses of trade, these fraudulent dealers habitually deceive a worthier class of victims by false promises of employment, and assist in thronging the already crowded avenues of simple labor with a host of competitors, whose first acquaintance with American faith springs from a gross imposture, and whose first feeling, on discovering the cheat, is reasonable mistrust, if not implacable revenge. The importation of the physical necessities of life may be burdened with duties which many deem extravagant; but the importation of vice and idleness, of seditious citizens and factious rulers, is not by a system which transforms the great patrimony of the nation, purchased by the blood of our fathers, into a source of bounty for the promotion of immigration.

Whenever an attempt is made to restrain this fatal evil, native and adopted demagogues protest against it as an effort which threatens to deprive them of their most important tools; and such is the existing organization of our established political parties, that, should either of them essay the reform of an abuse which both acknowledge to be fraught with ruin, that party sinks, upon the instant, into a minority, divested of control and incapable of result.

From such causes has been derived a body, armed with political power, in a country of whose system it is ignorant, and for whose institutions it feels little interest, except for the purpose of personal advancement.

This body has formed and encouraged associations under *foreign names,* to promote measures of foreign policy, and to perpetuate foreign clannishness among adopted citizens of the United States, in contravention of that spirit of union and nationality, without which no people can legitimately claim a place among the nations of the earth.

It has employed the power of associations to embroil the people of this country in the political disputes of other lands with which the United States are anxious to encourage peace and amity.

It has introduced foreign emblems, not only of national, but of partisan character, in the civic processions and public displays of bodies of men, claiming the title of American citizens, and sworn to American fealty; by which means it has fomented frequent riot and murder.

It has adopted national costumes and national insignia foreign to the country, in arming and equipping military corps, constituting a part of the national guard, with its word of command in a foreign language, in open defiance of our military code; by which means it has weakened the discipline of the militia, and rendered it less available for defence in time of war.

It has entered into the strife of parties as a separate organization, unknown to the laws, suffering itself to be addressed and led to the contest—not as a portion of the great American family of freemen, but combined as sectarians and as *foreigners;* thus virtually falsifying its oaths of allegiance, and proving beyond denial its entire unfitness for political trust.

It has formed and encouraged political combinations holding the balance of power between opposing parties; combinations which have offered their votes and influence to the highest bidder, in exchange for pledges of official position and patronage.

It has boasted of giving governors to our states and chief magistrates to the nation.

By serving as an unquestioning and uncompromising tool of executive power, it has favored a political centralism, hostile to the rights of the independent states and the sovereignty of the people.

It has facilitated the assumption by the national executive of the right to remove from office, without the consent of the senate, persons who only can be appointed with such consent; which assumption is an obvious evasion of the spirit of the constitution.

Economic Nativism: Statement of Effects of the Competition of Immigrant Labor

Thomas R. Whitney was a leading nativist during the Know-Nothing period of the 1850s. In 1852 Archbishop Hughes of New York sought the passage in Albany of a measure which would have permitted Church authorities to hold title to Church property. Under a 1784 law, the legislature had required that lay trustees chosen by the congregation control all Church property within the state. Embittered by the Archbishop's effort, Whitney, then in the state legislature, was one of three sponsors of a bill making clerical ownership of Church property illegal. Subsequently, Whitney was elected to Congress and was one of the most influential of the forty-three Know-Nothings present when the Thirty-fourth Congress convened. He introduced into the House a proposal to extend naturalization to twenty-one years. Failing to make headway with the bill, he and his Know-Nothing colleagues turned to a measure that would have prohibited the entry of foreign paupers, criminals, idiots, and insane and blind persons. After a long debate, the question was referred to the House Committee on Foreign Affairs. One of the sources upon which the committee relied was Whitney's work *A Defense of the American Policy, As Opposed to the Encroachments of Foreign Influence*. Eventually the committee decided that the matter should be left to the state legislatures with their police powers.

In the 1850s a chief nativist weapon was the warning to workingmen that immigrants represented a serious threat to their economic status. In *A Defense of the American Policy*, Whitney made one of the period's most effective statements on economic nativism.

SOURCE: Thomas R. Whitney, **A Defense of the American Policy, As Opposed to the Encroachments of Foreign Influence** (New York, 1856), pp. 306–11.

The Mechanics of America have heretofore occupied a position in society which has not been attained by their class in any other nation. In European countries, the word mechanic designates not only a class but a *caste* in society; and that too, of a low grade. The dignity of labor is not recognized in their *effete* social systems. But here it *has been* otherwise. The reasons of this difference are obvious. In all aristocratic systems, the sole protection of the aristocracy lies in distinctions of caste, and the broader those distinctions are made, the better for the aristocrats, and the worse for the producing classes. It is not because labor is disreputable in itself that aristocracy sneers at it, but because of this feigned distinction, which is essential to the very existence of a privileged class.

The effect of this distinction is threefold—moral, social, and financial. Its moral effect is to degrade the workingman in his own estimation, and render him easily subservient to the dominion, the whims, or the caprice of those who lord it over him. The social effect is to deprive him of his rights as a man; to place him in a position subordinate to others, and by closing the doors of promotion against him, dampen his ambition, and confine his efforts to the bare necessities of the present. The financial effect is the natural result of his moral and social condition. Owing to that condition of hopeless passiveness, the spirit of noble emulation is stifled in his bosom, and he entertains no aspirations for a loftier position in life. His necessities alone are present to his view, and to supply them is the burden of his ambition and his energies. He is willing to work for them alone, and the competition of poverty, brought about by these influences, compels him to be content with a mere pittance.

In the United States the only castes intrinsically recognized are founded upon merit. This is the natural and imperative result of our system of government in its unadulterated form. The American mechanic is morally, socially, and politically on a par with his fellow-citizens of every calling, whether rich or poor, and his *right* to the highest executive office of the nation is as complete, perfect, and undisputed as that of any other living man.

This being his attitude in society, his self-respect is stimulated, and his ambition awakened. He has an inducement to emulate the best in the land, and he strives by mental culture to qualify himself for the highest intellectual pursuits and enjoyments. How many of our American mechanics have been elevated to positions of lofty honor and responsibility! How many have given lustre to the name of America!

The question before us at the present moment is this: Can the American mechanic retain his rights and high social position against the competition of immigrant labor? "Coming events cast their shadows before." The view that I have given of this class is a view of the primitive, *natural* position of the mechanic, under the unadulterated workings of our system of government. It is a view of his position where all things and all men are in that state of *social* as well as moral and political equilibrium which is contemplated by our institutions. If that equilibrium is destroyed by any unnatural or uncontemplated antagonism between capital and labor—if the interests of capital become from any cause opposed to the interests of labor, it follows that the rewards of labor must be reduced, and although the intrinsic *rights* of the mechanic remain, his means of acquiring and assuming those rights are proportionately lessened.

Before the unequal competition of immigrant labor cast its shadow over the industrial interests of our country, every American journeyman mechanic was enabled, by the force of his industry, to maintain a financial position equal to that of his social, moral, and political position. He was sure of employment, at wages adapted to the dignity of his franchise; to the necessities of the present, and the vicissitudes of the future. He could dwell in his own cottage, supply his family with comforts and luxuries, rear his children respectably, find time for his own mental improvement, and lay by a little of his earnings each week for a rainy day. Neatness and cleanliness pervaded his home, and the cheerful hearth was to him the ever-welcome refuge from toil. But with a superabundant immigration from Europe came a train of evils which are now rapidly developing themselves. Many an American mechanic still lives in the enjoyment of all his just privileges, but how great the proportion of those who, from want of employment, or reduced compensation, or both, have been alienated from their homes, their comforts, their ambition! How vast the number of those who have been driven from their employments to make room for the under-bidding competition of the foreign laborer! The American mechanic cannot live upon the pittance demanded by his European competitor. It is not his custom—it was not the custom of his fathers—it is degrading to his sense of self-respect.

I will relate two instances of the manner in which this disparaging competition is carried on.

A German cabinetmaker, who received work from storekeepers, occupied a spacious loft in Ann street, in the city of New York. In that loft was his workshop and his dwelling. He employed three *apprentices,* all Germans, and with them was constantly occupied in manufacturing furniture. This man, under a plea of destitution, *obtained all his winter fuel, with other necessaries, from the Alms-House department of the city!*

The other case is that of a tailor, also a German, who obtained a constant supply of work from clothiers. He employed from eight to ten hands, all of whom *boarded* with him. This man kept his two children constantly employed *in begging for broken victuals from door to door, by which means his table was supplied with provisions!*

Here are the elements of competition which the American mechanic is called upon, by excessive immigration, to withstand—*Imposture and pauperism!* The elements are too unequal. The odds are against him. He cannot contend with them. His moral sensibilities—his sense of self-respect forbid it. The alternative presented is poverty or disgrace. He chooses the former, and quits his shop, in hopes that something will "turn up" to his advantage. He seeks in vain for employment at remunerating prices. It is not to be had. He must work at the prices of the *foreign pauper,* or remain idle. He turns to the country, but even there the same spectacle is presented. Foreigners are working the farms. The teeming earth, which has till now sent forth its abundance from beneath the hand of the hardy American farmer, struggles on in a succession of short crops, under the cheap system of European tillage.

In his pressing necessities, the discharged workman bethinks him of the public service. He determines, as a last resort, to obtain some subordinate public office, from the emoluments of which he may support his family with respectability. He has done good service to his party in times past, and he is sure it will not deny him an appointment. For the first time in his life he looks into the public departments, and applies for a situation. He finds every post occupied—*occupied by foreigners!* There is *nothing* left to him but submission or beggary. In the workshop, on the farm, and in the public offices, the aspect is the same. In every department he encounters the drudging and importunate foreigner.

To turn from the home of childhood and the associations of early life, and seek subsistence on the broad prairies of the far West—to build his house in the wilderness, and endure the hardships of a pioneer life, becomes his final recourse. But even there he finds the same competition. The foreign squatter has staked out the best portions of the public domain.

Thus the personal interests of the American mechanic are submerged, his rights neutralized, and his hopes thwarted by excessive immigration of the poor of Europe. These are the *direct* effects.

Indirectly, the effects assume a different phase. The introduction of this degraded element into the industrial arena of the country, is in itself calculated to promote *caste,* and stimulate a puerile aristocratic taste among the rich. In such hands, labor puts on a repulsive aspect—is shorn of all dignity. With them, the instincts of refinement, heretofore shared by the working-men of America, in common with *all* their fellow-citizens, are unknown. They present the positive distinction between *intellectual* labor and mere drudgery, and thus they themselves draw the distinguishing line which forms the basis of caste, and encourages an aristocratic, anti-republican sentiment.

Post-Civil War Nativism

Historians treating the Civil War and post-Civil War period present a picture of declining nativism. They hold that the call to the colors, the patriotic responses of immigrant groups to the war effort and the approach of the war helped to bring about the demise of the Know-Nothing Party and the fragmentation of the Order of United Americans. "Now the foreigner had a new prestige; he was a comrade-at-arms. The clash that alienated sections reconciled nationalities." Except for the temporary revival of know-nothingism resulting from the Draft Riots of 1863 and General Grant's wartime order expelling Jews from his military jurisdiction in 1862, nativism was overwhelmed by patriotism. Moreover, with the nation's material growth after the war, there was a great demand for immigrant labor. Merchants also began to see immigrants as part of a growing consumer market. In addition, there was great confidence in the Americanization process. Under these conditions political nativism remained dormant in the 1860s and 1870s.

Nevertheless, the period saw the revival of local units of the Order of United Americans. *The Irish-American,* a leading ethnic journal published in New York City, ever sensitive to all signs of nativism, branded the reappearance of the Order as part of a movement to strike at the immigrant's social status and "drive him from all lucrative employments." Furthermore, when jobs became scarce, especially during the panic of 1873, the daily advertisements that appeared in the newspapers indicated the discrimination that persisted against the Catholic Irish.

SOURCE: **The Irish-American,** June 28, 1873. **The Know-Nothing "Unions"**

A Member Rises to Explain And "puts his foot in it." The annexed letter reached us through the Post-Office, last week:—Englewood, N.J., June 18, 1873.

To the Editors of the Irish-American:

Gentlemen—I have noticed the articles, for several weeks back, in the *Boston Pilot,* with regard to the Anti-Catholic Association known as the "O.U.A.M.," and, more particularly, in this week's edition of the *Irish World, Irish-American,* and *Irish Democrat.* The *Irish-American* speaks of some order known as the "Order of the American Union." Now, what I desire to know, is whether this "Order of the American Union," spoken of by Captain Tanner, is the "Order of United American Mechanics;" and for this reason: I have been a member of the "O.U.A.M." for over a year, and I have found nothing in it proscribing a man on account of his religion. Show me a *native-born American, in good standing* in his community, and I care not whether he be a Catholic or not, he can join the "O.U.A.M.:" and there is nothing in the constitution of the Order to prohibit him. And, furthermore, the *Irish World* speaks of Orangemen being at the head of it. Now that is an absurdity, because every man who joins the Order is required to take an oath of allegiance to this country. And, again, if you will show to me a *foreign-born citizen,—no matter what his religion may be,*—who is a member of the "O.U.A.M." (unless he may have perjured himself to become a member,) you may count on my resignation, certain, with a few others.

Respectfully yours,
S. H. Springer

Whatever may have been the original intention of the writer of the above communication, the result he arrives at reminds us forcibly of the celebrated law suit in which Curran told the Judge that it was not necessary to introduce evidence for his own side, as his opponent had already proved his case for him. If Mr. Springer had read over Captain Tanner's speech, he would have seen that that gentleman expressly stated that he did not refer at all to the

"Order of United American Mechanics." It may be that the gallant Captain has not been posted on the peculiar tenets of that "Order," or he might not have taken the trouble to exempt them from his vigorous denunciation and well-merited stricture. For here we have the testimony of one who proclaims himself a member of this secret, oath-bound "Order," and upon its face, he shows that it is just as illiberal and proscriptive as the "Union" which Captain Tanner so effectually exposed. That it is political in its ultimate objects, and is run in the interest of a class of unscrupulous men, who are fast making American politics a hissing and a bye-word, no one who has watched the events of the last thirty years in this country need be told. But these miscalled and very un-American "Mechanics" are wise in their generation. Warned by the downfall of the original "Native" and "Know-Nothing" factions, they do not now aim solely at destroying the political privileges guaranteed to the adopted citizen by the Constitution of the Republic; they strike at this social status, take measures to crowd him to the wall, to drive him from all lucrative employments—in a word, they would nullify and reverse the decree of the Almighty by taking from a fellow-man (for the accident of birth,) that daily bread which the Creator, even in His anger, declared to be the rightful due of honest toil. It is a scheme worthy of the old serpent that first crept into Eden, to destroy its peace; but it will fail, as every idea that assails the truth and justice of God's providence inevitably does fail.

But let us put Mr. Springer and his associates on their own platform, and see how they look, thus elevated. He says that, if he can be shown that any foreign-born man has got into the "Order of United American Mechanics," he and many others will quit it, instanter. The declaration is the stamp of his illiberality, though the issue he raises is not material. We happen to know that Scotchmen and North of Ireland men have been taken into the "Order:" and Mr. Springer does not have to be told that it was not because they were Catholics. But, let us suppose that, in the late civil war here, Mr. Springer, full of love for his native land, had gone out to fight her battles, and, like Captain Tanner, had fallen wounded upon some glorious field. There he might easily have found himself side by side with some strong-armed *Irish* mechanic, who had stepped into the ranks of danger to show that he was not ungrateful for the shelter afforded him by the Republic, and that he was not unworthy of the citizenship with which her laws invested him. Their blood, poured out in a common cause, might mingle on the soil which it consecrated anew to liberty and human right. Or, perhaps, they might linger together for months in some hospital, tended patiently and impartially (as Captain Tanner describes it) by some angel in the form of woman and the garb of religion. But, when all that was over, and they were spared to return to their homes in peace,—at the door of the "Lodge" of the "Order of United American Mechanics," Mr. Springer would have to bid his Irish comrade farewell. Inside *that* threshold he could not take him: nay, he himself tells us he would not remain there if he thought that there was *one* foreign-born man admitted! The tricky American politician, whose every act is a perjury, may be there; the knave who took advantage of the hour of his country's peril, to coin her misfortunes and the blood of her soldiers into ill-gotten wealth, may be there; but the scarred and shattered veteran of a hundred fights for the Union is shut out, if it so chance that he was born on Irish or German soil.

Mr. Springer, we wish you joy of your company; and we hardly think you will need to abandon them,—at least until that inevitable disintegration which, sooner or later, attacks all unnatural combinations, shall relegate the "Order of American Mechanics" to the same oblivion that swallowed up the "Native" church-burners of '44 and the "Know-Nothings" of '54.

SOURCE: New York *Times,* June 28, 1873. **Situations Wanted Females**

CHAMBER-MAID AND WAITRESS.—BY A NEAT, TIDY ENGLISH GIRL with two years' reference; is a first-class waitress, thoroughly understands the care of silver, and can do chamber-work nicely. Call for two days at No. 631 6th av., between 36th and 37th sts., upstairs.

CHAMBER-MAID.—BY A RESPECTABLE PROTESTANT GIRL, AS chamber-maid and waitress, or as nurse and seamstress in a private family; City or country; good reference. Can be seen for two days at No. 321 West 42d st.

CHAMBER-MAID.—BY A PROTESTANT GIRL, AS CHAMBER-MAID; would assist in the pantry, or would do waiting. Call at No. 49 West 18th st.

CHAMBER-MAID OR WAITRESS.—BY AN ENGLISH GIRL, AGED SEVEN-teen, at chamber-work or waiting; good city reference. Address E.K., No. 254 West Houston st., between Varick and Hudson.

COOK.—CHAMBER-MAID, &C.—BY TWO NEAT, TIDY GIRLS (PROTES-tants,) who will work of a family between them; cook thoroughly understands her duties well; makes soup, bread, biscuits, pastries, &c.; Chamber-maid is a smart active girl, and a nice washer and ironer; good recommendations. Call at No. 138 West 11th st., cor-ner 6th av.

COOK, WASHER, AND IRONER.—BY A PROTESTANT WOMAN, WHO IS A superior cook and thorough washer and ironer, for moderate wages; city or country; has very best recommendations. Can be seen at the Institute, No. 138 6th av., above 10th st., over the drug store.

COOK.—BY A PROTESTANT ENGLISH YOUNG WOMAN AS FIRST-CLASS cook; can do all kinds nice cooking, boning, larding, &c.; is a good pastry cook and good baker; is very neat and tidy; country or city; has best City references. Apply at A. Pelton & Co.'s, No. 645 8th av.

COOK.—BY A PROTESTANT AMERICAN WOMAN, HAVING EXCELLENT recommendations for capability, sobriety, honesty; is punctual and obliging; will go city or country; wages moderate. Can be seen at the Institute, No. 138 6th av., above 10th st., over the drug store.

COOK.—BY A CANADIAN PROTESTANT YOUNG WOMAN, WHO IS A first-class cook; makes excellent bread and biscuit, soups, meat, desserts, &c., also bones and lards; can furnish the best reference from last employer; country preferred. Can be seen at Odell's Agency, No. 109 West 34th, corner Broadway.

COOK.—BY AN AMERICAN PROTESTANT WOMAN; IS A FIRST-CLASS cook; makes excellent bread and biscuit, soups, meats, desserts, jellies, pastry, &c.; bones and lards; can furnish the very best of reference. Inquire for H.D., at Odell's Agency, No. 109 West 34th st., corner Broadway.

COOK.—BY AN ENGLISH PROTESTANT WOMAN OF THIRTY AS PLAIN cook, and will assist with the washing; has excellent reference; is not afraid of work or the country; wishes a place where she will not have to leave in a month. Call at No. 106 6th av., over blue store.

COOK.—BY A PROTESTANT WOMAN, AS COOK; UNDERSTANDS GOOD family cooking; good reference. Can be seen at No. 220 West 18th st., first floor, for two days.

COOK.—BY A RESPECTABLE PROTESTANT WOMAN AS FIRST-CLASS cook; understands her business; willing to assist with washing and ironing; good references. Call at 590 3d av., between 38th and 39th sts.

HOUSE-WORK.—BY A PROTESTANT AMERICAN GIRL TO DO GENERAL house-work; is a good plain cook, good washer and ironer; is very neat and tidy; has five years' City reference from her last place. Apply at No. 645 6th av.

HOUSE-CLEANER.—BY A PROTESTANT GIRL, TO GO OUT BY THE DAY; is an excellent cleaner; willing and obliging. Call at No. 152 East 39th st., near 3d av.

LAUNDRESS.—BY A GERMAN PROTESTANT YOUNG WOMAN; IS A FIRST-class laundress; can do all kinds of French fluting, puffling, polishing, &c. has excellent City references from last employer. Can be seen at Odell's Agency, No. 109 West 34th st., corner Broadway.

LAUNDRESS.—BY A GERMAN PROTESTANT GIRL, AS FIRST-CLASS laundress; understands French fluting, fine muslin, &c.; has good City reference. Apply at A. Pelton & Co.'s, No. 645 6th av., near 38th st.

Henry George on Immigration: "Dumping Garbage"

Described by the historian Vernon Parrington as "our most original economist" and the leading exponent of the school of "Democratic Economics," Henry George saw immigration to America, particularly from Ireland, as a process of "Dumping Garbage." Just four years after the publication of his very important *Progress and Poverty,* the father of the single-tax concept discussed immigration in a work entitled *Social Problems.* He expressed grave concern for the nation's very heavy immigration in terms that could easily have placed his material with the rankest nativist literature of the 1830s and 1840s. Henry George's attack was mainly upon Irish immigration despite the fact that in the years just previous to the publication of *Social Problems* the number of newcomers from Germany and Scandinavia far exceeded those from Ireland. He was appalled by the poverty and ignorance of the Irish immigrants. George was especially concerned, however, with the importation of the evils of Irish landlordism into a system of landownership which he was trying to reform by having "unearned increment" on land diverted away from private interests to the government.

SOURCE: Henry George, **Social Problems** (Chicago, 1883), pp. 147–50, 155–57, 161–62.

Dumping Garbage

This gulf-stream of humanity that is setting on our shores with increasing volume is in all respects worthy of more attention than we give it. In many ways one of the most important phenomena of our time, it is one which forcibly brings to the mind the fact that we are living under conditions which must soon begin to rapidly change. But there is one part of the immigration coming to us this year which is specially suggestive. A number of large steamers of the transatlantic lines are calling, under contract with the British Government, at small ports on the west coast of Ireland, filling up with men, women and children, whose passages are paid by their government, and then, ferrying them across the ocean, are dumping them on the wharves of New York and Boston with a few dollars apiece in their pockets to begin life in the New World.

The strength of a nation is in its men. It is its people that make a country great and strong, produce its wealth, and give it rank among other countries. Yet, here is a civilized and Christian government, or one that passes for such, shipping off its people, to be dumped upon another continent, as garbage is shipped off from New York to be dumped into the Atlantic Ocean. Nor are these people undesirable material for the making of a nation. Whatever they may sometimes become here, when cooped up in tenement-houses and exposed to the corruption of our politics, and to the temptation of a life greatly differing from that to which they have been accustomed, they are in their own country, as any one who has been among them there can testify, a peaceable, industrious, and, in some important respects, a peculiarly moral people, who lack intellectual and political education, and the robust virtues that personal independence alone can give, simply because of the poverty to which they are condemned. Mr. Trevelyan, the Chief Secretary for Ireland, has declared in the House of Commons that they are physically and morally healthy, well capable of making a living, and yet the government of which he is a member is shipping them away at public expense as New York ships its garbage!

These people are well capable of making a living, Mr. Trevelyan says, yet if they remain at home they will only be able to make the poorest of poor livings in the best, taxes must be raised and alms begged to keep them alive; and so as the cheapest way of getting rid of them, they are shipped away at public expense.

What is the reason of this? Why is it that people, in themselves well capable of making a living, cannot make a living for themselves in their own country? Simply that the natural, equal, and unalienable rights of man, with which, as asserted by our Declaration of Independence, these human beings have been endowed by their Creator, are denied them. The famine, the pauperism, the mis-government and turbulence of Ireland, the bitter wrongs which keep aglow the fire of Irish "sedition," and the difficulties with regard to Ireland which perplex English statesmen, all spring from that the National Assembly of France, in 1789, declared to be the cause of all public misfortunes and corruptions of government —the contempt of human rights. The Irish peasant is forced to starve, to beg, or to emigrate; he becomes in the eyes of those who rule him mere human garbage, to be shipped off and dumped anywhere, because, like the English peasant, who, after a slave's life, dies a pauper's death, his natural rights in his native soil are denied him; because his unalienable right to procure wealth by his own exertions and to retain it for his own uses is refused him.

The country from which these people are shipped—and the Government-aided emigration is as nothing compared to the voluntary emigration—is abundantly capable of maintaining in comfort a very much larger population than it has ever had. There is no natural reason why in it people themselves capable of making a living should suffer want and starvation. The reason that they do is simply that they are denied natural opportunities for the employment of their labor, and that the laws permit others to extort from them the proceeds of such labor as they are permitted to do. Of these people who are now being sent across the Atlantic by the English government, and dumped on our wharves with a few dollars in their pockets, there are probably none of mature years who have not by their labor produced wealth enough not only to have supported them hitherto in a much higher degree of comfort than that in which they have lived, but to have enabled them to pay their own passage across the Atlantic, if they wanted to come, and to have given them on landing here a capital sufficient for a comfortable start. They are penniless only because they have been systematically robbed from the day of their birth to the day they left their native shores.

•   •   •   •

It is to maintain such a system of robbery as this that Ireland is filled with policemen and troops and spies and informers, and a people who might be an integral part of the British nation are made to that nation a difficulty, a weakness and a danger. Economically, the Irish landlords are of no more use than so many great, ravenous, destructive beasts—packs of wolves, herds of wild elephants, or such dragons as St. George is reported to have killed. They produce nothing; they only consume and destroy. And what they destroy is more even than what they consume. For, not merely is Ireland turned into a camp of military police and red-coated soldiery to hold down the people while they are robbed; but the wealth producers, stripped of capital by this robbery of their earnings, and condemned by it to poverty and ignorance, are unable to produce the wealth which they could and would produce did labor get its full earnings, and were wealth left to those who make it. Surely true statesmanship would suggest that if any one is to be shoveled out of a country it should be those who merely consume and destroy; not those who produce wealth.

But English statesmen think otherwise, and these surplus Irish men and women; these garbage Irish men and women and little children—surplus and garbage because the landlords of Ireland have no use for them, *are* shoveled out of their own country and dumped on our wharves. They have reached "the land of the free and the home of the brave" just in time for the Fourth of July, when they may hear the Declaration of Independence, with its ringing assertion of unalienable rights, read again in our annual national celebration.

Have they, then, escaped from the system which in their own country made them serfs and human garbage? Not at all. They have not even escaped the power of their old landlords to take from them the proceeds of their toil.

For we are not merely getting these surplus tenants of English, Scotch and Irish landlords—we are getting the landlords, too. Simultaneously with this emigration is going on a movement which is making the landlords and capitalists of Great Britain owners of vast tracts of American soil. There is even now scarcely a large landowning family in Great Britain that does not own even larger American estates, and American land is becoming with them a more and more favorite investment. These American estates of "their graces" and "my lords" are not as yet as valuable as their home estates, but the natural increase in our population, augmented by emigration, will soon make them so.

Every "surplus" Irishman, Englishman or Scotchman sent over here assist directly in sending up the value of land and the rent of land. The stimulation of emigration from the Old Country to this is a bright idea on the part of these landlords of two continents. They get rid of people who, at home, in hard times, they might have to support in some sort of fashion, and lessen, as they think, the forces of disaffection, while at the same time they augment the value of their American estates.

.   .   .

These Irish men and women who are being dumped on our wharves with two or three dollars in their pockets, do they find access to nature any freer here than there? Far out in the West, if they know where to go, and can get there, they may, for a little while yet; but though they may see even around New York plenty of unused land, they will find that it all belongs to somebody. Let them go to work at what they will, they must, here as there, give up some of their earnings for the privilege of working, and pay some other human creature for the privilege of living. On the whole their chances will be better here than there, for this is yet a new country, and a century ago our settlements only fringed the eastern seaboard of a vast continent. But from the Atlantic to the Pacific we already have our human garbage, the volume of which some of this Irish human garbage will certainly go to swell. Wherever you go throughout the country the "tramp" is known; and in this metropolitan city there are already, it is stated by the Charity Organization Society, a quarter of a million people who live on alms! What, in a few years more, are we to do for a dumping-ground? Will it make our difficulty the less that our human garbage can vote?

B. THE MELTING-POT MISTAKE: THE DANGERS OF THE NEW IMMIGRATION, 1880–1924

Newpaper Reaction to the New Immigrant

In the latter 1880s and early 1890s a series of events occurred which provided nativists with their most effective arguments for immigration restriction since the 1850s. With memories of the violence of the Molly Maguires and the 1877 strikes still fresh in their minds, most Americans were shocked by the Chicago Haymarket affair of 1886. The incident in which a bomb was thrown killing seven persons and causing numerous injuries convinced many Americans that America's immigration policy was too liberal. In addition, there was a revival of fraternal orders like the Order of United American Mechanics comprised of professionals, white-collar workers, merchants and skilled mechanics who seriously regarded the continued unchecked flow of immigration as a threat to their status. Moreover, there was a resurgence of anti-Catholicism resulting from the rapid growth of Church membership, the creation of new dioceses in the United States and renewed Catholic demands for a share of public school funds. Fears of a papal conquest of the United States led to the formation of many secret anti-Catholic societies, most notably the American Protective Association. Nativists also were alarmed by signs that the sources of immigration were beginning to shift away from northern and western Europe to eastern and southern Europe.

Of the "new" immigrants, there was special concern about the Italians. Even before the 1890s, an image of the typical Italian immigrant had been implanted in the minds of many Americans. He was a swarthy, stiletto-carrying, common laborer who probably was associated with the Mafia, a stereotype which "conditioned every major outburst of anti-Italian sentiment in the 1890s." It certainly colored the newspapers' reaction in 1891 to the tragic New Orleans episode in which eleven Italians, suspected of being implicated in the murder of the superintendent of police, were lynched by a mob.

SOURCE: **Public Opinion,** April 14, 1891, pp. 616–18.

The St. Paul Pioneer Press

The difficulty is not one difficult to remedy. It is not necessary to prohibit immigration; it is not necessary to prevent the income of a single man who has a right to be here. All that we need to-day is to establish, through our consular agents, such a system of supervision as shall require the immigrant to present a clean bill of moral health, certified to by the country from which he comes. If this simple requirement were enforced, neither John Most nor any Sicilian or Corsican bandit could ever have set foot upon our shores. If it had not already become a tragedy, it would be an international burlesque that any government of Europe should send to us those of its subjects steeped in crime and bound by oath to its further perpetration whenever the occasion might arise, and should then require satisfaction of us when they defy the law and give free reign to their diabolical dispositions. But it is our fault from beginning to end. For almost ten years past every representative of enlightened public opinion has urged and besought Congress to take action for the regulation of immigration. The only answer has been some fool laws pretending to prohibit the admission of contract laborers, powerless to reach the real evil, and ridiculed and evaded by the very men at whom they were aimed. Not only in these violent disorders in our great cities, but in the strained competition of labor, and in the lowering of wages by the willingness of these new comers to accept such mean compensation as fits their methods of living, are we reaping the whirlwind. This last lesson ought to be enough. We have our hands full already, but, if the evil is allowed to grow, another decade may make it too great for us to cope with. The first law which the Fifty-second Congress places upon our statute-books ought to be one for the most rigorous system of supervision and restraint of foreign immigration that can be devised.

The Philadelphia Enquirer

Agents of the ocean lines report that the coming season will be the busiest ever known. Every vessel will come over loaded down with new recruits for America. More immigrants will be landed this year than ever before in history. What kind of people are these new citizens? Some are honest men seeking a home. They will go West, take up land and add to the resources of the Nation. This is the desirable class. Others will get no farther than New York, where they will get on the police force, take out naturalization papers, sell themselves to Tammany and the corrupt politicians who feed upon their stealings from the city, and in time share in the plunder themselves. Others will join the hordes of Huns and Poles in the coal regions, hive together in hovels, live on refuse, save 90 per cent of their earnings and work for wages upon which no respectable laborer could exist. Others will come from the scum of Italy and Sicily, will become day laborers on the railroads, will live in shanties like the Huns, and after saving up a few hundred dollars will take their money back to their old homes. Most of these will seek citizenship only for the profit there may be in the sale of their votes at election time, for politics is to the vicious classes of Europe and Asia a legitimate field for adding to the yearly income. Others will be fresh from jails and prisons, brigands, outlaws, murderers, midnight assassins, cowardly thugs, like the Mafia of New Orleans. Isn't there food for thought in the greatly increasing number of immigrants? No respectable person seeking to settle down and become a worthy citizen is unwelcome. He may not have an education. He may not even know how to read, but if he will work at some useful trade or turn his attention to the cultivation of the soil America will open her arms to him. But what shall we do with the assassins and criminals driven to this country in the expectations of finding a new field for their villainy? Where is this thing to end?

The Chicago Herald

The new legislation for the sifting of immigrants ought, of course, to be applied with strict impartiality, but, if rigidly applied, it will probably be found to exclude at least as many Italians as people of other nationalities. It is true of the Russians and Poles as it is of the Italians, that they are coming to our shores in increasing numbers, and to some extent they are accessions of rather doubtful value. This country extends a cordial welcome to honest, industrious, and intelligent people from all parts of the world (China excepted), but it can not afford to become a land of refuge for criminals, paupers, and barbarians, whose highest ambition is to overthrow law and authority of every kind. People who respect law and are capable of understanding that liberty does not mean license are heartily welcome. As to others, we must adopt as severe measures as may be necessary to exclude them from the country.

Robert DeCourcy Ward of the Immigration Restriction League on the Immigration Problem

As a result of the shift in immigration to southern and eastern Europe, New England's intelligentsia became concerned with the future of their race and class. In 1894 a small group of young Bostonians formed the Immigration Restriction League. The League, which was to "spearhead the restrictionist movement for the next twenty-five years," launched a counteroffensive against the new "invaders." Having lost their confidence in America's assimilative ability, the restrictionists placed less emphasis upon environmental factors and more upon heredity and race. Reluctantly accepting the Irish as part of the Anglo-Saxon race, they were more fearful of the new immigrants than of the Irish and Germans. The League members saw in the new immigration the danger of hordes of criminals, illiterates, paupers and insane persons being dumped upon these shores and the eventual destruction of the basic American character. The organization's propaganda mill fed businessmen, labor leaders and politicians with their views and aims. The League's public strategy in checking immigration was to seek the passage of a literacy test bill. In 1896, with nativist feeling running high, it succeeded in getting Congress to pass such a bill. The measure, however, was vetoed by President Cleveland, and the League carried on the fight for twenty years before it secured the desired legislation.

One of the leading figures among the young Bostonians who formed the Immigration Restriction League was Robert DeCourcy Ward. In the 1890s Ward, as a scientist, shied away from racial theories. By 1906, however, he had become interested in the growing field of eugenics. As the League's secretary, he read papers on immigration before meetings of eugenicists. Ward used eugenics to supply arguments as to why immigration restriction was necessary for the preservation of the American "race."

SOURCE: Robert DeCourcy Ward, "The Immigration Problem," *Charities* (February 6, 1904), pp. 138–39, 142–43, 147–49, 150–51.

The immigration question is at once one of the most important and one of the most perplexing problems before the American people. It is important because it concerns, in the most intimate way, not only the present welfare of all our citizens, but the welfare and the character of the citizens of future generations. It is perplexing because of the variety of the interests which are involved in any discussion of it. So complex a problem does not lend itself readily to brief consideration. If we would consider it at all, we must confine ourselves to one or two aspects of it alone. It is my purpose to discuss this question in some of its broader aspects, in the light of the conditions which have developed as recently as during the last two years, and to include also some consideration of the immigration of future years and of its relation to the American race which is to live on after we are gone. I shall have something to say, in closing, on the question of the further restriction of immigration, and I assume, at once, without attempting to argue the matter, that my readers are agreed that every nation has the undoubted *right* to restrict or to prohibit immigration, if it sees fit. The sentimental predisposition of hospitality and of fraternity in favor of *absolute* freedom of immigration to this country—a feeling which used to be universal, as it was traditional—has of late years very largely, I may even say almost entirely, disappeared, in the face of the changed conditions of immigration, which have made it plain that a departure from this traditional policy is not only in the highest degree expedient, but even absolutely necessary for the welfare of the country and for the preservation of its standards of citizenship and of character. Our fathers were undoubtedly right when they openly welcomed the sturdy immigrants from northern Europe. Shall we say that we are wrong if we believe in maintaining American standards of living, and in selecting to some slight extent, if we may, the elements which are to make up the American race of the future?

In such a consideration of the immigration problem as that before us at the moment, there is no need of wearying ourselves with a lengthy examination of statistics of immigration. During the ten years, 1880–1890, immigration amounted to five and a quarter millions, or over one-third of the total immigration from 1820 to 1890. At its maximum, over one per cent was added to the population of the United States in a single year, and the average during the period 1886 to 1896 was 435,000 a year. Between 1890 and 1900, owing to the period of industrial depression which came in that decade, the numbers fell to somewhat over three and a half millions. There has always been a close relation between the number of alien arrivals in this country and the general state of business here. Periods of financial depression are soon followed by a smaller immigration, and periods of industrial activity bring in much greater numbers. Immigration has thus come to us in great waves during prosperous times, with a falling off in the intervals of financial crises, but, on the whole, *each wave during prosperity is higher than the last.* When a period of depression sets in, to the already large numbers of our own unemployed there are added thousands of immigrants with no occupation or skill. Our skilled workmen are thus deprived of the opportunities for employment in unskilled occupations to tide them over until better times, and our unskilled labor is reduced to a starvation basis through being underbid by immigrants who are willing to live in a way utterly incompatible with American habits and character. In times of ordinary business activity the same results are produced, though in a less degree.

It is perfectly true that there has been a great demand for labor during the past two or three years, but if material growth can only be secured through a degradation of our citizenship, is such material growth an altogether desirable thing?

.   .   .

With continued business prosperity; with an ever-increasing facility of transportation, and with a widening sphere of the steamship agent's influence, there is every reason to expect a still larger immigration during the current fiscal year, and in a few years, as the number and size of steamships increase still further, we may easily have two million newcomers every year. In fact, unless some action is taken by this country to prevent it, the tide will flow on so long "as there is any difference of economic level between our own population and that of the most degraded communities abroad," as the late Gen. Francis A. Walker put it.

No one who notices, even in the most casual way, the faces of the people he sees on the streets and in the cars, need be told that a most striking and fundamental change has taken place in the nationalities of our immigrants during the last fifteen or twenty years. A few years ago practically all of our immigrants were from northern and western Europe, that is, they were more or less closely allied to us, racially, historically, socially, industrially and politically. They were largely the same elements which had recently made up the English race. As experience has shown, they found little difficulty in assimilating with the American people, and what is more, they were as a whole eager to become assimilated. They intermarried among themselves and with the older American stock, which was akin to the English. Now, however, the majority of the newcomers are from southern and eastern Europe, and they are coming in rapidly increasing numbers from Asia. These people are alien to us, in race (at least, within reasonably modern times), in language, in social, political and industrial ideas and inheritances. Their standards of living are very different from ours. They have a very high percentage of illiteracy. (In 1903, for example, there were among the southern and eastern Europeans over fourteen years of age about forty per cent of illiterates). And most of them are unskilled laborers. In 1869, immigrants from Austria-Hungary, Italy, Poland and Russia were about one-hundredth of the number from the United Kingdom, France, Germany, and Scandinavia; in 1880, about one-tenth; in 1894, nearly equal to it; in 1903, three times as great. In 1903, Great Britain and Ireland sent us about 70,000 immigrants, Germany, 40,000 and Scandinavia about 70,000, whereas Austria-Hungary sent us 206,000; Russia, 136,-000 and Italy 230,000. Unless all signs fail, this startling change in nationality is destined to continue, and to become much more marked in the future, Asiatic races of which we have perhaps as yet hardly heard, playing a more and more conspicuous part in the years to come.

· · · ·

No argument is necessary to convince any American that the hope of this country lies in the assimilation of our foreign-born population. We want these aliens to become Americans with us; to love and to preserve our institutions; to speak our language; to live, so far as possible, up to American standards of living; to contribute to the well-being of society. But this most necessary process of assimilation which is of such vital importance to national unity, is becoming increasingly difficult every day because of the wide gulf which separates the majority of our latest immigrants from ourselves; and furthermore, and very largely, because so many of these immigrants are illiterate and because of their unfortunate, albeit perfectly natural, tendency to settle in communities of their own in our large cities. In a very valuable special report of the United States Commissioner of Labor, issued a few years ago, it was shown that persons of foreign birth or parentage form seventy-seven per cent of the total population of the slum districts in Baltimore, ninety per cent in Chicago, ninety-one per cent in Philadelphia, and ninety-five per cent in New York. Further, southeastern Europe has furnished three times as many inhabitants as northwestern Europe to the slums of Baltimore, nineteen times as many to the slums of New York, twenty times as many to the slums of Chicago, seventy-one times as many to the slums of Philadelphia. The slums of our large cities are thus chiefly a foreign product and a product of the countries which have sent us rapidly increasing numbers of immigrants during recent years. Of the slum inhabitants of the above-named cities the average illiteracy was, for those from northwestern Europe, twenty-five per hundred; for those from southwestern Europe, fifty-four per hundred; for native Americans, seven per hundred. In this connection it is worth noting that Dr. Shively has estimated that 23,000 tuberculous immigrants were landed in New York in 1902, and has pointed out the impossibility of making these persons take proper care of themselves because they cannot read the directions printed in almost all known tongues and distributed throughout the city. Our recent immigrants have also brought us other diseases, many of them almost unknown in this country before.

.   .   .

Most of the discussions of the immigration problem in the past have been concerned with its economic side. The question is, however, a racial as well as—I myself believe even more than—an economic one. With an easy-going, laissez-faire spirit we have said to ourselves: "Yes truly, we are receiving an enormous lot of foreigners—Jews, 'Dagoes,' Poles, Syrians—but they will all be assimilated and become part of our old Anglo-Saxon, American stock. The old American stock is, and will always be, very greatly in excess, and these foreigners will not affect the future of the country or of the race. Don't let us worry. It will settle itself." Within a few years, however, and chiefly within a year or two, a radical change has been taking place in the view of the problem which is being taken by thinking men and women. People are coming to see that we have spent too much time studying the economic sides of the question. There is a racial side which is even more important than all the economic aspects put together.

President Eliot did much to set people thinking on this question when he showed, in his annual report for 1901 and 1902, that of the graduates of seven Harvard classes in the 1870's, twenty-eight per cent are unmarried, and those who are married average only two surviving children. President Roosevelt, at about the same time, attracted considerable attention to the general subject of the American birth-rate by his use of the term "racial suicide," which has since often been quoted. Following along the same lines as those suggested in President Eliot's investigation, Professor Thorndike, in the *Popular Science Monthly* for May, 1903, discussed the question of the low birth-rate as shown by statistics from Wesleyan University, New York University and Middlebury College. His results in general confirmed those of President Eliot—to the effect that the birth-rate among college graduates, at least in the East, is too low to keep up their numbers. A very exhaustive study of the statistics of Massachusetts from 1885 to 1897, by R. R. Kuczynski, published in the *Quarterly Journal of Economics* for November, 1901, and February, 1902, has shown that the proportion of persons married among the natives is much smaller than among the foreign-born; that the birth-rate among married women of child-bearing age is much larger among the foreign-born, and that the marriage rate is decreasing among the natives and increasing among the foreigners. Mr. Kuczynski concluded: "It is probable that the native population cannot hold its own. It seems to be dying out." Dr. Bushee, in his investigation of *The Ethnic Factors in the Population of Boston,* likewise comes to the conclusion that the native whites are failing to keep up their numbers on account of their low birth-rate. Statistics, therefore, "put the whole native population of Massachusetts in the same position as college graduates, and the question accordingly seems to be one of the upper class or of the older part of the population, and not simply a question of the educated classes." The size of families is, of course, determined by the interaction of many diverse causes. Among them late marriages; the increase of luxury; higher ideals of education for children; the longing for freedom from household cares; greater prudence; interests of women outside the home, and indeed, actual racial infertility, have all been urged as contributing causes. As to race sterility, cases of animals which are bred for special purposes and which become sterile, are known, and it has been urged that selection for our civilization may have the same result. However this may be, one cause of a lowering birth-rate has been suggested which seems reasonable, potent, and of increasing importance. I refer to the effect of foreign immigration. This point was first brought out by Gen. Francis A. Walker, as a result of his studies as superintendent of two United States censuses. General Walker showed that, contrary to the usual belief, foreigners did not come here in the past because Americans despised manual labor, but that Americans gave up manual labor because they did not wish to be so closely associated with the less intelligent and less progressive foreigners. In his "Discussions in Economics," he wrote:

The American shrank from the industrial competition thus thrust upon him. He was unwilling himself to engage in the lowest kind of day labor with these new elements of population; he was even more unwilling to bring sons and daughters into the world to enter into that competition. . . . The great fact protrudes through all the subsequent history of our population that the more rapidly foreigners came into the United States, the smaller was the rate of increase, not merely among the native population, but throughout the population of the country as a whole, including the foreigners. . . . If the foregoing views are true, or contain any considerable degree of truth, foreign immigration into this country has, from the time it assumed large proportions, amounted not to a re-enforcement of our population, but to a replacement of native by foreign stock.

Thus, it has come about that Americans have not married, or if they have married, they have not been willing to increase the size of their families until they have had the means to enable their children to withdraw from competition with the lower classes of foreigners. As lower and more degraded immigrants come, it is to be expected that this process will apply to a larger portion of the people already here. Possibly we may feel that General Walker went too far in his view of this matter, nevertheless the United States Industrial Commission, which has made one of the most thorough studies of immigration ever undertaken, said in its report, p. 277: "It is a hasty assumption which holds that immigration during the nineteenth century has increased the total population."

Dr. Bushee has called attention to this law of population which was formulated by Dumont, to the effect that population increases inversely with "social capillarity." The stronger the competition, the greater the effort to maintain and raise the standard of living and the social position; the greater the effort, the greater the voluntary check to population. In large cities, the rearing of large families, sometimes even marriage at all, may become inconsistent with the maintenance of American standards of living in the keen competition which prevails on all sides. Competition is much more serious in its consequences when it is due to the immigration of races which are able and content to live under wholly inferior conditions.

It is the desire to live above the social stratum of the recent Jewish, Italian and Hungarian immigrants that operates to keep the native American from marrying or from having large families. On the other hand, while the native American white population is apparently destined to decline, the foreign elements are increasing very rapidly, not by immigration alone, but by their own natural high birth-rates. In Boston, it appears that "all the foreign-born groups show a high natural increase . . . (and) on the whole, the most recently immigrating nationalities have the highest birth-rates." The same thing is true for Massachusetts, and probably also elsewhere, where social conditions are similar. The foreigners who compete with the natives do not dread the lowering of the social standard nearly as much as do the natives, and hence the check on population does not operate in the same way in their case. Among the families of our newest immigrants, children are born with reckless regularity, the birth-rate being very high among the Jews and Italians. Furthermore, the Jews have extraordinary vitality. Although poor, and living under miserable conditions, the mortality of both children and adults is very low. Probably long generations in the Ghettoes of Europe have fitted them for their present conditions of life. It is likely that in a few generations the birth-rates of many of our more recently immigrating races will fall somewhat, for this has been the case with our older immigrants, the Germans and the Irish, for example. The Jewish birth-rate, however, will probably never fall as low as that for the other nationalities; because it has not done so in other countries. The Russian Jews are now surpassing all the other nationalities in their natural rate of increase. The birth-rate in Italy, also, is much higher than that in Ireland. In the second generation of Jews and Italians there is an increase of the death-rate, but the balance remains on the side of a rapid increase of population by excess of births over deaths. As regards second generations of immigrants in general, we may assume that, as Dr. Bushee has pointed out, "the second generation of those nationalities which tend to congregate in the slums shows a deterioration over the first." "With other nationalities, who are increasing less rapidly, and who live in more healthful surroundings, the second generation appears to have made an improvement over the first."

The question before us is therefore, a race question. Slav, Italian, Jew, not discouraged by the problem of maintaining high standards of living with many children, are replacing native Americans. The highest stratum is gradually being eliminated in the course of natural selection, because of the external pressure on the American stock.

There can, then, be absolutely no doubt that the recent change in the races of our immigrants will profoundly affect the character of the future American race. What the resulting physical and mental changes will be, Prof. Franklin H. Giddings, of Columbia, and Gustave Michaud have recently told us. The ethnic composition of an average immigrant has radically changed during the past few years, the Baltic and the Alpine stocks giving way to the Mediterranean. The dilution of the energetic Baltic blood, which, "combined with the conditions peculiar to a new country," has made us "preeminently an energetic, practical people, above all an industrial and political people," will, according to Mr. Giddings, inevitably cause a decline of this American push. The increasing proportion of Alpine and of Mediterranean blood will "soften the emotional nature, but it will quicken the poetic and artistic nature. We shall be a more versatile, a more plastic people, gentler in our thoughts and feelings because of the Alpine strain; livelier and brighter, with a higher power to enjoy the beautiful things of life," because of the Latin blood. "We may doubtless learn courtesy from many an Italian; virtue from many a Slav; family loyalty from many a Jew; the beauty and the refining influence of music from many a Hungarian." Turning to the physical side it is clear that the average stature will be reduced and that the skull will become broader and shorter. He would, indeed, be a hopeless pessimist who should maintain that this racial change will have *naught* but undesirable effects, mental and physical, upon the future American race. We probably need less nervous energy and push; we shall undoubtedly benefit by a quickening of our artistic and poetic nature; we shall probably not be injured by an infusion of some of the "conservative and contemplative stock which comes from eastern Europe." The good qualities of the new races we may need; their defects we should be willing to do without. Yet, when all is said regarding the benefits which we may, or even must, derive from these new elements in the blood of our race, are we not, as it were, giving away to the philosophy of despair? Are we not, most of us, fairly well satisfied with the characteristics, mental and physical, of the old American stock? Do we not love American traits as they are? May we not be rather reckless in assuming that everything will settle itself for the best? It may be that the American race of the future is to be a far better race in every respect than the old one. But we should remember that, as it has been put by a recent writer, "in forming a race of unknown value, there is being sacrificed a race of acknowledged superiority in originality and enterprise."

. . .

Evidently, the races which are destined most profoundly to alter the character of the future American race would be most affected by an educational test. I believe that if the educational test bill which passed Congress in 1896 had become law, there would now be little need of discussing the immigration problem. It is not likely, however, that an illiteracy test bill will pass Congress this session, although President Roosevelt is heartily in favor of such a measure. Those of us who believe in some further regulation of immigrant travel to the United States should stand together in support of whatever reasonable legislation may be proposed. It is certain that the steamship companies will fight it, whatever it be.

A last word: Our immigration is changing rapidly in character. Our people are being exposed to a competition unheard of in the past. A new race is being produced, perhaps better, perhaps worse, than the old. We have an opportunity which few nations enjoy of practising artificial selection in the choice of the blood which shall go into the new race. Is it not well to take advantage of this opportunity? Shall we not, at least, try to keep within some sort of reasonable limits the infusion of new blood, concerning whose ultimate effects the wisest of us know so little?

Henry Pratt Fairchild and the Melting-Pot Mistake

One of the most dramatic statements of America's ability to assimilate was made by an English author, Israel Zangwill, in a play, *The Melting Pot,* which had a popular run in 1908. Earlier, other writers had been intrigued by America's assimilative process. The French observer Crèvecoeur saw the American as a "new man" produced by the blending of several peoples. Nineteenth-century American authors like Ralph Waldo Emerson, Walt Whitman and Herman Melville expressed a similar idea of the fusion of many peoples into one. It was Zangwill, however, who did most to popularize the concept by describing America as a "melting pot" into which peoples from all over the world had been poured to produce a homogeneous, finer new nation. At the same time, the concept was receiving scientific support from a leading anthropologist, Franz Boas, who held that the American environment was actually changing the immigrant's bodily and mental characteristics.

Opposition to the melting-pot idea came mainly from two sources. Horace Kallen, a Jewish intellectual and one of the early exponents of cultural pluralism, held that true Americanism meant the conserving and fostering, not the melting down, of ethnic group differences. On the other hand, criticism of the melting-pot concept came from supporters of immigration restriction. They argued that the theory had never worked. They further held that since non-assimilation would result in the destruction of nationality and the immigration process of the previous fifty years did not result in assimilation, the free immigration policy would eventually destroy national unity.

SOURCE: Henry Pratt Fairchild, The Melting-Pot Mistake (Boston, 1926), pp. 9–13, 18–21.

These were the facts which gave to Israel Zangwill's little drama, "The Melting-Pot", when it appeared in 1909, a significance quite disproportionate to its literary importance. For one hundred years and more a stream of immigration had been pouring into the United States in constantly increasing volume. At first this movement had attracted little attention, and such feelings as it aroused were mainly those of complacency and satisfaction. As the decades rolled by certain features of the movement created considerable consternation and a demand sprang up for some form of governmental relief. In time this relief was granted, and the popular concern died down. In general, however, during practically the whole of the nineteenth century the attitude of the American people toward immigration was one of easygoing tolerant indifference when it was not actually welcome. But as the century drew to a close evidences of popular uneasiness and misgiving began to display themselves. These were due in part to changes in the social and economic situation in the United States, in part to changes in the personal and social characteristics of the immigrants, and in part to repeated warnings issued by those whose professional activities and opportunities gave them a wider access to the facts of immigration than was possible to the average citizen. In particular the American people began to ponder about the ultimate effect upon its own vitality and solidarity of this stupendous injection of foreign elements. Could we stand it, and if so, how long? Were not the foundations of our cherished institutions already partially undermined by all these alien ideas, habits, and customs? What kind of a people were we destined to become physically? Was the American nation itself in danger? Immigration became a great public problem, calling for judgment.

Then came the symbol, like a portent in the heavens. America is a Melting-Pot. Into it are being poured representatives of all the world's peoples. Within its magic confines there is being formed something that is not only uniform and homogeneous but also finer than any of the separate ingredients. The nations of the world are being fused into a new and choicer nation, the United States.

The figure was a clever one—picturesque, expressive, familiar, just the sort of thing to catch the popular fancy and lend itself to a thousand uses. It swept over this country and other countries like wild fire. As always, it was welcomed as a substitute for both investigation and thought. It calmed the rising wave of misgiving. Few stopped to ask whether it fitted the phenomena of assimilation. Few inquired whether Mr. Zangwill's familiarity with the intricate facts of immigration were such as to justify him in assuming the heavy responsibility of interpreter. America was a Melting-Pot, the apparent evidences of national disintegration were illusions, and that settled it.

It would be hard to estimate the influence of the symbol of the melting pot in staving off the restriction of immigration. It is certain that in the popular mind it offsets volumes of laboriously compiled statistics and carefully reasoned analyses. It is virtually beyond question that restriction would have come in time in any case. How soon it would have come without the Great War must remain a matter of conjecture. Be that as it may, when the concussions of that conflict had begun to die down the melting pot was discovered to be so badly cracked that it is not likely ever to be dragged into service again. Its day was over. But this did not mean that the real facts of immigration had suddenly become public property. Our symbol had been shattered, but we had not yet, as a people, been able to undertake the extensive investigation necessary to reveal the true nature of the case. The history of postwar movements is replete with evidences of the gross misconceptions of the meaning and processes of assimilation which characterized many even of those who devoted themselves directly to the problem. Even to-day, in spite of the fact that there is perhaps no other great public problem on which the American people is so well educated as on immigration, there is yet great need of a clearer understanding of the tremendous task that still confronts us.

*   *   *

The central idea of the melting-pot symbol is clearly the idea of unification. That is an idea which needs no logical demonstration to command general acceptance. Every one realizes, almost intuitively, that in any community, particularly a democratic one, unity is one of the essentials of stability, order, and progress. Every American citizen will admit without argument that if immigration threatens the national unity of the United States it is a matter of grave concern. The purpose of the melting-pot figure was to convince the American people that immigration did not threaten its unity, but tended to produce an even finer type of unity. It failed because it did not take account of the true nature of group unity, of the conditions of its preservation, or of the actual consequences of such inroads upon unity as are involved in an immigration movement.

*   *   *

In this process of progressive adaptation is to be found the first basis of group differentiation. It is therefore important to understand just why and how this adaptation took place and what is the nature of the results.

It has been observed above that every living species is adapted to some particular environment and also that no two individuals of a given species are exactly identical. This last fact is due to the principle of variation which operates throughout all organic beings, and brings it about that no two members, even of the same brood from the same mother, are completely alike. It follows that some individuals are more closely adapted to the surrounding environment than others. As long as the environment remains constant those individuals which are most closely adapted are those that come nearest to the average or type of the species. Those individuals which vary minutely on either side of the average will be able to survive, though with a slight handicap. But those which differ too widely from the type will not be able to hold their own in the fierce struggle for existence and will be eliminated. Thus the typical features of the species are kept constant.

Now at any given time there are always some members of the species living on the very edge of the habitat, that is, in close proximity to a slightly different environment. Among the offspring of these individuals there will be some whose variations constitute a handicap in the regular environment but afford an advantage in the adjacent environment. Some of those with these peculiarities will almost certainly drift over into this new environment and so be able to survive. Of their offspring, those will have the best chance of survival in this new environment which inherit the favorable peculiarities of their parents. Thus this variation tends to be perpetuated. Furthermore, some of these offspring will have variations fitting them to move still farther into the new environment, and here the process will be repeated. Differences in environmental features are the cause of changes in the characteristics of species. Variations occur in all directions according to the law of chance, but only those variations are perpetuated which happen to accord with some slightly different environment into which the individual which possesses them may find his way. If for some reason the original environment undergoes a change the same process, of course, takes place. These developments are indescribably slow, but given sufficient time they will eventually produce a distinctly different type. This new type is at first known as a "variety" of the old species. But as the process goes on the changes at last become so marked that the new type can no longer be considered to belong to the old species: a new species has come into being.

It was undoubtedly by such a method as this that mankind first began to separate into distinct types. We know something of the pathways and directions by which the outposts of the species made their way by infinitesimal stages out of the original central Asian habitat into new environments. Certain well-defined channels led northward and northeastward, into the inhospitable plains of Siberia and eventually across the Bering Sea into the northwest corner of the North American continent and thence southward until the whole of the western hemisphere was peopled. Other channels led eastward into the fertile plains of China. Still others took a southwesterly direction and led the primitive pioneers who followed them into Asia Minor, Africa, and thence northward into Europe. In every case the spread of the human species could take place only so fast as the physical variations could be developed necessary for life in each new environment. And in every case it was the contact with a new environment which was responsible for the perpetuation of these variations.

As observed above, man alone of all the higher species has been able to carry this process of variation to the extremities of the earth without losing his specific unity. Instead of having several more or less closely related species of men, as there are species of wolves, or bears, or sparrows, we have one great inclusive human species divided up into a number of varieties. To these varieties we correctly apply the term "the races of man."

C. WHO IS THE AMERICAN: ETHNIC AMERICA IN ITS OWN DEFENSE, 1875–1924

How It Feels to Be a Problem

The Italians were among the most maligned and ill-treated of the new immigrants. As the number of Italian immigrants rose annually, near the turn of the century, bitter prejudice against them increased. From 1880–1900, the number of Italians landing in America grew from 12,000 to 100,000, and in the decade that followed the yearly average was over 200,000. These figures were not lost on the nativists. The New Orleans lynching of eleven Italians in 1891 was followed by the systematic murder of six Italian workers during the 1895 strike in the Colorado coal fields.

A year later, three Italians were dragged from a jail in a small Louisiana town and hanged. Moreover, to millions of Americans, Italian immigration was the Vatican's latest instrument through which it hoped to subvert the United States, and the stereotype of the ignorant, violent Italian was readily accepted.

Against this background of discrimination and prejudice, Gino Speranza, a writer and second-generation Italian-American, raised the questions of how it felt to be an Italian in the United States and what were the causes of the retardation of assimilation. In the course of discussing the factors that either speeded or retarded Americanization, the writer took up the matter of what was an American. To Speranza, being an American was mainly a state of mind or a spiritual experience, the product of a long process in which the newcomers were taught and permitted to experience the "good and enduring" things in Americanism.

SOURCE: Gino C. Speranza, **"How It Feels to Be a Problem,"** *Charities* (May 7, 1904), pp. 457–60.

The American nation seems to like to do some of its thinking aloud. Possibly this is true of other nations, but with this difference, that in the case of the American, the thinking aloud is not suppressed even when it deals with what may be termed the "country's guests." Older nations, perhaps because they lack the daring, self-sufficiency of the young, prefer, in similar cases, to think in a whisper. All countries have problems to grapple with, economic, political or social; but with America even the labor problem is popularly discussed as if its solution depended on that of the immigration problem.

Now, considering the large percentage of foreign born in the population of the United States, it is a strange fact how few Americans ever consider how very unpleasant, to say the least, it must be to the foreigners living in their midst to be constantly looked upon either as a national problem or a national peril. And this trying situation is further strained by the tone in which the discussion is carried on, as if it applied to utter strangers miles and miles away, instead of to a large number of resident fellow citizens. Perhaps this attitude may be explained by the fact that to the vast majority of Americans "foreigner" is synonymous with the popular conception of the immigrant as a poor, ignorant and uncouth stranger, seeking for better luck in a new land. But poverty and ignorance and uncouthness, even if they exist as general characteristics of our immigrants, do not necessarily exclude intelligence and sensitiveness. Too often, let it be said, does the American of common schooling interpret differences from his own standards and habits of life, as necessarily signs of inferiority. Foreignness of features or of apparel is for him often the denial of brotherhood. Often, again, the fine brow and aquiline nose of the Latin will seem to the American to betoken a criminal type rather than the impress of a splendid racial struggle.

Then there is another large class of "plain Americans" who justify a trying discussion of the stranger within the gates by the self-satisfying plea that the foreigner should be so glad to be in the "land of the free" that he cannot mind hearing a few "unpleasant truths" about himself.

This is not an attempt to show that the tide of immigration does not carry with it an ebb of squalor and ignorance and undesirable elements. It is rather an endeavor to look at the problem, as it were, *from the inside*. For if America's salvation from this foreign invasion lies in her capacity to assimilate such foreign elements, the first step in the process must be a thorough knowledge of the element that should be absorbed.

Many imagine that the record and strength of the American democracy suffice of themselves to make the foreigner love the new land and engender in him a desire to serve it; that, in other words, assimilation is the natural tendency. Assimilation, however, is a dual process of forces interacting one upon the other. Economically, this country can act like a magnet in drawing the foreigner to these shores, but you cannot rely on its magnetic force to make the foreign *an American*. To bring about assimilation the larger mass should not remain passive. It must attract, *actively attract,* the smaller foreign body.

It is with this in mind that I say that if my countrymen here keep apart, if they herd in great and menacing city colonies, if they do not learn your language, if they know little about your country, the fault is as much yours as theirs. And if you wish to reach us you will have to batter down some of the walls you have yourselves built up to keep us from you.

What I wish to examine, then, is how and what Americans are contributing to the process of the assimilation of my countrymen who have come here to live among them.

I have before me a pamphlet which a well-known American society prints for distribution among arriving immigrants. On the title page is the motto: *"A Welcome to Immigrants and Some Good Advice."* The pamphlet starts out by telling the arriving stranger that this publication is presented to him "by an American patriotic society, whose duty is to teach American principles"—a statement which must somewhat bewilder foreigners. Then it proceeds to advise him. In America, it tells him, "you need not be rich to be happy and respected." "In other countries," it proceeds, "the people belong to the government. They are called subjects. They are under the power of some Emperor, King, Duke or other ruler," which permits the belief that the patriotic author of this pamphlet is conversant mostly with mediaeval history. There are some surprising explanations of the constitution, showing as wide a knowledge of American constitutional history as of that of modern Europe—but space forbids their quotation. "If the common people of other countries had faith in each other, there would be no Czars, Kaisers and Kings ruling them under the pretext of divine right." This is certainly a gem of historical exposition.

Then, in order to make the stranger feel comfortable, it tells him, "you must be honest and honorable, clean in your person, and decent in your talk." Which, of course, the benighted foreigner reads as a new decalogue. With characteristic modesty the author reserves for the last praise of his country: "Ours," he says, "is the strongest government in the world, because it is the people's government." Then he loses all self-restraint in a patriotic enthusiasm, "We have more good land in cultivation than in all Europe. We have more coal, and oil, and iron and copper, than can be found in all the countries of Europe. We can raise enough foodstuffs to feed all the rest of the world. We have more railroads and navigable rivers than can be found in the rest of the civilized world. We have more free schools than the rest of the world. . . . So great is the extent (of our country), so varied its resources, that its people are not dependent on the rest of the world for what they absolutely need. Can there be any better proof that this is the best country in the world? Yes, there is one better proof. Our laws are better and more justly carried out."

Between such instruction and the welcome the immigrant gets from the immigration officials, he ought to feel that this is certainly the "best country in the world."

Perhaps the first impressions the foreigners receive are not a fair test of what it really feels to be a problem—because the initial adaptation to new and strange conditions is necessarily trying to any one.

The real test comes after—years after, perhaps—and it is this aftermath that I wish to examine. Perhaps I come from a hypersensitive race, and what I say of my people cannot apply to the immigrants of other nationalities, but close and constant contact with Italians of all classes on the one hand and twenty years of strenuous American living on the other, seem justification for voicing the sentiments of my countrymen among a people, many of whom look upon us as a menace. And the fact that though many suffer, yet few cry out, may be a further justification for one from their common average to speak for them.

Naturally, when one speaks of the Italian in America, the American thinks at once of the ubiquitous unskilled laborer. He thinks of him as a class or a mass composed of more or less picturesque elements, with no particular individual characteristics. This is especially true of the men who employ such a class. Through the padrone system of engaging men, the employer never comes to know the employed. He gives an order to the padrone to get him "five hundred dagoes." The men are supplied, they do their work and are passed on to other jobs. However practical this system may appear, it is based on a vicious mistake. The chief characteristic of the Italian is his individuality, and a system that treats him as one of a homogeneous mass is essentially wrong and cannot yield the best results. When the Irishman supplied the labor market in America, it may have been a simple thing to deal with him in masses; to apply that system to the Italian is to lose sight of elemental differences.

In endeavoring to graft the system employed in the case of Irish labor on the Italian, employers discovered a new element which they did not care to study or did not know how. So they tried to patch up the difficulty by the introduction of the padrone. This Italo-American middleman is for the laborer, to all intents and purposes, the real employer. How can you expect assimilation of this vast class of laborers when you uphold and maintain a system which completely isolates the class from its American superior? It may be argued that the padrone system is a necessity in dealing with large bodies of Italian laborers; but this is an argument which stops short in its conclusions. It is like claiming that an interpreter is necessary in addressing a foreigner; he is, unless you learn the foreign language. And, moreover, if you depend too much on the interpreter you will oftentimes find he is not interpreting correctly. Against this it may be urged that it is the business of the foreigner to adjust himself to his American employer; but how can he when you interpose a padrone?

Now, as a rule, padrones are of a type hardly calculated to teach their men what is best in American life. They are generally shrewd fellows with a good smattering of bad English and well versed in American boss methods. But they know their men well; they count on their ignorance and implicit confidence, on their helplessness and loyalty to the *compaesano*—be he right or wrong. Naturally, the padrone will endeavor to keep the laborer from all contact with his American superior; he will make himself the final arbiter and supreme power. I know of several instances where, in order to prevent an appeal to the contractor, the padrone has taught the laborer to fear his superior as a cruel and unapproachable person. Hence this vast foreign mass touches at no point the American element or touches it in a way to make them desire to avoid it.

Is it a wonder that the intensely sociable Italian herds with his fellows and will not mix? Foreign urban congestion is a real problem, but may it not be that the remedy has to come from others than the foreigners? You begin by drawing a sharp line against him; you distinguish him from others. The cultured among you persist in seeing in him only a wearying picturesqueness with a background of mediaeval romance and Roman greatness; the uncultured among you see in every *meridionale* a possible *mafioso*, in every *settentrionale* one more mouth to fill from that "bankrupt Italy."

The better disposed tell us we are hard workers and earn every cent we make; but even these speak as from master to man. Perhaps it is our friends that make us feel most keenly that we are a problem. They take us under their wing, they are zealous in their defense, they treat us like little children. They speak of the debt the world owes Italy, they benignantly, remind their countrymen that these foreigners have seen better days. It is extremely trying—this well-meant kindness that disarms criticism.

Of course, criticism by the stranger within your gates seems ungracious; but whenever it is attempted it is suppressed by this common question: "If you don't like it, why don't you go back?" The answer is never given, but it exists. For the majority of us this is our home and we have worked very hard for everything we have earned or won. And if we find matter for criticism it is because nothing is perfect; and if we institute comparisons it is because, having lived in two lands, we have more of the wherewithal of comparisons than those who have lived in only one country.

Then there is the American press. How is it aiding our assimilation? It would not be difficult to name those few newspapers in the United States which give space either as news or editorially, to non-sensational events or problems with which Europe is grappling. As regards Italy, there is such a dearth of information of vital importance that little, if anything, is known by the average American, of the economic or political progress of that country. Columns on Musolino, half-page headlines on the mafia, but never a word on the wonderful industrial development in northern Italy, never a notice of the financial policies that have brought Italian finances to a successful state!

What is the American press doing to help assimilate this "menacing" element in the republic?

"Why is it," was asked of a prominent American journalist, "that you print news about Italians which you would not of other nationalities?"

"Well, it is this way," was the answer, "if we published them about the Irish or the Germans we should be buried with letters of protest; the Italians do not seem to object."

It would be nearer the truth to say that they have learned the uselessness of objecting unless they can back up the objection by a "solid Italian vote."

One result of the unfriendliness of the popular American press is that it drives Italians to support a rather unwholesome Italian colonial press. Why should they read American papers that chronicle only the misdeeds of their compatriots? Better support a local press which, however poor and ofttimes dishonest, keeps up the courage of these expatriates by telling them what young Italy is bravely doing at home and abroad. But this colonial press widens the cleavage between the nations, puts new obstacles in the way of assimilation and keeps up racial differences.

To feel that we are considered a problem is not calculated to make us sympathize with your efforts in our behalf, and those very efforts are, as a direct result, very likely to be misdirected. My countrymen in America, ignorant though many of them are, and little in touch with Americans, nevertheless feel keenly that they are looked upon by the masses as a problem. It is, in part, because of that feeling that they fail to take an interest in American life or to easily mix with the natives. And though it may seem far-fetched, I believe that the feeling that they are unwelcome begets in them a distrust of those defenses to life, liberty and property which the new country is presumed to put at their disposal. They have no excess of confidence in your courts and it is not surprising, however lamentable, that the more hot-headed sometimes take the law into their own hands. You cannot expect the foreigner of the humbler class to judge beyond his experience—and his experience of American justice may be comprised in what he learns in some of the minor tribunals controlled by politicians, and in what he has heard of the unpunished lynchings of his countrymen in some parts of the new land. What appeal can the doctrine of state supremacy and federal non-interference make to him? Imagine what you would think of Italian justice if the American sailors in Venice, in resisting arrest by the constituted authorities, had been strung up to a telegraph pole by an infuriated Venetian mob, and the government at Rome had said, with the utmost courtesy: "We are very sorry and greatly deplore it, but we can't interfere with the autonomy of the province of Venetia!"

I am aware that the question is often asked: If these people are sensitive about being discussed as a problem and a menace, why do they come here? It is a question asked every day in the guise of an argument, a final and crushing argument. But is it really an argument? Is it not rather a question susceptible of a very clear and responsive answer. They come because this is a new country and because you invite them. If you really did not want them you could keep them out, as you have done with the Chinese.

Americans by Choice or Spirit

In May 1921 Congress passed a temporary immigration law which introduced the principle of numerical restriction based upon nationality. The legislation remained as a stopgap measure until the passage of the Johnson-Reed Act of 1924, the landmark law in the long fight for immigration restriction. The act avowedly sought to maintain the dominance of the basic stock by reducing the proportion of immigrants entering the United States from southern and eastern Europe.

Prior to the passage of the new legislation, the House Committee on Immigration and Naturalization held hearings. Rabbi Stephen A. Wise, the leading spokesman for American Jewry, appeared before the committee, and in the course of his attack on the whole quota concept of immigration he presented his thoughts on what constituted an American. He held that there were people who were Americans by "geography" or birth and those who were Americans by choice or spirit. To Wise, Americanism meant "a great deal more than birth in America, or even than that racial background which you might say lies back of birth." He went on to reject the idea that the old immigrants came here for loftier reasons than the new immigrants; political reasons for emigration from the Old World were no more compelling and valid than economic ones. Wise attacked the whole quota system of recent legislation as the product of racist thinking built around the idea of Nordic racial supremacy.

SOURCE: **Hearings: Immigration and Labor** (House Committee on Immigration and Naturalization, 68th Cong., 1st sess., Washington, 1924), pp. 340–45.

Doctor Wise. I hope, Mr. Chairman (although I am not a native American, that was disclosed already and I shall continue to reveal it by the imperfect manner of my speech), I trust that if no Jew on earth were to be denied admission to America by any laws or statutes or regulations that might be devised, I would, as an American, with of course, the Jewish ancestry and background and I hope passion for and love for fair play, be just as eager to stand up to-day and assert the right—not the vested right, Mr. Congressman, of any European in America, but the right of every man outside of America to be considered fairly and equitably and without discrimination, as long as and in so far as it be the policy of this country, without fear or favor, to admit to this country men who will become of American residence and citizenship, and men calculated to enhance the wealth and to enlarge and enrich the moral and spiritual resources of your and my country.

Reference has been had to my foreign birth. I am sorry to say that I was born outside of these United States, not because I cherish any presidential ambitions, Mr. Chairman (there is an organization in certain parts of the country that would probably see to it that I was not elected President of the United States, even if I should have been born here), but I can not help sympathizing very earnestly with the attitude of the gentleman who was heard to-day, who stated that, after all, birth is a matter of accident; but not wholly a matter of accident, for birth carries with it, I grant you, sir, lineage, ancestry, racial hopes, racial tradition, national stock.

Mr. Box. And recent environment?

Doctor Wise. And all those environmental influences of the past which we call heredity, and all that extraneous heredity which we name environment. I quite agree with you, sir. At the same time I feel, Mr. Chairman and gentlemen of the Immigration Committee of Congress, that there is just a little danger of our overstressing the circumstance of birth, as if one birth and one lineage carried with them certain high qualifications, and as if another birth and lineage or ancestry carried with them, inevitably, certain disqualifications.

Now it may shock some of you to hear me say that I think there are many men born in America who are not Americans in any high sense of the term—not Americans in any high sense of term. They are geographically Americans; they are Americans in so far as they were born within this territory which is denominated the United States of America; but that is because I labor under the disadvantage of being a minister. I assume that America is a spiritual entity and that physical birth does not open the door to that spiritual entity unless one have other qualifications. In other words, I ofttimes put it—

Mr. Box. But you do admit that the fact a man is born in America gives him a vested right here to the exclusion of others?

Doctor Wise. It gives him that vested right which inheres in physical birth on the American soil: absolutely, sir. But I hold, Mr. Chairman, that no one of you, with your high conception of American ideals, would venture to deny that Americanism means a great deal more than birth in America, or even than that racial background which you might say lies back of birth.

If I may be forgiven a rather personal allusion, may I cite this: I happened to tell Colonel Roosevelt (one of the older friends of whom I never found it difficult to call him by another name)— I happened to tell Colonel Roosevelt in 1893, soon after I first met him, 30 years ago, about my father, who was a student in the German University at Leipsic in 1865, and I told Colonel Roosevelt that I had learned from two friends of my father (all of them, of course, Europeans; all of them Austrians, as my father was an Austro-Hungarian) that the three of them stood together in the Leipsic University room on the day after the assassination of President Lincoln and my father turned to the other two men (he was then 21 years of age, born in 1844, and could not speak one word of the English language) and said, "Some day I am going to live in the land of Lincoln—some day I am going to live in the land of Lincoln." Colonel Roosevelt turned to me and said, "When did your father come to America?" I said, "He came to America in 1874, almost immediately after my birth in Budapest." "And your father," he said to me, "said he was going some day to live in the land of Lincoln, in 1865?" I said, "Yes." Colonel Roosevelt then said, "Then I should say that your father was an American nine years before he ever touched the soil of America with his foot, because the soul of America, was his in the making and in the hoping, long before he dreamed physically of becoming a part of the United States."

Forgive this digression, but I think it not without significance, because it bears just a little upon the discussion of a moment ago with respect to the vested right of any European. No European has any vested right in America, but, Mr. Chairman and gentlemen of the committee, I point out to you that we may commit a wrong even against those who have rights visavis or respecting us. We may wrong one man if we deny him that which on any arbitrary and indefensible grounds we grant to another. And, Mr. Chairman, I dissent most heartily from the notion, most earnestly and solemnly from the notion that just because XYZ in Czechoslovakia, Yugoslavia, Rumania, have no vested rights in America, therefore the United States of America can do no wrong to them if we exercise, as against them, an attitude which is discriminatory. Discrimination, even though it cloak itself under the name "selection," is always fundamentally and eternally unjust.

Mr. Box. You spoke of your father being an American before he came here—

Doctor Wise. I quoted Colonel Roosevelt, sir.

Mr. Box. I understand that.

Doctor Wise. I quoted Colonel Roosevelt, who was a fairly good authority on American problems.

Mr. Box. I understand that, and it was a very apt saying of Colonel Roosevelt. But is there not a vast difference between a man like your father, who felt an affinity for American life and who came here because there was that in him which drew him to the land of Lincoln, and the great number of people imported here at the instance of employers and seekers of cheap labor, who come to get a job? I do not mean your people; I mean is there not a vast difference between the old immigration which came, prompted by the motive you mentioned and others—is there not difference between the motives of such men as your honored father and the men who are gathered up by the importers of labor to supply the needs of production, as they call it, which means the needs of profit making? Now, is there not a difference?

Mr. Dickstein. Mr. Chairman, may I be permitted to answer—

Mr. Sabath. He knows there is no such immigration now.

Doctor Wise. Let me answer; I want to answer him. I will tell you, sir, my father was looking only for and requiring only a political and spiritual refuge; but tens and hundreds of thousands of eastern and southern Europeans need very much more than that; they need a fair and decent opportunity to live. They have a passion for a country in which there shall be one law—just and equitable. They need and hunger for economic subsistence for themselves and for their families. On the contrary, I am prepared to say that the poor fellow in Czechoslovakia who dreams of America as a place where he can rear his children with some degree of decency and comfort, hungers for America even more than my father did, who, after all, was thinking in terms only of the spirit; he needs America more than my father did, because my father was not driven in any part by economic necessity.

I trust I answer your question, sir. May I proceed for just a few moments and point out that I, for my part, answering the questions that might later have been addressed to me by members of this committee, wish to say that I consider any quota arrangement undesirable, unfeasible, and in spirit unjust. The question was asked before, why, then do you accept it? Because we bow before the force of a public law of our country—of this country—at this time. I do not assent to the wisdom of the present law touching immigration. I believe that we have a highly and wisely selective and sifting immigration arrangement in the law often referred to to-day, namely, the law of 1917; and I for my part do not at all believe that arbitrariness—and it is arbitrary—the principle of arbitrariness of the 1910 quota or the proposed 1890 quota in any wise enhances the selective results of the immigration policy and principle embodied in the law of 1917. On the contrary, I see now why men like Mr. Marshall and other wise, farseeing Americans were and of necessity were opposed to the law which is to-day upon the statute books. They foresaw that it might become what it is evidently calculated and planned that it shall become the beginning, the first step, the thin-edged wedge. You cure the evils—and I maintain they are evils—by aggravating and by deepening them through this new, indefensible, arbitrary arrangement. When I say "indefensible," I have in mind it can be defended only on one ground, that already animadverted upon, namely, the necessity of these United States of America to put a premium upon one type of immigration and put at a discount, virtually within the limits that decency inhibits, every other type of immigration.

One word, and only one word, in supplement to what has been said about the Nordic race. I am no anthropologist, but I remind you, gentlemen, that anthropology is an upstart science; it is one of the newest of sciences, and we sit here listening to dissertations upon anthropology. The distinguished gentleman from Colorado, Mr. Vaile, I believe, quoted to us from the book of Madison Grant

—Madison Grant, who, after all, represents a group of men who are experts on the care of menageries, a group of men who are concerned with the problems of the American Museum of Natural History, men with a most expert acquaintance with the problems which arise in and out of the management of the Museum of Natural History, but which hardly constitutes adequate qualification for a decision as to the worthiness of one group of aliens and the unworthiness of another group of aliens.

But, Mr. Chairman, are you and your associates prepared to maintain, as you in substance do, that the Latin races, that the Gaelic races, that the Slavic races, are to be counted as inferior and treated as inferior; are you prepared to continue the discussion of the Nordic race, originated by the son-in-law of one of the great prophets of the German Empire, namely, Stuart Chamberlain, that you wish to shut out the southerners, that you wish to shut the door in the face of that great people of France, which is not Anglo-Saxon, which is not Teutonic, which by no stretch of the imagination would be called Nordic—those European people, those southern people, those Mediterranean people, those akin to the Latin races? And what about the Latins themselves; what about the great Italian people, who, after all, have made some of the most artistic and spiritual contributions to the treasury of the human spirit? I am reminded, gentlemen, of the unhappy term you sometimes meet with, the term "Asiatics." Of course, there is a great distinction, and that distinction is ofttimes ignored, between the Near East and the Far East. The Near East includes principally Egypt and Asia Minor, and it never has been for a moment confused—the Near East—with the civilization of the Orient, with the Far East, which, after all, does represent the antipathetical point of view and attitude touching the whole of life.

I remember some years ago I asked Charles Cuthbert Hall, one of the noblest Christian gentlemen I have ever known, I said, "Mr. Hall, will you give one of a series of addresses to my people in my synagogue on the founders of the great religions of the day?" He said, "Which would you have me speak on?" I said, "On your own religion, Christianity, the religion of the East." He pondered for a moment and then he put out his hand and said, "Of course I will, Rabbi Wise." Christianity is a religion of the East; it is a religion that had its rise in Asia Minor; excepting for one or two of the expounders and apostles of Christianity, none of them ever left the soil of Asia.

I am not pleading to-day for Asiatic immigration: on the contrary, I insist there is a great gulf fixed between the Near East and the Far East, in spite of the fact that John, Peter, Paul, James, Matthew, and Luke, even the founder of Christianity Himself, were in a very real sense of the term Asiatics and of Asia. I protest against the contemptuous and derisive use of the term Near Easterner or Asiatic as if the Asiatic were a term of reproach. The fact is, nearly every man in this room, whether Jew or Christian, lives by the spirit of the things that have come to us out of Asia, out of the Near East, out of that tremendous group of figures, the greatest the world has ever known, who gave us after all, the Bible of the East and the Bible of the truth and spirit of God, the spirit of the God of Love, the God of Righteousness, and the God of all those things which you as Christians and I as Jew hold in common. And I think, Mr. Chairman and gentlemen, I feel deeply the eastern and southern immigrants of Europe have certain cultural contributions to make to the spirit of America. May I be permitted to say that I yield to no man in America my reverence for the great things of Anglo-Saxondom. I know some things about Anglo-Saxondom; I know, after all, America in the highest sense was founded by the Pilgrims of Virginia and by the Puritans of Massachusetts; I know they brought with them the old England and here established the new England; I know we are living on the basis of Anglo-Saxon law; I know some of our greatest institutions and ideals have come to us through Anglo-Saxondom and out of Anglo-Saxondom, and I remind you of what perhaps you have no time to recall, that much that is best in Anglo-Saxondom rests upon the Hebrew Bible. The Puritans who developed New England in the early seventeenth century were men who were called magpies in their own day, and I wonder if you happen to remember when the first constitution of the Colony of Massachusetts was written there was a provision at the close that "any problem undecided by the provisions of this instrument shall be referred to the appended book of Mosaic Law," the law of the Mosaic Commonwealth decided for the founders of America, whether in Virginia or Massachusetts. They rested themselves upon Bible truths, rested themselves upon the Bible ideal; that ideal which had no little part in the deepening and confirming of the American passion for freedom.

Forgive me if I say I do not think it chance or accident; I believe in all my heart it is providential design. In an outer room of that building the light from which first proclaims liberty to the rest of the world, there is inscribed the words taken from a chapter of the Book of Leviticus, a Mosaic law, "And he shall proclaim freedom throughout the land unto all the inhabitants thereof." I say it was providential design, for those men inevitably went back to these Bible ideals and the Bible passion for freedom. "Let my people go that they shall serve me," said He, and the founders of America went back to Bible ideals.

PART III
The Slum as a Home

———————

INTRODUCTION

Having survived the horrors of the crossing and the exploitation of runners and brokers at the port of debarkation, the immigrant faced the greater ordeal of terrible living and housing conditions. For wretchedness, there rarely has been the equal of the slums of major nineteenth-century American cities, particularly New York City. By the time of the Civil War, the modern slum had become an integral part of American city life.

The need for providing shelter for the many immigrants that poured into the early-nineteenth-century cities resulted in new forms of housing. The largest percentage of city dwellers, especially immigrants, rented living quarters. The type of urban dwellings that developed was influenced by the city's geography, transportation system and tradition. Along the horse-drawn lines of Chicago and St. Louis, the "three-decker" building, with the bottom floor rented, emerged. New York City's pattern of dwellings was dictated mainly by the narrowness of the island of Manhattan. Here, in the 1850s and 1860s, old buildings in the lower part of the city were either converted or torn down to be replaced by the "railroad" type of house or early tenement. Into these structures were crowded tens of thousands of immigrants. One of the largest, Gotham Court, a five-story edifice lacking plumbing and heating, housed about five hundred tenants.

The tenement became the symbol of slum living. Overcrowding, disease and filth were the conditions of tenement life. Speaking of the New York City tenements in 1865, a city agency revealed, "The Tenement houses, for size, numbers, and multitudes of persons who inhabit them are unequalled in any city in the civilized world." Making a tour of wards heavily populated by immigrants, a veteran newspaper reporter was shocked by what he saw. To enter a house on Baxter Street, he had to pass through a hog pen, and he found a room measuring eight by twelve in which fifteen persons slept on a vermin-covered floor. A bedroom at 14 Roosevelt Street had two feet of water whenever it rained. Many houses were situated near stables, fat-boiling plants and slaughter-houses. Samuel Gompers, the famous American labor leader, whose family had lived in a building located opposite a slaughter-house, remembered, "All day long we could see the animals being driven to slaughter and one could hear the turmoil and cries of the animals. The neighborhood was filled with the penetrating, sickening odor." He could not eat meat for many months after the family had moved to another neighborhood.

One of the worst aspects of the tenements was the cellar dwellings. In 1871 there were 25,000 persons living in New York City in these quarters. The cellar abodes in the lower part of the city were particularly deplorable. That part of Manhattan, being very flat and lacking adequate sewerage, did not afford rain and waste means of descending toward the rivers. At low tide, when the mouths of the sewers were open, a terrible odor was forced up through all of the street openings by either an east or west wind. The stench drifted through the cellar dwellings' openings especially during the summer when windows and doors were kept open.

The introduction of the "dumbbell" type of tenement in the late 1870s was hailed as an improvement because it provided for at least a window in every bedroom as required by the Tenement House Law of 1879. The rapid growth of the city, however, resulted in crowding even greater numbers into the dumbbell structures. These buildings then became the main target for housing reformers. By 1900, 42,700 tenements in New York City housed 1,585,000 people. Though not in New York City's class for substandard housing, Boston, Cleveland, Cincinnati and Chicago had their own slums.

The heavy nineteenth-century influx of immigrants also caused residential areas of the larger cities to resemble a mosaic of immigrant neighborhoods. Nationality groups tended to live in certain sections. Eventually the newer immigrants displaced the older ones. For example, New York City's Lower East Side first was occupied by the Irish and Germans, and then the Italians replaced the Irish and the Jews the Germans. Sometimes the patterns followed provincial rather than nationality lines; in New York City, instead of one "Little Italy," there were districts of Neapolitans, Calabrians and northern Italians.

The immigrants' tendency to congregate in urban areas continued through the nineteenth century. The Dillingham Report of 1910 revealed that an even larger percentage of the new immigrants settled in cities than that of the old immigration. In addition, the new immigrants tended to live in larger cities than their predecessors. The arrival of over five million newcomers in the 1880s produced some striking figures of urban living. In 1890, Greater New York had more foreign-born residents than any city in the world, and it had twice as many Irish as lived in Dublin and as many Germans as in Hamburg.

One of the more serious aspects of the growing concentration of immigrants in American cities was the continuing pattern of immigrant poverty. Throughout the nineteenth century, a high percentage of paupers in American cities were foreign-born. Moreover, since there was a close relationship between poverty and crime, it was not surprising that a high incidence of crime existed in immigrant neighborhoods. The notorious Five Points of New York City was an area of heavy Irish concentration. In 1860, when half of the city's population was foreign-born, about 80 per cent of those convicted of crimes were immigrants.

The immigrant slums also presented serious health and sanitation problems. Methods of removing waste and providing for decent drinking water were totally inadequate during most of the nineteenth century. As late as the 1870s, there were only a few miles of sewers in cities like New York, Boston and Chicago, and these were inadequate. The sewerage of most cities was emptied into nearby rivers. The East and Hudson rivers received New

York City's wastes while the residents of Chicago complained of the stench that came from the refuse in the Chicago River.

Crowding, poor sewerage, filth and poor drinking water exposed nineteenth-century cities to terrible epidemics. Yellow fever, typhus, typhoid and cholera were not uncommon visitors to the nation's urban centers. As late as 1865, there was a typhus outbreak in New York City, and a year later cholera took over a thousand lives in that city. Most of the victims lived in those wards with large immigrant populations. In 1878 Memphis was struck by a yellow fever outbreak which caused nearly five thousand deaths. Not until the late 1890s were the full implications of dirty drinking water and the importance of adequate sanitation duly understood by urban leaders.

An increased concern for the life-style of urbanites, especially those in the slums, led to an important reform movement in the late nineteenth and early twentieth centuries. The way was led by the work of social workers such as Jane Addams, the efforts of journalists like Jacob Riis and the research of groups such as the Charities Publication Committee. Lawrence Veiller, one of the early professional sociologists, probably had more to do with the improvement of housing than anyone. Under his urging, a state commission was created in 1900 to study tenement housing conditions and recommend legislation. His ideas were incorporated into the Tenement Law of 1901, which forbade the further construction of the dumbbell dwelling and required improvements in existing buildings. The commission created by the new law processed nearly half a million complaints in its first twelve years. By 1920, forty other large cities, usually following the New York model, had tightened their building codes and had provided for improved enforcement.

A. CONDITIONS OF LIFE IN THE ETHNIC GHETTO

Street Gangs and Ghetto Society

As soon as the immigrant family arrived, by necessity they were forced to rent unsanitary quarters which had been vacated by their predecessors. That being the case, the children were raised in "tenements, in attics or cellars, in rooms unlighted and unheated, where broken-down stairways, rotten woodwork, defective plumbing and overflowing garbage boxes all [taught] a disregard for laws that [were] not enforced."

The head of this household, perhaps an unskilled worker, would take what employment was offered, sometimes paying the greater part of his wages to an exploitive employment agency or agent. In the hope of raising the family's standard of living, the mother too became a wage earner. She would take in washing, scrub floors by day or clean office buildings by night. Consequently, the parents were unable to pay close attention to the needs of their children. Their children then took to the streets and sought the fellowship which was no longer available at home. There they joined the gang, lived the life of the gang and shortly became juvenile criminals. Soon, street gangs became endemic to ghetto society.

Jacob Riis, a New York City police reporter, was an eyewitness observer to the ghetto street gang of the 1890s. In "The Harvest of Tares," a chapter from his book *How the Other Half Lives* (1891), he described the juvenile delinquent as "the ripe fruit of tenement-house growth."

SOURCE: Jacob Riis, **How the Other Half Lives** (New York, 1891), pp. 164–66, 169–71, 173–74.

Along the water-fronts, in the holes of the dock-rats, and on the avenues, the young tough finds plenty of kindred spirits. Every corner has its gang, not always on the best of terms with the rivals in the next block, but all with a common programme: defiance of law and order, and with a common ambition: to get "pinched," *i.e.,* arrested, so as to pose as heroes before their fellows. A successful raid on the grocer's till is a good mark, "doing up" a policeman cause for promotion. The gang is an institution in New York. The police deny its existence while nursing the bruises received in nightly battles with it that tax their utmost resources. The newspapers chronicle its doings daily, with a sensational minuteness of detail that does its share toward keeping up its evil traditions and inflaming the ambition of its members to be as bad as the worst.

The gang is the ripe fruit of tenement-house growth. It was born there, endowed with a heritage of instinctive hostility to restraint by a generation that sacrificed home to freedom, or left its country for its country's good. The tenement received and nursed the seed. The intensity of the American temper stood sponsor to the murderer in what would have been the common "bruiser" of a more phlegmatic clime. New York's tough represents the essence of reaction against the old and the new oppression, nursed in the rank soil of its slums. Its gangs are made up of the American-born sons of English, Irish, and German parents. They reflect exactly the conditions of the tenements from which they sprang. Murder is as congenial to Cherry Street or to Battle Row, as quiet and order to Murray Hill. The "assimilation" of Europe's oppressed hordes, upon which our Fourth of July orators are fond of dwelling, is perfect. The product is our own.

Such is the genesis of New York's gangs. Their history is not so easily written. It would embrace the largest share of our city's criminal history for two generations back, every page of it dyed red with blood. The guillotine Paris set up a century ago to avenge its wrongs was not more relentless, or less discriminating, than this Nemesis of New York. The difference is of intent. Murder with that was the serious purpose; with ours it is the careless incident, the wanton brutality of the moment. Bravado and robbery are the real purposes of the gangs; the former prompts the attack upon the policeman, the latter that upon the citizen. Within a single week last spring, the newspapers recorded six murderous assaults on unoffending people, committed by young highwaymen in the public streets. How many more were suppressed by the police, who always do their utmost to hush up such outrages "in the interests of justice," I shall not say. There has been no lack of such occurrences since, as the records of the criminal courts show. In fact, the past summer has seen, after a period of comparative quiescence of the gangs, a reawakening to renewed turbulence of the East Side tribes, and over and over again the reserve forces of a precinct have been called out to club them into submission. It is a peculiarity of the gangs that they usually break out in spots, as it were. When the West Side is in a state of eruption, the East Side gangs, "lie low," and when the toughs along the North River are nursing broken heads at home, or their revenge in Sing Sing, fresh trouble breaks out in the tenements east of Third Avenue. This result is brought about by the very efforts made by the police to put down the gangs. In spite of local feuds, there is between them a species of ruffianly Freemasonry that readily admits to full fellowship a hunted rival in the face of the common enemy. The gangs belt the city like a huge chain from the Battery to Harlem—the collective name of the "chain gang" has been given to their scattered groups in the belief that a much closer connection exists between them than commonly supposed—and the ruffian for whom the East Side has become too hot, has only to step across town and change his name, a matter usually much easier for him than to change his shirt, to find a sanctuary in which to plot fresh outrages. The more notorious he is, the warmer the welcome, and if he has "done" his man he is by common consent accorded the leadership in his new field.

.　.　.

In Poverty Gap there were still a few decent people left. When it comes to Hell's Kitchen, or to its compeers at the other end of Thirty-ninth Street over by the East River, and further down First Avenue in "the Village," the Rag Gang and its allies have no need of fearing treachery in their periodical battles with the police. The entire neighborhood takes a hand on these occasions, the women in the front rank, partly from sheer love of the "fun," but chiefly because husbands, brothers, and sweethearts are in the fight to a man and need their help. Chimney-tops form the staple of ammunition then, and stacks of loose brick and paving-stones, carefully hoarded in upper rooms as a prudent provision against emergencies. Regular patrol posts are established by the police on the housetops in times of trouble in these localities, but even then they do not escape whole-skinned, if, indeed, with their lives; neither does the gang. The policeman knows of but one cure for the tough, the club, and he lays it on without stint whenever and wherever he has the chance, knowing right well that, if caught at a disadvantage, he will get his outlay back with interest. Words are worse than wasted in the gang-districts. It is a blow at sight, and the tough thus accosted never stops to ask questions. Unless he is "wanted" for some signal outrage, the policeman rarely bothers with arresting him. He can point out half a dozen at sight against whom indictments are pending by the basketful, but whom no jail ever held many hours. They only serve to make him more reckless, for he knows that the political backing that has saved him in the past can do it again. It is a commodity that is only exchangeable "for value received," and it is not hard to imagine what sort of value is in demand. The saloon, in ninety-nine cases out of a hundred, stands behind the bargain.

For these reasons, as well as because he knows from frequent experience his own way to be the best, the policeman lets the gangs alone except when they come within reach of his long night-stick. They have their "club-rooms" where they meet, generally in a tenement, sometimes under a pier or a dump, to carouse, play cards, and plan their raids; their "fences," who dispose of the stolen property. When the necessity presents itself for a descent upon the gang after some particularly flagrant outrage, the police have a task on hand that is not of the easiest. The gangs, like foxes, have more than one hole to their dens. In some localities, where the interior of a block is filled with rear tenements, often set at all sorts of odd angles, surprise alone is practicable. Pursuit through the winding ways and passages is impossible. The young thieves know them all by heart. They have their runways over roofs and fences which no one else could find. Their lair is generally selected with special reference to its possibilities of escape. Once pitched upon, its occupation by the gang, with its ear-mark of nightly symposiums, "can-rackets" in the slang of the street, is the signal for a rapid deterioration of the tenement, if that is possible. Relief is only to be had by ousting the intruders.

.   .   .

A bare enumeration of the names of the best-known gangs would occupy pages of this book. The Rock Gang, the Rag Gang, the Stable Gang, and the Short Tail Gang down about the "Hook" have all achieved bad eminence, along with scores of others that have not paraded so frequently in the newspapers. By day they loaf in the corner-groggeries on their beat, at night they plunder the stores along the avenues, or lie in wait at the river for unsteady feet straying their way. The man who is sober and minds his own business they seldom molest, unless he be a stranger inquiring his way, or a policeman and the gang twenty against the one. The tipsy wayfarer is their chosen victim, and they seldom have to look for him long. One has not far to go to the river from any point in New York. The man who does not know where he is going is sure to reach it sooner or later. Should he foolishly resist or make an outcry—dead men tell no tales. "Floaters" come ashore every now and then with pockets turned inside out, not always evidence of a post-mortem inspection by dock-rats. Police patrol the rivers as well as the shore on constant look-out for these, but seldom catch up with them. If overtaken after a race during which shots are often exchanged from the boats, the thieves have an easy way of escaping and at the same time destroying the evidence against them; they simply upset the boat. They swim, one and all, like real rats; the lost plunder can be recovered at leisure the next day by diving or grappling. The loss of the boat counts for little. Another is stolen, and the gang is ready for business again.

The Daily Struggle for Air and Space

Though the immigrant ghetto dweller created no new health problems, he complicated existing ones. Thus, some educational programs were undertaken to make the newcomers aware of the advances in preventive medicine. Although public health officials were sincere in their attempts to correct the deplorable conditions in the working-class districts, they found it extremely difficult to explain to those who understood little English the precautions to be taken to prevent communicable disease. In addition to the language barrier, the fact that most of these people had come from rural surroundings and had had no experience with congested urban life further compounded an already hard-pressed situation.

In the selection which follows, "Tuberculosis and the Italians in the United States," Dr. Antonio Stella examined the relationship of this dreaded illness to the "daily struggle for air and space."

SOURCE: Antonio Stella, **"Tuberculosis and the Italians in the United States,"** *Charities* (May 7, 1904), pp. 486–89.

In spite of the traditional renown of Italy as the paradise of Europe and one of the most healthful countries on earth, notwithstanding the fact that she really yields less victims annually to consumption than any other nation on the continent under similar demographic conditions, it is an undoubted fact, and a truth sadly brought daily to the attention of physicians, social workers, and others in a position to know, that tuberculosis is very prevalent among the Italians emigrated to these shores.

To have an idea of the alarming frequency of consumption among Italians, especially in the large cities of the Union, one must not look for exact information to the records of the local boards of health and the registry of vital statistics; they are, for the very reason of the mobility of the Italian emigration, very fallacious, and show a low figure; but one must follow the Italian population as it moves in the tenement districts; study them closely in their daily struggle for air and space; see them in the daytime crowded in sweat-shops and factories; at night heaped together in dark windowless rooms; then visit the hospitals and dispensaries; and finally watch the outgoing steamships, and count the wan emaciated forms, with glistening eyes and racking cough, that return to their native land with a hope of recuperating health, but ofttimes only to find a quicker death.

This desire and tendency on the part of all Italians, whether rich or poor, to go back to their homes as soon as informed that they are affected with phthisis, is the chief cause of the discrepancy between the *actual high* number of consumptives existing among the Italians in the United States and the *official low* figures of the various health boards.

* * *

From some tenements in Elizabeth and Mulberry street, there have been as many as twelve and fifteen cases of consumption reported to the Board of Health since 1894. But how many were *never* reported? How many went back to Italy? How many moved away to other districts?

My personal experience with some of the houses in that particular neighborhood is that the average has been not less than thirty or forty cases of infection for each tenement yearly, the element of house-infection being so great. I remember some rear houses in Elizabeth street, and one in Mott street, now torn down, through the operations of the new tenement law, that yielded as many as twenty-five cases in the course of a year to my personal knowledge alone.

And how could it be otherwise?

When we consider the infectious character of tuberculosis on the one side, and the overcrowded and filthy conditions of some tenements on the other, where a population of men, women and children is herded together at the rate of eight and ten in every three rooms (in some "flats" on Elizabeth street this number can often be doubled), a population, besides, made up chiefly of agriculturists, fresh yet from the sunny hills and green valleys of Tuscany and Sicily, abruptly thrown into unnatural abodes and dark sweat-shops—a population, at that, over-worked, underfed, poorly clad, curbed with all the worries and anxieties of the morrow, and only free, thank God!—from the worst ally of consumption—alcoholism—where could the Koch bacillus find victims more prepared, where a soil more fertile than among such surroundings?

. . .

No one will deny that the integrity of our respiratory organs depends chiefly on the quantity and quality of air we breathe. Every individual in normal condition should have at least 35 cubic meters of air as it is reckoned for hospitals, and the air we breathe in should not contain more than one per cent of all the expired air. In many tenements, on account of the overcrowding, the quantity of air left for each person is reduced to three or four cubic meters, and the expired air in the sleeping-rooms represents one-half or one-sixth of all the air available. We can well say, then, that the atmosphere of those places is largely made up of the emanations from the bodies of the various persons living together.

What deleterious effect on the lungs and on the system in general the sojourn and sleep in these rooms must have, is beyond all calculation. The haematosis and oxygenation are first affected, and then appears that train of obscure and insidious symptoms (persistent anaemia, progressive fatigue, emaciation, etc.), which represent the ante-tubercular stage, and actually prepare the ground for the bacillary invasion.

Those that feel this change most keenly, and fall victims to tuberculosis with marked rapidity, are not the second generation of immigrants, as generally believed, but the very first arrivals, especially those coming from the rural districts of Italy, unaccustomed yet to the poisoned atmosphere of city life.

Among those—and they are the large majority—who seek work in factories and shops, instead of pursuing their natural occupations in the open air, the stigmata of progressive physiological deterioration and general low vitality are most apparent. Six months of life in the tenements are sufficient to turn the sturdy youth from Calabria, the brawny fisherman of Sicily, the robust women from Abruzzi and Basilicata, into the pale, flabby, undersized creatures we see, dragging along the streets of New York and Chicago, such a painful contrast to the native population! Six months more of this gradual deterioration, and the soil for the bacillus tuberculosis is amply prepared.

For the Italians, though, besides the abrupt passage from rural to urban life, and the unsanitary housing accommodations, which stand among the foremost influences responsible for the spread of tuberculosis among them, another potent factor must be mentioned, and this refers to certain trades and occupations, that are especially favored by our countrymen, and which may well be called phthisiogenic, on account of the important role they play in the development of tuberculosis.

Suffice it here to mention the rag-sorters, sweepers, bootblacks, hotel cleaners, continually exposed to the inhalation of dust contaminated with dried tubercular sputum; the plasterers, marble and stone cutters, cigar makers, printers, pressmen, upholsterers, cabinet makers, barbers, tailors, brass and glass workers, who all stand near the head of the list in the mortality from consumption, and among whom we find thousands of our Italian immigrants.

In many of those occupations, besides the direct irritation to the bronchial mucous membrane from the inhalation of dust, the work itself requires a sitting position (cigar makers, tailors), in which the chest is bent forward, and thus prevents the expansion of the lungs, and directly interferes with the proper aeration of the pulmonary apices.

Still worse is the condition where the sweat-shop system flourishes at home, either as extra work, done late in the night, by young men and women already exhausted by ten hours of work in a crowded factory, or as a regular practice, by poor housewives, desirous of adding to their husbands' earnings.

Words can hardly describe the pathetic misery of these Italian women compelled to sew two or three dozen of pants for forty cents, using up their last spark of energy to make life better, when in fact they only accomplish their self-destruction. For their health is usually already drained by a too-productive maternity and periods of prolonged lactation; they live on a deficient, if not actually insufficient, diet; they sleep in dark, damp holes, without sunshine and light, and have already had enough to exhaust them, with the raising of a large family and the strain of hard housework.

This practice explains in a measure the somewhat higher death-rate from phthisis of Italian women than men, especially among Sicilians, and the fact that we often find among them consumption in the quick form, that is, miliary tuberculosis of the subacute or the very acute type, which, rather than a clinical rarity, is of quite common occurrence in this class of patients.

. . .

In view of these facts and the present state of our emigration, we must then consider the prevalence of tuberculosis among Italians as a function of their special economic and social conditions in their new environment, and if any remedies can be expected in the future to stop the spread of the scourge among them, they must be found in the betterment of those conditions and thorough change of their present aspirations.

. . .

Not every one knows that the Italians in this country represent almost exclusively the working class, and in some quarters the very poor class. To raise them to a higher social level, economically speaking, besides being a matter of slow evolution, implies a problem of such magnitude and such distant realization at the present, that we can only hint at it in passing by, and leave the social workers and economists the full discussion of it.

B. THE OPPRESSION OF THE TENEMENTS

"Woe in Strata; Poverty . . . and Filth in Layers"

Long before Jacob Riis, the late-nineteenth-century reformer, called attention to *How the Other Half Lives* others had become concerned with the problem of housing in American cities. A New York *Star* reporter was struck by the different grades of degradation that existed among and within the tenements. For example, the cellar abodes of Water Street were "lower" than those of the

Five Points, and those of the Five Points were lower than those of Fifth Avenue. Similarly there were varying grades of tenements. Generally the worst tenements were occupied by the poorest people, the laborers and the lowest elements in the socioeconomic scale. Moreover, a particular tenement might even have its own class structure graded by floors. In an article entitled "Woe in Strata" the *Star* reporter did a sociological study of one of the city's tenements that recently had been erected on a midtown street.

SOURCE: New York *Star,* August 21, 1870. **Woe in Strata**

Tenement Houses and Their Horrors

Poverty, Crime, Starvation and Filth in Layers—The Height of Tenements and the Depth of Crime—Awful Revelations—How the Landlords Squeeze the Poor to Make a Profit

That one half the world does not know how or where the other half lives, is a dreadful truth. And if the unwitting half had some notion of the unwotten half's manner of habitation, it is still questionable whether the sufferer would cease to endure or the wealthy to be oblivious of the sufferer's condition. The instinct of residence somewhere, bred and nourished the love for home, which can be bounded by the mud walls of a hovel, or the marble corridors of a regal palace. Man must live somewhere, whether in the cave habitations of the Troglodytes, in the trees of the Malayan Dyaks, in the rice boats of the Chinese rivers, in the turf thatched cottages of Ireland, in the shanties of the East Side, in the brownstone piles of the Avenue, in the tent of nomadic Arabs, in the wagon of the settler, in the hut of the frontiersman, in the tenement house of the Fourth Ward.

The tenement-house system, mal-administered as it is, stands responsible for

HALF THE DANGEROUS CLASS

now so largely on the increase, and for which the defences of our society are altogether inadequate. Its workings are apparent in the shiftless, nomadic, unhappy characteristics of a great portion of our laboring community. It effects all the mischievous demoralization on which disorder so generally depends. It abolishes the attachment to home, which is the sheet anchor of society, and casts its victim abroad with less to connect them with comfortable stability than the relation of the limpet to his rock. It saps the ties that bind the young and restless to the interests of order, by bringing them up within the influences of constant riot and turbulence, by offering them no attraction to domestic tranquility, by depriving them of all chances for the soft attention of household happiness and of sincere neighborly intercourse.

Perhaps there is hardly

A CRIMINAL OF DESPERATE CHARACTER

who cannot be traced to a tenement house when his habitation is a matter of police research. And of the more ignoble and vicious criminals an immense majority will be found to have come to the criminal surface from the criminal dregs of a low-class tenement house. Their constitution, as we have said before, fosters lawlessness and debases fast and permanently all respect for twin institutions of law and order.

THE TYPICAL TENEMENT HOUSE

of New York is as local as the "blocks" of Chicago and Cincinnati. Nowhere but in New York could they be permitted, by the careless contempt of the influential and the wealthy, to contain so large an account of misery as at present fills them all.

There are several varieties of the article, all of which possess distinctive features. Some of them approximate closely to the furnished hotels of Paris. Others, again, are little better than the pauper lodging-houses of London. Some of them are lofty edifices, reared in an atmosphere of respectability. Others are

EXAGGERATED HOVELS,

filled to overflowing with the dissolute parasites of society and their dirty and drunken families. Some are not destitute of the delicate comforts of a detached and separate home roof. Others compress degraded humanity into limits of space, of cleanliness and decency, into which no hog-pen could squeeze its unfragrant inmates.

The best and most elegant variety of the superior tenement-house "in an unexceptionable neighborhood" may be found in some of the mid-town cross-streets. Some speculative capitalist has probably run up, at lightning speed, and with rather more care for the condition of his purse than the comfort of his tenants, a pretentious block of stores. As soon as they are let the second floor is generally occupied by the lessees of the shops below. They, perhaps, are also responsible for the high floors. Having no personal use for the amazing number and variety of rooms thus placed at their disposal, they immediately advertise a "desirable suite" on each landing. The advertisements are answered and an astonishing mixed crowd of individuals take possession of the building. The most curious and heterogeneous collections of furniture arrive, and variety in every floor, almost in every room, indicates the distinctive proprietary interest of the house. On the third floor probably is a decent mechanic, with wages of $25 or $30 a week. Perhaps his family, including as a matter of course, a squalling baby, only demands the accommodation of four rooms. A few cheap articles of furniture are crowded into the remainder, which are duly let to young and long suffering men of respectable occupation and character. The lower floor tenants therefore have a tenant with a tenant. Upstairs again on the fourth floor probably resides a dressmaker or milliner, with a drunken husband and a half a dozen weary apprentices. She may squeeze three of the latter into a small hall bedroom and eke out her own rent by distributing it among her own tenants. On the fifth floor, probably, are two or three females who never meet but to quarrel over their respective water privileges, and who do everything in their power to disturb and implicate in their wars the unoffensive neutral below them. Way up, under the sky, on the sixth floor, are three wild, noisy families which, as a matter of course, are just as well off, as regards the number of their children, as they are lacking in less vivacious but more current wealth.

THE SECOND FLOOR PEOPLE

are exclusive, and rather look down upon the tenants overhead, while they scarcely do more than notice the monthly recurrence of the attic families on rent day. The daughters may flirt with the young men lodging up stairs, and the frequent rencontres on the stairs or in the passage may lead to consequences of a more serious nature. But in all probability the second floor has a young male boarder or two of its own, and in such a case the amatory attentions of the young ladies are confined to their own direct tenants instead of being allowed to fasten on the more elevated youths who look down upon their lessees in the light of landlord and superior.

THE THIRD FLOOR PEOPLE

are a quiet sober set, yet who pay their bills promptly, who are never behindhand in their rent, and who exercise a paternal supervision over their two or three young and naturally erratic lodgers. They furnish their rooms with dull but scrupulously well-brushed carpets, with irreproachable, though slippery horse-hair sofas and chairs, with highly respectable, though woodeny and knubbly beds, with gorgeously impossible pictures, of which the frames and the variety of paint laid on are more remarkable than any mere superficial, esthetic point of superiority. They look rather pityingly on the dressmaker overhead, and may exchange remarks on minor topics three times a day, with some of the apprentices. As to the top floor they profess a clearly contemptuous ignorance.

THE FOURTH FLOOR TENANTS

are a pale, sickly set, in whose ears ring perpetually the clatter of sewing machines, and whose daily toil is as monotonous as it is under paid. Their conversation is as feeble and colorless as themselves. They read the *Chimney Corner* and the *Fireside Companion* when the brief holiday interval comes in between their hours of work, and all of them look for the day when a knightly cavalier shall rescue them from the dragon Toil and woo their bonely hands in marriage. All but one, and she, the mistress, wakes up every now and again from her few day dreams to wait on her drunken prize in the next room, for whose maintenance in idleness and detestable small vice, the needles are principally piercing other people's clothes. They are only sorry that the life tide has no faster ebb, if it must ebb to its utmost before a bright and blessed turning can ensue.

THE FIFTH FLOOR PEOPLE

are noisy and clamorous, always naggling with one another, and always in a state of warfare among themselves. They are, as a rule, backward with their rent, but not behindhand with excuses for its non-appearance on the day when it is due. Their rooms are apologetically furnished. They are fearfully unclean, and have a habit of strolling about the passages in a state of acute undress. The men attached respectively to each of them are vigorous smokers, and affect the cheaper and nastier varieties of tobacco. Slop pails are fairly numerous about the passages, and fairly well filled with domestic garbage. They generally end their tenancy by a reluctant evacuation of the premises for which they are in arrears.

THE SIXTH FLOOR PEOPLE

are of a low order, under a cloud most of the time, unreasonably jubilant on other scattered occasions. Their elevation preserves the respectable tenants from too close a connection with their broils, their battles, and their sprees, while their immediate under-holders are of too disreputable a character to be much disturbed by the competitive turbulence overhead. They have but little to pay and they generally pay it. They never pretend to any acquaintance with the house inmates below the floor just underneath them, and with these even they are never intimate. They are content with the scantiest imitational furniture. They affect the same license in matters of dress, or, rather, undress, as the noisy crowd below them, and while their manners are, perhaps, less corrupted, are naturally more boisterous and less desirable as neighbors.

This is a fair representation of a tenement house of the better class. Sometimes, of course, the gradations are not as distinctly marked, but to all pertain the unpleasant characteristics inseparable from the co-operative system of householding. The variety of interests in the house, the imaginary or actual social degrees of importance attached to each floor, the mixed noises, the mixed smells, the mixed everything, make the very best of them a very undesirable place of residence for anybody who is fortunate enough to have an alternative.

But if the better class of tenement houses can be so repulsive and so forbidding to those who are sensible of delicate instincts, what will the poorer and unfortunately more disgusting varieties suggest? Built for the poor by the rich, they embody in their dumb brick and mortar all the neglect which capital shows to labor when labor has done all it can for capital and has no more in its power.

They are let furnished—with conditions that degrade, with inseparable influences that corrupt, with effects that created misery, and with other effects that intensify it. They are, most of them, designed with deliberate, with wanton disregard for the pressing necessities that even poverty is environed by in such narrow limits as are imposed by the cupidity of these builders. Literally, flesh and blood is squeezed into hard cash.

CUBIC FEET OF AIR

are stolen by the thousand from those who have a free and inalienable right to its inhalation. Inlets of health and outlets of foul breath, foul smells, foul organic corruption, are blocked up, lest a stray dollar should flutter from the landlord's grip through the sanitary loophole. Bonner's horses breathe sweeter air, and swallow more of it than the poor who are always with us and for whom the familiarity of poverty has bred among us such direful contempt.

The vilest and most pestilential tenement-dens are of course to be found where the poor are attracted by cheapness. To this, all else is sacrificed. They forget the chances of life and death, the certainty of squalor, the terrible unseen concomitants which invisibly conduct to crime. The cheap accommodation, however monstrously dear it may be otherwise, attracts their regard, and they mutually huddle together in joint wretchedness.

IN THE FOURTH WARD

these tenements are generally numerous. For the most part they are vast brick piles, dingy without, from their very internal foulness; on the ground floor, a rum shop; in the attics, death and disease. They are often the hideous fungi extending from a fortune made out of poisonous whiskey. Venders of the great moral virus who have turned human depravity into wealth, and who have made the vitiated appetites of others the stepping-stones on which they themselves proceed to fortune, take a fiendish revenge on their dupes by building, with the money out of which they have been deluded, these monster hot-houses of wretchedness, of squalor, of sickness, and of crime.

The pavement at the base of one of these woeful piles is awfully uneven, and

SLIPPERY WITH PESTILENTIAL STEAMS.

A sullen gutter stagnates on each side of the street. On these a thick, green, oily scum, which sometimes turns to purple, invariably mantles. Garbage, decayed and decaying vegetation, filthy rags, filthy pieces of wood, fragments of boots, fragments of food, fragments of dress, slimy bits of ribbon, sloopery hats, all these and a thousand leavings of the left poor, combine to rot and to fill the simmering air with the fumes of putrefaction.

The crazy door is always open. So rusty are the hinges that they have forgotten how to move. The paint is blistered, and the sun has forced great cracks to rend the unseasoned panels. The entrance hall reeks with the foul, greasy steam of dirty flesh, made gross by dirty feeding. The floor planks are rotten and the inexperienced foot plunges with a dull splash into pools, of whose composition an unwary visitor can never be over certain. Out in the vaporous backyard—more like a huge well with a moistly decaying bottom, shut in as it is by six-story walls on every side—three sickly women are, for form's sake, dabbling rotten clothes in muddy water.

THEY ARE ALL HALF DRESSED.

Their single skirt is scarcely more illusive in the outlines than the sarong of a Kaffir. The half open bodies of their garments hang loosely about their flabby figures. Modesty is nearly dead in them, but they are old, and the immodesty is neither immoral nor voluptuous. Up stairs, one flight, families live in two rooms apiece, cooking, living, sitting, working, eating, sleeping, all go on in two compartments, neither of which is twelve feet square, between both of which is only one window and in one of which is generally a stove. And yet six and seven forlorn, panting images of God have squeezed out each other's lives, and breathed each other's breath, and watched each other die over and over again in these holes blacker than Hyder Ali's Black Hole ever dreamed of being. For those who died in war a nation lamented and execrated. For those who die here in peace, a nation has no word of comfort. The very city where it all goes on from year's end to year's end, hardly knows of it.

Trades are carried on in these narrow pest-houses, chiefly those of the tailor and the cobbler. Then in addition to the pitiable family of tenants a still more pitiable group of journeymen often come to intensify the horrors of such a place, and to rob one another of a gasp of oxygen.

The furniture of these

DENS OF MISERY

is of the scantiest character. A table, a cracked stove, two chairs, two mattresses and a couple of boxes comprise their whole outfit. Their inmates are correspondingly squalid and miserable. The children who hang about them listlessly are wolf-eyed, ravenous, and half naked. They die off faster than exotics in the frost. Scarcely a family but represents only a half of its original constitution. Death riots in such a playground as this, but, most tenderly, takes away the children before they more than understand their miseries and try

THE WRONG REMEDY.

Is it a wonder that, with such surroundings and so fostered by circumstances, crime should have a frightfully rapid and rank growth in these places?

Is it a wonder that—poverty always pinching, hunger always gripping, sickness always demoralizing—vice should be so monstrous and so potent as it is?

In one of these places, but lately, there were four typical, four tragic incidents of simultaneous occurrence, which, with dreadful perspicuity, illustrate the horrors of such a life.

On one floor a party of ruffians, feverishly delirious for a fight, with the fever of blood and inwardly developed disease, nearly murdered a man. He was frightfully beaten with all kinds of weapons; his head gaped with several dreadful cuts; his side was perforated with two or three knife stabs. He is now in the hospital, dying.

ON ANOTHER FLOOR, ELEVEN JEWS

were at work tailoring in a room eight feet by eleven, a woman was cooking at a stove, a sick man tossed on a mattress, three awfully pale children moaned, ignorant of their malady; one window let in the air from a back yard, the thermometer would have marked 94 deg. as the pitch of temperature, and ice was

SIXTEEN CENTS A POUND!

On another floor the father of a family numbering nine, and including a baby at the breast, had come home mad drunk. He was a car-driver and had just been discharged for an accident for which he was not to blame. What could he do but go on a spree? He was beating his wife fiendishly, the children were screaming, the neighbors grinned maliciously or else were callous and inattentive.

In a room on this floor a woman lay dead with a whiskey bottle in her clammy clutch. Her head was pillowed on a bundle of old and fever-haunted rags. Thousands of flies buzzed in the hollow of her damp, dead mouth, in her ears, eternally deaf, in her nostrils already purple with the touch of dissolution. She was wrapped in an awfully foul linen skirt and was swollen with the gases of her rotting bowels. . . . There she lay with only hungry flies and hungry rats to watch as she grew hourly bigger and more hideous. At last the police came, and they who had been her only acquaintance while she breathed and got drunk, buried her when she was putrefying. Whiskey had murdered her, and, not satisfied with her life, had made her a hideous human monument in death.

Housing Conditions in Philadelphia

While investigating housing problems in the nation's cities, Jane Addams contrasted the tenement conditions of New York, Boston and Chicago with the "happy condition of Philadelphia." Having no firsthand knowledge of the Quaker City, she merely voiced what seemed a general belief.

Her representation of Philadelphia's state was comforting, but far from corresponding to the facts. In special reports of the United States Commissioner of Labor, *The Slums of Great Cities* (1894) and *The Housing of the Working Classes* (1895), serious evils were shown to exist. In addition, Dr. Frances C. Van Gasken, for years an inspector of the Philadelphia Board of Health, in an address in 1895, gave an eyewitness description of Philadelphia's tenements and alleys as anything but a happy condition.

In 1903 the Octavia Hill Association, a stock company organized for the purpose of rehabilitating homes, decided to undertake an investigation of the Philadelphia situation. The author of the article which follows was given a leave of absence from the New York Tenement-house Department for the purpose of aiding in the work. Representative streets were chosen which were considered typical of those in which poor housing conditions existed. A house-to-house canvass was made in these blocks and detailed reports were filled out for each tenement and each apartment.

The first section investigated was Little Italy; the second comprised mixed nationalities, mainly Russian, Austro-Hungarian, German, Irish and Polish. An impression of the character of the tenants was gathered from a list of the principal occupations in which the heads of the families were found employed: laborers, unskilled workers in factories, small shopkeepers, tailors, peddlers, ragmen, teamsters and expressmen, barbers, leatherworkers, laundrymen and laundresses and waiters.

SOURCE: Emily Wayland Dinwiddle, **"Housing Conditions in Philadelphia,"** *Charities* (April 1, 1905), pp. 631–38.

The housing and sanitary conditions are totally different from those in New York. The general impression that Philadelphia is a model city in respect to workingmen's homes is based apparently upon the absence of the dumb-bell tenements, the large proportion of one-family houses, and the small density of the population per acre. In contrast to these undoubted advantages, conspicuous evils are to be found. William Penn would doubtless be shocked if he could see today the results of his original plan, by which he intended that each house should stand in the middle of the "breadth of his ground, so as to give place to gardens . . . such as might be a green country towne which might never be burnt and might always be wholesome." It was with this object that he laid out the large blocks which have since lent themselves so readily to being cut up by a network of small alleys, in which many of the worst conditions in the city are found.

"Out of sight, out of mind" is a familiar proverb, and dilapidation and neglect are common in these dark corners of the city. In an accompanying photograph is shown the bad repair of an alley dwelling, the front rooms of which were still occupied at the time when the picture was taken. The tenant of this house informed the writer that she had been living there and paying rent for fifty years and during that time the landlord had never made a repair. In a house in an Italian court, where the roof had been leaking badly for many months, the occupants rigged up shelters of boards and tarpaulin, which they hung over the beds to keep the water off.

Insufficient lighting and ventilation are common in the alley houses. A large proportion have no yards and where yards are found, they are frequently so small as not to deserve the name. Half the alley buildings in the first block investigated received no light or air from the rear or side and thus had no through ventilation. The blank wall at the back sometimes faced on the yard of a neighboring lot. In other cases a second row of houses immediately adjoined at the rear. Such buildings were back-to-back houses of the type long denounced abroad, where a number of investigators showed a terrible increase in mortality among the tenants of buildings of this class in excess of the death-rate, among the general population.

Not only are a considerable proportion of the alley houses thus cut off from through ventilation, but frequently the court on which they front is but a narrow, dark passageway. A row of five houses without yards in one of the districts inspected faced on an alley varying in width from three feet two inches to three feet eleven and a half inches. A four-story building formed the opposite boundary of the alley and also closed in the end away from the street. Needless to say, the tenants of the houses were obliged to keep lamps burning during the day. The relation between such conditions and the prevalence of tuberculosis need hardly be pointed out.

Filthy and disease-breeding conditions are frequently seen in the courts. Some have no under drainage and are defectively paved and graded, so that slops thrown out into the gutters remain stagnant before the houses. Accumulations of garbage and rubbish are common. In one alley inspected a large stable adjoined the houses, and the pit into which the refuse from this was thrown partly blocked the access to the miserable toilet rooms used by the occupants of seven of the houses and built directly against the wall of the stable. In this alley were fourteen families, consisting of eighty-three persons. These were housed in forty-one rooms, including all the kitchens as well as the bedrooms. One family had a lodger in the yard, where there was a sofa bed in the open woodshed. Two of the houses in the court were dilapidated frame buildings said to have been made over from an old stable. The water supply for the entire court consisted of one hydrant for ten of the houses and another for the remaining four.

The wretched alleys of Philadelphia are by no means confined to any one section, but are scattered throughout the city, and not infrequently found back of handsome residences or opening off business streets. In the three districts inspected forty-two per cent of the houses were on little alleys or courts. In a small special study of alley conditions and in the course of visits with building and health inspectors numbers of others were seen in widely separated neighborhoods.

Somewhat similar to the state of affairs found in the alleys is that in the tenement houses of the city. A tenement house is defined in Philadelphia as in New York, as a building occupied by three or more families living independently of each other and doing their cooking on the premises. There are a little over four thousand such buildings, most of which were originally constructed for private residences. The tenants live together on much the same terms as the families in the alleys. They share the use of halls and yards instead of courts and usually the water-supply fixtures and sanitary accommodations of every kind are in common. The same conditions of dirt and neglect result in both cases from the divided responsibility. No one tenant feels any obligation to clean what is used by all. There is often a marked difference between the cleanliness of the individual rooms and the extreme uncleanliness of the public parts of the house. Lack of light and ventilation is frequently similar in the two types, yard space being sacrificed in each case in order to crowd the largest possible number of families upon the lot. Twenty-three per cent of the houses inspected had no yards, either at the rear or side. Three per cent without yards were on the corners of two streets or of a street and an alley, so that at least an open space adjoined on two sides. The remaining twenty per cent were interior houses, for which lack of yard space is very serious.

Overcrowding of rooms, however, is even more important than the overcrowding of land space. Because of its low buildings the density of population per acre in Philadelphia is small, but the crowding within the rooms in some sections is very great. One tenement house, the largest inspected, contained thirty families, one hundred and twenty-three persons, in thirty-four living rooms. In the Italian district more than one family in every four, almost one in three, had but one room for all the purposes of kitchen, dining-room, and bedroom. One hundred and four single-room "house-keeping apartments" were found in this one block. Five instances were met with in which as many as seven persons of all ages and both sexes slept in one room, which served as kitchen, as well. One family was found sharing three rooms with eighteen lodgers. A family of eight occupied an "apartment," consisting of one room and a bath. They naturally used the bath-room for sleeping purposes. The total proportion of overcrowded rooms found in the districts inspected in Philadelphia was greater than that discovered in similar investigations made in Chicago and Jersey City. The situation apparently is growing steadily worse, because of the fact that numbers of the foreign immigrants and of the negroes coming in from the South, are settling in the already congested districts.

Inadequacy of water supply fixtures is an evil mainly confined to the tenement and alley dwellings. In the first district investigated more than one-fourth of the families were dependent on fixtures used in common by from six to eleven families each. In a court where one hydrant was the sole provision for the supply of seven houses, the water supply was cut off for a period of over three months, and the occupants of the houses were compelled during this time to draw water from a hydrant belonging to another building. A colored woman in another alley said to the writer: "I'm sorry to have you see my house lookin' dis way, lady, but 'tain no use tryin' to be clean; we ain' got but one hydrant for dese yere five houses and we ain' had no water for a week, since di pump busted." Indoor water supply was considered a luxury, sixty-three per cent of the houses having no water within the building.

The toilet accommodations were only slightly less inadequate in number than the water supply fixtures. Health and decency are sacrificed in the cases where individual toilet rooms are used by a number of families. The cleanly tenants suffer unjustly from the filthy habits of others and every facility is given to the spread of disease.

The plumbing of the houses was as a rule, of the most anti-

quated type. Forty-one per cent of the sinks were not sewer connected, discharging on yards, courts, or alleys, though all the
houses were in the closely built-up parts of the city, where one
man's drainage becomes a stench in the nostrils of his neighbor.
Fifteen per cent of the sinks were sewer-connected, but were not
trapped, a dangerous condition, involving direct connection between the air of foul drain pipes and that in the rooms.

Over half the toilet accommodations were yard vaults. The foul,
malodorous wells still exist in the crowded blocks, with butchers'
shops and bakeshops, kitchens and sleeping rooms closely adjoining. These vaults may with reason be held in part responsible for
the high typhoid fever rate in Philadelphia. That the contagion of
the disease can be carried from such wells by house flies has been
clearly proved.

As a result of defective plumbing, leaky vaults, and broken
paving beneath surface gutters in yards and alleys, much damp-
ness of cellars was found. No less than forty-four per cent of the
cellars were noticeably damp, wet, or covered with standing water.
Five houses in one court, of which four were occupied, had cellars
flooded with sewage from a leaking soil pipe, the foul water
standing about a foot deep in all but one. There was sickness in
each of the buildings and one of the patients was told by his physician that his only chance for recovery lay in being removed to
more sanitary quarters.

Filthy conditions resulting from the keeping of animals on the
premises were found in a number of instances. In one tenement
house visited two rooms on the top floor were given up to the
raising of fowls. In another chickens were kept in a fenced-off
corner of a third story room, used at the same time as a kitchen
and bedroom. Under a shop in one dwelling-house white mice and
rats, guinea pigs, rabbits and dogs were kept for sale.

Apart from the insanitary condition of the houses, many of the
tenements were in a dangerous state because of lack of fire protection. Of the sixty-five tenement houses found among the buildings covered in the investigation, fifty-five made no pretense of
complying with the law requiring fire-escapes. One house was only
two stories high. The remaining nine, which had fire-escapes, were
not all adequately equipped. In one, the fire-escape, so-called, consisted only of an inside non-fireproof stairway at the rear of the

ordinary stairs. The house containing thirty families had an iron fire-escape extending from the top floor to the ground, but this was accessible at each story only from a hall window and a window of one apartment. If a fire started in the hall, or originating elsewhere, spread through the hall, as is usually the case, such a means of escape would be almost useless. The Allen street holocaust in New York might be repeated at any time.

C. MEN WITHOUT COMPASS: THE STRUGGLE FOR SURVIVAL

"Italian Immigrants and Their Enslavement"

The author of "Italian Immigrants and Their Enslavement" chose two typical male immigrants for study—the peasant and the *signore,* his born master. As a rule, the peasant sold his farm and/or mule in order to bring to America a meager amount of money. The *signore* brought "nothing except, perhaps, a criminal record as a bankrupt merchant or commission-agent." Immediately, the farmer sought work, and in his eagerness to gain employment accepted almost any terms offered. The *signore* looked for an opportunity which enabled him to gain more than bread alone. Since he had little chance to victimize the native American workman, he sought his humbler countryman as his legitimate prey.

On the other hand, the peasant became a common laborer: the house painter, the stonecutter, the ditchdigger. Wandering from job to job, he found little inducement to become permanently established. The salary of this unskilled worker was entirely arbitrary, and he received lower wages than his American-born colleague, even when working side by side with him.

SOURCE: S. Merlino, **"Italian Immigrants and Their Enslavement,"** *The Forum* (April 1893), pp. 184–90.

The Italian laborer does more than his share of work and receives less than his share of earnings; for as a matter of fact, the laws enacted with regard to this matter oppress the laborer and assist rather than hamper the contractor. Even supposing that the contractor does not succeed in importing contract labor, he finds in the market a large number of men entirely at his mercy, with not even the weak support of a promise to defend themselves against his greed. The few dollars which the immigrant possesses on landing are skillfully taken out of his pocket by the hotel-keeper before the hotel-keeper gives him a chance to work. When he is reduced to absolute indigence, the lowest kind of work imaginable is offered him and he has to accept it. He walks through Mulberry Street and sees a crowd around a bar in a basement. He enters the basement and finds a man employing men for a company. He adds his name to the list without knowing anything about the work he will be called upon to do, or about the place where he is to be transported, or about the terms of his engagement. Perhaps, however, he passes a banker's establishment and stops to read on a paper displayed at the window a demand for two hundred laborers, supplemented with the significant assurance that the place of work is not far distant. He enters, enlists, takes his chances, and falls in the snare set for him.

I once witnessed the departure of a party of laborers and I shall never forget the sight. In foul Mulberry Street a half-dozen carts were being loaded with bundles of the poorest clothes and rags. One man after another brought his things; women and children lounged about, and the men gathered together in small groups, chattering about the work, their hopes, and their fears. For these men *fear*. They have heard of the deceit practised upon those who have preceded them and of their sufferings. Each man carried a tin box containing stale bread and pieces of loathsome cheese and sausage, his provision for the journey. Some had invested whatever money they had in buying more of such food, because, as they told me, everything was so much dearer at the contractor's store. The sausage, for instance, which, rotten as it was, cost them four cents a pound in New York, was sold for twenty cents a pound at the place of their work. Presently our conversation was interrupted by the appearance of the contractor; the groups dissolved, the men took leave of their wives and friends, kissed once more their children, and made a rush for the carts. Then the train started for the railroad station, where the laborers were to be taken to their unknown destination. Of course, this destination and the wages and the nature of the work have been agreed upon in some informal way. But the contract is a sham. I do not believe there is a single instance in which a contract was honestly fulfilled by the contractor. When we think of law-breakers we instinctively refer to the lowest classes. But the contractors are systematic law-breakers. As a rule, the laborer is faithful to the letter of his engagement, even when he feels wronged or deceived.

The contractor is sure to depart from the terms of the contract either as to wages, or hours of labor, or the very nature of the work. Contractors have been known to promise employment, to pocket their fees, and then to lead the men to lonely places and abandon them. Some employment agencies agree with the employers that the men shall be dismissed under pretext after a fortnight or two of work, in order that the agents may receive new fees from fresh recruits. As a rule, however, the men obtain more work than they want or can stand. The contractor, who has acted thus far as an employment agent, now assumes his real functions. Him alone the employer (a railroad or some other company) recognizes, and all wages are paid to him. He curtails these for his own benefit, first by ten or twenty per cent or more, and he retains another portion to reimburse himself for the money he has spent for railway fares and other items. Wages are generally paid at the end of the second fortnight; the first fortnight they remain unpaid till the end of the work, in guarantee of the fulfilment of the contract by the laborer. Meanwhile the men have to live, and to obtain food they increase their debt with the contractor, who keeps a "pluck-me-store," where the laborers are bound to purchase all their provisions, inclusive of the straw on which they sleep. The prices charged are from twenty-five to one hundred per cent and upward above the cost of the goods to the seller, and the quality is as bad as the price is high. At sunset the work ceases and the men retire to a shanty, very much like the steerage of a third-class emigrant ship, the men being packed together in unclean and narrow berths. The shanty is no shelter from wind or rain. Only recently the shanty where the Chicago National Gas-Pipe Company huddled its Italian workmen, near Logansport, Ind., was blown down by a wind-storm and several men were killed. Neither the number nor the names of the dead were known, as Italian laborers are designated only by figures.

The brutality of the contractors toward their subjects baffles description. The contractor is a strongly-built, powerful man; he has acquired the habit of command, is well armed, protected by the authorities, supported by such of his employees as he chooses to favor, and, sad to say, by the people, who are hostile to the laborers. He often keeps guards armed with Winchester rifles to prevent his men from running away. His power has the essential characteristics of a government. He fines his men and beats and punishes them for any attempted resistance to his self-constituted authority. On Sunday he may either force them to attend church service or keep them at work. I have been told of contractors who taxed their men to make birthday presents to their wives. A feudal lord would not have expected more from his vassals.

There are numerous cases where the contractor objects to paying wages. One day last July, as I was walking in King's Bridge, near New York City, I met two laborers loitering in the rear of their shanty. They were evidently afraid to talk, and it was with much difficulty that I learned from them that they were the only members of a gang of about two hundred who had dared to strike work, because their contractor had employed them for three months without paying them. I made my way to the shanty and entered into conversation with a woman who was engaged in cooking. She told me, with tears, that she had saved a little money and had invested it in feeding the men. "Now, if the contractor will not pay us," she said, "I shall be ruined." I denounced the outrage in the Italian press of New York, but ineffectually. A few days later some Italians who worked in a locality near Deal Lake, New Jersey, failing to receive their wages, captured the contractor and shut him up in the shanty, where he remained a prisoner until the county sheriff came with a *posse* to his rescue. I could mention a half-dozen more such cases, all recent. The latest came to my knowledge in Cleveland, Ohio. A contractor had run away with the money, and neither the press nor an attorney employed by the men succeeded in compelling the company which employed him to pay the workmen. Old laborers have the same tale to tell. Nearly all have the same experience. Every one will grant that robbing a poor man of his well-earned wages is a shameful crime; yet in no instance, to my knowledge, has a contractor been made to suffer for his fraud. He generally disappears for a few days and starts again in another place. In this way many, no doubt, have been enriched.

But this is not the worst form of outrage of which contractors are guilty. There have been cases where Italian laborers have suffered actual slavery, and in trying to escape have been fired upon by the guards and murdered, as happened not long ago in the Adirondacks. A similar case was told to me by one of the victims. He said:

"We started from New York on November 3, 1891, under the guidance of two bosses. We had been told we should go to Connecticut to work on a railroad and earn one dollar and seventy-five cents per day. We were taken, instead, to South Carolina, first to a place called Lambs(?) and then after a month or so to the 'Tom Tom' sulphate mines. The railroad fare was eight dollars and eighty-five cents; this sum, as well as the price of our tools, nearly three dollars, we owed the bosses. We were received by an armed guard, which kept constant watch over us, accompanying us every morning from the barracks to the mines and at night again from the work to our shanty. . . . Part of our pay went toward the extinction of our debt; the rest was spent for as much food as we could get at the 'pluck-me' store. We got only so much as would keep us from starvation. Things cost us more than twice or three times their regular price. Our daily fare was coffee and bread for breakfast, rice with lard or soup at dinner-time, and cheese or sausage for supper. Yet we were not able to pay off our debt; so after a while we were given only bread, and with this only to sustain us we had to go through our daily work. By and by we became exhausted, and some of us got sick. Then we decided to try, at the risk of our lives, to escape. Some of us ran away, eluding the guards. After a run of an hour I was exhausted and decided to stay for the night in the woods. We were, however, soon surprised by the appearance of the bosses and two guards. They thrust guns in our faces and ordered us to return to work or they would shoot us down. We answered that we would rather die than resume our former life in the mine. The bosses then sent for two black policemen, who insisted that we should follow them. We went before a judge, who was sitting in a bar-room. The judge asked if there was any written contract, and when he heard that there wasn't, said he would let us go free. But the bosses, the policemen, and the

judge then held a short consultation, and the result was that
the bosses paid some money (I believe it was forty-five dollars),
the policemen put the manacles on our wrists, and we were
marched off. At last, on April 1, we were all dismissed on account
of the hot weather. My comrades took the train for New York. I
had only one dollar, and with this, not knowing either the country
or the language, I had to walk to New York. After forty-two days
I arrived in the city utterly exhausted."

. . .

At best, the workman, after years of hard labor, saves just
enough money to purchase his return ticket, or possibly a hundred
dollars more to pay off the debts contracted in his absence by his
family, or to buy up the small farm which was foreclosed by the
government because he failed to pay the land tax. The boss or contractor, the hotel-keeper, and the banker accumulate fortunes and
buy villas or palaces in their native towns, whither they eventually
return after the time has passed when their sentence to punishment is no longer valid, covered with all the honor and glory accruing from the possession of wealth.

The Lodging House

In every large city thousands of single males found nightly shelter in cheap lodging houses. Judging by investigations carried out
by the Young Men's Christian Association of Chicago, 80 per cent
of these houses could not be entered without being "reasonably
sure of leaving . . . infected with any one of a dozen diseases."
The sanitary and ventilating conditions in more than half of the
shelters observed were found "not only deplorable, but criminal."
In most of them, no laundry accommodations were furnished, and
in many, there were no baths. In addition, common towels and a
single drinking cup serviced an entire floor of one hundred men.

In one house, an investigator found a ladder leading to an attic.
The attic had practically no ventilation and "showed no signs of
having been cleaned since the building was erected." This was discovered to be a "parlor bedroom" for drunks, men in the last
stages of disease and "old fellows so infected with vermin that
even the most hardened lodger [would] have none of them."

"For men, the only alternative to the lodging house was cooperative housekeeping in non-family groups." In this circumstance, the living and sleeping conditions were far from satisfactory. In most cases, economy led men to choose homes for which rents were low, and consequently in dilapidated condition. These houses were originally planned for a family of four or five, and were totally unsuited for the purposes to which they were put.

SOURCE: **Report of the Massachusetts Commission on Immigration** (Boston, 1914), pp. 64–68.

For the men the only alternative to the lodging house is cooperative housekeeping in non-family groups,—an arrangement even more unsatisfactory so far as the health and morals of the young men are concerned. For this reason the majority of Poles, Lithuanians and Italians in Massachusetts choose to lodge with their married friends. Among certain nationalities of recent immigration, however, the opportunities for lodging with families are rare, owing to the very small percentage of women in this country. This was found to be especially true in Massachusetts of the Armenians, the Greeks and the Turks.

. . .

It is natural that among immigrants who have come from countries where the present emigration is comparatively new the number of males should be far in excess of the number of females. Single men are, of course, the most free to come. Married men come first alone and try the experiment of life in this country before sending for their wives and children. Moreover, wherever the immigration is to some extent temporary, and men come with the idea of returning to their homes in the future, these men are of course unlikely to bring their families with them. The newness of the immigration is in part responsible for the present conditions among the Armenians and the Greeks, and so the preponderance of the men over the women is, more or less, a temporary condition, which, to some extent, will be remedied by time. The Turks, on the other hand, have strong, permanent motives in their religion and in their attitude toward women for not wishing to bring their wives to this country.

In the investigation of the commission, 35 non-family groups were studied, representing a total of over 300 men. Twenty-three of the groups were Greek, nine were Armenian, and three, Turkish. They were located in the larger cities,—Boston, Worcester, Springfield and Lynn,—and in the smaller cities or towns,—Chicopee, Stoneham, Ipswich and Northbridge. The conditions found are believed to be typical of hundreds of such groups throughout the State.

* * *

The method of living is similar. The men hire an apartment, or sometimes a house, and share the rent, which generally amounts to between $1.50 and $2.50 a month for each. Sometimes one of the men acts as boss, and runs the apartment for the others, cooking the meals himself perhaps. A few instances were found where the boss was married, or where his sister lived with him. In three of the 23 Greek groups visited, a woman was living. In the Armenian groups visited, no women lived, while in the whole Turkish colony at Worcester, of 400 or more men, there is probably not one Turkish woman.

Occasionally, the men club together and hire a cook, each paying usually $1 a month. In most of the groups visited, however, the men do their own cooking, either acting each one as his own commissary, or taking turns at buying and cooking the food. Occasionally, especially among the Greeks, the men eat at restaurants or coffee-houses.

* * *

It is generally impossible to do more than estimate the size of the group, as the men understate the number. Police and health officers testify that day and night shifts are frequently found. In one case an investigator was told that a house of seven rooms was occupied by fourteen Turks, sleeping two in a room. On a visit at five in the afternoon he found eighteen men who apparently lived there, while four others who worked at night were sleeping in an adjoining room. Making a night inspection, he discovered seventeen men occupying the seven rooms. This investigation was made by the commission early in the autumn. In the winter, when the men drift back to the cities of Massachusetts from construction work all over New England, the numbers are greatly augmented.

.   .   .

With the men in the non-family groups the most serious difficulty is their general forlornness. They do not touch the outside world, they have no normal family or social relationships in their own group, they work long hours for low wages and are open to every temptation. That abnormal vice develops dangerously among them is not surprising.

Most people appreciate the dangers and temptations which American country girls or young men face in the change from rural to city life, and many agencies are at work on the problem of their proper housing and recreation. For these young immigrants the dangers are more serious because the change is even greater, and the crisis they are facing is therefore more difficult. So far as their housing conditions are concerned, the young men, as we have said, must choose the demoralizing non-family groups or a household which can hardly be so equipped as to offer men and women lodgers proper protection. For this reason it is necessary, as Mr. Veiller of the National Housing Association points out, to "recognize that there is need of some place in which the large number of single men that come to our shores . . . can be cheaply lodged. . . . Where there is a considerable alien population we must carefully find out the facts as to the need of housing accommodations for single laborers of this kind, and see to it that lodging houses of the very best type are provided for their accommodations, placing one of these in each alien center, and not attempting to house the various races in the same house."

The Immigrant in the Courts

The immigrants' initial contact with the nation's laws came with their first experience in the courts. Consequently, respect for the judicial system was largely determined by the treatment they received at that time. Unfortunately, due to their ignorance of English and total lack of knowledge of American law and court procedure, many aliens were prevented from securing justice.

In addition, the dual standard in the enforcement of the law by the police and/or in the application of the law by the courts existed in many states. According to the Massachusetts Commission on Immigration, "this double standard, one American and the other immigrant," was practiced not because of intent, but due "to the careless indifference" of many bureaucratic court systems.

SOURCE: **Report of the Massachusetts Commission on Immigration** (Boston, 1914), pp. 107–11.

The municipal or police courts are, to the immigrant, the courts of surpassing importance as object-lessons in American justice or injustice. In many States the police judges and justices of the peace have been accused of the grossest abuse of their power in cases where immigrants are concerned, so that the worst possible lesson has been learned by the immigrant in his first conscious contact with American law.

.   .   .

In these courts the immigrant appears as complainant or defendant, ignorant not only of American law and court procedure but of the language as well. The judge is therefore dependent upon the interpreter for his knowledge of the facts; the intelligence, honesty and impartiality of the interpreter are as important as his own.

In this matter, as in education, the importance of planning to care for the immigrant in accordance with American standards of justice has never been really faced. Instead of responsible interpreters, those provided are too often dangerously incompetent. Recent improvement has been made in the Municipal Court of Boston. In 1912 a law was passed authorizing the justices of this court to employ official interpreters. In the autumn of 1913, when the justices desired to appoint under this statute an interpreter for the Slavic, Lithuanian and Yiddish languages by civil service examination, they found that the Civil Service Commission had no authority to certify interpreters. The commission agreed, however, as a matter of courtesy, to hold the examination. This examination, which was mainly a test of the applicant's ability to translate these languages, brought out the fact that many of the men who had been for years interpreting about the Boston court had totally inadequate vocabulary both in English and in the foreign language.

The Municipal Court of Boston now has two official interpreters who are paid $1,500 a year, and are used for court work and in the probation service. In South Boston and East Boston and in other parts of the city that are not under the jurisdiction of the Municipal Court of Boston, and in the other cities and towns of the State, there are no official interpreters. Men who speak Italian, Polish, Greek and other foreign languages hang about the court in the hope of being called as interpreters. The judge usually calls the same one over and over, and therefore a few, although never really appointed as interpreters, come to do practically all the interpreting of the court. There is no uniformity in the matter of their selection or their pay. Some receive $2 for every case, some $2 for every day they are used, no matter in how many cases; others are paid $3, and some as little as 60 cents for a day's work. Most of these interpreters, although they may have some other business, are practically dependent for support on their employment about the court.

Owing to this method of selection and payment the legitimate earnings of the interpreter are wholly inadequate and, in consequence, he may be tempted to take money from those interested in the outcome of the case, and to arrange for division of fees with some "shyster" lawyer for whom he acts as runner. In every city in which investigations were made by the commission complaints of dishonesty on the part of present or former interpreters were heard. Police officers and clerks of court said that men ignorant of English as well as of the language they were attempting to interpret are constantly accepted as interpreters because no others are available. In order to determine the general truth of this statement, interpreters who are used in four different cities were selected quite at random by the commission and given a very simple test as to their command of the languages they testified they were interpreting in court. One of the men met the tests given satisfactorily; the others were quite incompetent. For example, one man who regularly interprets Polish and Lithuanian in the South Boston court was asked to translate from a Polish newspaper a paragraph which, translated, reads as follows:—

Rochester, N.Y.—Frank Zgodzinoki, sixteen years of age, was arrested for stealing coal from the New York Central Railroad yard. During the hearing of the case it was learned that the boy was sent by his mother to get coal. The boy was discharged, but the judge threatened to send his mother to jail if she taught the boy to steal.

Of this, the interpreter, after reading and re-reading, was, according to the stenographic report, able to make out the following:—

Rochester, N.Y.—There was arrested 16 March Francis Zgodzinoki for—something about the mother. I understand some the mother was arrested in some affairs. Central President, that is New York Central.

The man realized his inability to translate it and offered various excuses; that questions are asked in court in a "quite different way entirely;" that "when the man comes upon the stand to testify we know what he is going to say;" and that in important cases the judge allows him to use a dictionary. Another interpreter who claimed to speak and understand Polish but not to read it, and who was sure he could translate this same paragraph if it were read to him, translated sentence by sentence as follows:—

It was arrested about sixteen years ago a man by the name of Francisco Zgodzinoki. The charge was the larceny of the New York Central. He was tried and acquitted. His mother sent a boy. He was asked the question whether he was going to learn the children to steal.

An Italian interpreter translated a paragraph taken from an Italian newspaper as follows:—

Accusing of fraud in damage of certain Siegfrid Maas, collector of electric house. The fellows William Tantoni and Romeo Rinaldi they appeared before Magistrate Tennant. The day of 12 last May in Massachusetts Avenue aggressed and robbed of $9. They were arrested and those present auditor of the fraud further Rinaldi and Tantoni and a certain William King they are confession the crime. They probated and they return to Rahway Reformatory. The Tantoni and Rinaldi so they got out and proved their innocence and they were set free.

It is unnecessary to give the correct translation here. The man's ignorance of English is sufficiently clear to indicate that he was capable neither of properly putting the questions of the court and attorneys nor of interpreting the answers of a witness, yet he has been doing such work about the courts for the last fifteen years. He said he interpreted both the Sicilian and Calabrian dialects also, but when tested he failed even more completely with these. According to his testimony he is often employed by lawyers to help work up the evidence before the trial, and he usually has some lawyer to whom he refers Italians who come to him with their troubles. This man's own statement seemed to confirm the reports which the commission received that he is not only ignorant but dishonest, and is deliberately using his position to exploit his fellow countrymen and defeat justice.

A common complaint is that an Italian undertakes to translate dialects that he does not understand. The Pole who knows Polish is likewise allowed to translate Russian, Bohemian, Slovak and the other Slavic languages. He may perhaps in rare cases have learned all these, but as a general rule he is able to understand something of what is being said only because of the general similarity of the languages. That means, of course, that he is entirely unable to make the accurate translation that is essential in the administration of justice.

D. WOMEN OF DESPAIR

Prostitution and Poverty: The Story of the White Slave Trade

Many immigrant women arrived in the United States alone. Illiterate and ignorant, some young women lost their way and became prey to hordes of exploiters. What became of them no one knew; confused, desolately lonely, they went where they were led and believed what they were told. Domestic service and work in sweatshops were the most available areas of employment open to them. It was this group which was most easily exploited, as they were invariably at the mercy of their employer. He might fire them at a moment's notice.

Soon after came the almost inevitable—the plausible "white slaver"—and the way of least resistance. Commenting on this form of prostitution, sociologist Henry Pratt Fairchild remarked: "The victims of the white slave trade are most often alien women. *They are most particularly desirable to the promoters of the traffic because of their lack of connections in this community.*"

In the article which follows, "The Daughters of the Poor," George Kibbe Turner described the extent of the trade in the early 1900s.

SOURCE: George K. Turner, "The Daughters of the Poor," *McClure's* (November 1909), pp. 45–46, 48–50, 52–58.

There are now three principal centers of the so-called white slave trade—that is, the recruiting and sale of young girls of the poorer classes by procurers. The first is the group of cities in Austrian and Russian Poland, headed by Lemberg; the second is Paris; and the third the city of New York. In the past ten years New York has become the leader of the world in this class of enterprise. The men engaged in it there have taken or shipped girls, largely obtained from the tenement districts of New York, to every continent on the globe; they are now doing business with Central and South America, Africa, and Asia. They are driving all competitors before them in North America. And they have established, directly or indirectly, recruiting systems in every large city of the United States.

· · ·

Up to this time prostitution had existed in the United States—as most people assume that it exists to-day—without having attracted the business management of men to securing and exploiting its supplies. So far as it had management, it was entirely a woman's business. Its supplies came, as they must always come, from poor and unfortunate families. From 1850 to the present time, the poorest and most unprotected class has been the newest European immigrants. The most exposed and unprotected girls are those in domestic service. For over half a century this class of population has been called upon to furnish the great bulk of the supplies of girls in our large cities, and this class of employment far more than any other.

.   .   .

In the freedom of the Van Wyck administration of the late '90's, the latest type of slum politician that New York has developed demonstrated further his peculiar value to politics, and the great rewards of politics for him. Like the saloonkeeper before him, he had large periods of the day to devote to planning and developing political schemes; there were a great many dependents and young men connected with the business; and there grew up in the various political and social centers of the East Side so-called "hang-out joints," saloons and coffee-houses, where these men came together to discuss political and business matters. It soon became evident that these gangs were exceedingly valuable as political instruments in "repeating," or casting a great number of fraudulent votes.

Yet, in spite of this growth of an entirely new element of political strength, Tammany Hall was defeated in the election of 1901, largely because of a revulsion of popular feeling against some phases of the white slave trade. This feeling was especially directed against the so-called cadets—a name now used across the world to designate the masses of young men engaged in this trade in and out of New York, exactly as the name of maquereau is used to designate the Paris operator. As the women secured for the business are at first scarcely more than children, the work of inducing them to adopt it was naturally undertaken most successfully by youths not much older than themselves. In this way the specialization of the business in New York produced the New York cadet— the most important figure in the business in America to-day. The Committee of Fifteen—which made a thorough and world-wide investigation bearing upon the conditions of life in New York developed by the disclosures of 1901 and 1902—defined this new American product as follows:

"The cadet is a young man, averaging from eighteen to twenty-five years of age, who, after having served a short apprenticeship as a 'watch-boy' or 'lighthouse,' secures a staff of girls and lives upon their earnings. The victim of the cadet is usually a young girl of foreign birth, who knows little or nothing of the conditions of American life."

.   .   .

In Chicago the New York operators secured an even stronger hold. Several hundred New York dealers came into the West Side section after the Low administration and established there an excellent reproduction of the red light district. At its height it contained between seven hundred and fifty and a thousand Jewish girls from New York—largely new immigrants, who could scarcely speak the language. Local crusades have sent a great number of the New York men farther west; but the cadet is now one of the prominent features of the local slum life, and a considerable number of New York Jews still remain in positions of business and political leadership there.

A detailed statement of the spread of activities of the New York dealer and cadet through the United States since the exodus from New York after 1901 would serve as a catalogue of the municipal scandals of the past half dozen years, and would include the majority of the large cities of the country. The New York Jewish cadets were found to be present in hundreds in San Francisco at the great exposé there, and took a prominent part in the rottenness that preceded it; they were strong in Los Angeles before the disclosing of conditions in their line of business changed the administration there a year ago; and two of the most notorious dealers of New York's East Side were prominent figures in the political underworld uncovered by Folk in St. Louis. To-day they are strong in all the greater cities; they swarm at the gateway of the Alaskan frontier at Seattle; they infest the streets and restaurants of Boston; they flock for the winter to New Orleans; they fatten on the wages of the Government laborers in Panama; and they abound in the South and Southwest and in the mining regions of the West.

It is interesting to see how the picking up of girls for the trade in and outside of New York is carried on by these youths on the East Side of New York, which has now grown under this development, to be the chief recruiting-ground for the so-called white slave trade in the United States, and probably in the world. It can be exploited of course, because in it lies the newest body of immigrants and the greatest supply of unprotected young girls in the city. These now happen to be Jews—as, a quarter and a half century ago, they happened to be Germans and Irish.

The odds in life are from birth strongly against the young Jewish-American girl. The chief ambition of the new Jewish family in America is to educate its sons. To do this the girls must go to work at the earliest possible date, and from the population of 350,000 Jews east of the Bowery tens of thousands of young girls go out into the shops. There is no more striking sight in the city than the mass of women that flood east through the narrow streets in a winter's twilight, returning to their homes in the East Side tenements. The exploitation of young women as money-earning machines has reached a development on the East Side of New York probably not equaled anywhere else in the world.

It is not an entirely healthy development. Thousands of women have sacrificed themselves uselessly to give the boys of the family an education. And in the population of young males raised in this atmosphere of the sacrifice of the woman to the man, there have sprung up all sorts of specialization in the petty swindling of women of their wages. One class of men, for instance, go about dressed like the hero in a cook's romance, swindling unattractive and elderly working-women out of their earnings by promising marriage, and borrowing money to start a shop. The acute horror among the Jews of the state of being an old maid makes swindling of Jewish women under promise of marriage especially easy.

But the largest and most profitable field for exploitation of the girls of the East Side is in procuring them for the white slave traffic. This line of swindling is in itself specialized. Formerly its chief recruiting-grounds were the public amusement-parks of the tenement districts; now for several years they have been the dance-halls, and the work has been specialized very largely according to the character of the halls.

The amusement of the poor girl of New York—especially the very poor girl—is dancing. On Saturdays and Sundays the whole East Side dances after nightfall, and every night in the week there are tens of thousands of dancers within the limits of the city of New York. The reason for all this is simple; dancing is the one real amusement within the working-girl's means. For five cents the moving-picture show, the only competitor, gives half an hour's diversion and sends its audience to the street again; for five cents the cheaper "dancing academies" of the East Side give a whole evening's pleasure. For the domestic servant and the poorer shop-girl of the East Side there is practically no option, if she is to have any enjoyment of her youth; and not being able to dance is a generally acknowledged source of mortification.

There are three main classes of dance-halls, roughly speaking, which are the main recruiting-places. In two of them are secured the more ignorant, recent immigrants, who appear in the houses kept by the larger operators of the Independent Benevolent Association. The halls of the first class are known by the East Side boys by the name of "Castle Gardens." To these places, plastered across their front with the weird Oriental hieroglyphics of Yiddish posters, the new Jewish immigrant girl—having found a job—is led by her sister domestics or shop-mates to take her first steps in the intricacies of American life. She cannot yet talk the language, but rigid social custom demands that she be able to dance. She arrives, pays her nickel piece, and sits—a big, dazed, awkward child—upon one of the wooden benches along the wall. A strident two-piece orchestra blasts big, soul-satisfying pieces of noise out of the surrounding atmosphere, and finally a delightful young Jewish-American man, with plastered hair, a pasty face, and most finished and ingratiating manners, desires to teach her to dance. Her education in American life has begun.

The common expression for this process among the young dance-hall specialists of the East Side is "to kop out a new one." Night after night the cheap orchestra sounds from the bare hall, the new herds of girls arrive, and the gangs of loafing boys look them over. The master of the "dancing academy" does not teach dancing to these five-cent customers; he cannot, at the price; he simply lets his customers loose upon the floor to teach themselves. Some of the boys are "spielers,"—youths with a talent for dancing, —who are admitted free to teach the girls, and are given the proceeds of an occasional dance. The others pay a ten-cent fee. The whole thing, catering to a class exceedingly poor, is on a most inexpensive scale. Even the five-cent drink of beer is too costly to be handled at a profit. The height of luxurious indulgence is the treat at the one- and two-cent soda-stands on the sidewalk below the dance-hall. Contrary to the common belief, intoxicating liquor plays but a small part in securing girls from this particular type of place.

.   .   .

A class very similar to this, but of different nationality and religion, is furnished by a second kind of dance-hall on the East Side. Just north of Houston Street are the long streets of signs where the Polish and Slovak servant-girls sit in stiff rows in the dingy employment agencies, waiting to be picked up as domestic servants. The odds against these unfortunate, bland-faced farm-girls are greater than those against the Galician Jews. They arrive here more like tagged baggage than human beings, are crowded in barracks of boarding-houses, eight and ten in a room at night, and in the morning the runner for the employment agency takes them with all their belongings in a cheap valise, to sit and wait again for mistresses. Every hand seems to be against such simple and easily exploited creatures, even in some of the "homes" for them.

Just below this section of the Poles and Slavs lies the great body of the Jews, and in the borderland several Hebrews with good political connections have established saloons with dance-halls behind them. For the past five or six years the Jewish cadets have found these particularly profitable resorts. These girls are so easily secured that in many cases the men who obtain control of them do not even speak their language.

.   .   .

The American-bred Jewish girl does not attend the "Castle Garden" dancing academies for "greenhorns." Generally she is able to take dancing lessons, and her dancing is done at weddings or balls. A large number of these balls are given by the rising young political desperadoes, who form for the East Side girls local heroes, exactly as the football captains do for the girls in a college town. The cadets, who make up these men's followers, become acquainted with the girls upon the street at noon hour or at closing time, when the young toughs hang about the curbings, watching the procession of shop-girls on the walks. Nothing is more natural than the invitation to the ball; and nothing is more degrading than the association, at these balls, with the cadets and their "flashy girls."

There is liquor at these dances, which plays its part in their influence; but the tale of drugging is almost invariably a hackneyed
lie—the common currency of women of the lower world, swallowed
with chronic avidity by the sympathetic charitable worker. The
course of a girl frequenting these East Side balls is one of increasing sophistication and degradation. At its end she is taken over by
the cadet by the offer of a purely commercial partnership. Only
one practical objection to the life remains to her—the fear of arrest
and imprisonment.

"That's all right; you won't get sent away," says the cadet. "I
can take care of that."

His indispensable service in the partnership is the political protection without which the business could not exist. How well he
performs his work in New York was demonstrated by the recent
testimony, before the Page commission of the legislature of the
immunity of women of this kind from serious punishment by the
local courts.

These three classes of girls form the principal sources of the
supply that is secured in New York. The ignorant "greenhorns"
are taken over more by the larger operators into the houses. The
American-bred girl is the alert and enterprising creature who is
going through the cities of the United States with her manager,
establishing herself in the streets and cafes. The cadet in the past
was almost always Jewish; now the young Italians have taken up
the business in great numbers. There are a number of "dancing
academies" in the Jewish section near the Bowery, where the Italian cadet secures immigrant girls. He attends and conducts balls
of his own, which are attended by both Christian and Jewish girls,
and he has developed an important field for Slavic and Polish girls
in the saloon dance-halls of the employment agency district just
north of "Little Italy" in Harlem.

.   .   .

Meanwhile, New York, the first in the development of this European trade in America, remains its center, and its procuring interests are the strongest and most carefully organized of all. The
young cadet has his beginning, as well as the woman he secures.
These boys learn in the primary schools of the farther East Side,
from the semi-political gangs in the dance-halls; step by step, as

they grow in the profession, they graduate into the Third Assembly District, the chief "hang-out" place of the procurer in the world. In all the East Side districts of Tammany Hall these youths have representatives who look out for their interests; but here two thirds of the active workers are or have been interested in markets of prostitution.

Around the district's eastern edge in lower Second Avenue hang the mass of the Jewish cadets, who are members of the strong East Side political gangs. Many of them are determined thieves as well. Farther along is a mixture of the more leisurely class, who devote all their attention to their work as managers of women. Among them are scores—and through the near-by East Side hundreds—of youths who have women at work throughout this country, especially in the West and South-west, or abroad, but who prefer to remain, themselves, in the companionship and comfort of the national headquarters of their trade. Correspondence on the condition of the white slave trade comes here from all over the world. On the lower Bowery and in Chatham Square are the Italian cadets.

There are scores of "hang-outs" for cadets in the Third District, and in all the notorious saloons the waiters are managers of women, and receive their jobs on the recommendation of politicians. Special lawyers defend the cadets when they are caught, and all have their direct access to the political machine, largely through the political owners of their special "hang-outs." Altogether, it is a colony of procurers not equaled throughout the world in its powers of defense and offense.

* * *

The exploitation of a popular government by the slum politician is a curious thing, always. I sat some time ago with a veteran politician, for many years one of the leading election district captains of the Tammany Bowery organization, conversing sociably in the parlor of his profitable Raines-law hotel.

"The people love Tammany Hall," said my host. "We use 'em right. When a widow's in trouble, we see she has her hod of coal; when the orphans want a pair of shoes, we give it to them."

It was truly and earnestly said. As he spoke, the other half of the political financing was shown. The procession of the daughters of the East Side filed by the open door upstairs with their strange men. It was the slum leader's common transaction. Having whole-saled the bodies of the daughters at good profit, he rebates the widow's hod of coal.

The so-called "human quality" is the thread-bare defense of slum politics. But all its charitable transactions have been amply financed. From the earliest time it has been the same old system of rebates to the poor. First, the rebate of the tenement saloon at the death of the drunken laborer; then, the rebate from the raking-up of the last miserable pennies of the clerk and laborer and scrubwoman, by the pool-rooms and policy; and now, smiling its same old hearty smile, it extends to the widow and orphan its rebates from the bodies of the daughters of the poor.

E. THE TRUANTS OF THE STREETS

Foreign-Born Children in the Primary Grades

Jane Addams had the opportunity to work with immigrant chil-dren during and after the period of their short school life. Her ob-servations of the Italian youngsters in the Nineteenth Ward of Chicago, with certain modifications, could be applied to most of the children of that city's Bohemian and Polish communities.

In a speech to the National Educational Association in 1897, she asserted that the primary aim of education was to give the child's own experiences a social value. She concluded, that due to the isolation of the schools from the realities of urban ghetto life, American education had failed the children of the foreign-born peasant.

SOURCE: Jane Addams, **"Foreign-Born Children in the Primary Grades,"** *National Educational Association,* Journal of the Proceedings and Address of the 36th Annual Meeting (Chicago, 1897), pp. 106–10.

It is the children aged six, eight, and ten who go to school, en-tering, of course, the primary grades. If a boy is twelve or thirteen on his arrival in America, his parents see in him a wage-earning factor, and the girl of the same age is already looking toward her marriage.

Let us take one of these boys, who has learned in his six or eight years to speak his native language, and to feel himself strongly identified with the fortunes of his family.

Whatever interest has come to the minds of his ancestors has come through the use of their hands in the open air; and open air and activity of body have been the inevitable accompaniments of all their experiences. Yet the first thing that the boy must do when he reaches school is to sit still, at least part of the time, and he must learn to listen to what is said to him, with all the perplexity of listening to a foreign tongue. He does not find this very stimulating, and is slow to respond to the more subtle incentives of the schoolroom.

.   .   .

Too often the teacher's conception of her duty is to transform him into an American of a somewhat snug and comfortable type, and she insists that the boy's powers must at once be developed in an abstract direction, quite ignoring the fact that his parents have had to do only with tangible things. She has little idea of the development of Italian life. Her outlook is national and not racial, and she fails, therefore, not only in knowledge of, but also in respect for, the child and his parents. She quite honestly estimates the child upon an American basis. The contempt for the experiences and languages of their parents which foreign children sometimes exhibit, and which is most damaging to their moral as well as intellectual life, is doubtless due in part to the overestimation which the school places upon speaking and reading in English. This cutting into his family loyalty takes away one of the most conspicuous and valuable traits of the Italian child.

His parents are not specially concerned in keeping him in school, and will not hold him there against his inclination, until his own interest shall do it for him. Their experience does not point to the good American tradition that it is the educated man who finally succeeds. The richest man on Ewing street can neither read nor write—even Italian. His cunning and acquisitiveness, combined with the credulity and ignorance of his countrymen, have slowly brought about his large fortune.

The child himself may feel the stirring of a vague ambition to go on until he is as the other children are; but he is not popular with his school-fellows, and he sadly feels the lack of dramatic interest. Even the pictures and objects presented to him, as well as the language, are strange.

The school, of course, has to compete with a great deal from the outside in addition to the distractions of the neighborhood. Nothing is more fascinating than that mysterious "down town," whither the boy longs to go to sell papers and black boots; to attend theaters, and, if possible, to stay all night, on the pretense of waiting for the early edition of the great dailies. If a boy is once thoroughly caught in these excitements, nothing can save him from overstimulation, and consequent debility and worthlessness, but a vigorous application of a compulsory-education law, with a truant school; which, indeed, should have forestalled the possibility of his ever thus being caught.

It is a disgrace to us that we allow so many Italian boys thus to waste their health in premature, exciting activity; and their mentality in mere cunning, which later leaves them dissolute and worthless men, with no habits of regular work and a distaste for its dullness.

These boys are not of criminal descent, nor vagrant heritage. On the contrary, their parents have been temperate, laborious, and painstaking, living for many generations on one piece of ground.

Had these boys been made to feel their place in the school community; had they been caught by its fascinations of marching and singing together as a distinct corps; had they felt the charm of manipulating actual material, they might have been spared this erratic development.

. . .

The school is supposed to select the more enduring forms of life, and to eliminate, as far as possible, the trivialities and irrelevancies which actual living constantly presents.

But in point of fact, the Italian child has received most of his interests upon the streets, where he has seen a great deal of these trivialities, magnified out of all proportion to their worth. He, of course, cares for them very much, and only education could give him a clew as to what to select and what to eliminate.

Leaving the child who does not stay in school, let us now consider the child who does faithfully remain until he reaches the age of factory work, which is, fortunately, in the most advanced of our factory states, fourteen years. Has anything been done up to this time, has even a beginning been made, to give him a consciousness of his social value? Has the outcome of the processes to which he has been subjected adapted him to deal more effectively and in a more vital manner with his present life?

Industrial history in itself is an interesting thing, and the story of the long struggle of man in his attempts to bring natural forces under human control could be made most dramatic and graphic. The shops and factories all about him contain vivid and striking examples of the high development of the simple tools which his father still uses, and of the lessening expenditure of human energy. He is certainly cut off from nature, but he might be made to see nature as the background and material for the human activity which now surrounds him.

·   ·   ·

No attempt is made to give a boy, who, we know, will certainly have to go into one of them, any insight into their historic significance, or to connect them in any intelligible way with the past and future. He has absolutely no consciousness of his social value, and his activities become inevitably perfectly mechanical. Most of the children who are thus put to work go on in their slavish life without seeing whither it tends, and with no reflections upon it. The brightest ones among them, however, gradually learn that they belong to a class which does the necessary work of life, and that there is another class which tends to absorb the product of that work.

May we not charge it to the public school that it has given to this child no knowledge of the *social meaning of his work?* Is it not possible that, if the proper estimate of education had been there; if *all the children had been taught to use equally and to honor equally both their heads and hands;* if they had been made even dimly to apprehend that for an individual to obtain the greatest control of himself for the performance of social service, and to realize within himself the value of the social service which he is performing, is to obtain the fullness of life—the hateful feeling of class distinction could never have grown up in any of them? It would then be of little moment to himself or to others whether the boy finally served the commonwealth *in the factory or in the legislature.*

But nothing in this larger view of life has reached our peasant's son. He finds himself in the drudgery of a factory, senselessly manipulating unrelated material, using his hands for unknown ends, and his head not at all. Owing to the fact that during his years in school *he has used his head mostly, and his hands very little,* nothing bewilders him so much as the suggestion that the school was intended as a preparation for his work in life. He would be equally amazed to find that his school was supposed to fill his mind with beautiful images and powers of thought, so that he might be able to do this *dull mechanical work,* and still live a real life outside of it.

"Mister, Do You Need a Shine?": A Twentieth-Century View of the Greek Padrone System

The exploitation of children which existed from America's colonial inception was still a thriving activity on the eve of World War I. As industrial America grew, youthful workers were employed in increasing numbers in factories and textile mills, and on the streets of the nation's urban centers.

The selection which follows described the operation of the Greek padrone system in the twentieth century. Similar to their Italian counterparts in the late 1800s, exploitive Greek promoters imported boys to be used as bootblacks. Requiring cheap labor to compete with blacks and Italians, Greek padrones wrote letters to their relatives and friends urging them to send over their youthful kinsmen. Thinking these "businessmen" were concerned with the welfare of their children, Greek families unknowingly sent thousands of youngsters into quasi-slavery in the United States.

SOURCE: **"The Greek Padrone System in the United States,"** *Reports of United States Immigration Commission,* II (1911), pp. 394–95, 398–401.

The movement to import Greek boys and use them as bootblacks in the United States commenced about fifteen years ago simultaneously with the first efforts of Greeks here to invade the field of the shoe-shining business, which was then almost entirely in the hands of Italians and negroes, confined, however, to booths and stands or chairs located within or just outside of saloons and hotels.

.   .   .

As the demand from the United States for boys increased . . . recruits were drafted from . . . sections of Greece and from Turkey. The padrones continued to open new places in various cities of the United States. From the ranks of those who worked under the system new padrones sprang up, started new places, and enforced the rules of the system as rigidly on their help as they had been applied to themselves. The capital required to embark in this business is inconsiderable, the fixtures, chairs, and all paraphernalia being available on credit. Hence it became easy for Greeks with a little capital to operate such places, provided they could procure the necessary help. This was an easy matter for them to arrange. They wrote letters to their relatives or friends in Greece and brought over all their youthful kinsmen, or sons of their friends, who naturally regarded them as guardians and protectors.

In the year 1903 Smerlis and some other padrones conceived the idea of organizing a trust of the shoe-shining business in this country, and several conferences were held with that end in view. They felt that they could entirely control their labor by having the parents of boys in Greece give mortgages on their property to some representative of the padrones, guaranteeing the time of service of their sons in their employ in the United States. The padrones thought this could be easily accomplished, as it had been successfully tried in individual cases. They proceeded to make arrangements for the consolidation of their interests, but investigations directed by the Bureau of Immigration at this time resulted in the deportation of many boys and gave the padrones the impression that their prosecution was intended under the criminal statutes.

.   .   .

The Bureau of Immigration was instrumental in indicting and convicting quite a number of padrones under the conspiracy statute of the immigration act, and these convictions were purposely given wide publicity in the Greek press. This had a discouraging effect on some importers and rendered others extremely careful in importing youths from Greece. They now import their labor indirectly through relatives in Greece in a manner that places the padrones almost beyond the reach of our criminal statutes. The fact that boys are in great demand in shoe-shining places in the United States has been in the past and is now well advertised throughout Greece. Since the passage of the act of February 20, 1907, and the insertion of the provision in section 2 which excludes at the discretion of the Secretary of Commerce and Labor or under such rules and regulations as he may from time to time prescribe, all children under 16 years of age unless accompanied by one or both of their parents, it is not uncommon for parents of youths destined to the system in the United States to accompany their children in order to insure their landing at the ports of entry. Without exception, during primary inspection or before the boards of special inquiry they state that they bring their children to this country for the purpose of placing them in schools and giving them an education, and that it is their bona fide intention to send for their families as soon as they are able to do so.

Under the present immigration statutes such statements, if aliens are physically eligible, generally land them, for their likelihood to become public charges is easily overcome by having some one of their friends, relatives, or townsmen telegraph to the officers at the ports of entry their willingness and ability to befriend the aliens. A week after landing the father will deliver his son into the hands of the padrone as prearranged, directly or indirectly, through correspondence. In some few cases, where no agreement exists, the father generally proceeds to Chicago to one of the Greek saloons or restaurants on South Halsted Street, where he is sure to meet friends and be taken care of. As Chicago is regarded the most likely market to hire boys who are brought there by their parents, padrones throughout the United States have some relative or friend represent them in that city in securing the boys' services. Within a week of the arrival of any boy in Chicago he can find his way into some shoe-shining establishment, east, west, north, or south.

Chicago offers the best advantages for boys destined to the system in the United States in violation of law; next to Chicago, other cities in the interior, away from the ports of entry, are desirable. Destinations to cities not distant from the ports of entry are studiously avoided, because the heads of the system here, and those interested in Greece in its behalf, know well that the nearer to a port of entry the destination of a young alien is the more likely he is to be detained by the immigration authorities; his examination is more rigid, and those relatives or friends he claims to have are required to call in person. On the other hand, the farther the destination from a port of entry, the less rigid the examination is if the aliens are provided with a good address and their railroad tickets; the likelihood of requiring their relatives or friends to call in person is further removed. In other words, they know that their cases can not stand a searching investigation and they plan accordingly. In addition to these reasons, Chicago is advantageous to padrones because every province of Greece is there well represented in the Greek colony, and this enables them to have some friend to meet those they expect and direct them to their destination.

.   .   .

Early in 1907 many Greek boys landing in the United States either came in charge of pseudofathers or falsely claimed that they were destined to cities in the interior to some one who they alleged was their father. Pseudofathers were adult immigrants bearing distant or no relationship at all to the boys they brought in as their sons. They did this either for pay or, in the majority of cases, as a favor to the parents of the boys in Greece or the padrones in the United States to whom the boys were destined. In such cases the boys assumed the surname of the pseudofather and the claim was made during primary inspection that they were father and son. The examining inspectors at the ports of entry, being unable to devote much time to such cases by separating them and putting them through a rigid examination to determine the truth or falsity of the relationship claimed, generally passed them. In like manner boys were instructed in Greece to assume the surnames of persons residing in the interior of the United States and claim at the ports of entry that they were en route to join their fathers, each naming as his father the party whose name he had assumed. If the boys were not landed the parties whom the boys claimed as fathers sent affidavits to the immigration officers at the ports of entry embodying the false statement that the detained boys were their sons.

Upon receipt of said affidavits the immigration officers, in the absence of any evidence to the contrary, generally allowed the boys to land.

.   .   .

Boys employed as bootblacks live in insanitary quarters and are absolutely ignorant of the necessity of fresh air. They and their employers close all windows to prevent the contracting of colds, and in addition, sleep with their heads covered, this being the manner of sleeping in their native villages. Wherever space will allow, two and three beds are placed in one room, three and sometimes four boys sleeping in one bed. In some places no beds at all are used, but the boys roll themselves up in their blankets and sleep on the floor.

As the shoe-polishing shops are opened between 6 and 6:30 in the morning, the boys are compelled to get up between 5 and 5:30 o'clock, and in large cities, where living quarters are some distance from their place of work, they rise as early as 4:30. They remain at work from morning until 9:30 or 10 at night, excepting in some small cities where the shops are closed about 8 or 8:30 o'clock, and on Saturday and Sunday nights the closing hour is usually later. After the doors to the shoe-shining establishments are closed the boys have to mop the floors, clean the marble stand and other fixtures, and gather up the rags to take home. They then proceed to their living quarters, where supper has to be prepared, although in places where upward of ten boys reside, one of them usually acts as cook in the morning and prepares the night meal. Of the meal prepared in the morning the boy cook at noon takes part to the shop, the other part being left at the house for supper. In the rear of nearly every shoe-shining establishment a small space is partitioned off. This is almost without exception filthy and nauseating. Into this place the dinner is brought. Each boy then disappears behind the partition and devours as fast as he can his share of the food, the padrone or his manager apportioning it. They eat singly, and if customers arrive the boy has to suspend eating his dinner and attend to patrons. In the majority of places the noon meal consists of bread and olives or cheese. When the shops are closed and the boys go to bed, all so completely exhausted that many retire with their working clothes on, divesting themselves of only their coats and shoes. Two of the boys have to remain up to wash the dirty rags used at the shop and hang them around the stove to dry, so that they may be available for use the following day.

In some few places beds and sheets are used, and the boys live under fair conditions; these are exceptions, however, and occur in places run by Greeks who are somewhat Americanized, are married, and have their wives taking care of the living quarters.

Some padrones running shoe-shining establishments in the business sections of the larger cities, in order to save a few dollars in rental, lodge their help nearly an hour's walking distance from their place of business, and as no car fares are allowed by the padrones, the boys have to walk. The time consumed in covering this distance the boys pay by loss of sleep, that is, they have to get up early enough to have breakfast, walk downtown, and be in the business district in time to open the shops by 6 or 6:30 a.m. They have to work every day in the year, as they are permitted no days off. In a good many shops the boys are not continuously at work and are enabled to get breathing spells, but they are nevertheless confined to the place during the entire year. So absolute is this confinement in most cases that boys have been in the United States and in the same city three or four years and upward and yet their knowledge of the city they live in is limited entirely to their work place, their living quarters, and the streets they traverse in going to and from work.

Padrones forbid the boys to have much to say to Greeks coming to the shop unless the padrones are present. By this means of complete isolation they are enabled to keep their help in ignorance of the English language and the labor conditions in this country, thereby preventing them from receiving information by contact with persons of their own race and learning that they can do better in other occupations and elsewhere. The boys are constantly watched by either the padrone, the manager, or relatives of the padrone; in every shoe-shining place the padrone has relatives laboring for him who act as spies on the other boys. The moment an outsider engages a boy in conversation those interested crowd around to hear. In nearly all instances the boys refuse to answer questions concerning their ages and their work in the presence of the padrone or his spies; if they do answer, they lie, making such false statements as they have been instructed to make by their employer. To frustrate further any attempts of outsiders to induce them to leave, either for places of like character or for other occupations, many padrones insist on reading, or having their managers read, all letters the boys receive while in their employ and likewise examine letters they send out, not excepting those to their parents. Through this method the padrones are enabled to prevent complaints against themselves from the boys to their parents in Greece, whose good will the padrones are anxious to retain. They dislike to have it reported in Greece that they are mistreating their help, as information travels from village to village easily and creates a tendency to blacklist them, thereby closing in a measure their source of procuring new recruits. In some instances boys are physically punished by padrones . . .

PART IV

The Working Class in Industrialized America: Exploitation of the Helpless, 1860–1915

INTRODUCTION

Women were among the most pitifully exploited members of the nineteenth-century working class. Even the girls who worked in the early so-called model factory towns of Lowell and Waltham, Massachusetts, were subjected to the most tyrannous type of regimentation. Growing industrialization, with its division of labor, resulted in the widespread use of women in factories. Employers sent recruiters into rural districts and to immigrant depots to seek girls. As the factory system grew, working conditions worsened. Twelve to fifteen hours of toil, often starting at 5 A.M., at extremely low wages and under wretched conditions, was common. A group of New York City reformers observed, "No picture of human life deservedly excites the sympathy of benevolent minds than that of poor working women defrauded of their little earnings—women, who by patient industry and by severe toils of their own hands, furnish the only support of aged parents or of crippled or diseased sisters and brothers, and ofttimes of large families of their own." Many women sought to supplement their income through prostitution, and it was commonly known that the term "seamstress," appearing in newspaper advertisements, often was used interchangeably with the word "prostitute."

The Civil War brought many women into factories, a large proportion of whom remained employed after the war. Generally the women earned much less than the men for the same work. In 1870 a survey revealed that in New York City 7,000 working women could afford to live only in cellars and that 20,000 of them were near starvation. In 1875 a Massachusetts investigator reported that lady compositors employed in the printing trades could not endure the prolonged attention and confinement the work required and broke down. In the cotton mills of New England and the South tens of thousands of women toiled long and dreary hours often under conditions that were beyond human endurance.

Between 1870 and 1900 the number of female breadwinners continued to increase. In 1870, 15.8 per cent of all persons employed in manufacturing were women; by 1900 that percentage had risen to 19.4. The 1900 census revealed that of all females ten years of age or older engaged in gainful employment, 16.5 per cent were foreign-born. Since a large proportion of women were in unskilled trades where competition was most intense, many females did not receive a living wage.

Like women workers, children also were a convenient source of exploited labor especially in the early years of the nation's industrial development. At the start of the nineteenth century, the apprenticeship system protected the young workers. With the rise of the merchant-capitalist in the 1820s and 1830s, however, the system began to break down and apprentices often were excuses for cheap labor. In 1832, it was reported that two fifths of all persons working in New England factories were children under the age of sixteen. Reformers warned that if children continued to work in their "deadly prison" from dawn to dusk, irreparable damage would be done to generations to come. Efforts to reduce working hours were met by employers' arguments that the shorter workday would have a bad influence on the youngsters.

The nation's lack of concern for the child labor problem was seen in the fact that no significant statistics on working children were collected before 1870. The federal census of 1870, however, reported that there were three quarters of a million working children. Ten years later, this figure rose to over one million. In addition, these statistics did not include the many children whose age had been falsified.

During the last two decades of the nineteenth century, although the number of working children increased markedly, little was achieved to improve their conditions. In 1880, it was reported that 1,118,356 children from ten to fifteen years of age or 16.8 per cent of all youngsters in that age group were employed. In 1900, those figures rose to 1,750,178 or 18.2 per cent. In many manufacturing trades, children worked under conditions that sacrificed "their future efficiency as adults by severe, unsuitable or unhealthful labor." In glassworks, more children were employed than in any division of manufacturing except textiles. It was stated that each man employed as a glass blower needed a helper and that "veritable child slavery exists." In the textile mills, there was "little industrial training" which fitted the youngsters for adult labor.

Moreover, working children often were required to work such long hours that they were too exhausted to enjoy the pleasures that young people sought. In manufacturing, working hours depended upon state law and its proper enforcement. Where no legislation existed, 11 or 12 hours a day or 66 hours a week were common. Many children, especially those employed in glassworks, furniture factories and silk mills, worked nights. One of the most unwholesome occupations employing large numbers of children was the manufacturing of tobacco goods. The tobacco factories often were unsanitary and poorly ventilated, and the atmosphere was polluted with poisonous tobacco dust.

Then there were the newspaper boys, mainly the children of immigrants, who were exposed to all of the evils of the large city street trades. Usually working for a corner man, they toiled for long hours and very little pay. Thousands of children worked long hours with their immigrant families residing and trying to make a living in tenements. At the turn of the century, a special agent for the National Child Labor Committee held that "tenement work seems to me one of the most iniquitous phases of child-slavery that we have." Jacob Riis found in seven back-yard factories in New York City sixty-three children at work who were under fourteen years of age. Most of these children could hardly speak English. There also were the many young Italians virtually enslaved under the padrone system. The greatest evil of child labor, aside from the physical effects, was the moral and mental losses that children suffered from the loss of education and instead being subjected to a drudgery of daily monotonous, unrewarding toil.

Charles Loring Brace, founder of the Children's Aid Society, was one of the early reformers who thought that the child labor problem could be best attacked through an effective compulsory education law. In the 1870s and 1880s the Knights of Labor and American Federation of Labor made the abolition of child labor a primary objective. By the early twentieth century most states had legislation restricting the employment of children, but the first significant decline in the evil did not occur until the 1920s. Effective federal action came with the New Deal.

All workers—men, women and children—were faced with the harsh problems created by the early stages of industrialization in an unplanned society. The greatest threat, especially to the breadwinner, was that of job insecurity. Workers were constantly faced with the threat of unemployment resulting from depressions, recessions and seasonal slowdowns. For example, the outbreak of the Civil War resulted in a depression that put 30,000 men out of work in New York City alone. During the 1867 winter, the *Workingmen's Advocate,* the nation's leading labor newspaper, reported that there were 50,000 unemployed in New York.

During hard times, Castle Garden, the nation's major immigrant entry depot, was the scene of hundreds of "hangers about" or immigrants who either had not been able to find work or had been sent to the country for jobs that did not exist. Jacob Riis remembered the hard times of the 1870 winter when, as a recent arrival, he could not find work and had to sleep in doorways, tenements and police stations. The depressions that followed the panics of 1873 and 1893 caused unprecedented unemployment and suffering.

Workers also were exposed to the hazards of heat exhaustion in working at forges or in sugar refineries on torrid days. Unguarded machinery, inadequate inspection and defective equipment maimed and killed workers; the existing legislation ostensibly designed to protect the workingmen were either inherently ineffective or poorly enforced. Breadwinners complained of unfair labor competition; employers frequently used prison and immigrant contract labor and fraudulent apprenticeship arrangements to "knock down" wages. The legislatures and courts generally were unsympathetic to the workingmen's pleas for amelioration. Moreover, in the latter nineteenth century, the modern American labor movement was just coming into its own and the working class would have to wait until the early twentieth century for reform legislation.

A. THE WOMEN WHO TOIL

The New York City Working Women

The Civil War was one of American history's greatest catalysts in the industrial employment of women. During and after the war, reformers and social-minded newspapers became particularly concerned with the plight of working women. The effects of wartime economy were felt most sorely by "these women who were dependent upon the needle and the various factory employments for their daily bread." A group of New Yorkers, including Moses Beach, editor of the New York *Sun,* helped to form the Working Women's Protective Union. In addition, the city's journals devoted considerable space to working women's problems. During the Civil War, Horace Greeley's *Daily Tribune,* always interested in reform movements, reported the proceedings of a working women's mass meeting held at Cooper Institute, New York City. Similarly, in the 1860s, James Gordon Bennett's New York *Herald* opened its columns to reports of injustices suffered by the city's working women, many of whom were immigrants working in "tenement pens."

SOURCE: New York *Daily Tribune,* March 22, 1864. **A Meeting of the Working Women of New York**

The large hall of the Cooper Institute was well filled last evening with the working women of New York and their friends. A number of prominent ladies and gentlemen occupied seats on the platform, thus giving countenance to a good cause and showing sympathy with an oppressed and suffering class in our community.

The Hon. Chas. P. Daly presided. He said that when called upon to preside he had submitted to him a constitution which should attract the attention and admiration of all who felt interested in the welfare of working women, 30,000 of whom reside in this city, who are employed in all branches of business.

The accomplished speaker proceeded to show that it was not the intention of the meeting to make an attempt to regulate wages, but to take steps to aid the poor working women in their laudable attempts to obtain that which is justly their due.

The Secretary of the meeting then came forward and read an exceedingly interesting statement. He was followed by Miss Teresa Esmonde, who read a song written for the occasion by Mrs. Stephens. One verse will serve as a specimen of its style and sentiments:

> The war about that rings from battle
> Thrills through the answering crowd
> When you free the slave as a chattel,
> The joy of freedom is loud
> But the prayer that comes from women,
> When she asketh bread for toil,
> Is met with a clamor inhuman,
> 'Mid an eager rush for spoil.
> Work! Work! Work! This is the answering cry
> "Our wives are fond of jewels,
> and widows were made to sigh!"

Miss Esmonde was followed by a smart working woman of middle age, who came forward and in a business like manner exhibited specimens of the sewing done by the working women of this city. She spoke distinctly and with a clear voice making an impression upon the minds and hearts of her hearers that will be long remembered. The following are some of the statements she made to her deeply interested hearers:

A pair of drawers of white cotton drilling, 1800 stitches, sewed on the machine, and well made. Completely finished with buckles, button-holes, straps and strings.

The woman who made these drawers was a smart operator and could finish four pairs per day, working from 7 a m until 9 in the evening, receiving four and .16 cents a pair, or sixteen and .64 cents for her day's labor; resting, she says, long enough to make herself a cup of tea and eat a piece of bread.

Another very large pair of canton flannel drawers, 2,000 stitches, done by hand. Double seams, filled; with eyelets, button-holes, buttons, stays and strings; the working woman to furnish her own thread—a rule adopted by employers since the price of a spool of cotton had risen from four to eight and ten cents.

This woman, the mother of three children, was very poor, and came to the rooms of the Working Women's Protective Union, No. 4 New Chambers street, where she threw down the work, saying she had been working on these drawers for seven months and could not work any longer for the price paid. Said she: "I may as well starve without work as to work and starve at the same time." An inquiry revealed the fact that the wealthy firm who employed her paid 5½ cents per pair for these drawers, of which she could make two pairs per day, remarking, "If I get to bed about daylight, and sleep two or three hours, I feel satisfied."

A haversack packet, made by hand, containing upward of 600 stitches and three button-holes—two yards of sewing.

This article was made by a woman who supported her sick husband and four little children. Each packet required one hour's faithful labor, and the compensation received was 1¼ cents or 12½ cents for ten hours' work. She furnished the thread . . .

A fine white cotton shirt, with a fine linen plaited bosom, nicely stitched and well made throughout, containing 11,500 sewing machine stitches, six button-holes, felled seams etc.

Two of these shirts are finished each day by the operator, who employs nearly every moment of her time, finds her own thread, and receives for the garments 16 cents each, or 32 cents for more than twelve hours' labor. These shirts sell for $3 to $3.50 in retail stores. Their total cost to the employer may be summed up as follows:

Three yards fine muslin, at 33 cents	— 99
Half yard fine linen	— 38
Labor and thread	— 16
Buttons	— 6
Total Cost	1.59

Ladies' collars and cuffs, containing 1,700 fine sewing-machine stitches, the outer edge being ornamented with the insertion of various colored trimmings.

These articles of ladies' wearing apparel made for twenty-one cents per dozen sets—a set consisting of the collar and two cuffs. Three dozen are made per day by a good operator, working early and late. The thread is paid for by the woman who takes out the work.

A dozen sets will cost as follows:

Fourteen yards of trimming at 8¢ per yard	—	$1.12
One yard of linen	—	90
One yard of muslin	—	35
Labor and thread	—	21
Total Cost		2.58

The retail price per set in the Broadway and Bowery stores is seventy-five cents. The wholesale prices are not less than five dollars per dozen sets . . .

While this lady was speaking, a white-haired old gentleman frequently called for the names of the manufacturers who grind the faces of the poor. He was assured that their names would be given to the public when the proper time arrived. At the close of this exercise, the meeting was addressed by the Rev. Mr. Milburn and Mr. Beach of "The New-York Sun."

SOURCE: New York *Herald*, November 27, 1869. **Our Working Women**

JUSTICE NOT CHARITY, DEMANDED—FACTS AND
FIGURES—DESTITUTE CONDITION OF THE WORKING
WOMEN—THEIR AVERAGE WAGES AND WORK-
ING HOURS—THE WORKING WOMEN'S PRO-
TECTIVE UNION—THE FEMALE CHARITIES
OF THE CITY—THE CHEAPEST LIVING
IN THE WORLD—"A SHROUD
AS WELL AS A SHIRT."

If "man's inhumanity to man makes countless thousands mourn," his indifference to the trials and tribulations of the poor and the weak of the other sex produces widespread misery and is far more reprehensible. The icy philosopher who stops to look with disdain upon the aged and decrepit woman who wanders about our streets, worn, wearied, shattered and penniless, after a life of industry and frugality, who stretches forth her hand for his paltry alms, little considers how her fate has been a struggle for the merest existence, and how her tedious years have been rendered fruitless by the cupidity of unscrupulous employers. He would not only countenance the injustice, but deny her the feeble comfort contained in a stranger's pittance. This is the natural result coming from the pound of cure rather than the ounce of prevention. And thus charity, inculcated by the religious as a duty, yet used by the unfortunate as a willing refuge, becomes responsible for the ills which lie at the root of injustice.

It is to remove the unjust customs which oppress and degrade the working women of New York, and not to inaugurate and support high-sounding charities instituted to relieve them, that constitutes the basis of all true philanthropy, and embodies the only principle that should be written as a humane rule. They do not ask for charity; they crave justice. They do not implore luxury and idleness; they demand equity and fairness. They do not sue for ease and elegance; they are satisfied with fair pay and cleanliness. They do not seek even for equality with men; but they do feel that all the avenues of labor should be opened to their industry, and that all facilities should be extended for their success. What a trifle is sought, what a task to accomplish!

Ever since this island has been growing denser in its population this problem of female labor has been crystalizing into a more inflexible mass, swelling with the large influx of country girls, and increasing with the inpouring of immigration, the female labor community has at last grown to such proportions, that destitution and general pecuniary distress accompany any and every prostration of trade. Out of such sufferings come all species of benevolence, until at last it is considered that homeless girls, friendless orphans and bereaved widows should be placed in institutions and left to solve the future of their own helpless lives in idleness. Too much Utopian is this, because it is purely charitable.

What the working women require is opportunity, and not alms; and let this once be understood and the efforts of interested people combined, can yet be made to lift up this essential portion of the body politic to the level where it belongs.

TENEMENT PENS

How is it at this hour over every inch of ground in this city where working women can be found? They live in nasty tenement houses, often in cellars. Their quarters are generally unfit for human habitation. Badly lighted, poorly ventilated, if clear air is accessible at all, their rooms are situated in pools of foulness, where every impurity is nurtured and where every vice flourishes. The home accommodations are scanty. A dirty and carpetless floor; a stained, patched and dingy wall; a low and smoky ceiling; a rickety bed with meagre coverings; a broken down stove, second hand cooking utensils, and furniture to correspond—these make up the inventory of the most industrious. Often in quarters of such limited space as not to have sufficient area for one person whole families live, breed and die. Amid such misery as this dwell those who are accounted the most successful in the minor fields of labor. But what squalor and poverty surround those who are driven by the savage masters of avarice into nooks and corners of hovels where hogs would be uncomfortable! Yet such is not an overdrawn picture of the actual sufferings that may be witnessed any day of widows and young girls who have mainly to depend upon the fruits of their labor.

A REMEDY

And what is the remedy? This has often been asked. The reply is simple. Give to women the wages they can and do earn; allow them hours that will enable them to attend to their household affairs so as to attain neatness and cleanliness; provide good and comfortable buildings in healthy situations where rooms can be rented at moderate prices, and the result will then depend upon their virtue and industry; and the 75,000 working women of New York will not disappoint the most sanguine expectations. The fall trade, now about over, has not been what was expected, and the work for the holidays does not promise much. The consequence is, that the winter will be unusually severe, and thousands upon thousands will be driven to the last ditch. In the season of privation and suffering coming there can be no doubt that a great many can be relieved by charitable workers, yet the majority can better be supplied by opportunities for employment. Whatever is done, the prospect may well appal the most indifferent. There never were so many women in the city, and never so many helpless to supply the most ordinary wants of daily life . . .

THE SOCIAL EVIL—CAN IT BE AVERTED?

Moralists may say what they will, and statisticians may endeavor to blind the public regarding the identity of this crime with the present condition of the laboring women, but the facts remain to show, beyond a doubt, that the life of luxury obtained by debauchery is the true reason that accounts for the excessive numbers of abandoned women. In the first place the quarters of working women in tenements are not habitable, their dress can never be otherwise than plain, and their food coarse and indigestible, servants rarely suffer these inconveniences, being under the generous eyes of provident mistresses. Then, too, the extravagant dress now the fashion excites envy, and the knowledge that it can be obtained is often sought without counting the cost of how it is obtained. Deplorable as it is, hundreds rush into the vortex because they have no refuge from a depraved public taste, and nothing but a choice between plenty and destitution. The former is chosen at the sacrifice of virtue. Like other drawbacks mentioned this can only be averted by organized labor, better homes and more advanced wages . . .

SUMMARY

With our almost exhaustless subject we have only been able to give but the merest outlines, and many of them indistinctly. But we have shown that justice, and not charity, is demanded by the working women of New York; that their wages are inadequate and will not average six dollars per week; that their hours of work, not including household service, will average one-half of the twenty-four; that female competition, lack of organization, want of funds, protracted labor, and the flash extravagance in dress, all operate to depress the wages of the working women; that the Working Women's Union is a noble and beneficent institution, and deserves the aid and encouragement of all charitably disposed; that new departments of labor are opening and that old branches are developing and that the recognized charities are performing their missions. These are all questions of vital interest, for in them is the salvation or destruction of the working women on this island. The severe winter is here. Chill blasts begin to penetrate the damp and cheerless abodes of the nimble fingered widows. Orphans grow sick, suffer from the cold, wither from hunger and die; but the world moves on, and with it a misdirected, misap—ed philanthropy. Still the needles ply and still capital feasts upon the prostrate form of labor.

> O men with sisters dear;
> O men, with mothers and wives!
> It is not linen you're wearing out,
> But human creatures' lives!
> Stitch—stitch—stitch,
> In poverty, hunger and dirt,
> Sewing at once, with a double thread,
> A shroud as well as a shirt.

The Working Girls of Boston

As American industrial growth advanced in the last decades of the nineteenth century, women played an increasingly important part in the nation's economy. The problems of the New York City working women were shared by their sisters in other manufacturing cities. Carroll D. Wright, the chief of the Bureau of Statistics in the Massachusetts Labor Department and one of the earliest systematizers of social statistics, sent out a team of investigators to interview Boston's working girls. A pioneer in the use of the modern sociological-interview technique, he dispatched teams to gather anecdotal as well as statistical data. The material compiled by this research group was made the basis of a significant study published in 1889.

SOURCE: Carroll D. Wright, **The Working Girls of Boston** (Boston, 1889), pp. 114–18.

Girls living away from home, in boarding and lodging houses, the latter especially, are oftentimes obliged to practice very close economy in living, one girl being reported as taking her meals at restaurants, and often going without her supper as well as other meals, because she did not have the money to pay for them; another, as going without meat for weeks, eating bread only without butter, and seldom able to buy a baker's pie, while in the case of three sisters living in one room with all meals at restaurants where employed, they are only able to get a bare living without any of life's comforts; they economize in every way possible, buy food and cook it themselves Sundays, and when invited out to dinner (which is only rarely), they make a "field-day" of it.

In the same way, girls speaking of their dress, say that it is almost impossible in many cases to buy new clothes, they depending largely upon what is given them in the way of old dresses and other garments by relatives or friends; others spend little or nothing for clothes each year, or have a new suit once in two or three years. One girl says "it costs every cent she earns for board and other expenses," and that she was obliged to take ten dollars that she had saved for a new dress and pay a doctor's bill, and that she is in consequence nearly destitute of clothing suitable for street or store wear. This matter of dress, she says, has a great deal to do with one's success in seeking employment, a poorly dressed woman being refused on the score generally of "just hired," while a shabbily dressed girl is entirely ignored.

Touching the question of income, and in addition to and explanatory of the savings or debt table, are the facts reported by some of the working girls as to how they have been able to make some slight saving each year, or the causes which have led them into debt. Some of the girls report that it takes about all they ever earn to meet expenses, and that it is only by the strictest economy that they can lay by anything; two others, sisters, say they want for nothing, live frugally and manage to save a little something, while another says she pays all of her money to her mother, but thinks it is being saved for her ultimate benefit. Four sisters report that they each expect to receive $200 from the estate of a deceased uncle, while one girl says that the $40 saved the past year she intends to send to her parents. Of those who have saved in past years any considerable sums, two are reported as having $500 in savings banks, in one case the result of seven years' savings; two others, as having $100 saved, in one case during four years of work; one other girl says her savings in all amount to $300, while still another says that in three years she has almost paid for a $300 piano. A tailoress, earning ten dollars a week, says she has lost money in various savings banks, $300 of which was in Mrs. Howe's "institution," but notwithstanding these losses she has about $5,000 saved. Another woman well advanced in life, says she has during the past year built a little house to provide for old age, and that in her working career she has accumulated some hundreds of dollars, but could not have done so if she had not been with friends and not obliged to pay any board. In still other cases, one girl says she is using her money towards clearing a debt on a farm left her by her father, while another says three years ago she saved up money enough to pay the passage to this country of her mother and brother. From those in debt, or without savings, comes the report that through the sickness of the girl herself or her mother, the savings of years have been eaten up by medicines, etc.; in one instance, a girl reports that during a ten weeks' sickness two years ago she spent the savings of eight years and was $20 in debt. Another says she has incurred a debt of $75 on account of the expenses of her son's illness; another that she placed some money, the savings of many years, in the hands of a friend who has lost it by speculation, while still another says she opened in company with another woman a boarding and lodging house, but owing to the bad management, as she says, of the other woman the venture was a failure and she suffered a loss of $500 in money; she has had some money left her, and that with what she has earned make her savings now amount to $500.

In a few instances, girls are reported as having come to Boston from other states and countries, on account of the favorable reports received of plenty of work, and good pay, and with the expectation of making a great deal of money, but in all these cases they are dissatisfied and intend to return at their earliest opportunity; they report the work duller here even than from whence they came, and that they have been unable to find sufficient good paying work upon which to live. Others say that during work-life there is little chance for amusement, while others think girls in many cases would be much better off at housework or some kindred occupation than in shops or factories. One girl left her work to do light housework in a boarding house, but found there were thirty boarders to work for, and so left and went back to her usual occupation.

It is interesting to note the "life" experiences of a few who have been at work for a number of years and have a history, and from them learn what the future of working girls entirely dependent upon their own labor may be, if the conditions developed in regard to small pay, etc., should continue.

A carpet sewer, 34 years of age, and now earning six dollars a week, says she was married at 29 and lived with her husband until, on account of his dissipated habits and neglect of her, she finally left him and went to work, earning $2 a week and running up a board and lodging bill of $35. She has received since a little money from her husband's lodge and makes a little extra by crocheting tops on woollen mittens at ten cents per dozen pairs. She gets her own meals on a little parlor stove and is compelled to live in a small way in order to keep herself and boy alive; she spends scarcely anything for clothing.

A coat maker, earning six dollars a week, says that at the age of fourteen she had a fever and for lack of proper medical care it settled in her right leg, causing decay of the bone; although a great sufferer, she has worked for 26 years and taken care of herself without assistance. She had one hundred dollars in the bank in December, but in consequence of dull times was obliged to draw it out to meet expenses. Eleven years ago, she made the acquaintance of another lame girl, and formed with her a partnership both in their work and housekeeping. They share everything in common and their relations have been of a most affectionate and self-denying character.

In a garret, four stories up, was found a machine operator on men's clothing who said she was married at the age of 20; her husband was consumptive but lived 16 years after her marriage. During her married life she worked more or less, at home and in stores. She has two children, a boy of 11 and a girl of 5, but they do not now live with her; up to a short time since, the boy lived with her and went to school; her work failing, she could not pay his board in advance, and he was sent to live with relatives. At night, after working through the day, she makes clothes for her children and does her own sewing and washing; she has not had a new dress for three years, and she says it sometimes costs a good deal more than she earns to provide for herself and children, and that she has often had to go without her supper.

In another instance, a very bright, smart and most intelligent woman was found living in a small attic room lighted and ventilated by the skylight only. In her younger years, she said she taught school in summer and went to school in winter, studying music and preparing herself to enter the Normal school to become a teacher. Disappointed in this respect, she has had a rather hard life since, and now has a little child to support. While at work, she leaves her little girl at the Day Nursery and pays five cents for the privilege. In the dull season, she has lived on less than a dollar a week for food for herself and child. When seen she was doing quite well as compared with her experience for some years; she had paid her rent to date and had the first five dollars in her pocket over and above living expenses for many a day, with a prospect of earning sufficient to fully meet running expenses. She felt quite elated over what seemed good fortune to her, it being something new in her experience as a working woman.

In the same way, a very intelligent, well-educated and good-appearing lady, apparently quite comfortably situated with relatives, reported that five years ago her husband was sun-struck and two years after he was obliged to be confined in an asylum, where he died. During his illness and after his death, having no money or property, the support of the family including two children, now six and eight years respectively, devolved upon her, and she went out sewing, making cloaks and suits, and in dull seasons doing nursing and such other work as she could find. Being quite smart, she succeeded in making, as she says, $400 a year for almost four years. Constant application to work, often until 12 at night and sometimes on Sundays (equivalent to nine ordinary working days a week), affected her health and injured her eyesight. She has been treated for her eyes and was ordered by the doctor to suspend work, stay in doors and keep out of sun and lamp light; but she must earn money, and so she has kept on working. Her eyes weep constantly, she cannot see across the room and "the air seems always in a whirl" before her. She complains that women having husbands employed, work in shops for rates of pay less than girls who are dependent solely on themselves can afford. On account of her poor health, the past year has been a bad one for her, and she has been unable to meet her expenses. She was obliged to sell some of the furniture bought when married and other articles, and owed when seen three months' board for self and children; she gets aid from relatives in the shape of clothing for children, and that is all. She hopes something may be done for working girls and women, for, however strong they may be in the beginning, "they can't stand white slavery for ever."

The Working Women of Pittsburgh

Despite the growing importance of women in the nation's industrial system, the opening years of the twentieth century found the working conditions of women little improved over what they had been during the previous fifty years. At this time, however, one of the areas of investigation that commanded the attention of social workers was the plight of America's working girls.

In 1905 the Charities Publication Committee, including Jacob Riis and Jane Addams, was formed to conduct comprehensive surveys of urban social problems. The committee's organ, *Charities and the Commons,* attracted much attention in special issues in 1905 and 1906, dealing with the problems of blacks in northern cities. With financial help from the Russell Sage Foundation, which made possible the hiring of trained social workers, the committee launched an ambitious systematic study of Pittsburgh, Pennsylvania. Two years later, the findings were published in the important six-volume social study, *The Pittsburgh Survey.*

During the two years of the Pittsburgh project, condensed aspects of the study were published in *Charities.* Among these articles were studies of the working women of Pittsburgh, many of whom were immigrants.

SOURCE: Elizabeth B. Butler, **"Pittsburgh's Steam Laundry Workers,"** *Charities and the Commons* (April–October 1908), pp. 549–52.

The modern steam laundry is the latest instance of the routing of a home industry. Solitary washtub and red-armed washwoman —these are industrial types that are passing, as surely as individual loom and shuttle have passed, and the individual dye-vat for cloth. They are beaten back by the advance of the machine which has invaded and overcome the province of one kind of hand work after another. The type in the ascendant to-day is the low stone building with its washing machines, mangles, and steam ironers of a dozen kinds, its system of marking worked out in minute detail, and its network of agencies and drivers' routes to gather in trade from hotels and factories, from railroads and private homes. Here and there circumstance gives added reason for the growth of the newer type. A railroad center with its stream of travellers demanding quick, efficient service, its stations and Pullman-cars with their immaculate porters, its hotels and cafes, sending out wagon loads of table-linen—these are consumers who scarcely can wait until it is the whim of the sun that their linen be dried. The commercial laundry is the only possibility.

Of this, Pittsburgh laundrymen have taken advantage, and of the black smoke, too, and the smoke-filled fog, conspirators both against all fine fabrics. The knot of railroad lines, the travellers, the hotels, but most of all the black dust from the mills, have helped to make the industry prosperous. From the lower city to the East End there are no less than thirty-two steam laundries, four of them in charitable institutions, but all of them commercial, with a force of 2,402 employes, of whom 2,185 are women. As employers of women, exclusive of clerical work, the laundries stand third. Mercantile houses rank first and the stogy industry second.

The division of labor is carried far as in a factory. There is specialization for speed. Most of the women are young, as factory girls are young. Yet the differences of type among them are greater than one finds in any other industry. In the several departments,—washing, mangling, starching and ironing, checking and sorting,—there are different kinds and conditions of work, differences of mental and physical demand, and wide differences of personnel.

As it nears seven in the morning, one may see the girls coming down the street. Bleak and dull-red and square, the low buildings stand against the gray light. A single driver's wagon is in the alleyway. Several men, high-cheeked Slavs, have just gone in, but close behind them is a group of American girls, collarless and rough-jacketed, with shoes much worn and old. There is pride in their look, but none of the almost defiant independence which one instinctively reads into the stubborn pace of the three Polish girls who follow. These come linked together in the spirit of "we against the world," even if "we" be only three feeders at a mangle, and the world, that large impersonal thing which is represented by the foreman. There are young girls, too, girls out of school only a month or two, lacking the training of eye or hand or brain which might set them a step higher at the start. A rough-armed Irish-woman, a grandmother, walks with them. She has seen her trade go, together with her early strength, and has found here her only chance to get a steady job. There are others, women who have spent their youth too quickly, and have sold their strength at a little price. There are women worn out at other trades. And there are girls with fresh faces and bright eyes, girls who step quickly, surely, with the pride that comes from the consciousness of a trained hand and a clear brain. There are only two of these, but of the others there are many. The whistle from a neighboring factory shrills out the hour, there is the slow sound of an engine starting, a gathering whirr of belts and wheels, and the last girls disappear to take their places at the machine.

At the preliminary processes of washing, mangling, and starch-ing, place is found for the beginners and the girls of lowest grade. There are only a few women in the washroom, for this is preemi-nently the man's part of the laundry, and such women as work there are employed only on pieces which it is convenient to have done by hand. The washermen, who are frequently American, and the wringermen, who are nearly always Slavs, have full charge of the washing machines,—huge cylinders full of hot water and steam-ing clothes,—and of the extractors, which twist the clothes and fling out the water by centrifugal force. With haste always behind them, the men do not wait to let all the water run out before they lift the dripping garments into trucks and wheel them over to the metal wringers. The results are a wet floor and a cloud of steam, which affect not only the workers here but all the workers on the floors above, for the washroom is usually on the first floor or in the cellar. The convenience of the drivers, and a tradition, refera-ble perhaps to the washtubs in the kitchen, is responsible.

From this point of view, the washroom is the most important department in a laundry. On its construction and on the regulation of its work, depend the health of workers in all parts of the build-ing. Its location, its drainage, provision for the escape of steam and for forced ventilation, become matters of much significance.

Yet there is only one laundry in Pittsburgh, in which the washroom is on a floor above the other departments, and so shut off by concrete walls that the rest of the building is not filled with steam. One other has a second floor washroom, but the rest choose first floors or cellars with fine disregard of the discomfort and positive ill-health that may result. Yet we might expect that even if location were not considered carefully in the arrangement of departments, such provision would be made for the escape of steam and for adequate ventilation as to make the workrooms more tolerable. But in considering provision for the escape of steam, we have to meet a situation characteristic of Pittsburgh. In only one case is there any outlet except through the windows, and on a foggy day the windows are useless. For the Pittsburgh fog is not the fog that a coast town knows; it is moisture permeated with coal dust and grime, perilous to the eyes and throat of the pedestrian, and of a fatal, penetrating quality wherever open door or window gives it a chance to enter. It has to answer for many a spoiled lot of clothes which it seized on their way from washing machine to extractor,— a mishap not discoverable until they reached the ironing room and had to be sent back ignominiously for a repetition of the process from the beginning. What wonder, then, that there are orders for doors and windows to be kept closed? What wonder that in seven cases the washroom windows are so small and low, not over three feet by three, that air cannot come in nor steam fly out; or that in three cases there are no windows or other openings at all?

But to the girls standing just above, the hot boards seem scorching. The steam seems to work its way through cracks and crevices, and to attack them like a vicious thing until in dismay they give up their jobs and try what chance may have for them elsewhere. One girl told me that as long as she worked in a laundry, she always went home by a back street so that no one would see the old shoes which she had to wear. Tightfitting shoes were unendurable. "I never knew anyone who worked in a laundry long," said another girl. "The work's too hard, and you simply can't stand the heat."

Sometimes electric fans are provided, by the slit of a window at the far end of the room or near the stairway, but a single fan, or even two, is a feeble defense against clouds of steam rising from two to six boiling cylinders, ten hours a day. Even iron pipes to admit outside air, a device used in one basement washroom, are powerless in the presence of a hot six-roll mangle and a row of washing machines, cellar-wide.

Good drainage makes ventilation less difficult. In all but three cases, gutters run under the washing machine to carry off the waste, and where the floor is convex, there need not be much waste water under foot, if reasonable care is used in lifting the clothes. Yet in the majority of the rooms, nineteen cases, I found that the floor was either flat or sunken and filled with holes and that the water stood in pools. Sometimes this was in a cellar, closed in by rough, damp stones and lit by a flaring gas jet; sometimes it was on a first floor, a few steps away from the mangle-room and just beneath the ironers. Often it was in a basement, half lit by small, dim panes of glass, and foul with the odor of soiled linen and of steam that had risen and cooled for months without once being cleared by a sweep of fresh air.

For the women who work in these washrooms, there are few mitigating circumstances. In twenty out of the twenty-eight laundries, no women are employed regularly, but in the rest thirteen women work regularly, and more under extra pressure of trade. "You can't get a young woman to do this work," managers say. They are women whose strength has gone at other trades, housewifery mainly. For a dollar a day they work ten hours over the tubs, at flannels and socks, and sometimes fine things, that would need to be handled by an extra machine if they were machine-done. From a visit to one laundry, I have taken the following: "Cellar washroom; eight men employed. Two women hand washers for flannels. The firm finds that its trade in articles of this kind has doubled since it began to do this work by hand. The washroom is not well drained. Gutters beneath washing machines, but the floor is straight and has sunk in places. Windows are small, three feet by three. Ceiling low, less than ten feet. No escape for steam, and the air is foul." It is incongruous to find this survival of the home industry, with its discomforts, incorporated in a department of a factory industry imperfectly developed. It is questionable whether this survival is necessary. Some laundries succeed without it. Whether it be true or not that fine goods can be treated without undue wear and tear and yet without recourse to the washtub, one wonders what solution will offer itself when the present generation of old women has passed away. There is little hope for recruits from among the young women, to whom the factory tradition, the idea of collective work, is fundamental.

To the hand washers, and to all the other women in the plant, the location of the washroom below rather than above other departments, the imperfect drainage, inadequate ventilation, and lack of provision for the escape of steam, make work unnecessarily hard, and take too great a toll from their store of strength.

Opening out of the washroom or on the floor just above it, is the room where the mangle stands. Under the steam heated metal rolls of the great machine, or around the steam cylinder, winding in tortuous ways through inner recesses, go table and bed linen, towels, and all manner of flat things, to come out smooth and dry at the farther end. There is almost a fascination in watching the even pace of the continuous apron that carries the sheets along, the developed efficiency of this socialized household ironing day. The work is done by the machine. The responsibility on the mangle girls is relatively small.

B. THE BITTER CRY OF THE CHILDREN

Italian Slave Children

Among the most pitiful victims of child labor were the offsprings of immigrant workers. Strangers in a new land, these children were exploited by not only native employers but members of their own ethnic group. Some of the most notorious dealers in child labor were the Italian padrones, or masters. Either through contractual agreements with parents or through the kidnapping of the children, the padrones "employed" or "enslaved" the youngsters. Sent out as mendicant musicians by the masters, hordes of these juvenile minstrels roamed the streets of New York City and Philadelphia.

In 1873 the *Gazzetta del Popolo* of Turin contained an item that had appeared in the *Reforma* of Rome "showing the enormous proportions to which the traffic in children between Southern Italy and New York has reached." New York City newspapers, notably the *Herald* and *Sun,* also became concerned about the padrone problem. They gave prominence to cases that were being brought by the authorities against padrones under the Civil Rights Act. The reported testimony revealed the charges of cruelty and exploitation made by the young victims against their masters. On September 16, 1873, the New York *Herald* contained the contents of a report on the "Italian Slave Children" of Philadelphia made by the police there.

SOURCE: New York *Herald*, September 16, 1873. **Italian Slave Children**

A Heavy Haul of Philadelphia Padrones and Their Victims.
One Hundred and Fifty-nine Arrests by the Police.

SCENES AND INCIDENTS

A Large Batch of Children Let Go, but the Trade Effectually Broken Up.

THE PADRONES ON THE MOVE

Philadelphia, Sept. 15, 1873.

About five weeks ago a letter was sent to the Mayor of this city, by an official adjunct of the Italian government, and this letter was worded in the form of a complaint. The letter was turned over to the Chief of the Police, and the officers were detailed to make an investigation and report. The officers, following the young street Arabs and musicians, discovered that they all reached a certain locality of the city, and that the home of one, in many instances, was also the home of ten, twenty, thirty, and even more slaves of an Italian padrone.

Last night I received word from a police official to be on hand at five o'clock this morning, as the hovels of the Italians were all to be thoroughly examined. At the very early hour indicated the Chief of Police, along with several of his captains, left the Central Headquarters, and, unknown to anyone, proceeded to the corner of Eighth and Washington streets. There they joined a reserve of forty select officers, and, along with them, set out in the direction of the dismal and dreary Italian quarter of the town. To reach this region it was necessary to pass along thoroughfares familiar to me, for the filth in the gutter and the tottering forms in the rum shops indicated that the officers were hard by Alaska street and St. Mary's. I passed ten minutes in rear of the policemen in this dreadful neighborhood, and the negroes peeping out from behind broken shutters and crumbling door posts, jeered at, insulted and cursed me at every step. One sight that met my eyes was that of a delirious mulatto, drunken and frenzied by gin, fighting the air with his fists, and striking an iron post with his head. There was no time to take cognizance of scenes like these, for the Italian quarters were several squares below. At last the officers reached them. They begin at No. 733 Carpenter street, and run regularly along for an entire block. The officers forced an entrance in No. 733.

AH! WHAT A SIGHT

There were three rooms in the house and three beds in a room. In them were huddled, with and without clothing, men, women, and children. The latter were exceedingly numerous, and laid there under circumstances of the most abject poverty and woe. The onset created the greatest consternation. The air was filled with cries of terror, anguish and distress, blended with growls and hisses of displeasure. Dark, dire faces—some young, some old, some fearstricken and devilish and lowering—peered from every corner, as, in a moment, forms were supported upon their elbows or mingled in indescribable confusion in the centre of the room. One bed held four occupants, while the children leaped up from rude straw heaps upon the floor. Some were clothed in tattered undergarments, filthy and foul from wear, and some were destitute of any garments at all. Some dashed for escape to the windows, while others clasped their hands as if in fear and prayer.

There seemed to be a central figure upon whom the children fixed their eyes, as if for aid, and by this the officers knew that he was the stern, hard master they obeyed. He was arrested and the house thoroughly searched. Harps, violins, tamborines and musical instruments of every nature filled up the narrow spaces in odd corners about the rooms or else hung suspended by rude strings from the wall. At the rear of the house was a musical repair shop, with tools and instruments scattered about in reckless confusion. From this one house the three rooms of which each measured by rule eight feet by ten, forty-six parties were taken and hurried to the Second district station house. The next house entered was also located in Carpenter street, No. 821. This place was fouler still. It contained two rooms, which measured 12x10. There were the same features as in the other house, but there was something more. Beneath the front room there was a cellar and in this cellar were many human forms—all these of small children. I have already described the cellar of Alaska street, and this underground apartment was almost the same. The hole was full of filthy garbage, cabbage, leaves and the decaying relics of many unfrugal meals. It was an abominable place, the breeding spot of disease and the abode of roaches and vermin. Some of the children screamed as the officers came down, and naked younglings crouched in terror and anguish against the damp and clammy juttings of the walls. There were no musical instruments in their underground den.

THE AWFUL CHILL AND DAMPNESS

would have ruined their strings. Strange is it to a good and Christian people that the raw catgut of a violin should have been of more import than the delicate and tender cords of a human heart. The children were ordered to put on their garments. Why need I tell you what they were. Look at the ragamuffins at every corner. Behold the dirt and filth ground in the web and woof of all they wear, smearing the skin wherever they touch, and breeding mortification in the lips of the slightest wound. Such were the garments they put on, and stretching out their dark and slender arms the children, grasping with their little fingers the forms of those above them, frightened and weeping ascended the stairs. Sixteen were arrested here and sent away in the dawning light of early morning to join those sent on before. In describing their house, I have also described the one next to it, for it was modelled precisely the same. Fourteen occupants were found herein.

I do not wish to repeat the same sad story over and over again, as it was seen in different lights under a dozen different roofs, and so I pass to No. 1003 in the same thoroughfare.

To describe this place is impossible. Any accurate delineation of it would meet with no belief. Its foulness was terrible, and its stench caused several of the officers to withdraw to the door. There were six rooms which, by rule, measured eight feet by ten. A small tobacco shop, in front, upon the ground floor, kept back its filthiness from the curious gaze of pedestrians, but beyond that store were conditions of filth which no one could imagine humanity could bear. The floor was strewn with rinds of melons, apples, and other seasonable fruits, along with heaps of animal and vegetable matter in every stage of decay. The children positively lay directly in the midst of all this noxious manure, and every breath they drew sucked in its poisonous fumes. Roaches, fleas, and lice even, in the dim light that found its path in hidden rays across the dingy floor, could clearly be seen clustering at each point where filth and decay had wrought the fullest work, and the voice of youth and innocence was not strong enough to send its token to the charitable world from the quarters of its wretched prison. Fathers and mothers imagine your children sleeping there; for naught but such a reflection will touch your heart with the woe and misery of these little spirits, which, to some one in a distant land, are as dear as the happiness of your offspring is to you.

Picture your own dear ones going out at day-break, weak, faint, wan, weeping, bearing heavy harps upon their shoulders, and then picture them returning to dreary homes like those I have described, only to be struck, beaten and lashed, because the world had been less generous to them than the brutal, greedy and pinching soul of a domineering fiend imagined that it would be. Take this picture, hang it up in your dwellings, for nothing else can move you to look at this matter in its proper light. This "Italian system" has been brought up before you time and time again—mine is no new story —and yet the system lives and grows, and becomes more heinous every day.

I have no heart to carry this matter to further particulars; suffice it to say that 159 arrests were made, and, in one instance, 32 children were found ruled by the curse and the lash of a single man. This afternoon, at five o'clock, these children will give their evidence and tell the story of their woes. An interpreter will be furnished by the authorities of the Italian government residing here, and strange things will, no doubt, be revealed.

THE ANTI-CHILD-LABOR CRUSADE

At the turn of the century, organizations known as child labor committees, formed by social workers and public-minded citizens, played an important role in the fight for effective child labor legislation. One of the first and best known of these groups was the New York City Child Labor Committee. Florence Kelley, a prominent social worker, was a prime force in the formation of the New York body. Having come to New York City in 1899 from Chicago, where she had gained an outstanding reputation as Governor John P. Altgeld's chief factory inspector (the first American woman to hold such a position), she joined Lillian Wald at the Henry Street Settlement House. Called the "Joan of Arc" of the social workers, Kelley made child labor "her first concern." She and Lillian Wald succeeded in getting the representatives of the city's settlement houses to form a temporary child labor committee. In 1902, with the help of educators, "socialist millionaires," civic-minded groups and individuals, Kelley and her colleagues formed a permanent Child Labor Committee to raise funds, collect and disseminate child labor information and seek effective legislation. A year later, the New York body sponsored and achieved the passage, in Albany, of four key pieces of child labor legislation: (1) the Finch-Hills Acts which strengthened the laws regarding the hiring of children in factories and mercantile houses; (2) an amendment to the compulsory education law; (3) an enactment to tighten provisions against parental perjury; and (4) the nation's first street trades law. Encouraged by their legislative success and realizing that child labor was a national problem, in 1903 the New York City Committee took the lead in the formation of the National Child Labor Committee. Members maintained a militant propaganda campaign through their frequent literary contributions to such socially concerned publications as *The Annals, Charities and the Commons* and the National Committee's own *Child Labor Bulletin*.

Below are samples of articles that appeared in these social-conscious publications. One of many anti-child-labor articles presented by *The Annals* attacked the important problem of "Children in American Street Trades." In 1914, while Congress was considering the first federal anti-child-labor legislation, the Palmer-Owen bill, Florence Kelley wrote an article for the *Child Labor Bulletin*. Her organization, the National Consumer League, had attempted to carry the fight on the state level. Finding local progress too slow, the League sought national action in 1904, and succeeded in securing the passage of the first federal child labor law. Although the act was declared void by the United States Supreme Court, the movement had served to make the nation child-labor conscious.

SOURCE: Myron E. Adams, **"Children in American Street Trades,"** *The Annals* (May 1905), pp. 23–26.

Although the method of distributing the daily papers may seem to vary in different cities the means remain ever the same. The newsboy has always been regarded as indispensable for securing a satisfactory delivery or distribution. The purpose he serves is so evident, his place in the system seems so determined by necessity, that much thought has been given to the labor, but very little to the laborer. In truth the public has grown to look upon him as one of the factors in everyday life, able to care for himself and to work out his own salvation. That some do this there is no doubt. The newsboys who have gone from the street into business and even into larger affairs of state and of the nation refer with pride to the road over which they have traveled.

The newsboy has become a part of our city environment. A familiar figure, rather undersized as we know him best, flipping the street cars, or standing on street corners holding his stock in trade under his arm. A veritable merchant of the street, who scans each passer-by as a possible customer. Quick of wit and intent upon his trade he reads their peculiarities at a glance, and makes the most of their weaknesses. The public sees him at his best and neglects him at his worst. He is not considered in the problem of child labor, because he works in the open and is seemingly apart from the associations which are so hostile to the health and happiness of the factory child.

It seems the part of the iconoclast to controvert the popular conception of the newsboy. His energy and enthusiasm in the few hours when his work is at its best add to the picturesque in the city's life; his sacrifice and his service have always been the peculiar field of the melodrama or the boy's story book. It is very hard to throw these early impressions ruthlessly aside. This class of boys have the ability to do things which attract and to conceal those things which repel.

Undoubtedly in the early days of paper selling and before the child of foreign parents secured such a monopoly of street trades, there were some features of paper selling which were more attractive than they are to-day. With the changing character of the street there has also come the realization that the ordinary boy has little or no future there. The opportunity for him in the business of the paper is small. In fact the uncertainty and license of the street provides but a poor education for any occupation which requires either regular or persistent effort.

With the demand for more effective restriction of child labor and with compulsory education laws the fact has become obvious that the laborer on the street is one of the chief offenders against these laws. Investigations conducted by persons familiar with the problem have disclosed the fact that while street trading offered temptations to which the street boy was particularly susceptible, there has been little or no attempt to regulate and improve existing conditions.

It has also been noticeable that similar conditions prevail in most American cities. The dangers of the street trades are not limited to the great cities of the East, but are equally true of the western cities and of the smaller cities throughout the country. This matter has been more carefully considered in our great cities, and we shall take as the best illustration of the general dangers of street trading those found in the city of Chicago.

Chicago is particularly fortunate in the character of its street trades. Many forces have combined in the newspaper industry to make possible a system of distribution, which, both in simplicity and completeness, excells that of most of American cities. A system has been gradually developed in Chicago which excludes many of the deplorable tendencies in other cities. This allows the paper to pass from the publisher to the reader with the least possible waste of time or energy, and insures in the case of many of its workers the establishment of newspaper selling as an industry. The industrial possibilities have been largely due to the practical interest that the Chicago papers have taken in the newsboy, and in the development of a regular and methodical system of paper selling. This interest has not merely been evident in the desire to give some pleasure to the newsboy, by means of gymnasium, drill-halls and other forms of practical helpfulness, but also, to a much greater degree, in the attempt to put the work on a basis that would insure him a business and a regular livelihood.

Chicago is mapped out by carefully defined boundaries into "routes," assigned to men known as "route carriers." A wagon representing each paper covers these routes, not once, but several times during the day. At regular points along the route the driver is met by the men who are owners of the routes. These men are often accompanied by boys, waiting for a supply of papers for house to house delivery, and for sale on street corners in residence districts. They are the news dealer's assistants, and as a rule prove themselves reliable as well as prompt. In fact the competition for this employment is so keen that the boy must "hustle" or another will be given the coveted position.

In the early phases of newspaper selling the street corner in the downtown district was the scene of physical battles for supremacy. For many years the Irish lad held absolute possession. With strong fist and ready tongue, backed by many friends, he seemed almost invincible, but back of it all there was a certain lack of persistence that proved to be his undoing. The Jewish boy came next. He would not fight the Irish lad with the weapons of his choosing, he knew a better way. Every day he was at his post, in winter and summer, in good weather and bad, the customer could depend on his appearance with the paper. So his trade increased, and at last he gained a monopoly of the corner. In turn he fell, and the Italian, the prince of street venders, because he possessed both of the strong points of his predecessors, secured the monopoly of most of the good corners. He was both a ready fighter and a persistent worker.

Meanwhile the circulation managers of the newspapers came into the field with assurance of assistance to him who possessed the corner. The corner, which had been merely a prize for a physical contest, now came to have a quasi-legal position that implied

pecuniary value. Its value was so great that it could not pass unnoticed by the circulation managers, and protection of some sort
seemed necessary. The social privilege must have a more stable
backing than merely the "good will" of the street. Protection finally
came from the newspaper in the form of a card bearing the name
of the dealer and the position of his corner, with the condition
that no one could buy early papers without presenting this card. In
this way they were able to regulate the transfer of the corner. "For,
while they did not often interfere with the transfer of a corner
from one boy to another, if they knew him to be in the pay of another paper, or if they suspected that he was getting possession
of a number of corners in order to speculate on them, or to hold a
monopoly, they did not give him a card." This protection gives the
dealers confidence in their position, and inspires them to be both
regular in their trade and courteous to customers if they would
establish a business.

The plan which was so well adapted to the downtown district
was established on a more liberal scale throughout the city. The
principal corners in the outlying districts were occupied by so-
called "Canadian" boys, a title often given to the dealer who de-
livers papers to the smaller boy, and who controls the circulation
in his district. The dealers are empowered by the papers to arrange
the territory each boy is to cover. Some of these boys receive a
small salary from the newspapers, others are dependent upon the
small sum which they derive from the sub-letting of their districts,
and they manage to earn a very fair salary when they combine the
actual selling of papers with their other duties. Among the men
and boys who own corners outside the downtown district there is
a great divergence, both in age and nationality, but the boy finally
chosen as overseer is usually the best representative of the district
in which he lives.

SOURCE: Florence Kelley, **"Protection for American Children,"**
Child Labor Bulletin (May 1914), pp. 14–19.

We are to speak tonight in behalf of the Palmer Bill, which
proposes to give to all the children employed in manufacture

throughout this whole nation certain minimum degrees of protection. My only possible contribution to this discussion consists of a few observations of the absurd discrepancy between Uncle Sam's care for industry and for the inanimate world, and the way he shirks his duty towards his children. For instance, in a little village in Maine where I spent the summer several years ago, one of the neighbors lives in a wretched boat about five miles out at sea. He is a man without a country. He cannot land on American soil, though he is a native of Maine. He will probably never be able to land again on American soil, because some years ago he went into Blue Hill Bay and gathered there 1,560 scallops. On the shores of Maine scallops are important items of food, for the people are poor. Their food supplies are very meagre compared with the food supply of New Orleans. Every one is interested that fish and shellfish should be protected by the federal government. We never hear complaints there that the law is too rigidly enforced in behalf of lobsters and scallops. The federal government places a fine of a dollar a scallop for every one taken illegally. This man had taken 1,560 illegally, and will never in the world have $1,560 with which to pay that fine. So he spends the winters in the inclement climate to the north of us, on Canadian soil, and comes back in the summer as near to the home village as he dares, and fishes all summer; and the old neighbors (all of whom say that it is right that the law should be enforced and the fisherman never ought to have taken those scallops), sail out and buy fish and carry him some of the necessaries of life, and there he spends year after year and will, so far as anyone can foresee, as long as he lives.

In the village there is a factory where such herring as are caught in the weirs, and such scallops and oysters and clams and other things as the neighbors might put up legally, each in its own season, are canned for the market. The law of Maine requires that children shall not work in a factory or a cannery until they have completed a specified part of the public school curriculum and until they are at least fourteen years of age. But the factory inspector lives in Augusta, and the nearest Justice of the Peace is twenty-eight miles away, and the roads are often bad.

What effect must it have upon the moral discernment of all the people in that region around about to have that man punished, justly (and the people recognize that it is just, that the food supply should be protected to the uttermost)—what must it do to the moral discernment of the children especially, that the punishment inflicted by Uncle Sam is so rigorous in behalf of the food supply, but that the children may break the law from the time they are nine and ten, and eleven and twelve years old; that they may be taught not to go to school, though they know the law requires attendance; that they may be taught to go to work, though the law forbids it? Because all of that part of the enforcement of the law is politely left by Uncle Sam to the local authorities, who do nothing for the children, while he himself protects the food supply.

I have seen another very curious and sinister example of that same thing in a different part of the country. For four years I was responsible for the enforcement of factory legislation, including the child labor law, in the state of Illinois. One part of the duty of my staff was to enforce the law in the stockyards. I am haunted by a hideous memory of one of the hottest days in the hot month of August, in the year 1894. I was in one of the great cooling rooms, where icicles hung from the ceiling, because the preservation of meat required that the temperature there should never be allowed to rise above the freezing point. All day long wretched little boys at the doors of that cooling room were employed in swinging open at short intervals one of the heavy doors, moving on wheels at the top and bottom, long enough to let a little electric train of flat cars come in on a little narrow gauge railroad, every car piled high with sides of beef. The day was such that three men working out of doors in the Yards died of sunstroke, and others were stricken and taken away ill from their work. But all day long these little boys went, at short intervals, out from the zero temperature of the cooling-room and held the door open in that torturing heat, while the little train passed in, and then came back swinging the door into the cooling-room again. That work was very simple, opening a door; any little boy could do it for the doors moved on wheels. But the effect of the changing temperature upon those children was such—the excess of chill when they were inside and the excess of heat when they were outside—that always during the warm half of the year there were kept in all those great meat-packing establishments three times as many children on the

payroll for doing that work as ever were employed at one time—
In all those plants the federal government was paying federal inspectors to examine the meat with a microscope and in other ways, to make quite sure that the food supply we were shipping to Germany was in a wholesome condition. It was my duty to see to the children. I was responsible for the inspection of every factory, workshop, laundry, sweatshop, tenement work-room in the whole state of Illinois. We had a total appropriation for a staff of twelve persons of $10,000, out of which had to be paid traveling expenses for the inspectors from one end of Illinois to the other, printing, postage and office rent, and counsel fees for defending the constitutionality of the statute and prosecuting offenders. It was an absurd and preposterous allowance of money for the care of the children and the inspection of workrooms. The state of Illinois had a perfect right to refuse to spend more money than that. The federal government recognized a duty to promote our trade with Germany by spending more money every year on its inspections of the meat of each one of the great corporations than the state of Illinois spent for the whole enforcement of the child labor legislation of the third great manufacturing state in the republic. How confusing to the moral sense of the people employed in that industry, that the federal government recognizes its duty to keep the meat wholesome, yet leaves it to the sense of duty—or the lack of sense of duty—of the state of Illinois to have all the working conditions of all the working people of the state of Illinois as wretched as any employer might choose to allow them to be.

Such confusing contrasts one can repeat in innumerable instances wherever one is alert to see how we express our sense of duty as a nation; how immeasurably more punctiliously we enforce the laws of the nation than the states feel bound to enforce their own laws for the protection of the most defenceless of their citizens, the young children, the young boys and girls whom poverty constrains to work for their living.

We are bringing on in this republic three classes of citizens, three classes of children. The children of the first class are those fortunate boys and girls who live on the Pacific Coast and in the northwestern states, where every child receives a generous education, every child of sane mind is compelled to receive a generous education. No child along the Pacific Coast may go to work illiterate, no child may go to work defective in stature, no child may work at night. Those will be citizens of the first-class—all the future citizens of Washington, and Oregon, and California, and Idaho and that whole congeries of northwestern states. We may look with confidence to the citizenship of that part of our country forty years hence, when we shall be in our graves and they will be the republic.

The second class of citizens are the immigrant children, who live in the northern and northeastern states. Subject to such derogations as I have been describing, it is still true that the children of the north barring perhaps certain textile manufacturing parts of New England and the mountain regions of the Catskills and Adirondacks, the children who come out of the steerage and settle in the cities, are getting a degree of education which most of us twenty years ago would have regarded as quite Utopian. In the City of New York, sinful as we are in many respects, we have at least prohibited the work of the children in the tenements. We have prohibited the manufacture of articles *for children* in the tenements. We have put the canning industries under inspection and investigation, under the penalty of the law. No immigrant or native child can today, without infinite difficulty, escape the requirement that the child must finish six years of the work of the public schools before it can work for wages, to whomsoever payable. I think the chances of those immigrant city children are far more brilliant than the chances of the village mill children in my native state of Pennsylvania, because there, I grieve to say, we do not enforce our laws.

Then we are bringing on children of the third class, future citizens of the third class, in Georgia, North Carolina, South Carolina, Alabama and every other state which lacks compulsory education and an efficient enforcement of such provision for the children as the Palmer Bill includes. These are native American white children, whom we are reducing to future citizens of the third class over a very great area of this republic.

I have spoken of the way in which the states fail to enforce their own laws, often fail to enact them. I will cite one more example which has fallen under my observation. During those years when it was my impossible task to enforce the child labor law in Illinois I made the acquaintance of the great Illinois glass bottle works in the city of Alton. No child was too young to work in that factory, though the laws forbade their employment below the fourteenth birthday. The superintendent of the works told me that, a few years before I made his acquaintance, when he was in dire need of some boys to carry bottles, a widow came to him with little children, one in knee pants and one still wearing little kilts. She said that their father had been killed on the railroad and she was penniless; she had gone to the mayor of the city asking help and he had told her to put her able-bodied son at work. The able-bodied son was nine years old. She went to the superintendent who, in his need of boys, yielded to temptation. He said he had remembered it six years with shame. He told that widow that he would not trouble with one little boy, but if she would take home the smaller one and put him also into knee pants and then bring both the children back, he would put them both at work on the night shift. The widow took her little boy home, changed his kilts for knee pants, and took both her little orphan sons back, and they went to work on the night shift in that glass factory. At the moment it was not illegal. Afterwards when I made the acquaintance of the situation the child labor law had been enacted and it was my duty to enforce heavy penalties for such cruelty as that. There were still violations of the law, there were still little children ten years old at work, though they could not legally work at night before they were sixteen. But though I prosecuted that corporation before the magistrates of the five surrounding counties I never secured a conviction.

After I ceased to be inspector the idea occurred to my successor that, if he should take those defendants and all his witnesses, including the little children, all the way across the state of Illinois to the northern counties, he might be able to obtain a conviction. He made the experiment and succeeded, but he exceeded his appropriation in the process, and the work of inspection had to cease after the prosecution had succeeded. Such a travesty was the enforcement of the law in the third great manufacturing state of the Union.

Now those processes do not occur in the federal courts. There the jurors are not the immediate neighbors of the offenders. I submit to you that in the interest of having one class of citizens in the future, we need one enforcing authority for our legislation for the protection of the children, the federal courts.

C. WORKINGMEN IN AN IMPERSONAL SOCIETY

The Sweating System

One of the most notorious aspects of nineteenth-century industrial life was the "sweating system." The term was applied to the process in which manufacturers distributed material to contractors who, in turn, subcontracted the work to people performing the tasks in their homes. Historically, the system began in the early nineteenth century among the native workers who then dominated the clothing trade. Later, when the Irish moved into that field, they inherited the in-resident method of production. At the turn of the century, nearly three quarters of the workers in Manhattan's sweatshops were Jews and the remainder Italians. Then the well-known sweating district of New York City, bounded by Eighth Street, the Bowery, Catherine Street and the East River, had some 450,000 persons, including many children, who lived and worked in their homes. The denizens of the sweatshops toiled long hours for low wages and under terrible conditions producing mainly garments and artificial flowers. Many youngsters found plying street trades, with their peculiar evils, preferable to working with the family at home.

One of the contributions of the famous American economist John R. Commons to the reports of the U. S. Industrial Commission (1901) dealt with the sweating system. A prominent figure in the progressive movement of the early twentieth century, Commons, like his colleague Edward A. Ross, was a nativist. Though these progressives believed passionately in the political processes of democracy, they were very pessimistic and distrustful of the new industrial society that was evolving. They joined other nativists in their fear of the newer immigrants, and their writings, though scholarly, underscored the evils of unrestricted immigration.

SOURCE: **Reports of the United States Industrial Commission on Immigration and on Education,** XV (Washington, D.C., 1901), pp. 319–22.

The term "sweating" or "sweating system" originally denoted a system of sub-contracts, wherein the work is let out to contractors to be done in small shops or homes. "In practice," says the report of the Illinois Bureau of Labor Statistics (1892, p. 358), "sweating consists of the farming out by competing manufacturers to competing contractors of the material for garments, which in turn is distributed among competing men and women to be made up."

The system to be contrasted with the sweating system is the "factory system," wherein the manufacturer employs his own workmen, under the management of his own foreman or superintendent, in his own building, with steam, electric, or water power. In the sweating system the foreman becomes a contractor, with his own small shop and foot-power machine. In the factory system the workmen are congregated where they can be seen by the factory inspectors, and where they can organize or develop a common understanding. In the sweating system they are isolated and unknown.

The sweating system has undergone significant changes during the past 50 years. The early part of the last century, when the term seems to have originated in England, it applied to ready-made new clothing in the form of army clothing given out to contractors. At that time each tailor usually made the entire coat at home. The manufacturer of ready-made clothing and army clothing would give his work to a contractor who was a responsible party, usually not a tailor himself. This boarding-house keeper or saloon keeper was a subcontractor, though not a tailor. He in turn would give this work out to the individual tailors whom he personally knew and who were responsible for the work. The money received by these subcontractors for their part was called "sweat money," implying that their profit was the difference between the price they received from the manufacturer or contractor and the price paid to the tailor for making the garment, and that they invested no labor in the transaction.

There was an agitation against this system in the early fifties because of the low condition of the tailors. They worked for very low wages and many of them were unemployed much of the time. The work used to be made in between seasons for one-third and one-fourth of the regular price.

In the sixties the influx of the Russian Jews in the ready-made clothing trade who replaced the native and Irish tailors, began to be felt. Here the incursion of the foreigner seems to have been irresistible. His success was due, not always to the lower wages he was willing to take, for he was competing with the outcasts of the English tailoring trade, the unskilled English woman and the wretched and often imported Irishman, whose wages were as low as the contractor was willing to pay. But the success of the immigrant was due to his willingness to change the mode of production by using the sewing machine and division of labor against which the native tailor showed a decided aversion. Here the influx of the foreign Jew has wrought a complete change in the contract system. The old contractor was a mere middleman and had no need for any knowledge of the tailoring trade, and was mostly a lodging-house keeper, who secured the work by giving a cash deposit for the goods he took from the manufacturer and distributed among the wretched tailors in the lodging house and the helpless women in his vicinity who completed the whole garment. He was replaced by the Jewish contractor, who made his work in a shop. This Jewish contractor was not a mere middleman; he was necessarily a tailor and an organizer of labor, for his work was done by a system of division of labor calling for various grades and forms of skill, viz., the baster, machinist, and presser, with various subdivisions, such as fitter, busheler, finisher, buttonhole maker, feller, basting puller, etc.

The position of the contractor or sweater now in the business in American cities is peculiarly that of an organizer and employer of immigrants. The man best fitted to be a contractor is the man who is well acquainted with his neighbors, who is able to speak the language of several classes of immigrants, who can easily persuade his neighbors or their wives and children to work for him, and in this way can obtain the cheapest help. The contractor can increase the number of people employed in the trade at very short notice. During the busy season, when the work doubles, the number of people employed increases in the same proportion. All of the contractors are agents and go around among the people. Housewives, who formerly worked at the trade and abandoned it after marriage, are called into service for an increased price of a dollar or two a week. Men who have engaged in other occupations, such as small business, peddling, etc., and are out of the business most of the year, are marshaled into service by the contractor, who knows all of them, and can easily look them up and put them in as competitors, by offering them a dollar or two a week more than they are getting elsewhere. It is the contractor who has introduced the Italian home finishers in the trade; he has looked them up and taught them the work, and is getting it made for less than half the wages that he formerly paid for the same work.

The contractor never has at one time a large amount of work. Through him the industry is scattered over a wide area, among all kinds of people, and he thrives as long as they do not know one another. The contractor is an important factor in the clannishness of the immigrant nationalities. It is to him due in part that we have in large cities the Jewish districts, Polish districts, Swedish districts, etc., with very little assimilation. The contractors establish their shops in the heart of the district where the people live, and since they can practically earn their living at home, they have no opportunity of mingling with others or of learning from the civilization of other people.

The following is a typical case. "A Polish Jew in Chicago," at a time when very few of the Poles were tailors, opened a shop in a Polish neighborhood. He lost money during the time he was teaching the people the trade, but finally was a gainer. Before he opened the shop he studied the neighborhood; he found the very poorest quarters where most of the immigrant Poles lived. He took no one to work except the newly arrived Polish women and girls. The more helpless and dependent they were, the more sure they were of getting work from him. In speaking about his plans he said: "It will take these girls years to learn English and to learn how to go about and find work. In that way I will be able to get their labor very cheap." His theory turned out to be practical. He has since built several tenement houses.

The contractor in the clothing trade is largely responsible for the primitive mode of production; for the foot-power sewing machine; for the shops in the alleys, in the attics, on top floors, above stables, and, in some cases, in the homes of the people. These small shops are able, on account of low rent and meager wages, to compete successfully, although with foot power, against the large shops and factories with steam or electric power. Usually it is not necessary to have more than $50 to start a shop with foot-power machines. As there is no investment in goods, the contractor runs no risk. Little managing ability is required, because the number of employees is small.

The unlimited hours of work, often 7 days in the week, is a feature of the contracting system. The contractor himself works unlimited hours. His shop is open most of the time. He deals with people who have no knowledge of regular hours. He keeps them in the dark with regard to the prevailing number of hours that other people work.

The contractor is an irresponsible go-between for the manufacturer, who is the original employer. He has no connection with the business interests of the manufacturer nor is his interest that of his help. His sphere is merely that of a middleman; he is practically useless in a large factory. He holds his own mainly because of his ability to get cheap labor, and is in reality merely the agent of the manufacturer for that purpose. In this he in the main succeeds, because he lives among the poorest class of people, knows them personally, and knows their circumstances and can drive the hardest kind of a bargain. A very large number of the people who work in the sewing trade for contractors usually hope to become contractors themselves. When they succeed in this they reduce the prices, since the contractor when he first takes work out takes it for less money than other contractors.

Usually when work comes in to the contractor from the manufacturer and is offered to his employees for a smaller price than has been previously paid, the help will demonstrate and ask to be paid the full price. Then the contractor tells them, "I have nothing to do with the price. The price is made for me by the manufacturer. I have very little to say about the price." That is, he cuts himself completely loose from any responsibility to his employees as to how much they are to get for their labor, throwing the responsibility on the manufacturer who originally gave him the work. The help do not know the manufacturer. They can not register their complaint with the man who made the price for their labor. The man who did not make the price for their labor—the contractor— claims that it is of no use to complain to him. So that no matter how much the price for labor goes down, there is no one responsible for it.

In case the help form an organization and send a committee to the manufacturer, the manufacturer will invariably say, "I do not employ you, and I have nothing to do with you;" and when they go back to the contractor and file their complaint, he will invariably say, "I am not making the price for your labor. I am simply paying you as much as I can out of what I get from the manufacturer." This is also true with regard to any agreements of a labor organization that may be made. If an agreement is made with a contractor, it is usually worthless, because he has no property invested that can be levied upon. If the agreement is made with the manufacturer, it does not hold, because he is not violating it. In this irresponsible state of the business it is extremely difficult to devise any way in which organizations can make agreements and enforce them.

There is always a cut-throat competition among contractors. A contractor feels more dependent than any of his employees. He is always speculating on the idea of making a fortune by getting more work from the manufacturer than his neighbor and by making the work cheaper. Usually when he applies for work in the inside shop he comes in, hat in hand, very much like a beggar. He seems to feel the utter uselessness of his calling in the business. Oftentimes the contractor is forced to send work back, because he can not make it under the conditions on which he took it, yet he does not dare to refuse the offer for fear the manufacturer will not give him more of his work. So he tries to figure it down by every device, and yet, perhaps, in the end is forced to send it back.

Unemployment and Layoffs

The worker's greatest dread was unemployment resulting from business depressions and seasonal layoffs. America's economy has been subject to periodic business collapses which have thrown vast numbers of breadwinners out of jobs. Since the immigrant workers occupied the lower rungs of the occupational ladder, they generally suffered most from the adverse economic situations that developed in the nineteenth and early twentieth centuries, particularly those that followed the panics of 1873, 1893 and 1907. The depression years of 1873 to 1878 were the most severe in American history until that time. In addition to throwing tens of thousands of men out of work, the depression years of the 1870s permitted employers to cut wages, to make extensive use of lockouts and blacklisting and to launch successful attacks on labor unions.

The panic of 1873, which was signaled by the closing of the banking house of Jay Cooke and Company in September, undermined the nation's whole credit system. By the end of the year, there had been more than five thousand commercial failures with liabilities totaling one quarter of a billion dollars. The items below contain newspaper accounts of hardships among workers created by the debacle.

SOURCE: New York *Herald,* November 9, 1873. **Labor Depression in Brooklyn**

The Record of a Very Dull Week—Closing Factories and Curtailment of Expenses Upon Every Side—Heavy Discharge of Hatters.

There certainly has been no improvement in the labor market of Brooklyn during the past week, despite the confident assurance of many employers of an early resumption of the old standard of business a few days ago. Every branch of industry and trade is more or less seriously affected, and the greatest sufferers are, of course, the producers, the working people. The storekeepers, dry goods, lace, hosiery, glassware and jewelry dealers, wholesale and retail, all complain of the falling off in their receipts since the last week in October. There is less shopping now among the ladies, who, strange though it may appear, are accredited with a sudden impulse to practice economy and not buy anything that they do not actually want for immediate use. Meanwhile many of these tradespeople who keep retail stores pretend that there is a wonderful falling off in the prices of articles. This impression they endeavor to give for the purpose of creating a market for their wares, although the observant purchaser fails to see any diminution in the prices. A representative of the *Herald* yesterday ascertained the following facts illustrative of the evil effects of the tidal wave of depression which has swept over the working people of Brooklyn:—

A SKIRT FACTORY

An extensive factory, a building about 200 feet square, situated on Nostrand avenue, near Myrtle, seems "like a hall deserted." Such is really its condition. It has ceased to manufacture felt skirts, in the making of which it, up to within a few days past, employed about 200 men, women and children, who earned from $5 to $30 per week. The proprietor does not hold out much inducement calculated to inspire the discharged operatives with the hope of early employment.

PAPER PRINTERS AND STAINERS' FACTORY

On the corner of Walworth street and Willoughby avenue stands the paper printers and stainers' factory. There are seventy-five girls and boys employed here, but they are working on two-thirds time, with an early prospect of "being knocked out of time." The wages paid are at the rate of from $2 to $25 per week. The demand for stock is very small, and payments are obtained with difficulty.

A PICTURE FRAME FACTORY

on the opposite corner of Willoughby and Walworth streets, until recently kept 125 men busy and paid good wages. They have been compelled to discharge fifty men this week, and have reduced the pay ten per cent . . .

GLASS WORKS

The glass cutting establishment on North Eighth street, near Fifth, E.D., has reduced the working force from 180 to one-half that number. The time has also been reduced . . .

STEEL WORKS

A steel works factory, which is located on Kent street, near Hopper street, has been closed entirely upon two occasions within the past few weeks, owing to the fluctuation in the price of gold, which influences the value of iron, steel and all other metals. When business is good 150 men have been employed here. Now sixty constitute the force. . .

SOURCE: New York *Herald,* November 11, 1873. **The Working Women**

Hardships of the Unemployed Female Operatives of the City

Amid the general depression that prevails owing to the tightness of the money market, and the consequent tightfistedness of everybody who has anything to close his hand upon, there is one class in the community to which special attention should be directed. While the effects of the present embarrassment are felt in almost every quarter, none suffer more keenly from the dulness of the times than the working women of this city. A lengthened visit yesterday, by a *Herald* representative, through several well known extensive dry goods and millinery establishments, confirmed the impression previously formed, that the outlook for the respectable young women who earn their living in the various departments of large mercantile concerns is anything but encouraging. In several prominent firms the milliners, dressmakers, cloakmakers, seamstresses, shoebinders and vestmakers have been placed on what is known as "three-quarters time," while those who have hitherto depended on casual piece work will be compelled to await better opportunities than at present offer themselves. It is gratifying to think, however, that many of the foremost houses entertain a cheering view of the condition of affairs, hoping that a favorable change will shortly ensue. The firms more extensively engaged in business where women comprise the larger number of employes are very reluctant to discharge those depending upon them, but are compelled by the stringency of the times to shorten the hours of labor, thereby curtailing their usually heavy expenses. The poor dressmakers generally engaged in private families have little to expect, since the fall fashions are far behind, and with a poor prospect of a fair or plentiful exhibition. The vest and pantaloons makers are also among the sufferers, the falling off in business having been so great as to necessitate the reduction of a large number of hands. In view of the situation it would be well if some means were devised by which some relief could be extended to those at present suffering from want of employment. Of all the classes requiring aid few call for such prompt attention as the destitute young women. Neglect in this particular feature in the present embarrassing condition of affairs will assuredly entail the most serious consequences. There is a large and noble field open for the philanthropic and benevolent. Perhaps even those wealthy religious institutions might be induced to countermand the orders to the gentle missionaries about to set forth for foreign parts to reclaim the heathen and donate their travelling expenses to the penniless Christians at home. Indeed no effort should be spared to counteract the influences of the present gloomy situation.

SOURCE: New York *Herald,* November 17, 1873. **Connecticut**

Factory Production Reduced Fifty Per Cent in the Eastern Part of the State—Along the Oxeboxe River.

Killingly, Nov. 15, 1873.

The effect of the panic throughout this county of Windham is more severely felt than in any other section of the State. There is a large distribution of industries, and some of the mills are of considerable size and importance. Cotton forms the chief staple of manufacture. The foreign element among the operative class is not so considerable as in the western part of the State, where it is fully fifty per cent. The foreigners have less forethought and frugality than the natives, and, in consequence, suffer more in hard times like these, for which they are unprepared. In this town there is quite a number of cotton and woolen mills, all of which are suffering from the general depression. The Valley Mill, the Oriental, the Albion, the cotton mill of Thomas Pray, Jr.; the Elliotville cotton mill, employing 350 hands, and three smaller woolen mills are all running on reduced time, and in some cases with reduced help and wages. The Williamsville Cotton Company, employing over 200 hands, are on half time, and also the Atawangan mills. At Danielsonville R. S. Lathrop, manufacturer of weavers' reeds, has discharged more than half of his hands, and is running five days a week. Young & Co., shoe manufacturers, employing 75 hands, intend to close in a few days for a period of temporary repose . . .

Pennsylvania

Stagnation of Trade and Suffering Among Laborers—Glass Factories Stopped—No Resumption Probable Before January.

Pittsburgh, Nov. 14, 1873.

One of the most absurd statements ever impressed in printers' ink appeared in an Eastern paper a few days since, in a correspondence from this city, which was to the effect that probably less than 10,000 men were out of employment in Pittsburgh, and that there was comparatively little or no depression in the manufacturing industries of the city and no cause for uneasiness among the workingmen. There is no necessity whatever for an exaggeration of the effects of the present crisis, and still less for making light of a truly serious matter by misrepresentations. There is nothing to be gained by

A CONCEALMENT OF THE TRUTH

in matters of such grand import as this. Facts in connection with the situation as it exists now, may not be pleasant reading and may not be fruitful of benefits to the interests of the city, nevertheless there is no reason for withholding them from the public. When I say there is a great depression here in the manufacturing industries and in business generally, that there are thousands of workingmen out of employment, and that there is suffering among the families of such, I state truths substantiated through careful inquiry into the matter in question, and from personal observation. Yesterday and the day before it had their dreary quota of banking failures, or what is usually termed by the officials of such concerns "temporary suspensions." The collapse of these money depositories of course had not a tendency to dissipate any part of the gloom hanging over the manufacturers' interests and look hopefully for a revival of trade.

AMONG THE GLASS MANUFACTURERS

. . . "There is no money whatever for the employers in the glass business this winter, and only to save our men the suffering that would follow an entire suspension of operations have we consented to go on. With the reduction of 10 per cent in wages we feel confident of running all winter . . ."

Another manufacturer said to me that the complaint of a scarcity of orders was general, and if matters continue this way for a much longer period the factories would be compelled to close up entirely, a state of affairs which he hoped would be avoided in some manner.

"The Death Roll of Industry"

Upton Sinclair's classic study of the Chicago meat-packing industry, *The Jungle* (1906), served not only to expose the dehumanizing effects and unsanitary conditions existing in that trade but the terrible physical hazards faced by the workers as well. Industrial accidents were an ever present threat to employees especially in the nineteenth and early twentieth centuries. Unguarded machinery, cramped quarters and defective equipment caused numerous accidents. Workers were injured or killed by explosion, burning, electric shock, asphyxiation, falls and crushing. In 1865, after a rash of boiler explosions in New York City, it was reported that there were only seven inspectors for the city's ten thousand stationary boilers, and that many engineers were woefully ignorant of their jobs. In 1891 about 300 men were killed and over 2,000 injured in Pittsburgh's steel mills. There also were pathetic accounts of children losing either limbs or life while operating machines. Mining took a fearful toll; in 1910, 323 miners were killed in the Colorado mines.

With the nation's rapid industrial growth in the late nineteenth century, the incidence of accidents increased precipitously. Although some states had passed laws ostensibly to protect the wage earners against these hazards as far back as the 1870s, the legislation was either inherently weak or poorly enforced. The courts generally placed the full burden of proving the employer negligent upon the employee. Moreover, the workers had to prove that neither he nor his fellow workers were contributory to the accident. This situation continued until the end of the nineteenth century.

The "American safety movement," or fight for worker protection against industrial hazards, did not get under way until 1907. In the next several years, the revelations of the Pittsburgh survey and the exposés of the muckraking magazines brought the nation's attention to the problem. In 1907, the social magazine *Charities and the Commons* published an article appropriately entitled "The Death Roll of Industry."

SOURCE: Arthur B. Reeve, **"The Death Roll of Industry,"** *Charities and the Commons* (February 2, 1907), pp. 791, 793–802.

To unprecedented prosperity such as the past year showed and the present year promises, there is a seamy side of which little is said. Thousands of wage earners, men, women and children were caught in the machinery of our record-breaking production and turned out cripples. Other thousands were killed outright. How many there were no one can say exactly, for we were too busy making the record production to count the dead.

France, Germany, Holland and England have come pretty close to counting their death-roll of industry and to shortening it. America does not even count the lives. We know the number of cattle and hogs slaughtered for food, but we do not know the number of men, women and children whose lives and limbs are crushed by the wheels of industry running at top speed.

Yet though we do not know this total exactly, all methods of estimate lead to the conclusion that it must be in the neighborhood of half a million—equal to about one-half the number of immigrants who come to us from abroad in the same period. This loss happens at a time when throughout the country the demand goes up for more men in every branch of industry.

First of all it is necessary to examine the facts which we already possess. The first step in the program of reform should be prevention—before the fact; the second, restitution—after the fact. Placing more safety devices on our machinery, taking more sanitary precautions in our shops, and strengthening in general our present weak preventive legislation, make up the first part of the program.

Concurrently comes the alternate side of the program—restitution. Salvage work has been attempted in "bureaus for the handicapped" where wrecks of dangerous trades may be made as far as possible self-supporting. The ultimate goal of such a program will probably be workingmen's insurance against accidents—the theory being that the wear and tear on human life is a cost of production as much as the wear and tear on machinery and that the more equitable method of apportioning the risk of trade is on the consumer *en masse* rather than on the individual worker or on the charity of the community.

In considering the problem of public responsibility and industrial accident let us piece together the fragmentary information on the subject that we already possess. For the sake of convenience it is well to adopt the classification of industries followed by W. F. Willoughby in his monograph published as a bulletin of the Department of Labor in 1901. Mr. Willoughby includes (1) railways; (2) mines and quarries; (3) factories and workshops; and (4) building and construction work. If to these be added (5) agriculture and lumbering and (6) personal and domestic service, these six great groups of industry will almost cover the 29,000,000 wage earners of the United States.

In none of the other great groups of industry in the United States, are equally complete and accurate statistics of accidents to employes gathered as in the first group, the railways. When the Interstate Commerce Commission made its first report in 1889, it found that of the 704,743 railroad employes, 1,972 were killed and 20,028 were injured, a total of 22,000 for the year. During the latest year for which statistics are complete, 1905, of the 1,382,196 railroad employes, 3,361 were killed and 66,833 injured, a total of 70,194. In other words though our railroads do not employ twice the number of men they did in 1889, they kill or injure nearly three times as many.

. . .

In the mines and quarries of the United States the figures that are gathered by the several states are fairly complete as far as fatal accidents in coal mining are concerned. For years Frederick L. Hoffman, statistician of the Prudential Insurance Company, has gathered the statistics for this branch of industry. He shows in the *Engineering and Mining Journal,* that in eighteen states of the United States there were for 1905, 2,159 fatal accidents in the coal mines:

The fatal accident rate in American coal mines during 1905 was 3.44 per 1,000 employes, against an average of 3.11 for the decade ended 1905. There was, therefore, an increase of 0.33 per 1,000 equivalent to 210 lives more than if the rate during 1905 had been the average for the decade 1896–1905. With the exception of 1902, the rate during 1905 was the highest on record during recent years.

As for the non-fatal accidents, Pennsylvania reported in the same year 1,123 killed and 2,365 injured in anthracite and bituminous mining, a total of 3,488. This was an average of one killed or injured for every 55,000 tons mined.

. . .

Mine accidents, as the readers of the newspapers know them, are the spectacular events of explosions and cave-ins. As a matter of fact, the individual accidents which under present conditions are passed over as of comparatively small importance, outnumber these in their tally of lives lost. Falls of roof or slate, coal-cutting machinery, and electricity are probably responsible for more deaths than the "deadly" fire-damp and the "careless" handling of dynamite.

The introduction of coal-cutting machinery and the great influx of foreign labor, says James E. Roderick, Chief of the Department of Mines of Pennsylvania, are the two chief causes of the constantly increasing number of accidents from falls of coal, slate and roof. He continues:

Scores of foreign workmen annually meet their fate in this way and the question arises: Who is responsible for this great loss of life? It would be a most humane act if the foreigners could be prevented from working in the mines until they have acquired at least the rudiments of the English language, unless they can be put to work with competent men of their own nationality. It is my opinion that a foreman who allows incompetent foreigners to work together who do not understand the English language, should be held guilty of manslaughter in case of fatal accident to any of these men.

The dangers cannot be entirely eliminated but they can be lessened greatly if the common and well-known precautions are taken.

      •   •   •

There are over 7,000,000 American workingmen in the manufacturing and mechanical trades, but only ten states make any effort to secure reports of accidents . . . Massachusetts, Rhode Island, New York, New Jersey, Pennsylvania, Ohio, Indiana, Minnesota, Missouri, and Wisconsin. As far as real value attaching to these reports is concerned, no statistician has ever used them seriously, for in no case is it even claimed that complete returns are obtained, nor is it even known to what number of employes the figures obtained are applicable. The definition of what constitutes an accident differs in almost every state, and as for anything like compulsory reporting, it does not exist.

      •   •   •

New York is getting probably the best reports of accidents in manufacturing. Since 1902 the number of accidents so reported has increased over 100 per cent. A new law makes these reports confidential and they cannot be subpoenaed in court proceedings, a plan which should disclose a further and amazing increase when the figures for 1906 are tabulated. During the first quarter of 1906, 3,261 accidents were reported, nearly half the total number for 1905. This, of course, does not mean an increase of accidents but better reporting.

The most common type of factory accident is what the newspapers call being "caught in the machinery." Judged by a newspaper clipping record of 612 accidents, made as an experiment, thirty per cent of factory accidents are of this nature. A large proportion of such accidents could be prevented by merely screening off moving parts of machinery. This is often prescribed by law but frequently not attended to.

Cases of this sort could be multiplied indefinitely. Recently a man was picked up on the streets of New York for begging. His hands and fingers were partly off—a sacrifice to the speeding up the machinery of a harvester company in Chicago. He was an Armenian, unacquainted with our laws, and easily put off by the manufacturer on the community for support.

Young girls as well as foreigners are heavy sufferers. Cases in the big laundries of loss of arms and hands in mangles are frequent; almost never is there any compensation for the injury. In the jute mills about New York, scores are injured. A case that came to notice recently was that of a girl of seventeen, who had been injured two years before while operating a feeding machine. She instituted a suit but the probabilities were against her recovering anything. Another victim with an artificial hand has been added to the list with nothing to show for it.

A type of accident dreaded in the factories is to be caught in the leather belting or struck by it when it snaps or flies off the shaft. Adequate protection from accidents of this sort is not especially difficult. Again, fly-wheels, revolving too fast on account of overload or over-speed, burst, showering the men with as deadly fire as an exploding shell from hidden artillery. Last year a partial and incomplete record showed seventeen men killed and thirty-five seriously injured from this cause alone in seventy-seven such accidents.

. . . .

In foundries, machine shops, steel-mills, iron moulding shops, blast furnaces, car-shops, locomotive works, rolling mills, and wire mills thousands of men are every year caught in machinery, struck by heavy ingots, or by travelling steel cranes, or steel rails,—burnt, mangled and tortured. It is not to be supposed that all factories are charnel houses or that all employers are ruthlessly slaughtering their men and coining their blood into dollars. Yet there is a reverse side to what we ordinarily look on as peaceful industry that is ghastly.

Here is the statement of Joseph G. Armstrong, coroner of Allegheny county, where are blast furnaces and rolling mills:

The number of deaths of foreigners in the mills in Pittsburgh and vicinity has come to be nothing short of appalling, and after careful investigation of the matter, I am convinced that a great many are due to lack of proper protection. Conditions are such.

"If even the present laws were enforced conditions would not be so bad," said the Austro-Hungarian Consul, Adelbert Merle, at Pittsburgh. Hungarians, it was alleged, "disappear" from the tops of blast furnaces, where one misstep means a death worse than hell. One of the clippings of a newspaper record was headed "Slav spitted by red hot rail."

Within the past month came the horrible explosion in Pittsburgh in which thirteen were killed by a belching of molten metal from a blast furnace. The deputy-coroner, after investigating, claimed that the furnace had not been working properly for two weeks and that many men in fear had quit their jobs. The accident, he said, could have been avoided had the furnace been shut down when the trouble first became apparent. The rush of orders kept the company from making the needed repairs in time.

It should be borne in mind that this article does not deal with trade diseases. We are dealing with physical accidents, plain to the eye and countable. If these are uncounted, we can only guess at the human price of deadly white lead and its "wrist drop" and paralysis, of phosphorous matches and the disease called "phossy jaw," of "potter's consumption," of hatter's "shakes" and "miner's asthma" and "anthracosis" and the myriad of insidious diseases, like tuberculosis, that lurk in the materials and the work rooms. We are almost as ignorant of the extent and character of industrial accidents as we are of industrial diseases.

From the mining of the iron, the quarrying of the stone, and the felling and planing of the timbers; from the manufacture of the steel beams and hauling them to their destination; from the excavation and blasting for the foundation of a modern skyscraper as well as the sinking of the caissons; from all these things to the riveting of the steel into its superb frame and clothing that frame with stone, the process of modern building construction involves a continuous spilling of human blood.

For example, Chicago's skyscrapers last year exacted the heaviest toll of human life recorded in the history of building operations in that city. Figures compiled in the annual death-roll of the Bridge and Structural Iron Workers' Union showed a great increase in fatalities among the men. Of a total membership of 1,358 men in the union last year, 156 either lost their lives or were totally or partially disabled. During the year before twenty-six were killed, twenty-six were so injured that they could not resume their trade, and the number of minor injuries totalled about eighty. The increased loss from ten to twelve per cent of the membership of the union, was attributed to a speeding up of the work which it was claimed compelled the men to become less careful.

Falling I-beams kill almost as often as they maim. When they maim the effects are terrible. Such was a recent case in which two men were killed. The third was rendered deaf and dumb, his ears were cut off and "recovery" meant apparently a state of helplessness. He is now making scarcely half his original wage working on patent paper clips.

It is the falls from steel structures which make bridge building all but head the list as a dangerous trade. A large percentage of accidents in construction work is due to falls from insecure scaffolds, loose flooring and the collapsing of flimsy structures. Accidents of this sort are in most cases preventable. Death is dealt by falling bolts, cement blocks, bricks, tools, etc., by falling derricks, by numberless other foreseen and unforeseen accidents. Sometime or other at every point from foundation to roof, human life pays the price.

One of the most remarkable developments of modern engineering is in driving subaqueous tunnels by means of a hydraulic shield and compressed air. There is one tunnel job about New York where not a man has been lost by the "caisson disease," but this is not the case for all tunnel systems that are being put through. The coroner of New York reported sixty-eight deaths in tunnel work last year.

Dynamite and blasting powder are fatal in peace as well as in war, from their manufacture to their use. In a blasting powder factory men work face to face with death, and when death comes,—as it does frequently,—it is widespread and unescapable. High wages tempt men to come but few to stay.

But it is the reckless use of dynamite by the men themselves, and the lax rules of their employers that are responsible for most fatalities. Last year in New York city reckless handling of dynamite caused a special investigation that resulted in the summary removal of a city official who had failed to enforce the law.

PART V

The Seedtime of Unionism: Ethnic Participation in the American Labor Movement, 1860–1920

INTRODUCTION

The American labor movement was an important means through which immigrants were able to make an adjustment to their new life. Many immigrants, especially those in large urban areas, joined local labor unions. They looked to these associations to help solve their economic problems and provide them with a measure of security in a strange new industrial society. In turn, the newcomers made significant contributions to the leadership and ideology of the American labor movement.

The factors that induced them to come to America were primarily socioeconomic. The causes of the migrations existed both here and in Europe. Thousands of Irish and German peasants, forced off the land by recurrent crop failure, "swelled the tide of immigration." Samuel Gompers remembered: "It became harder and harder to get along as our family increased and expenses grew. London seemed to offer no response to our efforts toward betterment." Even more important than European conditions were those existing in the United States. When times were good in America, European workers left the old country to enjoy higher American wages. For example, during the depression that followed the 1857 panic, immigration to the United States suddenly dropped sharply.

The uncertain conditions that accompanied the coming and out-break of the Civil War resulted in even lower immigration figures. Not until the Union victories of 1864, accompanied by higher wages and the efforts of both government and private agencies to encourage the flow, did immigration again assume "stupendous proportions."

Civil War and post-war immigrants arrived in time either to wit-ness or to participate in an unprecedented revival of the American labor movement. In cities like New York, Boston and Philadelphia moribund unions reappeared and new ones were formed. Whereas the local unions of the 1820s, 1830s and 1850s were extremely short-lived, many of the unions of the Civil War decade displayed a high degree of continuity. The 1860s also saw an unprecedented number of national unions organized. Moreover, in 1866, the na-tion's first federation of unions, the National Labor Union, was launched at a convention held in Baltimore. Its major goal was the eight-hour day, and the new congress also sought the boycott of prison-made goods, abolition of slums and encouragement of co-operatives. The National Labor Union's demise in the early 1870s has been attributed to its increasing involvement in political labor reform at the expense of trade unionism. The entire labor move-ment was sent into a decline as the result of the depression that followed the panic of 1873.

During labor's renaissance of the 1860s and early 1870s many immigrant workers entered and became important participants in the American labor movement. Irish leaders and members began to dominate English-speaking unions in the large eastern urban centers. They were particularly prominent in the building trades. Since few Germans came with trade union experience because of the strict anti-combination laws that existed in many German states, some German workers, followers of Wilhelm Weitling and Joseph Wedemeyer, became socialists. Many more, however, turned to the labor movement. While some Germans joined English-speaking unions, others found membership in the "German union" more suitable. In 1869, there were at least twenty-six associations in New York City that called themselves "German unions," such as the German Cabinet Makers' Association and the German Cigar Makers' Protective Association. Moreover, the German Working-men's Union was a close rival to the city's main central labor coun-cil, the New York City Workingmen's Union.

Though less numerous than either the Irish or Germans, the English immigrant workingmen had the greatest influence upon the American labor movement of any immigrant group. In the post-Civil War period, Richard Trevellick and John Hinchcliffe, "pillars of the National Labor Union," were British immigrants. Andrew Carr Cameron, publisher of the important Chicago *Workingmen's Advocate*, and William Harding, the leading figure in the New York City labor movement of the 1860s and a founder of the National Labor Union, also came from England. Furthermore, many Irish workers who rose to leadership positions in America had been exposed to British trade unionism while working in English mill towns before coming to the United States.

These leaders, however, could not avert the decline of the National Labor Union. Eventually the Knights of Labor, originally a secret society formed by some Philadelphia garment workers, moved into the vacuum left by the Union. The Knights grew gradually until they reached a peak membership of 700,000 in 1886. Organized as an industrial union, the new group afforded many unskilled and semi-skilled immigrant workers their first opportunity to join the labor movement. The failure of a strike against the Gould railroad system, coupled with the aftermath of the Haymarket affair, helped to bring about the downfall of the Knights.

The 1880s also saw the rise of the American Federation of Labor. The leading founders, Samuel Gompers and Adolph Strasser of the New York City Cigarmakers' Union, both immigrants, felt that the labor movement had been too concerned with reform rather than bread-and-butter issues. They admired the "new unionism" of the British trade union movement which emphasized the centralized control of locals, the building of strike funds and economic objectives, especially wages and working conditions.

As the tide of immigration from southern and eastern Europe continued to rise, the number of unorganized unskilled and semi-skilled newcomers increased sharply. The American Federation of Labor persisted in its policy of concentrating on organizing the craft lines. In 1905 radical western workers joined with left-wing easterners to combat the Federation and formed the Industrial Workers of the World. The new body, rejecting "business unionism," was avowedly revolutionary and dedicated to the overthrow of the capitalist system through militant labor action. It welcomed into its ranks lumbermen, textile workers, farm hands, longshoremen, construction men and the employees in the rubber, automotive, electrical and other mass production industries. These workers were largely underpaid Serbs, Italians, Slovaks and blacks. The IWW, or "Wobblies" as they were called, led several publicized and successful strikes, most notably the one at Lawrence, Massachusetts, in 1912. Reports of police brutality won the strikers some public sympathy. Eventually, charges of violence and murder, however, made the movement extremely unpopular. Moreover, though its militant leadership won gains for the many unorganized workers, especially immigrants, it failed to build stable local unions. Millions of workers came under its influence, yet the IWW never had more than 60,000 permanent members. During World War I it engaged in a number of strikes, and its enemies saw an excellent opportunity to crush the movement by prosecuting and harassing thousands of its members under the wartime Espionage Act. The post-war Bolshevik scare completed the destruction of the IWW.

In the early years of the twentieth century a noted authority on immigration and labor argued that economic developments within the American economy were more responsible for the failure of organized labor to weld together effectively the majority of workers than immigration from southern and eastern Europe. He contended that improved technology had eliminated the need for the apprenticeship and training programs upon which craft unions had been established. Moreover, the growth of giant combinations had reduced the competition among employers for labor. The next important organizing period for the unskilled and semi-skilled had to await the New Deal era and the emergence of the Committee for Industrial Organization.

A. ORGANIZE OR PERISH: THE AWAKENING OF THE WORKING CLASS, 1860–80

"The Revolution in New York"

The outbreak of the Civil War unleashed forces which helped to usher in the start of the modern American labor movement. Having passed through the depression of the late 1850s, workingmen faced the hard times of the periods of impending war and the start of hostilities. The first economic effect of the war was to throw the North and West into severe panic. As the wartime economy took over in 1862 and business revived, American workingmen then faced the start of one of the worst inflations in the nation's history. They justifiably complained of the "enormous prices of every article." Wages failed to keep pace with the rising cost of living, and workers embarked upon their "advanced wages movement." In the latter part of 1862, workingmen started to reorganize dormant unions and form new ones. Some employers granted wage increases willingly, but many of them had to face strikes.

The rising tide of labor reached unprecedented proportions in 1863. Hundreds of new locals appeared and many national unions were formed. New York City, fast becoming the nation's leading industrial center, was the main focus of the labor upsurge. In 1861 there had been only fifteen local unions in the city; during the 1863 upheaval well over a hundred unions were formed. Moreover, that year the city saw at least twenty-nine trade-wide strikes despite the wartime emergency. Observing New York City's dramatic labor revival, *Fincher's Trades Review,* then the nation's leading workingmen's newspaper, reported: The Revolution in New York.

SOURCE: *Fincher's Trades Review,* November 21, 1863. **The Revolution in New York**

The upheaving of the laboring masses in New York, has startled the capitalists of that city and vicinity. The previous efforts of a few trades were but the rumbling of the volcano, which has burst forth in all its fury. The tide of reform has become relentless, and the cry for a "fair day's wages for a fair day's work," rings out trumpet-tongued all along the shores of the Harlem and East rivers.

The machinists are making a bold stand, and seem to act upon the belief that "in union there is strength." We publish their appeal in another column.

The City Railroad employees struck for higher wages, and made the whole population, for a few days, "ride on Shank's mare." This tax upon the lazy drones of Gotham soon brought the Company to terms, and now "all's well" with the railroad men.

The house painters of Brooklyn, have taken steps to counteract the attempt of the bosses to reduce their wages.

The house carpenters, we are informed, are pretty well "out of the woods," and their demands are generally complied with.

The safe-makers have obtained an increase of wages, and are now at work.

The lithographic printers are making efforts to secure better pay for their labor.

The workmen on the iron clads are yet holding out against the contractors, who have appealed to the Government for help.

The window shade painters have obtained an advance of 25 per cent.

The horse shoers are fortifying themselves against the evils of money and trade fluctuations.

The sash and blind-makers are organized and ask their employers for 25 per cent additional.

The sugar packers are remodelling their list of prices.

The glass cutters demand 15 per cent to present wages.

The coopers are now enabled to place an estimate on their own labor, and get what they ask.

Imperfect as we confess our list to be, there is enough to convince the reader that the social revolution now working its way through the land must succeed, if workingmen are only true to each other.

The stage drivers, to the number of 800, are on a strike, and demand $1.75 per day, instead of $1.25, as formerly.

The confectioners of New York and Brooklyn, are arranging their list of prices.

The United Tin Plate and Sheet Iron Workers of Brooklyn demand $1.50 to $2.50 per day, according to the branch of work.

THE UPRISING IN BOSTON

The workingmen of Boston are not behind their fellow-toilers in the great labor agitation of the country. The notes of preparation are sounding, and rapid organization is progressing. The old Bunker Hill spirit is fairly aroused, and well we know there will be no short-comings with the "Boston boys" and their neighboring co workers. In addition to the strike at the Charlestown Navy Yard, (which we now learn has happily been terminated in favor of the workmen,) the following trades are falling into line:

The journeymen segar-makers are organizing a Union, and regulating prices.

The varnishers and polishers are doing the same.

The wood sawyers of Chelsea, demand higher wages.

The riggers are on a strike for $3 per day.

At this writing it is rumored, says the Boston *Post,* that a general strike is contemplated among the workmen in the iron establishments at South Boston, and other parts of the city.

THE TRADE MOVEMENT IN PHILADELPHIA

Although the Trade movement in this city has not been attended with the excitement peculiar to other localities, it is nevertheless progressing—gradual, it is true, but steadily and firmly. Among the trades now in process of remodelling their list of prices, are the journeymen shoemakers, (ladies branch,) the manufacturers of earthenware, the sail makers at the Navy Yard, the segar makers, the curriers, the box trunk makers, tailors, ship joiners, with other trades, are organizing, and preparing for an increase of wages adapted to their necessities.

It is thought that the majority of employers in this city will concede, without resistance, all the journeymen will ask in reason. The unprecedented tax upon workingmen for all they consume, seems to have turned the tide of public sentiment in their favor; and we anticipate less of strife in Philadelphia than in almost any other city. We sincerely hope that our anticipations may be fully realized.

THE REVOLUTION PROGRESSING

New York is still convulsed with the efforts of workingmen to secure an advance of wages. In some cases, the workmen have succeeded—in others, the struggle is still going on, and has assumed an earnestness that promises well for the masses. Now is the time for mechanics and workingmen to stand firm, for no more auspicious moment was ever presented. The public expect it, the bosses know the men are right, and justice pleads as she never pled before. Even the women of New York are setting an example to that portion of the sterner sex who still halt between two positions. But, the time for argument must be monopolized by action. Those who hang back from motives of policy or fear, are only retarding the progress of others, and if success is to crown our efforts, *all* must move and act together.

The machinists of New York still "hold their position" manfully, and have already awakened the sympathy of their brethren throughout the country. It may be proper to state that the machinists' strike is in no way connected with the "Machinists' Protective Union" of that city; but the strikers have formed an impromptu organization, known as the "Machinists' Association of New York and vicinity." The strike once over, however, they will no doubt unite with the great National organization of their brother mechanics.

From other parts of the country we have cheering news of the emancipation of labor from the serf standard of wages. The trial may be severe to many, and deprivations may make the stoutest heart quail; but it will only be for a brief season—and oh,

> "What can we not endure,
> When pains are lessened by the hope of cure!"

Immigrant Labor Pioneer: William Harding

Labor leaders of the nineteenth century were truly labor pioneers. Biographers of nineteenth-century labor figures have dwelled upon the heroic organizing trips upon which many of these men embarked. Some of the most impressive organizing tours taken in the post-Civil War period were those of an English immigrant, William Harding. A coach painter, arriving in the United States in 1860, Harding found work in New York City's various coachmaking factories.

In the mid-'60s, he played an outstanding part in the reorganization of the city's central labor council and the revival of the whole city's labor movement. After the war, together with the nation's leading labor figure, William Sylvis, he launched the National Labor Union.

As president of the Coachmakers' International Union, Harding made five organizing trips, between August 1866 and November 1867, which covered well over 10,000 miles. Leaving his family in Brooklyn, the coach painter went on extended trips through New England, the Midwest, the Border States and Canada. Traveling mainly by train, he endured the hardships of rain, snow, rail washouts and crude accommodations.

Arriving at a city or town, Harding first sought a contact man with whom he visited the local shops trying to explain the advantages of unionism to both the employers and men. He found shelter either in a local hotel or a worker's home. Wherever he went he would try to sell subscriptions to the organization's publication, *The Coach-Makers' International Journal.* The journal contained Harding's reports of trips, information on local business conditions, impressions of interesting and historic places, as well as his views on trade unionism.

The passage from the *Journal* presented below included Harding's reports of an organizing trip that he undertook in the winter of 1866–67 through upper New York State, the Midwest and the Border States covering over 3,200 miles.

SOURCE: **Coach-Makers' International Journal,** II, no. 5, January 1867 (Philadelphia, 1867), pp. 69–72.

Mr. Editor:—Leaving Cleveland on the 28th of November, I visited Warren, where there are two, or we might say three shops, employing about twelve or fourteen hands, most of which were favorable to the Union, but did not seem to think they were, though enough so, after getting one subscriber to the *Journal,* I left for Ravenna. The work built in Warren is chiefly buggies, and they are sold in the South and Southwest generally. Arriving in Ravenna, I saw some of the men employed, and found them favorable towards establishing a Union, so concluded to make that the headquarters for four towns, namely: Warren, Ravenna, Tallmadge and Akron. With that view, I visited Akron, being compelled to pass by Tallmadge on account of the trains not running often enough to visit the two places in one day. I found the man in Akron quite ready to unite with Ravenna, and obtained the subscription of the employers to the *Journal,* as also one of the hands. They have a very excellent carriage shop in Akron, and make some very good work, chiefly light buggy bodies; about twelve hands employed.

Returning to Ravenna, I organized the Union there; the members of which are all young energetic men, that have yet to make their mark in the world. Leaving them, I next proceeded to Gallion, but found no business there in carriage making, though they are building shops there, and preparing for a large business in the spring. If they fill all the shops with hands next spring in the western section of the country, there will be a great scarcity of carriage-makers.

There being comparatively nothing doing in Gallion, I next visited Mansfield, still in Ohio, and found some men here ready to go for a Union, but it being Saturday evening, no meeting could be got, so I determined to go on to Columbus; at which place I arrived at 3 o'clock A.M., on Sunday morning, and, after taking a few hours rest, soon found that sterling friend and faithful worker in the labor cause, J. B. Peck, Corresponding Sec. to No. 8, with whom we were quite at home. Taking our things from the hotel, we took up our quarters at his house for the remainder of our stay. On Monday we were completely prostrated by sickness, but through the kind attention of Mrs. Peck, we soon recovered so as to be able to address the meeting in the evening, and we here take this method of returning our sincere thanks to friend Peck and his very amiable wife, for their kind attention to a stranger.

On Tuesday we took a look through the shops under the guidance of our friend and Mr. Miller. Business is not so very brisk in Columbus at the present moment, but the prospect looks good for the opening of the season. We also visited the jail here which the famous raider, John Morgan, made his escape from. On entering, we found our friend as well known inside as outside the prison, but for how long a term he had been in there we were unable to learn . . . The Capitol here is a very fine building, and has an excellent library, where any one that wishes may go and read the most valuable books that can be bought. This Union here is growing strong again, and will soon be all right. There were twenty-three present at the meeting, and no doubt No. 8 will soon be herself again.

As usual in all cases, those men who forced on the strike are now in business, and denouncing the Union that gave them the means to do what they are now doing; but I have tarried long in Columbus, so must take leave from all my friends here . . . At 4:10 P.M., we reach Porkopolis [Cincinnati], which, freely translated, means the City of Hogs. A committee had been appointed to meet us at the depot, but we did not apprise them of our coming, so found our way to one of the shops where the motto used by most carriage-makers was staring us in the face, namely, "no admittance—call at the office." How is it that carriage-makers alone should submit to this degradation? We have during our travels visited almost every other kind of work-shop and factory, yet was never asked our business, but have frequently been introduced by the employers themselves. Machinists, molders, carpenters, and, in fact, every trade but ours refuses to submit to so degrading a system of slavery. It is only when capital has fastened its fangs on labor that it presumes to do this; they never do it in a small shop where they are not so far removed by wealth from the journeymen.

. . . This being meeting night, we attended the union, where we found a good attendance, it being the night before their ball. After discussing various matters in connection with the trade in the city, it was deemed advisable to appoint a committee to wait on Mr. Gosling, the leading boss-coach-maker in the city to explain to him the true principles of our Union.

We found him [the] next day in his office, and were most cordially received. He entered into the subject with spirit, fully prepared to defend his course of action, denouncing the Union as a combination of demagogues, yet he himself had issued circulars throughout the United States, demanding of other employers that they should employ no Union men, and in one instance was successful, that of Frederick Wood, of Bridgeport; but he at last saw through the trick and took his hands back again. We endeavored for two hours to explain all our principles to Mr. Gosling, and think, to some extent, we succeeded in enlightening his mind on many points; but this much we must tell the carriage-makers of Cincinnati, that the rate of wages they pay their hands is far below the general standard . . .

Next morning, at 6 A.M., we were on the road to Covington, Ky. Found business there very dull; every thing being in a transition state. There are but three shops and but few hands employed. So after obtaining two subscribers to the *Journal* we started for Louisville . . . Next day we went through the shops. There are no carriage-makers' mottoes posted up down there; every one is free to go in and out as he pleases; the consequence of this is an excellent feeling between the men and the employers, quite refreshing to meet. In the evening we held a meeting, the Molders' Union adjourning early to let us have the hall, for which they will please accept our thanks; all the members remained to hear our few humble remarks. Quite a large number of our own trade was present. The meeting adjourned, and we held a session of the Union, where the propriety of visiting Nashville and Memphis was discussed. We stated that the funds of the I.U. [the International Union] would not admit of our taking so long a journey as 800 miles, when a motion was at once carried to vote a donation of $30 to send us down there, and to No. 11 is due the establishing Unions in Nashville and Memphis, which proposition we very kindly accepted, thanking the Union for their very great kindness . . . The City of Louisville is one of the best we have been in during our travels, being well laid out, and very picturesque, indeed, on the banks of the Ohio River.

Next morning we took our departure for Nashville . . . At 8 P.M., we arrived in Nashville, no longer the seat of war. We went to speak of Union, and right well were we received. We found a sportsman trimmer cleaning his gun, who left the weapon of war and took us around to the shops to make arrangements to hold a meeting in the evening. On going into Myers & Hunt's shop, we were quite taken by surprise at the very cordial manner in which we were received, an old New Yorker himself. He was right glad to see us, and also pleased to find what our mission was, saying, "all the men employed in my establishment are ready to join your Union, and so am I . . ."

Arriving in Memphis on Saturday evening, after a somewhat perilous journey, many parts of the railroad being under water, we rested on the Sabbath, as in duty bound. Early on Monday morning we proceeded to the shop of Bruce & C., to find friend Hughes, to whom we had letters of introduction . . . On making ourselves known to friend Hughes, and handing him our passport, we were most heartily received, and spent the remainder of the day in looking around the city, which is most celebrated for its muddy streets, eclipsing all in that line we have ever seen. In the evening the local Union of Memphis met, and unanimously adopted the Constitution of the I.U., and was duly initiated, and then the hospitality of the South shone forth. As Louisville had paid our fare down there, they sent us on to St. Louis, between 300 and 400 miles further, for which they have our sincere thanks. After making all the necessary explanations with regard to our principles, the Union adjourned, and we took leave of our new brothers, promising to see friend Hughes in the morning before leaving; a promise we duly kept. Taking dinner with him, we bade him farewell, and turned ourselves Westward for St. Louis, where we arrived after a 20 hours' hard ride, quite prostrated, having traveled over 800 miles, and organized two Unions, in four days.

On our arrival in St. Louis, we found the worthy Secretary of the Machinists' and Blacksmiths' Union, also friend Hinchcliffe, Editor of the South-West *Advocate,* who received us very kindly, and lent all the assistance in their power to organize a Union. Going into one of the shops, we found friend Moty, who at once took us around the city, and on going into Freeman and Green's, (who are turning out some of the very best work I saw in St. Louis, or in New York in fact,) who should take us by the hand but friend Turney, of Bridgeport, whom we were glad to see, knowing that he was a friend we could rely on at all times. He introduced us to friend Smith, who happened to be disengaged, and henceforth our course was clear in St. Louis. We got some bills printed, and carried them into the shops for a meeting on Saturday night, when a good number were in attendance, and St. Louis was within the circle, destined to be a large Union. After being organized, they donated $10 to the I.U. to help the cause along. The meeting adjourned, and we took leave of our friends in St. Louis with the exception of one or two, who promised to see us off.

Labor Uprising in the 1870s: The Great Eight-Hour and Railroad Strikes

Labor militancy and violence has generally been associated with the 1880s. Yet the 1870s were a decade of great labor upheaval. Labor historians have devoted much attention to the turbulent story of the Molly Maguires in the western Pennsylvania coal fields. Nevertheless the two most significant labor uprisings that occurred in that decade were the near-general strike of 1872 in New York City and the great railroad strikes of 1877.

In 1866 the National Labor Union had made the eight-hour day one of labor's primary objectives. Subsequently there were sporadic attempts to gain the shorter workday. In 1872, however, the workingmen of New York City made the first serious effort to gain the eight-hour day. Abandoning political action as the means of gaining their end, the city's trade unions struck for the shorter day. Before the movement had ended, the nation witnessed one of its greatest strikes: between April and July 1872 almost 100,000 workingmen, or one third of the entire labor force, or two thirds of those engaged in manufacturing, struck mainly for the eight-hour day. Some went out primarily for wages.

Among the strikers were thousands of members of Irish and German locals. Many workers achieved their objective though their gain may have been short-lived. But the movement served to revive organizations and reaffirm workingmen's confidence in trade unionism.

In 1877, an attempt by the Baltimore and Ohio Railroad to cut wages set off a series of strikes that virtually tied up the nation's transportation system. Within a month the stoppage had spread to the Pennsylvania, New York Central and Erie Railroads. At Martinsburg, West Virginia, nine persons were killed and President Hayes had to send federal troops to restore order. Pitched battles involving strikers and militiamen occurred in major cities. In Pittsburgh, the mob surrounded the state troops, burned down machine shops and destroyed Union Station. In that city twenty-six persons were killed and huge property damages were suffered. *Harper's Weekly,* the nation's leading picture magazine, contained vivid cartoons of the violent scenes, including a front-page picture of the 6th Maryland Militia firing point-blank at the demonstrators, as well as an account of "The Great Strike."

SOURCE: New York *Sun,* June 24, 1872. **The Uprising of Labor**

The situation as ascertained by the *Sun's* Reporters.

The Pluck of the Strikers—The Iron Men's Organization Another Bank of England—A Strike that cannot be Starved—Beginning the Eighth Week of the Fight

The eighth week of the eight-hour campaign begins to-day. Since the beginning, eight weeks ago, 95,000 men of different trades have been on strike for shorter time. Of these, 60,000 are working on eight hours, 25,000 are on strike, and 10,000 have resumed on the ten-hour system. The movement, it will be seen, has been successful. The coach painters only have been defeated, although many of the cabinet makers and piano manufacturers have been induced by the increase of compensation to return.

The men on strike are more determined than ever. Large sums of money are being forwarded from the workingmen of other cities for their relief, and it is evident that they will be able to hold out several months. Meanwhile the contagion spreads. Delegates from Boston, Philadelphia, Bridgeport, Worcester, Wilmington, Newark, and other cities report to the iron and metal workers that active preparations are making for a strike. In Wilmington and Philadelphia, where the iron and metal workers have strong unions, the members are pledged to pay $1 each, weekly, in aid of the New York strikers. Their combined membership is about 13,000.

The iron and metal workers made their first distribution of funds on Saturday night, handing out several thousand dollars, rejecting no applicant, and still having abundant means. The society formally disclaimed the Cooper Institute meeting [an eight-hour-day rally, led by radical groups] and its resolutions. The President repeated what he has daily said, that force would not be resorted to even to save the cause. Nearly every other trade on strike condemns the utterances of the speakers, and even the Eight-Hour League, the originators of the demonstration, say the speakers did not represent the sense of their organization.

The iron workers have about 9,000 men unemployed. King of Brooklyn gave eight hours on Saturday. Aside from the report of a committee sent to Chester, Pa., the men have everything to encourage them, and they are confident that within ten days their victory will be complete. They are daily strengthening their already strong organization by the addition of members, several hundred having recently joined.

THE SUGAR REFINERS' STRIKE

At the largely attended meeting of the sugar refiners yesterday, speeches were delivered by many members urging fidelity and courage. It was said that the employers were not prepared for the movement, and already had lost tens of thousands of dollars during one week of idleness. They cannot hold out. The Chair appointed a committee to wait on employers to-day, and learn what offers they were willing to make. The determination not to resume until $2.50 a day is offered was more conspicuous than on any former occasion . . .

WIRE WORKERS THREATENED

A card published by the employing wire manufacturers informs the men that the eight hours cannot be granted, and every man not at his post at 7 o'clock this morning will be discharged.

THE STRIKE IN WESTCHESTER

On Saturday about forty iron workers and foundrymen on strike in New York visited the foundries of Jordan L. Mott at Mott Haven, and the Messrs. Janes in Melrose, their object being to induce the employees there to strike for eight hours. No definite answer was given them. The same committee is expected to appear again to-day.

THE BROOKLYN STRIKES

The Workingmen's Union of Kings county have appointed a committee to wait on the Board of Supervisors and demand the Eight-Hour law in all public works.

The wire workers still hold out.

On the sugar refinery doors are posted "Laborers wanted." None of the refineries have their full complement of men.

Yesterday afternoon the livery stable keepers visited Chief Campbell and requested that a detachment of police be sent to Flatbush to protect their drivers. They feared that the strikers would waylay the men returning from funerals. The Chief promised to give sufficient protection.

SOURCE: "The Great Strike," *Harper's Weekly* (August 11, 1877), p. 263.

Meanwhile the situation at Pittsburgh had grown more desperate. The sheriff of the city endeavored to suppress the disorder: but his authority was defied, and call was made upon the State for help. Governor HARTRANFT issued a proclamation and ordered the military to support the sheriff. The arrival of the military served to increase the crowd, and the excitement grew in intensity. There was no violence offered, but the freight trains were not allowed to leave the city.

The Pittsburgh, Fort Wayne, and Chicago firemen and brakemen struck on the same day, and so did the men on the Western and Buffalo divisions of the Erie road, extending from Hornellsville to Dunkirk and Buffalo. The strike occurred at Hornellsville. The firemen and brakemen quitted work in a body, and there were no relays to take their places. No trains were allowed to go either way.

The sixth and seventh days of the revolution, July 21 and 22, were the darkest and bloodiest of all. The city of Pittsburgh was completely controlled by a howling mob, whose deeds of violence were written in fire and blood. The strikers remained at the Union Depot all through the previous night, but no demonstrations were made by them until the afternoon of the 21st, when Sheriff FIFE, at the head of the military, attempted to arrest some of the ringleaders. One of the mob approached the sheriff, waving his hat, and, calling to the crowd and the strikers, said, "Give them hell." Immediately a shower of stones was hurled into the troops, and one revolver-shot fired into the ranks. The soldiers returned the shots, and for three minutes a fire in all directions was kept up. There were no blanks, and the greatest havoc ensued. Sixteen of the crowd were killed and many wounded. The crowd fled in dismay, including the strikers, who sought shelter in every direction. Immediately after the firing, crowds of excited people sprang up as if by magic from all directions. Loud and deep were the imprecations against the Philadelphia troops, who were blamed by the strikers and the mob as being responsible for the trouble. Hundreds of people in no way connected with the railroad expressed their determination to join with the strikers in driving the soldiers from the city. These remarks were interspersed with loud and bitter threats that the company's shops, depots, and buildings should be laid in ashes that very night. And the rioters kept their word.

The news of the slaughter of the mob spread through the city like wild-fire, and produced the most intense excitement. The streets were rapidly crowded, and the wildest rumors prevailed. When the news reached the large number of rolling mill hands and workmen in the various shops of the city, they were excited to frenzy and by eight o'clock the streets of the central portion of the city were alive with them. A large crowd broke into the manufactory of the Great Western Gun-Works, and captured 200 rifles and a quantity of small-arms, and various other crowds sacked all the other places in the city where arms were exposed for sale, getting about 300 more. Among them were 1000 mill hands from Birmingham, on the south side. The different crowds consolidated and marched out to Twenty-eighth Street. In the mean time the strikers and the soldiers around the Union Depot had not been idle. At seven o'clock the Philadelphia troops, whose numbers had been swelled to over 800 men, withdrew into the large round-house at Twenty and Liberty streets, taking with them the two Gatling guns and two other pieces belonging to BRECK's battery. The round-house was a very solid building, with double walls, the outer one of iron, and the position was the strongest possible one for the troops. The strikers began to assemble rapidly, many arriving with guns procured at the Allegheny armory. By midnight 20,000 people were upon the ground, 5000 of whom were armed men. The mob laid siege to the round-house in which the soldiers had taken refuge, and opened a brisk fire upon it, which was hotly returned by the troops. Finding, after a number of efforts, that they could not dislodge the soldiers by this means, the rioters resolved to burn them out. Accordingly, just before midnight, an oil train was fired, and run by the mob down the track and against the sand house—a large building near the round-house. The former building caught fire and was destroyed, but the round-house was saved by the soldiers within, who played upon it from the railroad company's hydrants. The smoke of the burning oil nearly suffocated the soldiers, but they held their quarters until seven in the morning, when they vacated the building, and moved to Sharpsburg. On the way they were attacked by the rioters, and in the conflict numbers were killed on both sides. Once incendiarism was started, a new spirit of wanton destruction took possession of the mob. From the time the torch was applied to the first car, at eleven o'clock Saturday night, all night long, and the greater part of Sunday morning, car after car was taken possession of by the incendiaries, the torch applied, and the burning, fiery mass sent whirling down the track among the 2500 cars filled with valuable cargoes of freight of all descriptions, and costly passenger cars and sleeping and day coaches, spreading destruction on every hand.

After the departure of the militia, both the round-houses beyond the Union Depot were ignited, and 125 locomotives were destroyed. All the machine shops and railroad offices in the vicinity were also fired. The rioters planted a cannon in the streets near by, and threatened to blow in pieces any man who attempted to extinguish the flames. The firemen, thus intimidated, retired, and devoted themselves to saving private property only.

B. A RUTHLESS ANSWER TO HUNGRY MEN: THE TOIL AND TROUBLE OF THE GILDED AGE, 1880–1900

The Bread-Winners

Industrial strife in the post-Civil War era shook the confidence of the educated elite in democracy. John Hay, author and statesman, who had been President Lincoln's assistant private secretary, was in Cleveland during the great 1877 railroad strike. He was greatly moved by the event, and he wrote, "The prospects of labor and capital both seem gloomy enough. The very devil seems to have entered into the lower classes of working men, and there are plenty of scoundrels to encourage them to all lengths." He wondered if all the wonderful things that he had been telling Europeans about American democracy were really true.

No doubt the Cleveland experience colored his ideas when he sat down to write the novel *The Bread-Winners* several years later. The historian Vernon Parrington held that the work represented the views of the propertied classes alarmed by the rise of the labor movement and the industrial strife of the 1880s. Its immediate theme was a "satire of labor unions." Hay's biographer described *The Bread-Winners* as the "first important polemic in American fiction in defence of Property."

The passage below contains the author's description of a meeting of the secret Brotherhood of the Breadwinners conducted by the "oily" Anenias Offitt, "a professional agitator who lives off simple workmen whom he seduces." It contains much of the anti-labor bias of John Hay's class.

SOURCE: John Hay, **The Bread-Winners** (New York, 1884), pp. 82–84.

After the meeting had been called to order, and Sam had taken an oath of a hot and lurid nature, in which he renounced a good many things he had never possessed, and promised to do a lot of things of which he had no idea, Mr. Offitt asked "if any brother had anything to offer for the good of the order." This called Mr. Bott to his feet, and he made a speech, on which he had been brooding all day, against the pride of so-called science, the arrogance of unrighteous wealth, and the grovelling superstition of Christianity. The light of the kerosene lamp shone full on the decorated side of his visage, and touched it to a ferocious purpose. But the brotherhood soon wearied of his oratory, in which the blasphemy of thought and phrase was strangely contrasted with the ecclesiastical whine which he had caught from the exhorters who were the terror of his youth. The brothers began to guy him without mercy. They requested him to "cheese it"; they assisted him with uncalled-for and inappropriate applause, and one of the party got behind him and went through the motion of turning a hurdy-gurdy. But he persevered. He had joined the club to practice public speaking, and he got a good half hour out of the brothers before they coughed him down.

When he had brought his speech to a close, and sat down to wipe his streaming face, a brother rose and said, in a harsh, rasping voice, "I want to ask a question."

"That's in order, Brother Bowersox," said Offitt. The man was a powerful fellow, six feet high. His head was not large, but it was as round as an apple, with heavy cheek-bones, little eyes, close-cut hair, and a mustache like the bristles of a blacking-brush. He had been a driver on a streetcar, but had recently been dismissed for insolence to passengers and brutality to his horses.

"What I want to ask is this: I want to know if we have joined this order to listen to chin-music the rest of our lives, or to do-somethin'. There is some kind of men that kin talk tell day of jedgment, lettin' Gabrel toot and then beginnin' ag'in. I ain't that kind; I j'ined to do somethin';—what's to be done?"

He sat down with his hand on his hip, squarely facing the luckless Bott, whose face grew as purple as the illuminated side of it. But he opened not his mouth. Offitt answered the question:

"I would state," he said glibly, "the objects we propose to accomplish; the downfall of the money power, the rehabilitation of labor, the—"

"Oh, yes!" Bowersox interrupted, "I know all about that,—but what are we goin' to *do?*"

Offitt paled a little, but did not flinch at the savage tone of the surly brute. He began again in his smoothest manner:

"I am of the opinion that the discussion of sound principles, such as we have listened to to-night, is among the objects of our order. After that, organization for mutual profit and protection against the minions of the money power,—for makin' our influence felt in elections,—for extendin' a helpin' hand to honest toil,—for rousin' our bretheren from their lethargy, which, like a leaden pall—"

"I want to know," growled Bowersox, with sullen obstinacy, "what's to be done."

"Put your views in the form of a motion, that they may be properly considered by the meetin'," said the imperturbable president.

"Well, I motion that we stop talkin' and commence doin'—"

"Do you suggest that a committee be appointed for that purpose?"

"Yes, anything." And the chairman appointed Bowersox, Bott, and Folgum such a committee.

All breathed more freely and felt as if something practical and energetic had been accomplished. The committee would, of course, never meet nor report, but the colloquy and the prompt action taken upon it made every one feel that the evening had been interesting and profitable. Before they broke up, Sleeny was asked for his initiation fee of two dollars, and all the brethren were dunned for their monthly dues.

"What becomes of this money?" the neophyte bluntly inquired of the hierophant.

"It pays room rent and lights," said Offitt, with unabashed front, as he returned his greasy wallet to his pocket. "The rest goes for propagatin' our ideas, and especially for influencin' the press."

Sleeny was a dull man, but he made up his mind on the way home that the question which had so long puzzled him—how Offitt made his living—was partly solved.

Labor Organizations: The Greatest Menace to This Government

In June 1900 the Industrial Commission on the Relations and Conditions of Capital and Labor heard testimony from representatives of capital. On June 12, N. F. Thompson, Secretary of the Southern Industrial Convention and of the Chamber of Commerce of Huntsville, Alabama, appeared before the commission. His statement was an indictment of existing labor unions; he charged that labor organizations were "the greatest menace to this Government that exists inside or outside the pale of our national domain." Thompson asserted that many labor leaders were using the movement to spread socialist ideas; that labor organizations were destroying respect for authority; and that the American labor movement encouraged class warfare.

SOURCE: **Report of the Industrial Commission on the Relations and Conditions of Capital and Labor, VII** (Washington, D.C., 1901), pp. 755–57.

"Labor organizations are to-day the greatest menace to this Government that exists inside or outside the pale of our national domain. Their influence for disruption and disorganization of society is far more dangerous to the perpetuation of our Government in its purity and power than would be the hostile array on our borders of the army of the entire world combined.

"I make this statement from years of close study and a field of the widest opportunities for observation, embracing the principal industrial centers both of the North and the South. I make this statement entirely from a sense of patriotic duty and without prejudice against any class of citizens of our common country.

"If I could make this statement any stronger or clearer, I would gladly do so, for it is not until an evil or a danger is made strongly apparent that adequate measures of relief are likely to be applied. That such a menace is real and not imaginary the most casual investigation of existing tendencies among the laboring classes will make the facts discernible. On every hand, and for the slightest provocation, all classes of organized labor stand ready to inaugurate a strike with all its attendant evils, or to place a boycott for the purpose of destroying the business of some one against whom their enmity has been evoked.

"In addition to this, stronger ties of consolidation are being urged all over the country among labor unions with the view of being able to inaugurate a sympathetic strike that will embrace all classes of labor, simply to redress the grievances or right the wrong of one class, however remotely located or however unjust may be the demands of that class. To recognize such a power as this in any organization, or to permit such a theory to be advanced without a protest or counteracting influence, is so dangerous and subversive of government that it may justly be likened to the planting of deadly virus in the heart of organized society, death being its certain and speedy concomitant.

"Organizations teaching such theories should be held as treasonable in their character and their leaders worse than traitors to their country. It is time for the plainest utterances on this subject, for the danger is imminent, and in view of the incidents that have occurred recently in strikes it can be considered little less than criminal in those who control public sentiment that such scenes are possible anywhere in this country.

"This language may seem needlessly harsh and severe, but in some classes of diseases it is the sharpest knife that effects the speediest remedy, and so, in this case, if the public are to be awakened to their real danger the plainest speech becomes necessary.

"No one questions the right of labor to organize for any legitimate purpose, but when labor organizations degenerate into agencies of evil, inculcating theories dangerous to society and claiming rights and powers destructive to government, there should be no hesitancy in any quarter to check these evil tendencies even if the organizations themselves have to be placed under the ban of law.

That these organizations are thus degenerating is seen in the following facts:

"(1) Many labor leaders are open and avowed socialists and are using labor organizations as the propaganda of socialistic doctrines.

"(2) These organizations are weakening the ties of citizenship among thousands of our people in that they have no other standard of community obligations than what these organizations inculcate.

"(3) They are creating widespread disregard for the rights of others equally as entitled to the protection of organized society as their own, as evidenced in every strike that occurs and the increasing arbitrariness of labor demands on their employers.

"(4) They are destroying respect for law and authority among the working classes, as many have no higher conception of these than such as are embodied in the commands and demands of labor organizations and labor leaders.

"(5) They are educating the laboring classes against the employing classes, thus creating antagonisms between those whose mutuality of interests should be fostered and encouraged by every friend of good government; for the success of government hangs on no less a basis than the harmony and happiness of the people, embracing alike employers and the employed.

"(6) They are demanding of Federal, State, and municipal authorities class legislation and class discrimination utterly at variance with the fundamental principles of our Government, in that they are demanding of these various authorities the employment of only union labor, thus seeking to bring the power of organized society to crush out all nonunion workers.

"(7) They are destroying the right of individual contract between employees and employers and forcing upon employers men at arbitrary wages, which is unjust alike to other labor more skilled, and to capital, which is thus obliged to pay for more than it receives in equivalent.

"(8) They demand the discharge of men who risk life to protect employers' interests during strikes to reinstate those who were formerly employed, but who have been instrumental, directly or indirectly, in the destruction of life and property, thereby placing a premium upon disloyalty and crime.

"(9) They are bringing public reproach upon the judicial tribunals of our country by public abuse of these tribunals and often open defiance of their judgments and decrees, thus seeking to break down the only safeguards of a free people.

.   .   .

"A further law should be enacted that would make it justifiable homicide for any killing that occurred in defense of any lawful occupation, the theory of our government being that anyone has a right to earn an honest living in this country, and any endeavor to deprive one of that right should be placed in the same legal status with deprivation of life and property.

C. INTO THE TWENTIETH CENTURY: THE WORKINGMEN AND THE AMERICAN DREAM, 1900–20

A Report to the President on the Influence of Trade Unions on Immigrants

In August 1904, as the result of an editorial appearing in the Chicago *Tribune* entitled "The Union and the Immigrant," President Theodore Roosevelt asked Carroll D. Wright, the economist and statistician, to investigate the strike that was then in progress in the Chicago meat-packing industry. Making a personal survey of conditions there, Wright sent the President a report on the "Influence of Trade Unions on Immigrants."

The report was an excellent analysis of the positive functions of modern labor unions in a democratic society. It represented an advanced and enlightened approach to unionism at a time of rapidly increasing corporate control over the American economy and society. Though Wright conceded that immigration had a general tendency to depress wages, he observed that unions were a necessary means by which workers, both native and immigrant, could offset this negative aspect of immigration. Moreover, the economist noted that although the newcomers tended to be clannish, even in their unions, the labor movement often was the only means by which they were forced to work and come together. Long before the sociologists, Wright saw the value of unions in helping immigrants make their adjustment to American society and life.

SOURCE: **Bulletin of the Bureau of Labor,** No. 56 (January 1905), pp. 4–8.

The unions in the stock yards are controlled by the Irish, ably assisted by the Germans. As a Bohemian or a Pole learns the language and develops, he is elected business agent or other official. In the pork butchers' union, for instance, there are about 1,800 members, 600 of whom are Irish, 600 Germans, 300 Poles, and 300 Lithuanians and Slavs. This union recently elected a Pole as president of the local. In their business meetings the motions made, resolutions read, and speeches delivered are usually interpreted in five languages, though in some locals in only three. All business, however, is transacted primarily in English, although any member may speak to any motion in the language he best understands, his words being rendered into English for the minutes of the meetings and into all the languages necessary for the information of members. It is here that the practical utility of learning English is first brought home forcibly to the immigrant. In all other of his associations not only does his own language suffice, but, for reasons that can be well understood, shrewd leaders minimize the importance of learning any other. (The only notable exception to this is the National Polish Alliance, and even here only the Polish language is used. There is no apparent influence exerted, however, to create the impression that the Polish is all-sufficient.)

In his trade union the Slav mixes with the Lithuanian, the German, and the Irish, and this is the only place they do mix until, by virtue of this intercourse and this mixing, clannishness is to a degree destroyed, and a social mixing along other lines comes naturally into play. Not only is the Amalgamated Meat Cutters' Union an Americanizing influence in the stock yards, but for the Poles, Lithuanians, and Slovaks it is the only Americanizing influence, so far as could be determined in this investigation. It is true this Americanizing is being done by the Irish and the Germans, but it is Americanizing nevertheless, and is being done as rapidly as the material to work on will permit, and very well indeed. Again, the reaction is good in its results. The feeling among the Irish against the Dutch and the Polack is rapidly dying out. As the Irish in Chicago express it, "Association together and industrial necessity have shown us that, however it may go against the grain, we must admit that common interests and brotherhood must include the Polack and the Sheeny." It is also admitted that when the speech of the Lithuanian is translated in the meeting of the trade union the Irish and the German see in it the workings of a fairly good mind. Some of the best suggestions come from Bohemians, and mutual respect takes the place of mutual hatred.

The investigation disclosed the influence of the union in teaching the immigrant the nature of the American form of government. The records of this office, independent of this investigation, show that during an investigation of building and loan associations a few years ago information from the Bohemian, Polish, and other clannish associations of that character could be obtained only through the services of an interpreter. It was found that as soon as a Bohemian or a Pole heard the word "government," or "government agent," he closed his mouth, and it was impossible to secure any information.

This has been true in other investigations, notably in collecting family budgets; but with an intelligent interpreter, using their own language, the nature of the work was explained, and no further difficulty experienced. The union is breaking down this trait of character in the foreigners of the nationalities mentioned. This it is doing not as a matter of philanthropy, but from a selfish necessity. The immigrant must be taught that he must stand straight up on his own feet; that the ward politician is dependent on him— on his vote, etc.—and not he on the ward politician. In this way he first learns that he is a part of the Government, and while this is done by indirection, in a large sense, there is no other force that is doing it at all. The Pole, the Bohemian, the Lithuanian, the Slovak, and to a much lesser degree the Galician, have inherited the feeling that somehow government is a thing inimical to their natural development—a power forcing itself upon them from afar; an intrusive power for repression, taxation, punishment only; a thing which they must stand in awe of, obey, pay tribute to, and wish that it had not come among their people, even if they did not secretly hate it—a thing, in short, which ought not to be. Being weaker than it they must be silent in its presence, and if forced to speak, lie, as for them to tell the truth would mean imprisonment or death.

It is not necessary for these things to be true in order that the illiterate peasants should have believed them for generations. Seventy-five per cent of the stock-yards immigrants are of the peasant and agricultural laborer class of Europe, and comparatively few of them can read or write in their own language. To make such a people feel that the Government is their friend, that they are a part of it, that development and education, not repression, are its objects and its purposes with and for them, is an enormous task, and one which a trade union single handed and alone can not be expected to accomplish by indirection in a few years, with the flood of new ignorance that has been brought in by the high tide of immigration into the stock yards.

In every trade union, however conservative, there are members who will occasionally get the floor and advise their hearers to vote high wages and shorter hours at the ballot box. As the groups of Slovaks gather around after the business is over to have these things explained to them, many get their first real idea of what the ballot and election day mean, and the relation of these to the Government itself. In their own home countries the two essential, if not only, elements of the peasant and agricultural laborer's mind is to believe and obey, or follow. Advantage is taken of this fact here by clan politicians, as well as the clan leader in every department. Once the leader can make these people believe in him, he thinks for the entire group, and insists that their duty consists in following his lead implicitly. Necessarily, the trade union, in order to get them to break away from the leader that opposed the union on industrial lines, would be compelled to urge them to consider their own personal and group interests as wageworkers; to think and act for themselves along lines where they knew the real conditions better than any one else, and certainly better than their leader in a child insurance society, or something else as remote. Here, too, are the first germs of what may be called the departmental thinking implanted in their minds—that is, that while a leader may be worthy of their confidence in one thing, it does not necessarily follow that he is so in some other class of interests.

It is doubtful if any organization other than a trade union could accomplish these things, for only the bread and butter necessity would be potent enough as an influence to bring these people out of the fixed forms and crystallizations of life into which they have been compressed. Certain it is that no other organization is attempting to do this work, at least not by amalgamation, which is the only way assimilation can be secured among these various foreign elements. The drawing of these people away from their petty clique leaders and getting them to think for themselves upon one line of topics, namely, the industrial conditions and the importance of trade organization, result in a mental uplift. The only way they can pull a Slovak away from his leader is to pull him up until he is gotten above his leader along the lines of thought they are working on. The very essence of the trade argument on the immigrant is—unconsciously again—an uplifting and an Americanizing influence. The unionist begins to talk better wages, better working conditions, better opportunities, better homes, better clothes. Now, one can not eternally argue "better" in the ears of any man, no matter how restricted the particular "better" harped on, without producing something of a psychological atmosphere of "better" in all his thought and life activities. If better food, better wages, or even better beer, is the only kind of "better" one might get a Slovak or a Lithuanian to think about, then the only way to improve him is to inject the thought of "better" into the only crevice to be found in his stupidity.

Of course, many object to attempts to improve these people because the immigrants from Lithuania, Slavonia, and Russian Poland are better off here than they ever were or could be in their own countries; that, left to themselves, they would not only be perfectly satisfied, but delighted with their improved condition; that the union must first produce discontent and dissatisfaction with what would otherwise be entirely satisfactory before it can get these immigrants even to talk about joining the union. Again, it is urged that at home these people do not expect to eat as good food as other people, nor to dress as well, nor to live in as good houses; that, as peasants, they never compare themselves with other people or classes of people.

In opposition to all these things, the union begins by teaching the immigrant that his wages are not so good as another man's doing practically the same kind of work, while it neglects to tell him he is not doing it so well, so intelligently, nor so much of it perhaps; but the union gets him to compare himself not with what he was in Lithuania, but with some German or Irish family, and then "stings him with the assertion that he has as much right to live that way as anybody." The union attempts to show the immigrant that he can live better only by getting more money, and that by joining the union he will get it. If left alone he would be entirely satisfied, perhaps, with what he was getting before. It is perfectly true, probably, that in most cases the union does not care for the Lithuanian in the first instance, the real purpose being to protect their own wages by getting the immigrants to demand high wages for their labor. So later on some degree of fellowship is engendered, but self-defense is the real motive.

The union point of view is that for a Lithuanian peasant to be contented, satisfied, and happy with the Lithuanian standard of living in America is a crime, a crime not only against himself but against America and everyone who wishes to make individual and social development possible in America, and that whatever the union's motives for creating discontent, the fact that it does create a discontent among the immigrants—which is the first step toward their improvement and ultimate Americanization—renders the union so far a public benefactor.

Many persons were interviewed in securing information along these lines—bankers, professional men, and all classes. One gentleman, in the banking business in the stock-yards district for many years, stated that the Slavonians and Galicians have been buying homes within the last eighteen months to a most remarkable and unprecedented extent, and that this is in a measure true of the Lithuanians, but not to such a marked degree. He testifies that the union has given these people a sense of security in their positions. By mixing up the nationalities in the union meeting it has made them acquainted with each other and dispelled an undefined dread of pending race war or struggle between nationalities in the yards. Formerly most of the Slovak and Lithuanian immigrants were a floater class. About the only ones who return to their homes now are the Galicians, in whose country a more or less representative form of government prevails. Others testified in a similar way, although some thought the union had done little except to agitate for higher, higher, and higher wages, regardless of economic conditions.

On the police side of the problem, a sergeant of the twentieth precinct, known as "back of the yards," which is crowded with the Bohemian and Polish elements, stated that there had been the greatest improvement since the union was formed, in 1900—less disorder, better living, more intelligence, and more understanding of American institutions and laws; that they employ fewer policemen in the district, and that less crime is committed than prior to 1900.

The studies of the various nationalities involved in the present meat strike brings out some valuable points relative to the restriction of immigration. Among them there seems to be an unalterable opposition to laws excluding those who can not read and write in their own language, and their argument is that the peasant population of central and eastern Europe, from which they came, have more rugged morals, simpler lives, and fewer vices than the inhabitants of the cities and towns who can read and write, as a rule. They consider themselves not responsible morally or politically for the fact that Russia has fewer schools than Illinois and spends less money on education in a year than does that State. They claim that their ignorance is not of the kind that is synonymous with vice or with crime; that they are as innocent as ignorant, whereas a far worse town and city population would be admitted without question under such laws. They have some peculiar ideas about prohibiting absolutely any immigration for a specific term of years and then allowing only a certain percentage to come in each year thereafter; but the main point they make is as to the illiteracy of the peasant class, the most desirable we can secure, and the literacy of the criminal classes of the great cities, which could come in under such restrictive legislation. Such things are only a part of this study brought out by your two letters, and the study has seemed to me so interesting and, in a way, so novel, that I have taken courage to give you the results quite in extenso.

"Lo, the Poor Immigrant!"

It has been said of social worker Frances Kellor that she "probably did more than anyone to direct Theodore Roosevelt's reformist zeal toward the special plight of the urban immigrant." A pioneer in the movement to protect immigrants, Kellor became a national committeewoman for the Progressive Party in the 1912 presidential campaign. After Roosevelt's defeat, she continued her efforts in behalf of the newcomers. An event that left a deep impression upon her, as well as on many other Americans, was the Ludlow "massacre" of 1914.

In 1913 the coal miners of Ludlow, Colorado, struck for a wage increase and recognition of their union, the United Mine Workers. Over 14,000 foreign-born workers, from twenty-four different countries, had been employed there on the eve of the stoppage. The Rockefeller interests, which controlled the mines, rejected the demands, and a long, bitter struggle ensued. The strikers moved out of the company town and set up their own camp. On April 20, 1914, the militia attacked the camp, machine-gunning and setting fire to the tents. Thirty-three persons were killed, including women and children, and over a hundred wounded. Federal troops restored order but the strikers were beaten.

The Ludlow tragedy caused the thousands of immigrant miners there, as well as many throughout the nation, to question seriously the reality of the so-called American dream. The event and conditions under which foreign-born workers lived prompted Frances Kellor to bemoan the fate of the "poor immigrant." She observed of this kind of experience that it was not surprising the International Workers of the World found the immigrant workers a fertile field for organizing.

SOURCE: Frances A. Kellor, **"Lo, the Poor Immigrant!"** *Atlantic Monthly* (January 1916), pp. 59–63.

Go through the 'immigrant section' of a typical industrial town. Miserable shacks, overcrowded with lodgers because there are not enough houses; inadequate water-supply, lack of repairs, unequal enforcement of village laws—all these things characterize the section. Where the company owns the property, there is no security in the home, for eviction as trespassers follows the slightest protest. And on some of our great estates conditions are little better. The men who keep Tuxedo Park so beautiful for the fortunate families who live there are crowded into sodden communities, unable to get their houses repaired, or indeed to secure a sufficient number of houses at a reasonable rent to enable them to live with fewer than ten in three rooms. I had occasion to visit one of the great estates in Central New York in the process of its evolution from a forest to a country estate. I found the hundreds of employees housed in tar shacks on the slope near the foot of the hill, compelled to take boarders because there were not enough shacks, and each paying two dollars a month rent. Some of the shacks had no windows; others had leaky roofs and damp, cold floors. There were no drainage facilities, and after a rain the little clearing in which the shacks had been constructed was a veritable mud-hole. Even in dry weather, there were stagnating puddles of water. Since no provision had been made for garbage collection and disposal, the women were compelled to throw animal and vegetable refuse in the bushes near by. The wooden privy vaults close by the shacks were seldom, if ever, cleaned, and the residents were compelled to use the fields. The water-supply was a spring into which the surface draining of the hill poured. There were no bathing or laundry facilities.

On interviewing a number of the men and women, I found that this had not been their standard of living abroad. One had been a butcher in a small town in Italy, where he had lived in a small wooden house and had had a good-sized truck-garden. Another had been a house-painter who had come here to better his condition and bring his family here, but was now anxiously awaiting the moment when he should have sufficient funds to take him back to the old home. Another had been a farmer on a small scale; he had come here to go into farming, but through lack of proper advice and direction had drifted into construction work. His family was with him, but they were all going back as soon as possible.

This was really a community study in the methods by which American employers create the 'immigrant standard of living' in America, and incidentally the immigrant 'bird of passage' who contributes so much to American industrial instability. The determining factor in this place was one of the first families of America.

There are other phases of 'hospitality' which interest us greatly. There are Lawrence, Calumet, Trinidad, Roosevelt, Wheatland, Ludlow, where the sworn statements of witnesses lead us to doubt if we are living in free America. The report of the California Immigration Commission says of Wheatland:—

'There had occurred on August 3, 1913, on the Durst hop ranch near Wheatland, Yuba County, a riot among the hop-pickers employed on the ranch, resulting in the killing of two police officials and two pickers. It was the claim of the pickers that one of the primary causes of the discontent in their ranks, leading to riot and bloodshed, was the insanitary condition of the camp in which they were segregated on the ranch.' Before the trial of the men charged with inciting the riot and causing the murder, it was announced that 'evidence concerning the sanitary and living conditions in the camp would be introduced,' and the commission availed itself of the opportunity to conduct 'a careful investigation into the economic causes leading to the riot.'

They discovered that there were probably 2800 workers in camp at the time of the riot, of whom about half were women and children. Of the men, fully 1000 were foreign-born,—Syrians, Mexicans, Italians, Porto Ricans, Poles, Hindus, and Japanese. These people were expected to camp out in a desolate, treeless field. 'There were a few tents to be rented at 75 cents a week, but the majority had to construct rude shelters of poles and gunny sacks, called "bull pens," while many were compelled to sleep in the open on piles of vines or straw.' The sanitary arrangements were unspeakably inadequate, foul, and unhealthy; drinking water was scarce, and some of the wells were infected from the surface water which drained back from stagnant pools that formed near the toilets and garbage piles. There were cases of dysentery, typhoid, and malaria in camp. 'While the wage-scale and other factors contributed to the feeling of discontent, the real cause of the protest of the pickers seemed to come from the inadequate housing and the insanitary conditions under which the hop-pickers were compelled to live.'

Even more interesting is the Colorado situation. The investigation of the most recent Colorado struggle brought to light among other things this significant fact: that within ten years after their arrival every new force of immigrant workmen brought there reached the climax of their protest against the living conditions forced upon them. These successive revolts after years of helpless endurance have only one significance: left wholly to themselves, with little help in education or organization, these immigrant workmen not only attain in ten years a desire for the American standard of living, but are prepared to starve and die for it.

At one of the largest mines in New York State, owned and operated by the descendants of one of the oldest families in America, the writer found that the company practically owned the town except the saloons. It employed one of the justices and its counsel was county judge. A saloon-keeper and a padrone were the interpreters when one was needed. It was found in the case of both justices that bills and claims for fees had been presented to the supervisors and paid, which the docket did not substantiate; that they had failed to file records as required by law; that they had falsified accounts and settled cases in violation of law, there being no record kept; that they had neglected to transmit the fines to the clerk in their conduct of trials. How is an immigrant living and working in this town to learn to respect American hospitality or even to understand American justice?

There are graver evidences than these that the host, not the guest, is the violator of American hospitality. Some of the sons of the men who led the fight for the abolition of slavery in 1861 were fathering a peonage system among aliens in almost every state in the Union in 1909. The Federal Commission of Immigration verified the reports of the Department of Justice and found that foreign laborers were restrained in every state covered by its investigation, except Oklahoma and Connecticut, under conditions which, if substantiated by legal evidence, would constitute peonage as defined by the Supreme Court. According to the report of the Federal Immigration Commission, 'The peonage cases in the South relating to immigrants have been found to cover almost every industry—farming, lumbering, logging, railroading, mining, factories, and construction work. The chief causes of the abuses have been the systems of making advances to laborers, the operation of contract-labor laws, and the misrepresentations made to laborers by unscrupulous agents.'

And the cases of peonage in the North and East, described in the same report, are quite as flagrant.

The peonage conditions are sporadic. But the other conditions herein described prevail in many communities throughout our large industrial states. They have become an accepted accompaniment of industrial development.

These are the conditions, this is the community type, which we permit and which we make. Let us face the matter squarely. The immigrant, upon coming to this country, is suddenly freed from the most minute surveillance of his daily affairs, and from persistent official repression, direction, and advice. He understands that this is the land of liberty. He is suddenly freed from every familiar form of 'control'; in the midst of strange customs, institutions, and laws, he is more helpless than he was at home. Does America make the slightest effort to teach him the difference between liberty and license? No. At the very port of entry he is robbed by the cabman, and by the hotel runner, the expressman, the banker who exchanges his money, the steamship agent, and the hotel-keeper. His first lesson in 'property rights' in America is often the loss of his own small possessions. He is held in bondage by the hotel-keeper, who takes up his 'through railroad ticket' and keeps it until he has secured a fair return in board bill. The *padrone* gets him a job, and for the privilege of housing and feeding him at a price and under conditions about which the immigrant has nothing to say, keeps him in a job. If he rebels, he is promptly blacklisted. The employment agent gets him into debt with a prospective employer, and peonage results. In times of scarcity of labor, contingents of immigrant workmen have been made drunk, shut up in box cars, and landed in labor camps from which there is no return until spring.

After a year or two, or less, of 'American' experience of this kind, suppose the immigrant chances some noonday to hear an agitator of the Industrial Workers of the World. This agitator is often the first person to listen sympathetically to the immigrant's troubles. He represents America, he speaks of new liberty and new opportunity, and it is easy to convince the trusting ignorant alien that *his* way is the way out. No other way has been indicated. It is not that 'lawlessness and violence are the weapons he understands'; it is that they are the only weapons given to the immigrant. Moreover, the agitator addresses the immigrant in his own language. We forget the power of this appeal. In short, the I.W.W. has come to the immigrant, and the labor union has for years ignored him.

There are aristocracies among labor unions as among Pilgrims. And the immigrant, ignorant of English and with no facilities for learning it, listens and follows the only 'American' message brought him in a language he can understand.

What we descendants of the first Americans have done is to substitute for that ancient tradition of hospitality a system of heartless exploitation and of neglect, urbane or resentful according to the occasion. A strong nation, with its intrenchments of position, power, and property, has found it possible thus to deal with the weaker peoples who are its guests and admittedly its prospective citizens. The determining factor in our hospitality has been the necessity for laborers—slaves if you will. For years a war has been waged by the workers, backed by the unions and restriction leagues, chiefly fed by race-prejudice on the one hand and by the employers on the other, over the question of *admission*. We have been so busy fortifying one or the other of the positions of these contestants that we have paid no heed to the guests themselves. Left in new and strange circumstances to work out both their own welfare and their own conduct, they have been unable to do so in a manner satisfactory to us. It is small wonder that they have forgotten or have ignored or have been impertinent to their hosts.

If immigrants are lawless, what is 'the law' in America and how are they to know it? The Romans had one law. We have not only a mass of Federal statutes, but innumerable statutes in forty-eight states and many thousands of ordinances, all providing penalties of fine or imprisonment for their violation, and branding the accused as a violator of law, if not a criminal. How make the immigrant see what many of our oldest Americans fail to grasp? Is it the law that an immigrant may dig trenches in one state but not in another; is it the law that an immigrant may shave his countryman in New York but not in Michigan; that he may own a dog in Delaware but not in Pennsylvania; that he may catch fish in Louisiana but not in Florida? Is it the law that he is entitled to hear and understand the accusation made against him by means of an interpreter in one court, and that in another the accusing officer or the complainant is the interpreter?

Only a few months ago a New Jersey justice of the peace fined an old Hungarian woman for having in her possession on Sunday seven apples taken from a neighboring orchard. Although the woman had taken the apples with permission, and although the person who had given the permission testified to it in court, the justice still maintained that carrying the apples on Sunday was against public policy—and persisted in the fine. It is only fair to add that local sentiment in this case does not seem inclined to tolerate the justice's decision. However, a foreigner who could not speak English would, unaided, be helpless against such a decision.

Again, what is the immigrant to think when he commits larceny and the political leader gets him off if he promises to vote right at the next election? What is he to think when he is denied a license for a pushcart because he is an alien, but is advised to go on peddling and pay the fine each time he is caught, as his profits will cover the cost—with the proper influences? Wherever their own power and interests are at stake, it is the Americans who instruct him, not only to resent legal interference but to evade it.

PART VI
Cultural Conflict, Americanization and Assimilation, 1900–45

INTRODUCTION

In the first quarter of the twentieth century, the solutions to the problems of immigrant acculturation could be characterized as follows: (1) the "Americanization" theory; (2) the "melting pot" theory; and (3) the "cultural pluralism" theory. For the most part and in varying degrees, each of these theories focused upon culturally remaking the alien so that he was no longer recognized as an "outsider."

The advocates of Americanization claimed that prior to 1900, the United States was comprised of a homogeneous population with strong Anglo-Saxon affiliations. Thus they demanded that newcomers quickly divest themselves of all ethnic distinctions and adopt the customs, language and aspirations of the "established American prototype." Furthermore, they encouraged aliens toward a single-minded adherence to American life, and to forget their homelands and their traditions.

Those who espoused this view apparently had little understanding of the cultural and emotional conflicts which rapidly enveloped people thrust into a new life-style. In turn, these "assimilationists" discovered that their programs and methods met with dogged resistance within the immigrant community.

To most aliens, total assimilation and "forced" Americanization were inconsistent with the spirit of democracy which, in many cases, was integral to their immigration in the first place. Nevertheless, Americanization, as advocated in the early 1900s, was the accepted theory and to the bewilderment of many aliens was practiced by most agencies responsible for their adjustment.

As an alternative to Americanization, the melting-pot theory evolved as the new vision of the ultimate goal of American life. Popularized by Israel Zangwill's play *The Melting Pot* (1908), this conception of adjustment portrayed the United States as a nation "where all the races of Europe are melting and reforming!" As though he were standing at the nation's portals and delivering a welcoming address to the newcomers, Zangwill declared:

Here you stand good folk, think I, when I see you at Ellis Island, here you stand, in your fifty groups, with your fifty languages and histories, and your fifty blood hatreds and rivalries. But you won't be long like that, brothers, for these are the fires of God you come to— these are the fires of God. A fig for your feuds and your vendettas! German and Frenchmen, Irishmen and Englishmen, Jews and Russians, into the Crucible with you all! God is making the American!

The melting-pot theory, however, paralleled Americanization in that each were attempts to bring about the disappearance of divergent ethnic cultures. Nevertheless, many immigrants accepted the former as the lesser of two evils.

While Americanization was essentially associated with Anglo-Saxonism and did not permit the immigrant to make an original contribution to the nation's culture, Zangwill's theory *favored* the addition of new cultural elements within American society. In addition, the melting-pot advocates differed in their approach to assimilation. Immigrant morale was to be raised and pride in the alien's past was to be encouraged. Likewise, assimilation was to be gradual—taking into consideration the newcomers' language, customs and social environment. Old memories and ideals were not to be forsaken and the disintegration of families was to be avoided by keeping the second generation faithful to the old ways, while urging their parents toward the American life-style. Furthermore, the Anglo-Saxon was not to be singled out as the standard—

all groups which played a part in American life were considered as having a contribution to make.

Still, cultural annihilation was the price of the melting pot. For it was ultimately by losing their cultural identity that immigrants were conceived of as becoming part of the nation. As the American caldron "crystallized millions of aliens, of all nations, habits, and languages," it was only then that the new citizens were able to enrich the American spiritual heritage.

Although this postulate was more tolerant of ethnic differences, for many, it was as unacceptable as total Americanization. For essentially, in the right to maintain one's ethnic heritage, both ultimately led to cultural absorption.

Refusing to adhere to theories which destroyed Old World traits, immigrant leaders and their sympathetic American allies developed the idea of cultural pluralism, which, contrary to the other two theories, stressed the perpetuation of cultural differences.

According to this tenet, instead of eliminating or limiting the influence of ethnic distinction in favor of cultural homogeneity, its proponents would make the ethnic group permanent in its influence on American life, thus enabling the newcomers to maintain their European backgrounds while concurrently making an American cultural contribution. Hopefully, the result was to be an American culture characterized by "a symbiotic relationship of these several cultures existing side by side as distinct entities."

The proponents of this principle asserted that they were in accordance with America's democratic traditions. Arguing that the protection of their customs was an important reason for their migration, they pointed to the historical relationship between religious beliefs and cultural ideals. Highlighting the significance of this concern, they stated that total cultural absorption was as oppressive as the denial of the right to believe in the doctrines of one's own religion.

However, many who embraced this theory realized that the immigrants' cultural identity would not remain unchanged—for within time, assimilation would ultimately fuse them into the American mainstream. Although the continuation of their Old World traits enjoyed a greater protection with the "pluralist" approach, most foresaw this technique as creating conditions favorable for absorption. And, in the final analysis, they anticipated the gradual disappearance of ethnic distinctions.

All of the theories cited were utilized in the adjustment of the various ethnics. Although none was totally adequate to alleviate the cultural conflicts which assimilation created, these concepts were nonetheless facilitated by institutions and individuals in the acculturation of almost forty million new Americans.

A. OFF WITH THE OLD: ETHNIC MINORITIES IN CULTURAL CONFLICT

Challenge to the Old Order

While parents remained attached to their European cultural values, second-generation children of immigrants responded favorably to their new American environment. Invariably, this led to a clash of culture which few, if any, of the ethnics escaped.

In turn, many parents saddened by the total acceptance by their children of everything American bitterly resisted any change which might cause a cultural disorientation in the home. Others, while trying to maintain some cultural domination over their families, and seeing they were fighting a losing battle, were forced into what was termed "resigned toleration." According to sociologist William Carlson Smith, this attitude caused "the parents not to change their point of view but, in the interest of a tolerable peace, surrender and even allow the children to dominate the home." Lastly, some parents made a conscious effort to adjust to the problem confronting them.

This third group, although basically rejecting the new values, "redefined the situation in such a way as to prevent conflict and consequent family disorganization." Shortly after their cultural confrontation, in an endeavor to keep close ties to their children, they too joined the movement to Americanize.

In the following selections the major cultural conflicts which confronted immigrant families were recounted. In the first essay, "The Struggle in the Family Life," Mary E. McDowell described the conflicts which beset the Bohemian family. Concentrating her analysis on the struggle over the use of their native language, she suggested that all concerned be given an opportunity to find a common ground by using both English and Bohemian in the public schools. She asserted that the bilingual approach was needed to supply the "great need . . . of the homesick old country parents who [were] losing their grip on their children."

The second selection, "Special Problems in Italian Families," analyzed the particular internal conflicts of that ethnic group. Witnessing the breakdown of a close-knit family life, Ida L. Hull, Case Work Director for the Connecticut Charity Organization, reported that the basic cause of this dilemma was "the child who [was] secretly ashamed of being Italian."

The last article is "Jim's Own Story." Herein was contained the study of a clash of cultures in a California-based Jewish family. Pauline V. Young, author of the article, viewed this conflict from its cultural, economic, social and religious aspects.

SOURCE: Mary E. McDowell, **"The Struggle in the Family Life,"** *Charities* (December 3, 1904), pp. 196–97.

It is said that the criminals of the cities come from the ranks of the children of the immigrants, not from the immigrants themselves. Those who live near these transplanted people tell us of the struggle in the family life between the standards of the old country father and mother and those of the children who have learned the language and caught the spirit of the new country, and have become the important factor in the family life.

The child stands between the new life and its strange customs; he is the interpreter; he often is the first breadwinner; he becomes the authority in the family.

The parents are displaced because they are helpless, and must trust the children. This superficial, though very practical superiority forces the children and parents into a false position with relation to each other and towards the outside world. The parents have religious and social ideals, and an impassioned faith that in America is to be found liberty and independence. The children's ideals are formed by the teachers, the politicians and often the saloon-keepers. The parents' ideals are discredited; they are old fashioned; in some way the children enter into their parents' vague desire for freedom, but it becomes to them such freedom as is hurriedly realized in a do-as-you-please philosophy. They have lost the restraints of an old community feeling that surrounded the parents in their old home and have not yet become rooted in the new restraints by the public opinion of a neighborhood they do not know. The parents' values are belittled and their loyalties scorned. "Shut up talking about Bohemia," said a boy to his mother who was shedding homesick tears as she spoke of the beauties of her old home. "We are going to live in America, not in Bohemia." She had the vision of beauty, while she was living in the sordid ugliness of the stockyard district of Chicago, and her boy could never have her vision.

The children are determined to drop the mother tongue, and they very soon learn English, while the parents are past the age when it is easy to acquire a new language. One often hears of children refusing to answer in the language of the family. Everything seems to be done to develop and educate the children, forgetting that this cannot be done for the child independently of the family or the community. The school, the church, the social settlement all emphasize the child's importance. The parents are ignored, left behind and the breach between the new and the old in the family is not spanned as yet by any of the agencies in the community.

The American citizen in the making is left to become a rather pert, important self-deceived young person because he has been isolated in his education. How shall this breach be bridged? What is done will be experimental, but something must be done for the situation is serious and often tragic. The public school lectures given in the foreign tongues to adults are suggestive, and lead one to ask why not enlarge the usefulness of the schoolhouse to meet the need of foreign families.

To begin the bridge from the child's side: cannot the parents, their home country, its beauties, its heroes, legends, stories, history, songs, be made of interest to the children? Will it not place the parents in an atmosphere of poetry of idealization and make them an important factor to the children? Admiration is a strong element in education. Win back the parental authority by admiring all that is admirable in their past. Create a historic perspective that will give self-respect to the new citizenship and will lead to respect for authority in the home and the state.

Start the bridge from the side of the parent by giving to them in their native tongue, American history, constitutional history, old country songs, old country scenes, art, etc., with that of the new country.

Let the parents and children *together* have a special life in the schoolhouse, bring them together in social relation with English-speaking teachers and friends, let them sing together the national songs of America and of the old lands.

Patriotic Americans may think this dangerous and say the English language is the only one that must be used in the schools, forgetting that this closes all avenues of culture to the adult foreigners. It is more dangerous not to supply this great need of the hungry hearts of the homesick old country parents who are losing their grip on their children. The too early developed young Americans must gain reverence for their parents, and for authority in the home or we shall have an increase of lawlessness. Open the schools for the foreign parents who, with their children, may learn what true freedom is and what American hospitality is. What the new patriotic societies are doing for Americans, we can do for the foreigners; recall the best of their past, recognize their heroes and start an impulse of admiration for all that is noble in the old and the new.

SOURCE: Ida L. Hull, **"Special Problems in Italian Families,"** *National Conference of Social Work: Addresses and Proceedings* (1924), pp. 288–91.

The challenging of the old order is the privilege of youth the world over. This is as true in Italy as elsewhere. But misunderstandings between Italian parents and children in this country are due in large part to factors which would not have entered into the situation in their native land. Here differences of opinion are based largely on the conflicts, real or imaginary, of two cultures. The parents want to conduct their family life according to old-world patterns; but the children want to behave in what they consider the American way.

The immigrant brings with him the traditional family relationships, and transplants them into new soil. Sometimes they take deep root. The Italian of course knows that here he will have to make adjustments to new conditions outside the home, but within his own four walls is hallowed ground, which he consecrates to the customs of his fathers. His conception of family life is simple and clear-cut. In the home the husband and father is the unquestioned head of the family.

A jarring note in the harmony of the home is too often struck soon after the children go to school. They learn English quickly. They reach out eagerly to what they believe to be American ways. The Italian child soon learns in school that he has started on the way to becoming an American, and he is assured that no greater good fortune could befall him. His geography lesson shows him how big this country is; his history lesson thanks Columbus for discovering us—though really it is difficult to see how he could very well have missed such an expanse of land—and explains how Washington and Lincoln and a few lesser lights made this world what it now is; his civics lesson assures him that America, if not still the refuge of the oppressed, is indeed the home of the free. All these things are pleasant to hear about at school; but when he goes home at night, he feels a painful contrast between what he sees there and what he has been taught during the day. The teacher has said, for instance, that clean hands, clean clothing, and a toothbrush are essentials. But the father, as he comes home from work, and the mother at her household tasks, though they may not oppose these ideals, yet they hardly exemplify them.

Like all children, the Italian child tends to follow the crowd. He soon wants to go to the movies, to hike to the country, to join in all the amusements of his companions. It is the thing to do in America. The father is likely to object. What he has been observing has not given him confidence in his new surroundings. He has seen the boys of the corner gang indulging in hazardous fun which is likely to get them into serious trouble; and he has heard the loud laughter and the shrill voices of girls on the streets at night. What wonder that he determines to prevent his own children from joining such a dizzy dance!

An immigrant father finds it very difficult to understand what is happening to his children. If he thinks back to his own childhood, the surroundings in which he grew up are so unlike his present environment that it does not help much for him to try to remember how he felt and acted when he was a boy. His school days were probably few. While most Italian immigrants are not entirely illiterate, few of them have ever been in school more than four or five years. They come in large part from rural communities in the south of Italy. Many have been engaged in agricultural pursuits previous to emigration, and practically all of them have grown up in a relatively static community, in which a young man had few avenues open to him for the future. The concrete situations which the immigrant had to meet in his old home are so unlike those in which he finds himself here that his past gives him little definite help in solving his present problems.

Still more is he handicapped by the superficial character of his contacts with the America his children know, and so he cannot picture this country as they see it. The parents learn little English; their friends and acquaintances are of their own race; they live in a foreign colony, apart. When new problems come up, the father has not the necessary information for forming a new opinion; it is so much easier, too, for him to fall back on traditional lines of thought, as we all tend to do, and to solve the question with some proverb taught him by his grandfather.

The difficulties in making successful adjustments at home and in the community are in direct relation to economic and cultural status. The uneducated Italian parent is peculiarly handicapped by his inability to present to his children his own point of view. He does not know how to make vivid to them the glorious achievements of the race from which he springs. No matter how illiterate he may be, he is conscious of belonging to an old civilization. He may not be able to read a word or to speak anything but a dialect, yet he thrills when he hears the name of Dante, of Michelangelo, of Garibaldi. When the children begin to learn in school what they interpret to mean that the United States is as relatively important in all respects as in her size, a flood of protest wells up within him. But he cannot make himself articulate. Though he feels that the history and art and poetry of his past is being trampled upon by barbarians, he cannot translate his emotion into coherent words. How bitter his humiliation when it is slowly borne in upon him that in the eyes of his own children he is a "dago," an inferior being!

As the children learn English, they begin to interpret for their parents and so to have a voice in family councils. Soon they feel quite able to make their own decisions, and in no need of guidance from their parents. This dependence on the children is most irksome to the father, for it deposes him from his position of authority and makes his children at least partners, if not leaders, in family enterprises. Little by little the children break away from control. When this situation develops, some parents who are weak or who have been too much worsted in their struggles, give up the contest, and their children go their tumultuous way quite unrestrained. Few parents, however, relinquish control without a struggle.

The storm center of domestic tempests usually gathers around the daughters of the family. The boys are allowed more freedom of action, as befits their future as heads of families. But the traditional way of looking out for the girls demands that they be always with their mother or with some other responsible person until they are married. Permitting them even to go out to work in a shop is often a concession to new-world ways and to economic necessity. After the girl becomes a wage-earner she gains a sense of independence. She wants to look like other workers and to amuse herself as they do. She is attracted by movies, dances, clubs, suitors with admiring glances and flattering words. On all this the parents look askance. Social workers often fail to understand why permission is refused for the daughter to go out at night, even to properly supervised places of amusement. But the parents understand their daughter's passionate nature. They know, as social workers often do not, that going out unchaperoned at night may have for the girl a fascination akin to trying to see how close it is possible to walk to the edge of a precipice without actually going over the brink. And they realize as no American can, how their daughter may forfeit the respect of Italian men who see her disregarding the usual conventions. At the root of the parents' objection to the girl's freedom of action is always the fear that she may be so compromised that it will be impossible for her to get a good husband.

Marriage is the future toward which the parents are looking for their daughter, not with a passive hope that it may somehow happen, but with the conviction that it is their duty to arrange an honorable alliance at an early age. But the girl brought up here is apt to rebel. She insists on having some part in choosing a husband for herself, perhaps by the elimination of several admirers before she picks out the most favored one.

In considering the problem which Italian families have to face in working out their domestic relations, we should not forget that in the nature of things a part of the problem cannot be solved by the individual families. No, there is often too much that is wrong, and degrading, and dangerous in their environment. An unnatural strain on family relations is the inevitable result.

SOURCE: Pauline V. Young, **"Jim's Own Story,"** *Survey* (March 15, 1928), pp. 777–78.

"I am sixteen years old and I was a freshman in high school when I quit . . . We live in an American neighborhood, and there were hardly any Jewish boys in my class. We used to live in a Jewish neighborhood, but we moved so I would keep away from the gang. So my mother figured it out.

"I don't like to bring my American friends around. They were born here and so were their parents. My mother speaks 'English' to them, and they make fun of her. When I ask her to leave them alone she says: 'They are only goyim (Gentiles), ain't I good enough to entertain them?' Sure, she 'entertains' them—at my expense. My father won't allow us to play ball on the lot. He says it's a waste of time and a disgrace to make such a lot of noise over nothing. He was raised in Poland. But then he don't believe in sweatshops either, but has never been anything but a cutter in a sweatshop. It's awfully embarrassing to bring any American friends to the house. In New York it was different. We lived on the East Side, and those who were not Jews were something worse than that, and we did not care. My brother was raised there and he even went to Hebrew School, and to *shuhl* [the synagogue] with my dad.

"I hate to stick around here with no friends and nothing to do. My mother reported me to the judge of the Juvenile Court. He told me to stay off Augusta Street, and I did for a couple of days, but I was not going to be lonesome all by myself, and when I started to long for the guys, I ditched school and went out there to join them.

"They sure are a slick bunch, and we have a lot of fun together. We can play ball all we want to, besides there are many playgrounds in that neighborhood, and the directors are congenial fellows, but we don't stick around there all the time. We like to see the city, we like to go to the beaches. Some of the boys have a car and we drive around the city and sometimes go to the beach. We don't plan our doings, some one hits upon an idea and we all act on it. Sure we have to follow the leader. You got to, if you want to stick around a gang. Our leader is slick and smart, and his orders are worth taking. He is sure of himself, he plays fair and divides even. He is naturally boss.

"I got in trouble many times while with the gang. I was in Juvenile Hall several times. The longest I ever stayed there was two months. That was for truancy. But when I went back to my old school I started ditching school again. I did not like the teachers nor their subjects. It's pretty bad business to have a court record, the school knows about it, the guys tease you, and your parents worry and nag. Once I was arrested for fishing in a lagoon in a park. We didn't know we could not fish there, and we landed in Juvenile, but the night watchman looked us over and said: 'There ain't no use bringing them kids here, you just make criminals out-a them, and besides we ain't got no room.' And they let us go. Once a bunch of boys got arrested for trying to get money from milk bottles to go to Venice and have a good time. It costs at least a dollar to have fun. It costs fifty cents to rent a bathing suit. Sure, I have one but it got many rips and is the New Yorker kind. My mother figures that if I don't like that suit I won't go to the beach, but she has another guess coming. Then when you are at the beach you want to have fun at the Fun House, or at a show and some food. My parents don't believe in beaches and never go swimming. I don't like to stay home, and my parents don't understand what boys need, and they expect me to be old-fashioned and go to *shuhl*.

"I have never taken very much stock in religion. I don't see any sense in it. Our Sabbath begins Friday at sunset, but my father works in the shop all day Saturday. Oh, he sighs and hopes to be in the land of the 'faithful' before he dies, but that don't help him any. I don't see why a faithful people should suffer and be laughed at like we are. My parents nag me to go to *shuhl* on holidays. They make many sacrifices to keep their traditions, but they don't mean anything much in my life. It's different with my brother, he got a start in New York in a Jewish community, but I can't be friends with Gentiles at school and at work and stick up for European ways too.

That's just why I don't like to stay home. I don't want to hurt my parents and I can't follow their advice."

Jim is in almost daily contact with two divergent cultures: the older Jewish culture symbolized by the home, and the newer American culture symbolized by the school, industry and the larger community. The East-European Jewish family is a traditional social institution with a strict and thorough-going code of behavior. It is difficult to find the strictly traditional Jewish home in America because of the many changes the family have to make to adapt themselves to the American social environment. Family obligations, nevertheless, are still set in the foreground, and individual members are expected to conform to family traditions. Keen consciousness of family relations is associated with the individual's identification with family interests, practices and observances.

In the larger community, however, Jim tends to become an "American citizen." The English language and the associations at school open up to him a new world of social practices, customs, attitudes, and social values. This newer culture fosters, moreover, traits of independence, personal resourcefulness, individuality, and cultivates desires for personal distinction. When these traits are displayed in the home they clash with the older established order of life and tend to break it up. Jewish communal and family life in Europe developed and utilized much the same personality traits. All of the behavior of the individual was controlled by one general social code.

In America immigrant parents and children live for the most part in different worlds of interests and experiences. They hardly understand each other and they can not fully appreciate each other's feelings, and therefore, are unsympathetic to each other. There is little opportunity or incentive to share their individual experiences since they lack the common background necessary for mutually interpreting them. Their divergent cultures place them in different universes of discourse.

Frequently one sees Jewish parents struggling to adopt the new culture. The reverence with which they cherish their religious and racial freedom in America inevitably opens the door to many outside influences which change the situation at home particularly with regard to the control of the children. Yet they find it almost impossible to divest themselves of their heritages. These are habits deeply rooted in mind and body. They modify or even discontinue some social practices, but on the whole they are the victims of their social habits. A new code of behavior independent of their old cultures is exceedingly difficult to formulate, and many uncertainties and inconsistencies characterize their behavior. Not infrequently we find the parents as well as the children suffering from mental conflicts as a result of the irreconcilable social and cultural forces which they encounter in America. Tenacious observance of old and often meaningless traditions may be only a symbol of a mental conflict on the part of the parent. They may, indeed be self-defenses against the demands of Americanized children.

The situation is accentuated by the inability to resist successfully the invasion of the newer culture rapidly acquired by the children. The home situation requires a redefinition of the situation, but neither parents nor children nor outside social agencies are able to organize and integrate at will the incompatible elements. In the end each member comes to be bound by his personal code of behavior. Family chaos then replaces customary regulated behavior, and discipline is lost. In the case of the Jewish boy, emotional and family life produce strong attachments to the home. The cultural gap between parents and children may not therefore, express itself in as wide a variety of conflicts and anti-social behavior as may be observed among certain other groups.

Jim seeks to escape the results of family life through association with the gang. The gang is a unique and relatively independent unit with its own code of behavior. Jim can satisfy his dominant wishes in the gang provided he is prepared to follow the leader and stand by him through the various vicissitudes. Jim was in custody of the Juvenile court several times. But he represents a type of personal disintegration due to divergent cultural forces which is a challenge to the current philosophy and methods of dealing with juvenile offenders.

B. THE MENACE OF AMERICANIZATION: CULTURAL PLURALISM VS. ABSORPTION

Cultural Pluralism vs. the Melting Pot

The influx of millions of non-Anglo-Saxon Europeans into the United States in the early twentieth century motivated assimilationists to put forth programs for rapid Americanization. Perhaps the most significant theory proposed was that of the melting pot. According to this concept, the newcomers were to shed their European culture and replace it with a standardized American pattern. Although this theory had great support among native Americans, most ethnic leaders viewed it as an attempt to produce a homogenized conformity through the "negative process of denationalization." Nevertheless, most farsighted aliens realized that the problem of cultural adjustment would not be solved until a program was created which both sides could accept. Subsequently, led by their press, religious institutions and aid organizations, the immigrants associated themselves with the ideas of cultural pluralism. Through this concept, most felt that they would be able "to keep alive the spiritual attachment to the traditions of the land of [their] ancestors."

SOURCE: Emily Greene Balch, **Our Slavic Fellow Citizens** (New York, 1910), pp. 396–99, 411–14, 421–25.

Assimilation is much talked of in the United States. Its desirability is so taken for granted that any and every method of hastening it may seem acceptable, until something brings to our attention what bad company this very assimilation keeps. Wherever in the world there are people crying, "We are oppressed," there you are likely to find another set of people protesting, "This is no oppression; it is assimilation—benevolent assimilation." The shout of "Islam or the sword," wrought probably the most rapid assimilation on record.

It is a commonplace of history that while the constitution of centralized states on a territorial basis, putting an end to feudal disorganization, was the characteristic accomplishment of the sixteenth, seventeenth and eighteenth centuries, the active ferment of the nineteenth century has been the principle of nationalities. Each group with a racial or cultural unity, and above all with the type and sign of this, a common speech, has been eagerly struggling toward autonomy, or at least toward the right to develop along its own lines and to use its own language.

Everywhere this nationalistic movement has revealed fresh human treasures and called forth some of the rarest and finest blossoms of the spirit of mankind. In literature it has given us highly differentiated types of new and poignant beauty, doubly welcome in a leveling and cosmopolitan age. Folk lore, art and philology have also felt its vivifying touch. It has evoked the most intense devotion and been the cause of the most heroic sacrifices.

On the other hand, it has divided peoples who before were hardly conscious of differences, and has narrowed men's sympathies to their own little group,—in striking contrast to the cosmopolitan humanitarianism of the eighteenth century. It has lighted indescribable fires of bitterness. Perhaps no moral agony is greater than to see the language and tradition of one's fathers, one's spiritual birthright, strangled to death by a contemptuous rival. The Pole in Germany, the Slovak in Hungary, the little Russian in Russia—and how many more—all feel the hand at their throats. It is cruel enough in a case like that of the Germans of the Baltic provinces of Russia; though they see their children forcibly Russified, yet they know that across the border Germany is continuing her progress without thought of check. To the Slovak, who knows that if his idiom becomes obsolete in Hungary it nevermore can take its place among the living tongues of men, what must it be to see his school funds confiscated, his press harried and his children systematically taught to despise the language and nationality which he loves with a Slav's obstinate intensity?

With these things in mind one turns to the United States and finds there a process of Americanization going on which must be seen to be comprehended, and which becomes the more impressive the more it is studied. Here are over 75,000,000 people, representatives of an indefinite variety of human stocks, yet presenting in general an almost painful degree of uniformity. For local color, the short story writer must generally have recourse to sheltered and backward communities, to frontier outposts or to colonies of recent newcomers—all now rapidly losing their peculiarities. It reminds one of the old fable of the traveler's cloak; the wind which boasted that he could easily remove it only made him hug it the closer to him; in the warmth of the sun he felt it a burden, and voluntarily cast it aside.

Yet even in the United States assimilation is not quite without signs of difficulty and apprehension and conflicting purposes—signs of dread and jealousy, on the part of Americans, of the alien influences brought in by the streams of newcomers, and, on the part of the immigrants, of jealousy of American influence and dread of Americanizing pressure.

One comes sometimes with a sense of shock to a realization of points of view strange to one's own. Take, for instance, a conversation that I once had with a Polish-American priest. I had said something about "Americans," that they were not apt to be interested in Polish history, or something of the sort. Instantly he was on fire.

"You mean English-Americans," he said. "You English constantly speak as if you were the only Americans, or more Americans than others. The History of the United States, published by Scribners, is written wholly from the English point of view, and that is very common. Even such a great paper as the Chicago *Tribune* is written by men who are just over from England, and who yet speak of foreigners when they mean any Americans but English. For instance, in a recent bank failure they said that many 'foreigners' would lose, referring to German-Americans and others who had been in the country for generations. A priest born in Baltimore of Italian parents, speaking English and Italian equally naturally, will see priests, new from Ireland, promoted over him because he is a 'foreigner.' "

I remarked that if I went to Poland he would not consider me a Pole.

"No, that is different," was his reply. "America was empty, open to all comers alike. There is no reason for the English to usurp the name of American. They should be called Yankees if anything. That is the name of English-Americans. There is no such thing as an American nation. Poles form a nation, but the United States is a country, under one government, inhabited by representatives of different nations. As to the future, I have, for my part, no idea what it will bring. I do not think that there will be amalgamation, one race composed of many. The Poles, Bohemians and so forth, remain such generation after generation. Switzerland has been a republic for centuries, but never has brought her people to use one language. For myself, I do favor one language for the United States, *either English or some other,* to be used by every one, but there is no reason why people should not also have another language; that is an advantage, for it opens more avenues to Europe and elsewhere."

He was indignant at the requirement of the naturalization law of 1906, making a knowledge of English a condition of citizenship. I advanced as an argument for it the fact that the proceedings of Congress are carried on in English, and that to vote intelligently a man must be able to follow them. "In our Polish papers," he said, "the Congressional debates are as fully reported as in the English-American papers, and politics can be as intelligently followed." I did not feel that I could urge that many English-speaking voters seek familiarity with the debates in full in the *Congressional Record.*

The views that I have tried to reproduce here are, I think, not typical, but they certainly suggest a reconsideration of various questions, among others, "What are Americans?"

. . .

In America each immigrant group exerts a certain influence on the community into which it comes, and some newly imported customs take root, either because they are attractive or useful in themselves, or because the newcomers are so represented as to have local prestige; but the laws of imitation work out on the whole to effect a much greater change in the immigrants than in the old settled American community.

In the first place, the convenience of unity makes for Americanization. The different immigrant groups neutralize one another's influence. In the steerage of an eastward bound liner one finds perhaps Roumanians, Croatians, Jews, Germans, Italians, using English as their *lingua franca,*—men, some of them from the same village at home, yet unable to speak with one another until now. It is *E pluribus unum* in a new sense.

Again, in America the way to success on a large scale, (whether political or financial or social or literary success), the only way to a national influence or position, is the way out of the Ghetto, Little Italy or "Bohemian Town." Thus American ways have practical value, whether good or bad in themselves.

Further, the prestige of numbers is on the side of the American example, and the more so the more scattered the newcomers are. In a close colony the influence is the other way for those inside, yet even so, the attraction of the American mass makes itself felt. As in a teacup one sees the little bubbles drawn to the larger ones and merging instantly when once in contact, so the larger life tends to absorb the smaller group. Indeed, the prestige of America, and the almost hypnotic influence of this prestige on the poorer class of immigrants, is often both pathetic and absurd. They cannot throw away fast enough good things and ways that they have brought with them, to replace them by sometimes inferior American substitutes.

Especially deplorable is the way in which men alter or discard their family names. The mine boss or petty official hastens or inaugurates the process by refusing to be bothered with what he calls "outlandish" names which he cannot spell. One Lithuanian family explain carefully their real name and add, "We are called Bruno just because father was put down in the boss's book under the name of an Italian who had gone away." In the Pennsylvania mining towns one finds Slavs who call themselves by such names as John Smith or Tim O'Sullivan or Pat Murphy, in the effort to make Americans of themselves. It is a great pity. The descendants of these men have a right to their paternity and to the clue to family history given by a family name.

Thus under the joint influence of convenience, ambition and the natural human desire to be like other people, and especially to be like those who occupy the high seats in the synagogue, the unifying change goes on. The early Polish immigrants, patriots and men of education, melted into the common life so completely that later comers could find no point of attachment with them. The recent Slavic immigrants, Poles and others, have come in much larger numbers; they have formed considerable colonies, and their hearts are set, with a strength of desire which we can hardly conceive, on having their children speak their own language as their proper tongue. The consequence is some degree of success in this aim, but it means, I am convinced, only a retardation of the process.

In Cleveland a Bohemian-American teacher who took the school census found one or two young people in their early "teens," born in this country, yet unable to understand English. This was considered, however, very unusual. I was told of a Hungarian who went to live in Prague, but there in the capital of Bohemia he never learned the language, as he found he could get on with German which he knew. Later he moved to Chicago and lived in the Bohemian quarter, where he found it indispensable to learn Bohemian, and did so, with toil and pains. I have heard of graduates of Polish schools in Chicago and Baltimore who do not understand English. I have been in a Polish "sisters' " school where the children were singing Polish songs.

> "We are little exiles;
> Far from our dear home
> We weep night and day,"

or something like that, the little round-cheeked boys just in from play on a Chicago sidewalk were chanting.

A thousand more items to show the separateness of the foreign life in our midst might be piled together, and in the end they would all be as nothing against the irresistible influence through which it comes about that the immigrants find themselves the parents of American children. They are surprised, they are proud, they are scandalized, they are stricken to the heart with regret,—whatever their emotions they are powerless. The change occurs in different ways among the educated and the uneducated, but it occurs in either case.

The prestige of America and the hatred of children for being different from their playmates is something the parents cannot stand against. The result is often grotesque. A graduate at one of our women's colleges, the daughter of cultivated Germans, told a friend: "My father made me learn German and always was wanting me to read it. I hated to have anything to do with it. It seemed to me something inferior. People in the West call a thing 'Dutch' as a term of scorn. It was not till I was in college that I realized what German literature and philosophy have meant in the world, and that to be a German is not a thing to be ashamed of." Less educated parents, or those using a language less important than German, have a still more difficult task to hold the next generation. "I ain't no Hun, I'm an American," expresses their reaction on the situation.

In a Nebraska county town, in a district largely settled by Bohemians, one father of a family told me his experience. The older children, he said, spoke Bohemian excellently, they used to take part in private theatricals in the Bohemian opera house in the town and did well; but the younger children he simply could not induce to take to it. They knew so little that if he sent them with a message in Bohemian they were likely to make mistakes.

. . .

Is it strange that a Croatian physician wrote to me from Pittsburgh as follows?

"The great question appears to be how soon immigrants can be assimilated, to what degree, and if they are going to be good citizens. It has been found that everybody who gets Americanized becomes a good citizen, i.e., a shrewd business man who knows his value at the polls, who knows how to outwit the intricacies of the law, and how to be ashamed of his origin, his name and his religion . . . So far, good citizenship is associated with the ideal of a policeman, alderman, political boss, financier, and so forth, all of whom we can reach and see as good American citizens with rather dubious moral qualities, while educated and fine feeling people are out of reach; the immigrant knows nothing of their existence. There is no need to fear that, so long as the flesh pots are full in America, assimilation and the making of 'good citizens' will meet any obstacle; individuals, families, nations will readily submit to everything American if it only means their material advantage, while they don't expect in this country any moral profit, as there is none to get—for them. I think that it would be a good thing if some one would show to the Americans their real moral standing in the world. Unquestionably, with their freedom and their natural resources there should be much more feeling for righteousness, for tolerance and for art in this country. Had the Americans not the right men in Washington, they would develop in a few years into the most zealous worshippers of the Golden Calf and of nothing else. All this is, of course, merely my opinion, but it is based upon actual observation of the people during seven years. I believe in American, that is in human, ideas, and will hope that the minority will be able to win over the majority and make the people what they ought to be: first of all, honest."

. . .

Another view of what America is to the Slav is that of Father Tymkevich, whom I have already quoted. Economically he thought they gain by coming here, "physically and morally, no. In the city they need more morality." Then again, with deep wisdom, "They have no habits. The first step in civilization is to acquire habits, and where can they acquire them? On the streets? In the saloon?

"What my people need most is leaders,—leaders to form themselves upon, to give them a standard of ambition. Other people have leaders of their own, strong and influential men among the immigrant body, and Americans who know something about them and are ready to take an interest in them."

And again, almost like a cry, the phrase I have previously quoted, "My people are perishing for lack of vision."

"The Slavs are orphans in this country," he said. And it is in a sense true. It is not chiefly that they have no government of their own, concerned for them as Italy is concerned for the Italians; it is far more that coming to America they are cut off from the life of their old country, without getting into contact with the true life of their new home, from which they are shut off by language, by mutual prejudice, by divergent ideas. To them, both parents are dead, the fatherland that begot them and the foster-mother that supports without cherishing them.

In some ways this isolation is harder for the educated than for the laborer. A man like Father Tymkevich himself is in a position of almost intolerable loneliness. Intelligent, sensitive, separated from his own people by all that separates a scholar from peasants, he was a complete stranger in a community unused to look for friends and associates among foreigners.

What then ought we to be doing for these strangers in our midst? If we ought not to try to "Americanize" them, have we no obligations toward them at all?

It is obviously our plain duty to give the immigrant (and every one else) fair treatment and honest government, and to maintain conditions making wholesome, decent living possible. This is the minimum required at our hands, not by the Golden Rule—that asks much more—but by the most elementary ethic of civilization. Yet as a matter of fact, this simple, fundamental thing we cannot do. It is not in our power.

We can and must do what in the end will be a better thing. We must get our new neighbors to work with us for these things. If their isolation is not to continue, American must come to mean to them, not a rival nationality eager to make them forget their past, and offering them material bribes to induce them to abandon their ideals. We must learn to connect our ideals and theirs, we must learn, as Miss Addams has demonstrated, to work together with them for justice, for humane conditions of living, for beauty and for true, not merely formal, liberty.

Clubs and classes, libraries and evening schools, settlements and, above all, movements in which different classes of citizens join to bring about specific improvements in government or in living conditions, are of infinite value as they conduce to this higher unity, in which we may preserve every difference to which men cling with affection, without feeling ourselves any the less fellow citizens and comrades.

The Process of Denationalization

The Polish experience with the "imposition" of American cultural mores was similar to that of other European groups. While threatened with the inevitable process of Americanization, parents witnessed the deterioration of traditional family values. This new way of life, introduced into the home by the children, created a diversity of interest. In turn, the tension produced by this conflict often led to the breakup of the family unit.

In the article which follows, "The Unsolved Problem," the author reported that the "rate of Americanization among the children of the [Polish] foreign-born [was] too distressingly swift." He concluded that the tempo of denationalization placed the immigrant "in a kind of vacuum, cut off from the ancient moorings and far from the solid ground of [his] culture."

SOURCE: **"The Unsolved Problem,"** *The Interpreter* (January 1927), pp. 7–10.

The Immigrant's View of Progress

Among the Poles in particular there has of late been a movement toward concerted action against the too rapid Americanization of the younger generation. Their attitude toward the process of denationalization may be had very vividly (and in an American viewpoint not unamusingly) from a series of "Pictures of Polish-American Life" by a writer in the *Dziennik Chicagoski*, a Polish daily of Chicago. He tells, among others, of a Polish community in the Middle West settled forty years ago, in which the younger generation is wholly native-born:

In the local parochial school Polish has been the regular tongue along with English all the while. Some time ago a delegation of the Americanized youth called upon the pastor to abolish the use of Polish. The priest refused, and the controversy was submitted to the parish for decision. Out of a total population of some hundred and fifty families only one hundred and thirty-one ballots were cast, fifty-seven for dropping the Old World speech and seventy-four against. Polish was saved for the curriculum; but the significant thing is that the remaining parishioners who were entitled to vote were too indifferent to do so.

An even somberer "picture" is laid in St. Louis:

I have many relatives in St. Louis. Two years ago I was visiting some of them, and among others ran across a young priest who was entirely unable to speak or understand Polish. His father had come to America as a youth of seventeen, and he himself had of course been born here. Now he is a curate in an Irish parish, patiently waiting for his advancement on the day when the Poles shall be Americanized enough to be able to listen to a service in English.

At Stevens Point, Wisconsin, the old order was not so successful in resisting the tide of the times as in the unnamed parish referred to before. Here too the youth suggested that English supersede Polish, not in the schools but in the church, and the clergyman deemed it best to compromise.

The church was obliged to comply partially. The early morning services, which are attended largely by young folks are now conducted wholly in English. Now, I ask you, what is to become of these children? How can they remain Poles? Stevens Point, you are to remember, is nearly half Polish, six thousand out of a total population of thirteen thousand. Yet even in so concentrated a community Americanization has gone to such lengths.

Matters have deteriorated much further, according to this writer, in a number of other places.

In one town in Wisconsin a Polish society undertook a study to determine the degree of interest in Polish culture and affairs.

Its investigators have learned from a house-to-house canvass that out of one hundred and twenty families only sixteen took in a Polish newspaper, thirty-three read both languages, while seventy-one read nothing but English. In San Antonio, Texas, there is a parish whose beginnings go back to the sixties of the last century. The majority of the people in it, including its pastor, were born and raised in this country. Polish traditions and the Polish language have practically disappeared from its horizon. English is the language of the parochial schools and of the early church services. Only the high mass is still celebrated in the old tongue, but it is a mere matter of a few years before even that goes . . . I know a Polish family in Green Bay, Wisconsin, which has been in the place for forty years. Of the eight children only one, a daughter, is married to a Pole. The rest are married into various nationalities and are forever lost to the Polish community.

But while de-Polonization is naturally a distressing spectacle to the Pole, there is clearly an aspect to the evolution of the immigrant's children into Americans which cannot fail to make all of us pause. It is that vacuum stage, spoken of earlier. Discussing the existing situation, *Kuryer Polski,* a daily published in Milwaukee, comments editorially: "A young Pole reared in a Polish American environment is certainly an unattractive type. He is neither a Pole nor an American in any genuine sense of either word, but a species of transitional being . . . Having heard a great deal about liberty in America, he translates the notion into a license to do what he likes. He is impertinent and disagreeable to everybody (except to the policeman who carries a club and can put him in jail) and his behavior toward other people is such as to make a farmhand in the old country blush with shame. He thinks it perfectly proper to snub his parents, who are nothing but ignorant foreigners in his estimation, while he is a modern and progressive young person. He sneers with contempt at Poland, its language and civilization. All this makes him feel vastly superior to his elders, and he accompanies this display of his emancipation with oaths that would astonish a pirate and with a talent for long-distance spitting that would make a professional marksman gasp. Doubtless he believes that all this is American and calculated to win him the approbation of Americans. How should he know, poor soul, that decent Americans have a great deal more respect for a Pole who is genuinely and unaffectedly a Pole."

Looking to the Future

To remedy this distressing situation Polish responsible leaders are coming more and more to the conviction that their youth must be brought under the influence of their elders by drawing the boys and girls of Polish birth or descent into the Polish organizations. Says the weekly *Czas,* official organ of the Polish National Alliance, of Brooklyn, New York: "At the last Convention of the Alliance a program was worked out to increase the membership of the organization among the youth." And according to an appeal issued by the committee charged with the execution of the enterprise, the only hope of somehow bridging the ever-widening gulf between the generations is to bring back to the youth a sense of the value of the culture of the homeland.

"Our Mother country," it continues, "is destined to have a bright future and to exert much influence in this country. To assist our youth to share in this influence, it will be both desirable and necessary to educate them in the language and the traditions of Poland. We foresee great developments in commerce, industry and the arts of such a nature as to draw the two countries closer together, and this will make a knowledge of their languages and traditions very useful to those who possess both. It will therefore behoove such organizations as ours to look ahead and prepare our youth for the functions which in the future are bound to fall upon cultivated young people who can serve as intermediaries between Poland and America."

As one step in the desired direction, the committee proposes to print in its official newspaper a regular English department dealing with Polish history and affairs and designed especially to interest the young people.

The Polish National Alliance of Brooklyn is only the pioneer. The Polish National Alliance of America, with a membership of 236,000, is preparing likewise to take action in a situation which is disturbing the entire Polish population in the country.

What all this activity will accomplish, only the future can tell. But that America herself has a profound interest in a program whose purpose it is to guide the children of the foreign-born to a healthier development from the alien state to citizen-ship, is evident to everyone who has ever given the matter any thought.

C. NO LONGER ALIEN: ACTION AND REACTION

Education and Americanization

The concern over the immigrants' Americanization caused many assimilationists to advocate educational programs, particularly in the instruction of English, civics, American history and health. Consequently, numerous urban school systems began to register and educate millions of school-age immigrant children. In addition to providing classes for the young, most metropolitan Boards of Education instituted sessions of evening adult education. Interestingly, most of these voluntary educational programs were created at the insistence of the immigrants themselves.

SOURCE: A. R. Dugmore, "New Citizens of the Republic," *World's Work* (April 1903), pp. 3323–26.

At the corner of Catherine and Henry Streets in New York is a large white building that overlooks and dominates its neighborhood. Placed in the middle of a region of tawdry flat-houses and dirty streets, it stands out preeminent because of its solid cleanliness and unpretentiousness. It is the home of Public School No. 1. In it are centred all the hopes of the miserably poor polyglot population of the surrounding district—for its pupils the scene of their greatest interest and endeavor, and for their parents an earnest of the freedom they have come far and worked hard to attain.

The child of American parentage is the exception in this school. The pupils are of the different nationalities or races that have their separate quarters in the immediate neighborhood. If they were to be divided according to their parental nationality, there would be twenty-five or more groups. The majority of the pupils, however, are Swedes, Austrians, Greeks, Russians, English, Irish, Scotch, Welsh, Rumanians, Italians, Poles, Hungarians, Canadians, Armenians, Germans and Chinese. The Germans, Russians and Polish predominate, for there are a very large number of Jewish pupils.

The most noticeable thing in the school is the perfectly friendly equality in which all these races mix; no prejudice is noticeable. The different races are so scattered that there is no chance for organization and its attendant cliques and small school politics. This is particularly interesting in the face of the fact that the one thing more than any other which binds the boys together is their intense common interest in party and city politics. Also political news is followed and every question is heatedly debated in and out of class. This interest in politics and the training in argument and oratory it brings is probably due in large measure to the parents. To them this opportunity for political discussion is an evidence of the freedom of the new country which has replaced the tyranny of the old. The lack of organization and the lack of prejudice is shown by the fact that the "captain" or elected leader of a class composed with one exception of Jewish lads is the solitary exception—an Irish boy. In another class the "captain" is Chinese.

The interest in politics is only one of the evidences of a great desire to "get along in the world." Another is the fact that many of the boys are self-supporting. The number of boys working their way through can only be guessed. They are reluctant to tell anything about their home life or conditions. It is known, however, that about one hundred and twenty of the six hundred odd boys in the grammar department are self-supporting. A little Italian boy was late one morning and was asked for his excuse by the principal. After much questioning he told this story: His mother was dead, and his father, who worked on the railways, and consequently was away from home most of the time, could send him only enough money to pay the rent of the two small rooms in which he and a smaller brother and sister lived. To pay for their food and clothing he and his brother sold papers after school hours, making about $4 a week. The sister did the cooking and the housework. This particular morning she had been ill and unable to leave her bed, and it had taken him so long to care for her and attend to her work that he had been late. This was told quietly and quite as a matter of course. The boy was fourteen years old. He had no idea that his story seemed extraordinary. He had never thought of trying to get help of any kind. This earnestness is carried into all the school work. The boys, because of the sacrifices their schooling brings, realize more keenly how valuable it is to them.

Although the school is democratic, and although the public school has taught them the English language and a certain feeling of Americanism, their race shows itself often in the classroom. For example, the Russian and Polish Jews have a school standing far out of proportion to their number, and the Italians are unquestionably the most artistic in the manual training shops, while, as we have seen, the Irish talent for leadership and organization is not impaired by the public school. Very often this grafting of Americanism on foundations of foreign family tradition gives rise to very naive points of view—such, for instance, as that of the little Polish lad who gave the following definition of spring: "Spring, which is the first season of the year, is when flowers and business bloom."

The school course is similar to that in all the other public schools. There is, however one extra class called the "ungraded class." This class is divided into four subdivisions: those for (1) special discipline cases, (2) truants, (3) defective children—physically, mentally or morally, and that for (4) foreign born children who do not speak English. The work done with these boys is perhaps the most valuable single service of the school. Here the entire stress of the teacher's task is given to remedy the individual defect. The children are taught only those things which the teacher believes are within the understanding of each individual. Sand and clay modeling, drawing lines with colored crayons, weaving with colored splints, cutting, pasting and using peg-boards are some of the occupations through which the minds are stimulated. Gradually, as they develop, tool and other work is given, and the results are remarkable. Their defect may be of eyesight, hearing, muscular control, speech, moral sense. Some are afflicted with paralysis or epilepsy. Whatever it is, all that can be done to better their condition and to make them self-supporting is being done by tactful teaching.

It is a large task that schools of this kind are doing, taking the raw, low-class foreign boys of many nationalities and molding them into self-supporting, self-respecting citizens of the republic. The amount of this work done by the public schools in New York is indicated by the figures of the immigration bureau, for of the great body of foreigners who come into this country, more than two-thirds come through the port of New York, beyond which most of them rarely get. The results shown by the public schools seem little short of marvelous. There are many things in which, as a rule, the public consider that the public schools fail, but the one thing that cannot be denied—and it is the greatest—is that these boys and girls of foreign parentage catch readily the simple American ideas of independence and individual work and, with them, social progress.

SOURCE: **"Night Schools for Americanizing Immigrants,"** *Immigrants in America Review* (January 1915), pp. 35–36.

"Why are our immigrants un-Americanized?" is the question this country has been asking itself for the last year. How does it happen that an Italian or German or Pole who has been here for five or even ten years has remained a foreigner, ignorant of American life and perhaps indifferent to it—or even contemptuous?

This answer is not far to seek. Thousands of them have not learned American ways because they have never had a chance to learn our language. Their first consideration has had to be self-support; they have been obliged to go where they could get work. That often meant a brickyard, off on the outskirts of a sleepy little village, or a lumber camp in the heart of the woods, or a railway construction-gang settlement, not even near a village, or a quarry or coal or iron-mine village, with schools hardly large enough for the children, and no night schools at all.

The community is not always at fault, for often it would be impossible for a small town or village to carry the financial burden of installing night classes for several hundred men. Often, however, the community, whether large or small, has been blind to the civic and national importance, aside from motives of any other kind, of giving these dumb foreigners the power to hear us and to speak. In New Jersey, two or three years ago, local school authorities refused to allow a class to meet in the schoolhouse, although the leader was to be a volunteer and the school would be put to no expense whatever.

The prevalent theory that immigrants do not want to learn, and will not go to night schools when they are provided—due to their dropping out when the hours were too long for men wearied with a long day's labor in camp or mine, or when the teachers were incompetent or methods too childish for minds that, back of their present handicap, are mature—is proved untrue by the response immigrants make to any suggestion of aid. Some typical letters are given here that were written by immigrants who wish to learn English and become naturalized, but who live in communities where there are no night schools.

The first is a petition signed by sixty-six Lithuanian citizens of Melrose Park, Illinois:

"The undersigned citizens of the United States, of Lithuanian parentage, residing in Melrose Park, Cook County, Illinois, do respectfully petition your Honorable Body to install a free night school in our locality for the purpose of the education of the Lithuanian-American citizens in the English language.

"There is at present in our locality no free night school offering any opportunity for foreign-born citizens to become educated in the English language, although there are approximately three thousand (3,000) foreign-born American citizens in the village of Melrose Park, and surrounding territory."

.   .   .

"I am an Italian and it is two years since I am here coming from Europe and I have a strong desire to learn the American language good for to be soon as possible a citizen during this time. I went four months to school while I was living in a city, but now I'm working in a small town so I can't get the chance to attend night school. I would like have some advice how I could learn the language without going to school so I beg your goodness to advice me how to do."

.   .   .

"I am an emigrant who came to the United States.

"I like this country and I desire to become a citizen of the United States. I came to this country on January 15th, 1914. I filed my declaration on May 31, 1915.

"I came to Christopher, Ill. There are two public schools here, but there is no night school, and we immigrants are in the dark. We saw an ad. saying that the United States offer their services, which we accept with open hands. We immigrants want education and we wish voluntarily become Americans.

"We beseech you gentlemen to give us a helping hand to obtain education.

"We want education, we want citizenship.

"There is quite a number of us here."

.   .   .

"We, the undersigned naturalized citizens and 'future' naturalized citizens of the U.S., living at present in Dillonvale, O., beg to inform you that we would very gladly learn the American language. But taking private lessons in the same is to heavy burden for us poor coal miners of Bohemian and Polish nativity, and we think that if a Free Evening School could be established in Dillonvale, O., for the foreign-born citizens just during the winter season, that it would greatly benefit not only ourselves, but the whole community. Upon our inquiry at least 75 men and boys (above 14 years of age), and possibly some women, of the Bohemian population, would attend such evening school, and because these Bohemian men and boys have a pretty fair education in their native tongue, so there is no doubt about the result of such course."

.   .   .

"Dear Citizens:

"I read your notice in the Post Office, that you help those who desire to learn the English language, as well as those desiring to become American citizens. We Poles have settled in Danielson, Conn., with the intention of becoming citizens of this free country of America rather than be laborers (slaves) of the Czar or Kaiser. But the laws of this country require that all foreigners who desire to become American citizens have a knowledge of the English language and the laws. We Poles cannot do this here as there are no evening schools.

"We come to you, dear citizens. Please advise us what to do."

.   .   .

"I desire to learn the Englesh language to read and write and to etend night school. There are quite a number would like to teend but the supentend is oppose to it and therefore I write you as we are all laborers we cannot etend during the day. Please please write the Superentend in regard to same. I wish you would do something for us, as I want to git out my naliniles papers out next year."

.   .   .

"I would like to possess both, that is to learn English language and to become a citizen. Ther is a public school here, but there is no evening school. This is a small town and probably not rich and they do not want to make more expenses to establish an evening school. On the other hand a poor workingman who hardly make enough sometimes to pay for his living, cannot afford to pay somebody for English lessons and to learn at home without a teacher one can learn only to read and this not very good. Only the school can teach one good, or somebody who would give lessons.

"I was during one year in another town, where there was an evening school and where they teach very good. I went to this school during the entire winter and I learned a great deal but I have forgotten some during the summer and if I could this winter go to school as I did last, I could in spring already write and speak English good. To read I have learned quite well, only some hard words I cannot as yet."

. . .

These letters show clearly what the situation is, and sharply challenge America's claim that this is a democratic country where every man has a chance. For the sake of the country and for the sake of the country's need, let us see to it that the opportunity to learn English is put within the reach of foreign-born men and women in hamlet, camp, and city, in work-shop, field and mill.

Americanization and World War I

With the entrance of the United States into World War I, the immigrants' loyalty to their new homeland was put to the test. Shortly after President Wilson's declaration of war, the nation discovered that the alien hordes from Europe could not only be trusted, but were as patriotic as most native-born Americans.

The selection which follows is from a Hungarian newspaper, the *Magyar Tribune*. On April 21, 1917, it published the "Ten Commandments in Time of War." The editorial was only one of thousands which expressed immigrant loyalty during the duration of the conflict.

SOURCE: **Magyar Tribune,** April 21, 1917.

I. You must never forget that no one asked you to come to the United States. You came here of your own free will to make a better living and to save a few nickels for your old age.

II. When you stepped on the shore of the United States you were on free soil. No one asked you what you were doing here, and no one stood in your way. It was up to you and you only what you were going to do in this country. The nation immediately became your friend. You received the respect due to a guest when you entered the United States. Respect your host, and your host will respect you.

III. Keep your thoughts to yourself. Maybe the pope knows everything, but you are not a pope, and this does not mean that you know more than he does.

IV. Do not get involved in arguments in public places.

V. For six days do your work and attend to your duties. On the seventh day rest; that is what the Lord intended you to do. Six days out of the week are for labor, and during this time you should think of nothing but your duties. If you are engaged in respectable work, you will be considered a law-abiding citizen, so work for six days, and on the seventh day of the week devote your time to rest and to your family.

VI. Do not take part in any political movement. Trust people whose duty it is to think for you. Be satisfied, for you will not be able to change things anyway. In war, unity means strength.

VII. Have respect for the laws of the country which provide your daily bread. The laws defend your interests. Every law has a purpose. You must be familiar with the laws, and you must obey them.

VIII. Do not carry on your person any kind of firearm or other deadly weapon. Your only weapon of defense should be your self-respect.

IX. Keep your savings in the same place in which you had them in time of peace. Money should be kept in a bank and not on one's person or at the place where one lives. You yourself cannot guard your money so well as the bank can. The laws of this country insure that what is yours is yours only. Regardless of what the future may bring, your wealth will not be threatened by disaster in the United States.

X. Love your neighbor. All men are equal regardless of creed and nationality. We all came from the same parentage originally, and we are all brothers and sisters. After the world war will come brotherly love among the nations of the world. It is for this purpose that this country is fighting. No one asks you for sacrifice in this war; therefore you can lead a life of peace and happiness if you keep to the straight and narrow path.

Half an American

Describing America as a melting pot, assimilationists envisioned a nation in which immigrants replaced their traditions with American standards. The outcome of this movement was to be the creation of a composite of all types which had mingled to produce it. For many, Americanization worked well, and without too much difficulty they were able to withdraw from their cultural backgrounds. Nevertheless, countless others found the experience of this transformation frustrating and oppressive.

In the following article, the ordeal of assimilation was recounted. In "Half an American," Stoyan Christowe described the predicament of a "cultural vacuum"—no longer a Balkan, he was still not spiritually or linguistically an American.

SOURCE: Stoyan Christowe, **"Half an American,"** *Outlook and Independent* (December 1929), pp. 531, 555–57.

In my passion to liken myself to the Americans, to rub out from my personality all foreign traits and characteristics, I suffered agonies. I would not content myself with straight and safe English. Americanisms, native idioms and localisms would give a certain authenticity to my own Americanism. And I was not cautious in their use; with the result that often I made myself ridiculous, saying things entirely different from what I intended to say. Once in my college days a fellow student and I passed on the campus two lovers. I noticed as they came by us that the young man was holding the girl so awkwardly that she walked with difficulty. My intention was merely to remark to my friend on the un-natural way in which the young man was holding his companion and I could well have said, "What a stupid way to hold a girl!" but precisely what I said was, "Say, that fellow's got that girl in a bad shape!" My friend laughed uproariously, but genially, and I with him. In those days I was not very self-conscious about my mistakes. I knew that my whole being was in process of change, that I was in a state of turmoil. My English was in ferment.

Years have passed since then. And I am now a different person. Still I often ask myself these questions: What has been the result of this long and blind gestation in the womb of America? Have I become an American? Has the storm in my being lulled now that I have spent two-thirds of my life in a struggle for readjustment and adaptation? The one answer that pounds in my mind most is this: Despite the readiness and zeal with which I tossed myself in the melting pot I still am not wholly an American, and never will be.

It is not my fault, I have done all I could, America will not accept me. I shall always be the adopted child, not the real son, of a mother that I love more than the one that gave me birth. It is hard for a man with ingrained native traits and characteristics to remake himself in the course of one generation. There is still something outlandish about me; mannerisms and gestures that must strike as odd one born and bred here; tints and nuances in my speech that must betray my foreign birth soon after I open my mouth to speak.

I once believed that America demanded complete surrender from those who adopted it as their mother. I surrendered completely. Then I discovered that America wanted more—it wanted complete transformation, inward and outward. That is impossible in one generation.

Then what is my fate, and the fates of the thousands who fall into my category, or, should I say, into whose category I fall? What are we? Are we still what we were before we came to America, or are we half Americans and half something else? To me, precisely there lies our tragedy. We are neither one nor the other; we are orphans. Having forsaken our own mothers to become the foster children of another, we find ourselves orphans. Spiritually, physically, linguistically, we have not been wholly domesticated. And at the same time we have rendered ourselves incapable of resuming life in the old country.

While I am not a whole American neither am I what I was when I first landed here; that is, a Bulgarian. Still retaining some inherited native traits, enough to bar me forever from complete assimilation, I have outwardly and inwardly deviated so much from a Bulgarian that when recently visiting in that country I felt like a foreigner and was so regarded. My Bulgarian speech is now cramped and rusty, clumsy and inadequate for my thoughts. I cannot now speak that language half so fluently as I speak English; nor can I write it with half the facility with which I string English words upon this page. In my audience with King Boris during my visit there I found myself compelled to ask permission from the King to speak to him in English. In Bulgarian I stammered and was hopelessly inarticulate. I know hundreds who have been twenty and more years in America and who use English chiefly as their medium of communication, but speak it abominably, like foreigners, and speak their own tongues even less fluently. Some years ago I was interpreting in court for a Bulgarian who despite a continuous residence in this country of fifteen years still deemed himself unprepared to appear in court without an interpreter. We both found it more difficult to converse in Bulgarian than in English and the court was greatly amused when we had to discard our mother tongue and wrestle in English for understanding.

Later while I was traveling on a Bulgarian train the conductor came to tell me that in the adjoining compartment there was a Bulgarian who had been in America so long that his speech was no more comprehensible than that of a child of three. I asked to see my compatriot. I spoke to him in our native speech. He understood what I said, but when he attempted to reply his tongue was tied. Then I addressed him in English. His eyes lit up with joy and his face opened into a smile at the sound of English words in this land which was his birth soil. I was not surprised when I heard his English, which was only slightly more intelligible than his Bulgarian.

There are many such linguistic orphans in America. It is a difficult matter for one whose ancestors for centuries have twisted their lips in a certain manner, flung their tongues in this or that nook of the mouth, and otherwise adjusted and manipulated the speech organs to the articulation of peculiar native sounds to force these organs to the production of unnatural syllables.

Now I do not claim that America openly demands uniformity of the immigrant that has come to stay. The federal authorities when granting citizenship rights do not put one through a form of examination designed to ascertain whether he has attained to these qualities before they grant him his papers. But though the demand has not taken such concrete form it is nevertheless there palpably and none perceives it better than that immigrant who has been inoculated with the fever for Americanization. I have seen in the homes of foreigners certificates of American citizenship framed like college diplomas and hung on the walls. I have heard the owners of these diplomas of citizenship speak disparagingly of their own peoples and lands and exalt everything American, except prohibition. A kind of Americamania dominates their feelings and attitudes. Yet to the Americans themselves, I mean not the Americanized but the whole Americans, these proud citizens are Greeks or Bulgars or Polaks; not infrequently, Dagos, Wops, Bohunks.

What then eventually happens to these people? Do they continue living in a shroud of deception, or do they sooner or later see through the illusion and tire of their fidelity to America? At length I believe every immigrant begins to think of the old country. Many return with the thought of looking things over and remaining there. But they immediately find that while they have not made of themselves whole Americans, they have become so different from their own people and their mode of living has undergone such a drastic change that the prospect of resuming habitation in their native lands depresses them. There by their own people they are regarded as Americans and are looked upon with a not too approving eye. In America they are foreigners. What are they? They speak well neither English nor their mother tongues.

I cannot forget the experience I had with a Greek-American whom I encountered in my travels in the Balkans. I was driving in a Ford through Chalcidia when, tired and thirsty, I asked my Greek chauffeur to stop in a little village for a drink of *mastica* and a cup of Turkish coffee. A gendarme walked to where we had stopped and asked whether we would be good enough to take along with us to Polygiros, a town some fifteen miles distant, an American who had been stranded in their village. I started at the word American and quickly informed the gendarme that I myself was one. It would be a pleasure indeed to accommodate a countryman of mine.

Seated alone at a table on the terrace of the village cafe was the American, a short, chubby fellow with a round face. He was dressed in a blue serge suit, a gray cap was pulled over his forehead. The native Greeks in their baggy Anatolian trousers stood or sat at a respectful distance from him and watched his every movement.

His chest inflated, the man was surveying everything around him with a lordly air. Now he would sip his coffee, now finger the gold pendant on his watch chain, now pull up the legs of his trousers so that the crease might hang down straight. All these movements the villagers observed with profound and respectful interest. None dared to sit at his table or near him. Among them he was like an officer of an army of occupation. He was a sight! He seemed to be saying to everything and everybody around: "Look! I am an American! What are you? Nothing. Scum!"

The gendarme, the only person bold enough to speak to him, or probably the only person the man condescended to speak to told him that I was an American. That he should meet an American in these isolated places was enough to fill him with joy. He rose quickly and gladly extended his hand to grasp mine. But the instant he heard me speak in Greek to my chauffeur, he drew back to himself, like a hedgehog at the point of a stick, and eyeing me suspiciously, said in a contemptuous tone, "You ain't no American! You're a Greek!"

He reclined back in his chair and assumed his pose of superiority. It was not until I had shown him my American passport and dazzled him with a flow of English, which he considered learned, and later told me was like "the English in the newspapers," that he warmed toward me and accepted my lift to his destination.

All the way to the next town he cursed the Greeks. He had been born in a Greek community in Asia Minor and had emigrated to America years ago. Now he had come to the new parts of Greece to buy a place and settle down. But he was like a fish out of water. Time and again he reassured me that he could not live among the Greeks in the homeland and that he counted the days until his return to America where he planned to buy a soda fountain in Lansing. For twelve years he had been in that business in Michigan.

As he spoke derisively of the Greeks, his own people, of how filthy and backward and uneducated they were, I kept looking at him and could not help thinking that in Lansing he was a Greek.

But how about myself? In Bulgaria I am not wholly a Bulgarian; in the United States not wholly an American. I have to go through life with a dual nationality. When in the United States I long for the sleepy villages and the intimate life of the Balkans. When I am in the Balkans I dream of America day and night. An American made motor car seen on the street, an advertising poster announcing the showing of a motion picture made in the United States, anything closely or remotely connected with America is enough to send thrills through my spine. I was taking an afternoon nap in the house of a friend in Sofia and upon waking was told that I had been talking in my sleep. "What did I say?" I inquired, afraid of having revealed some secrets, with which one's head is always filled in the Balkans. "Nothing much," they comforted me. "You just kept blabbering about America!"

And shall I forget my joy upon my return to America! I was downright foolish. I felt like a child at the sight of his mother from whom it had been separated for months. Without unpacking my things, I left my room at the hotel and for nearly two hours walked up and down Broadway like a man possessed. Everything that my eyes beheld, I felt like embracing within my arms.

But here I am. A year has barely gone by and I am ready to embrace a Balkan donkey with fraternal affection. Yet I cannot leave America, though I am but half an American.

The Emotional Conflicts of the Second Generation

Europeans migrated to the United States because of the dissatisfaction with and rejection of Old World conditions. And for many, the adjustment to American life was "bought" with the repudiation of their native language, traditions and cultural values. In turn, as Americanization took hold on the immigrant family, second-generation youth began to reject the characteristics of their own ethnic groups which had become associated with alien inferiority and community isolation.

In the first selection, "The Emotional Conflicts of the Second-Generation," Evelyn W. Hersey analyzed those provocations for conflict which the children of immigrants encountered in their environment. Speaking before the National Conference of Social Work in 1934, Hersey discussed the "social background out of which develop the emotional conflicts of the second-generation."

The second selection presented, "Second Generation Problems," is taken from the Conference on Immigration held by the YMCA in New York in 1934. At this meeting, several youths of foreign parentage reviewed "with admirable sincerity" the problems each confronted as hyphenated Americans. Their testimony indicated that in spite of their ethnic diversity, the difficulties of each were strikingly similar.

SOURCE: Evelyn W. Hersey, **"The Emotional Conflicts of the Second-Generation: A Discussion of American-Born Children of Immigrant Parents,"** paper presented at the National Conference of Social Work, May 21, 1934. Reprinted in *Interpreter Release Clip Sheet,* July 10, 1934.

We all emphasize the necessity of a sense of security and of acceptance for the healthy emotional development of an individual. But these second-generation children lack these two essential elements necessary to emotional growth. The fact of "transplantedness" has already been felt by the parents. Many have come from tiny villages of a few hundred thatched-roof houses to make their homes in the alleys of a crowded industrial city. The protection of an intimate village set-up and customs is gone. The open fields and familiar farm work have given way to stevedore work on the docks or laboring work in a noisy subway. Fear and language barrier bar the way to quick understanding, and use of the resources of their new community. The children must be used as a medium of interpretation in the simplest contacts. It is Mary or Stanislaus who must talk to the gas man, the insurance man and the doctor in the hospital. However difficult the situation of these parents, they have nevertheless some sources of security. There are the neighbors of the same nationality living in the same street. Then too, there are those memories and stabilities built in their early years in a setting which they knew and understood and where they had found acceptance. With these strengths born of experiences before their migration they face the acute adjustments that have to come.

But their children's situation is much more difficult. Psychologists have been interested in the arrested development which sometimes follows when a child is forced early to face a bilingual situation. These children face not only a *bilingual,* but a *bi-cultural* conflict in their first contacts with the American schools and playgrounds. They have no previous experience of acceptance, no warm memories of "the other side" to give them security and a sense of their own value.

These children find when they ask questions about the world around them that their parents often say "I don't know", and instead of being sources of strength, lean in turn on the meagre information which the children have of the new community.

But this confusion and insecurity is not all the burden that these children have to bear. The American community has superimposed still another handicap by strongly rejecting all that is foreign. At the age when the little boys on Main Street find ego security in bragging *"My father"* the primary school son of a foreign born father is learning that his father's animated gestures and big beard and cap are causes of derision. His father is a "sheeny" or a "polack" or a "wop". Soon it becomes painfully evident to the child that this rejection includes him too. He grows to feel that his olive skin, his warm temperamental enthusiasm, his clothes—anything which marks him as different, also stamps him as inferior. To gain acceptance he must strive to make himself like this new unknown, strange pattern. Conflict within him is inevitable. He squirms, he fights, he breaks down, he runs away. But whatever he does, this rejection becomes a part of his life.

Instances of children's reactions to this community attitude are so common, as to go almost unnoticed. I shall never forget the picture of twelve year old Tony as he stamped his foot and shouted at his Sicilian father,—"I'll take nothing off a damn Dago like you". Adolescent defiance, yes, but with an added factor. He had acquired in his early years in American schools and playgrounds the idea that all that was Italian was to be rejected. In this instance, as in many others, the break of paternal authority had sad results. Three years later a probation officer struggled to pick up the pieces. Reluctantly I have come to believe that this pervasive feeling of rejection of "foreignness" is felt by all second-generation young people no matter how secure and adequate they seem.

.   .   .

Many firms refuse to employ girls whose names end in "s-k-y", and a bank reported recently that they had to discharge a very able young man because he "looked so foreign" the patrons objected. Some of these second-generation young people come to the definite decision to deny their background. I asked a very successful prominent caterer once whom I knew to be Czech, why he had changed his name to Alden. "Economic necessity. The elite of this city would not trade with a man with a Slavic name. I tried it." "Don't the old folks mind your losing the family name?" A shadow passed over his face as he answered, "It nearly killed my father, but he sees now it was necessary." It is to these experiences that we owe numbers of Bakers, Smiths, Davis's and Cabots in the Polish, Czech, Hungarian and Italian communities.

. . .

Added to this general feeling of rejection comes the definite conflict of customs and mores. The second-generation child very early meets at least two sets of standards and customs. He must choose between them or find some middle ground. How is he to choose, or where find a middle ground? He has a normal child's need to be part of a family group. How can he totally reject his parents and their customs? He has a normal child's need to be accepted by companions outside the home. How can he bear the rejection? There is nothing more alone than a second-generation child trying to find his way through this maze of conflict. His parents cannot understand his struggle and often reject him, as he tries to form some sort of compromise between the customs of his home and the outside world. He is constantly pulled in two directions. He feels he does not really *belong* anywhere.

. . .

The following is not an uncommon story. We have known similar stories of second-generation girls, who were forced to marry men from the "old country". George, a young Greek boy, was taken back to Greece by his family at the age of 18 and married to a beautiful village girl, the child of some of their former friends. He brought her back to this country. She was a country girl, unable to speak English, and with little education. George had graduated from the local high school and entered business.

He felt awkward and embarrassed about introducing his new wife to his friends. He tried to set up housekeeping with her, but she could not cook as he wished. She became more and more distasteful to him. He was miserable; he stayed out nights and went to the homes of relatives to live. He pleaded with his parents to find some way out of the situation. Of course, the young wife was desperately miserable too, but that is another story. The boy's conflict was very real and actually painful. He couldn't follow the customs of his family, his whole American adjustment had made it impossible to do so and be happy. His emotional tie to his parents had been too great for him to resist their plans. He recognized that he was hurting the helpless child who was his wife, and he was the sort of person who could not bear the harm and hurt he was doing. It was a long and complicated problem to untangle this situation so that both the boy and the girl could be free to live the life which might be possible for them.

These differences in custom involve not only marriage mores. They extend to the whole family set-up. The relation of father to children, parents to the oldest boy, boys to the girls, etc.

For instance, take the Flacco family. Mr. F. has been very successful financially and is very proud of his domestic wife and their three sons and five daughters. In spite of the fact that he owns a number of good sized houses, he still insists on living in their original small house down by the railroad. It seems that early the three older children, being boys, were allowed their freedom. They could come and go as they pleased and had plenty of spending money. Moreover, being boys, they were given authority over the five younger girls. They told them when they should come home, what allowance they could have, and meted out punishment for disobedience to their orders. As the American community threatened this power, the boys became more dominating and insisted more vehemently on their authority.

Clementina, the oldest, seemed to find some satisfaction in the prestige she received from being the oldest girl. Early she had sufficiently identified with her mother to take on the mother's attitude toward the younger children, and conduct of the home. She was interested in housewifely duties and the careful preparation of a hope chest. These interests gained her sufficient approval so that she was able to effect certain compromises for herself. She received a business training and was allowed to take a position. She became very efficient and felt the compensation of achievement. After some conflict, she was allowed to join a girls' club at the International Institute, with definite restrictions upon hours and frequency of attendance. For her own resentment at the dominance of her brothers, she compensated by wielding the same domination over the younger girls.

The next two girls, Mary and Rose (age 19 and 17) were brought to the office by way of the court. They had run away from home. Defiance mixed with cold sullen defensiveness, sounded in their measured tones as they repeated their refusal to return home. Both girls had a hunted, veiled expression in their eyes, and seemed really ill. "The family do not want us, it's their pride we've hurt by running away. They don't really care. Nobody in the world can understand what we've been through".

The Italian case worker made a visit in the home and found a furiously angry father and a weeping mother. "We are disgraced" they said. "We've tried to keep this from our friends, but soon they will know. No good girl stays away from home under a strange roof".

Clementina arrived in the office so choked with emotion she could scarcely talk. "They will kill my mother. Our family has always been together. Now it is broken and disgraced. I can't bear to go to see my friends. My life has been hard too, but I've stood it. Why couldn't they have waited until they could get out decently by marrying!"

Gradually we learned the long story of the increased withdrawal of the two younger girls, Rose and Mary. During early school days they had seemed normal, happy, friendly children. After they entered the Classical Girls' High School, their attitude at home changed. They were at first irritable, then remote, and felt increasingly that they were abused. Instead of taking part in the wordy and noisy family battles, they went upstairs to their room. For days they had refused to leave their bedroom even to eat. "They act as if they didn't belong to us", flashed Clementina.

Rose and Mary at first were almost unable to talk. Rose, the older, lived in a dream world of her own, where she was much superior to all others around her. Her dream satisfactions were so great that adjustment to the reality of earning a living or even casual social intercourse were impossible. Her family, to her mind, had thwarted her ambition. If it weren't for them, she would now be in college like her American schoolmates.

Mary was more able to tell how she and Rose had felt in the Girls' Classical High School, surrounded by well-to-do American girls preparing for college. "If only we could have had two decent school dresses apiece. There was money enough, but my father insisted it wasn't necessary. We were always different, never like the others. After we graduated we tried to find jobs and we couldn't. And home was unbearable. One morning Jack struck Mary so we both packed up and left".

.   .   .

The parents in the family have been at a loss to understand or accept the behavior of these girls in their attack on the sacred un-yielding family unit. Their act is *disgraceful, unbelievable!* The Italian family is the accepted social and economic unit. Each member contributes according to his ability and receives from the group according to his need. All wages are turned into the family coffer. Insurance, savings, property, all present and future economic security of all members, is provided for, not as individuals but as a unit. On the other hand, the costs of illness, misfortune, unemployment of any individual member, are borne by the group as a whole.

The role of the father and brothers is that of absolute authority, whose sacred duty it is to care for and protect the women, and who in turn expect obedience to their wishes. No daughter or son leaves this group except to marry and start a new and similar family unit. Even then there are certain close ties and obligations to be discharged to the original family group.

As one watches Rose and Mary, their agony is apparent. Rebellion and guilt, love and hate, resolution and hesitation, independence and unbelievable dependence, with a complex inconsistent code of behavior composed of old Italian mores, and confused pieces of a new standard.

SOURCE: **"Second Generation Problems,"** *Conference on Immigration Policy*, International Institute, Y.M.C.A., New York City. Reprinted in *Interpreter Release Clip Sheet*, April 25, 1935.

What Are the Problems of Second Generation Norwegians?
By Dr. George Aus.

1. The first problem I want to mention is the problem of adjustment in relation to the culture from which we came. We of the second generation cannot make the contribution to American life that we ought simply because we do not know, and therefore cannot appreciate, our past. We cannot truly interpret the present except as we are rooted in the past that has become the present—and at this point we of the second generation are not orientated. This condition is not without explanation. Let me mention several: 1. In the first place the first generation was so occupied with making a living in the New World that it did not have time to sit down and evaluate the culture from which it sprang. 2. In the second place this generation met an attitude on the part of their neighbors in the new home which told them that the best thing to do was to forget all about what they left behind. 3. In the third place the American school set out to make 100% Americans of the children on the assumption that this was to be done regardless of cultural background.

2. The second problem of adjustment to American life is the problem of taking our place in civic life. We of the second generation in New York have very little interest in the political and civic problems of our community. This phenomenon is all the more strange when compared with the rich civic life of the Norwegian people and with the contributions which our people have made in the Middle West. Why is it that we are so little interested in this phase of American life? Let me suggest a few reasons: 1. We are a minority group. 2. The political machine of the big city has "kept us in our place." 3. The first generation was too busy earning a living and making a home to have the leisure time which the active participation in civic life demands. 4. The first generation Nor-

wegian came late. It takes time to produce leaders. We are beginning, however, and one of the foremost of them—Major S. J. Arnesen—is in our gathering to-day.

3. The third problem which I want to mention is the problem of adjustment within the family. The adults arrived in one environment—youth is arriving in another. Wherever we have this condition there is bound to be tension and friction. At one place in particular is this true of our situation. The first generation Norwegian brought with him a high conception of the home. He finds it impossible to accept the "hotel" attitude toward the home that is so prevalent around him. He cannot regard the home as just a place to eat and sleep and he objects when his children begin to assume such an attitude toward their home.

4. The fourth problem which I have chosen is the problem of delayed maturity. In Norway the boy became a man at confirmation which was usually at fourteen. From then on he was to be independent—economically as well as mentally and socially. In America, however, childhood has been stretched to eighteen, twenty-two, and sometimes longer. Though it may be said that on the whole Norwegians are lovers of children and appreciative of the value of education, it cannot be said that we have been entirely set at liberty from the tension set up between the new and old world attitudes toward the beginning of maturity.

5. The last problem which I shall mention is the problem of adjustment to American amusement life. When the Norwegian is religious he is deeply so which tends to express itself in a pietistic attitude toward the world about him. Now if any institution can be said to hold the second generation it is the church. This being so, the second generation holds somewhat the same attitude toward the accepted standards of American "pleasure"—and that not without conviction. If we had had time this afternoon I might have mentioned some more problems of adjustment (not to speak of amplifying those I did touch), but in the time allotted these were the ones I felt should be mentioned. Thank you.

From the Ukrainian Point of View
By Stephen Shumeyko.

Before going into my little talk on some of the outstanding problems of the adjustment of American youth of Ukrainian descent to

American life, I wish to give you my conception of the meaning of this American life.

To me, the problem of American youth of foreign parentage in adjusting itself to American life is not that of outsiders striving to get within the portals of some exclusive precincts that are supposed to represent American life, but rather the problem is that of the youth of foreign parentage seeking means of cooperating with all the varied nationalities, from the Anglo-Saxon down to the Slavs that compose America, and together helping to build the real American life, and not the incomplete product that it is at present. This process of building the real America, of course, will not be confined to the present generation, for it will take many centuries before America will be able to realize fully all of its potentialities. The above conception of the meaning of the problem of adjustment is not at all clear to a great many of the youth of foreign parentage. Their conception, it seems, of adjusting themselves to American life is that of striving to gain what they suppose is equal footing with the predominant Anglo-Saxon element in this country. They are, however, really chasing after a mirage, and will discover this sooner or later. Bearing this in mind, we can now touch upon some of the problems of phases in the life of American youth of Ukrainian descent. Generally speaking, the American youth of Ukrainian descent is confronted with the selfsame problems that confront other youth, both of the so-called native as well as of foreign descent.

There are, however certain features or phases in the life of young American-Ukrainians that are peculiarly their own, that are not within the range of experiences of the youth of other nationalities. The two most prominent of these are: (1) The present American-Ukrainian youth is the first American-born younger generation of Ukrainian descent. Its parents are perhaps the latest arrivals to America of all immigrations. This fact gives our youth a host of problems that are not common to other youth—those of the older immigrations. (2) A perhaps more interesting phase in the American-Ukrainian youth life is what might be roughly termed as "double loyalty"—loyalty to America and loyalty, of a different sort, to Ukraine. It is upon this second phase that I wish to dwell.

The background of the American-Ukrainian youth is entirely different from that of other youth in America. They are the off-springs of a 40 million nation that has no national freedom, but is under the rule of four foreign states, namely, Soviet Russia which has the largest slice of Ukrainian territory, known as Greater Ukraine, and Poland, Rumania and Czechoslovakia. The latter three countries divide up among themselves that part generally known as Western Ukraine, with the newly-resurrected Poland having the lion's share. This fact, the oppression of the land of their parents, arouses a feeling of sympathy among the American-Ukrainian youth and a desire to help free Ukraine. This feeling is intensified at home by the parents. The parents of the American-Ukrainian youth, being the most recent arrivals, have not been as thoroughly Americanized as other immigrants. Although they know that America is their new homeland and will be the same for their descendants, yet their hearts and minds are across the seas in the land of their childhood days, the land they were forced to leave in search of freedom. Consequently it is not strange that their feelings towards the old country are greatly transmitted to their children, even though their children are thoroughly American. As a result, we have the rather unusual sight of a body of young people, loyal Americans to the core, yet deeply attached to the land from which their parents came—Ukraine.

At first this situation may strike some as being against the principles of Americanism, but closer examination of it discloses that there is no clash of loyalties here. On the contrary, in the opinion of the young folks, this attachment and loyalty to Ukraine is but an extension of one of the strongest principles of American life— the right of a people to govern themselves, a principle enunciated over and over again since the Declaration of Independence and finally embodied in Wilson's famous Self-Determination clause, which failed so lamentably when time came to apply it to Ukraine. This desire among the American-Ukrainian youth to aid the Ukrainian nation gain its freedom calls out the finest qualities in the youth, for, to serve this cause is to serve unselfishly, with no thought of recompense other than the moral satisfaction of seeing a people gain their rightful freedom. At present, this service expresses itself in various forms; chiefly, however, in becoming better acquainted with the Ukrainian language, song, dance, culture, history, tradition, etc.; for it is believed that this fundamental knowledge of their background will make the youth more useful in their self-appointed task and also help to acquaint other people with

Ukraine's plight. Needless to say, this begetting of knowledge of Ukrainian life is beneficial to America too, for it creates a better and more cultured type of an American citizen and also helps to enrich American culture.

Throughout the Ages, Youth has always inclined to be a Sir Galahad, a Sir Lancelot, but before it can assume this knightly role it must have its shining goal, its holy grail, its princess to set free from the clutches of some evil demon. In the eyes of our American-Ukrainian youth, Ukraine has the princess to set free— enslaved freedom; America, apparently, has not. This attitude was well expressed recently, when, in answer to a question, a young woman of Ukrainian descent said: "Ukraine needs me, America does not!" In Ukraine she sees an oppressed nation, and is determined to do her bit and help free her; in America she sees no such great and idealistic cause. It follows, therefore, that if Ukraine were a free nation then this American-Ukrainian youth would not be interested in it so much.

Such, briefly, is the position of many of the American youth of Ukrainian descent at the present time: loyal to America, loyal to Ukraine. To some this may seem inconsistent, a clash of ideals; to the American-Ukrainian youth it is most natural. It reasons as follows: We know we cannot have rights and privileges here in America without duties and responsibilities. We know that America gives us protection, education and opportunities, and that we in return owe her our love, obedience, service and loyalty. We know that our principal task here in America is not the making of money, but the making of America. And yet, we cannot forget that we are Americans of Ukrainian descent. We cannot forget how for centuries our Ukrainian forefathers fought and sacrificed their lives and fortunes in the cause of an ideal dear to all nations —freedom. From our minds the inspiring thought that there was once a Ukrainian state, self-chartered and self-ruled, can never be effaced, and the burning hope that there will again be one can never be extinguished. Knowing all of this, and remembering that one of the greatest of Americans, Woodrow Wilson, himself declared that each nation is entitled to self-rule and self-determination, we, American youth of Ukrainian descent, shall strive to make ourselves worthy and useful citizens of our America and also to do our bit towards the realization of that centuries old dream—the creation of a free and independent state of Ukraine.

The Ethnic Citizen and World War II

With the entrance of the United States into World War II, ethnic America was once again presented with programs for Americanization. Realizing the immense potential within these communities, the federal government sought out and utilized their vast pool of manpower and skills. The overwhelming response on the part of hyphenated Americans can be attested to by the number of second-generation youths who served in the military, and the thousands of "Rosie the Riveters" who manned the vital industries needed to fight the Axis powers.

In an effort to ensure and maintain the existing level of ethnic participation in the war effort, President Franklin D. Roosevelt designated May 17, 1942, as "I Am An American Day." He urged that it be set aside as a public occasion for the recognition of citizens who had been naturalized during the preceding year. Consequently, throughout the land, celebrations were held in honor of those who had chosen the United States as their new homeland.

In addition to loyalty, the government sought to tap their financial resources. Thus, specific guidelines were established in order to conduct bond drives in such communities as Polish Hill and Little Italy. In a speech entitled "The War Savings Division of the Treasury Department and the Foreign Born," Edward B. Hitchcock, Chief of the Foreign Origins Division of the United States Treasury, instructed his staff to appeal to their Americanism, "so that when [the government had] sold them War Bonds [they had] also [sold] them America." Needless to say, the response to the sale of bonds matched their enthusiastic response to the nation's military call.

SOURCE: **"I Am An American Day Ceremonies,"** *Interpreter Releases,* April 25, 1942.

The President has designated Sunday, May 17, 1942 as "I Am An American Day" and urged that it be set aside as a public occasion for the recognition of all citizens who have attained their majority or who have been naturalized during the year just preceding. In consequence, all over the country, plans for celebration are now under consideration and suggestions for programs based on typical celebrations held in 1940 and 1941 may prove useful.

Planning a Program

Patriotic music, flag ceremonies and speeches are, it would seem, the fundamentals in the "I Am An American Day" celebrations. Pageants, motion pictures and dances also frequently form part of the program.

It is generally recognized that music is a most effective means of providing the emotion and enthusiasm required in a good ceremony. Patriotic music, as the specimen programs attached to this Release show, would seem to be an indispensable feature of these celebrations. Furthermore it affords opportunities for audience participation, the importance of which cannot be stressed too strongly. Flag ceremonies such as the pledge of allegiance to the flag by the entire audience and the flag raising and lowering ceremonies with the audience standing at attention, serve similar purposes.

As for the speeches, experience has proved that there should not be too many of them and that they should be short, incisive and inspirational in nature. Government officials, judges, prominent members of the community are usually chosen for speakers; not infrequently naturalized citizens are asked to speak and often prove to be very moving and effective.

"Immigrant Gifts", "Parades of Nations" and the "Melting Pot" are some of the subjects around which pageants were built in the 1940 and 1941 celebrations. A pageant "Out of the Past", written, directed and produced by the combined personnel of the Americanization school for the District of Columbia, dramatized the Preamble to the Constitution of the United States, "weaving through its words the concepts which it embodies. These concepts were stated first by the voice speaking for America and echoed and enlarged upon by voices from the various countries".

At the celebration held in Salt Lake City in 1940, there was presented a pageant entitled "Immigrant Gifts to America", a tribute to the cultural contributions brought to the United States by persons from other lands. The different countries were presented as spokesmen for their people; Italy, for instance, spoke as follows:

"I am the Italy
In these Americas.
A whisper merely of mellow Rome
In the eager West.
Yet how shall you forget me?
Who gave you law and the procedure of law;
Who cradled Christ in the lean and bitter years
    of the beginnings;
Who brought the brilliance of Renaissance
To all the progenitors of America.
A man of mine planted the first banners
Of the white race on your shores
And another gave his name to half the world,
Columbus and Amerigo, and you honor them still—
Sons of me have built your roads,
Your tall buildings, dug your sewers and tunnels,
Rome has always been a builder.
And I gave you song, and singers to warm you,
Campanini, Da Ponte, Bertelatti—
How shall you forget these things?"

Folk dancers in national costumes add color and beauty to the ceremonies but in order that internationalism may be stressed rather than nationalism, the dances of more than one nation should be presented and American folk dances should be included.

Specimen Program

The following specimen program was derived from various sources. The first was copied from a pamphlet "I Am An American Day, of 1941," issued by the University Extension Division, Massachusetts Department of Education.

"I AM AN AMERICAN DAY" PROGRAM

1. Selection by a Band—(American Legion Band, for instance)
2. Posting of the Colors—Veterans' Organization
3. Pledge of Allegiance to the Flag—Entire Assembly

4. Invocation—A Catholic ⎫
         A Protestant ⎬ Clergyman
         A Jewish ⎭
5. Greetings—The Mayor
    or
   Reading of the President's Proclamation on "I Am An American Day"
6. Music by a Glee Club or Soloist or by a Band
7. Youth Speaks—Our American Heritage
    (by a young man or woman who has just reached voting age)
8. "What Citizenship Means to Me"
    By a newly naturalized citizen
9. Music—Patriotic songs by a Glee Club or Soloist or else Patriotic Music by a Band
10. Address by the Judge of the Naturalization Court, or by a Congressman or by a prominent citizen
11. "America"—(First and Last Verses)
    Played by a Band and sung by the Audience
12. Retiring the Colors—Veterans' Organization

SOURCE: Edward B. Hitchcock, **"The War Savings Division of the U. S. Treasury Department and the Foreign Born,"** *Interpreter Releases,* March 23, 1943.

The United States of America has the most mixed population of any country on the globe. It is too simple to say that our country is a melting pot. It has been called a polyglot zoo, a nationalistic anachronism, an alchemistic crucible, an international soup-kettle. It is indeed an international soup-kettle into which every nationalism on the earth has been poured, out of which has come what we think of as Americanism—which is the mingling and commingling and intermingling of nationalisms and racialisms and ideologies and creeds, of traditions and cultures, of languages and dialects, of literates and illiterates—where people have found a haven and a refuge, or a wider opportunity for them to work out their individual destinies. We like to think of our America as a nation of one people from many countries. You know as well as

I do, that Americanism is the sum of the whole, and it would not be the same if any of its parts were lacking. This Americanism of ours is really a new world order, an internationalism, which is the hope of the future.

The 1940 Census has figures on what it calls "The Foreign White Stock of the United States," where it is shown that 34,600,000 of our population—over 26 percent, more than one fourth—are either foreign born or of foreign or mixed parentage. About 11,400,000 are foreign born. The remaining 23,000,000 are of foreign or mixed parentage—of which number 15,200,000 had both parents foreign born, 5,000,000 had a father foreign born, and 2,700,000 had their mothers foreign born. The new census also shows that 80 percent of first generation foreign born whites live in cities. Hence the great problem of foreign born people exists mainly in the larger industrial and urban areas. And that is where your interest and mine mainly begins and ends.

.   .   .

The particular task of the Foreign Origin Section of the National Organizations Division of the War Savings Staff is to bring all these varied peoples into loyal and active participation in the war effort. It is our belief that we will thus be able to build morale for the present and a better world for the future, while engaged in our main job of selling War Bonds. It is certainly logical to assume that every individual of foreign birth or extraction who invests in War Bonds has thereby bought a share in the United States and is financially interested in the war effort.

I should like to make it quite clear to you that our principal task is a job of salesmanship. We have to so promote the Treasury campaign that all of the varied people of this country with money to invest will put it into these bonds. We are not directly concerned with the political attitude of these people. You have heard from those Government agencies concerned with such matters, very directly concerned, but it is not our function to pass upon the political beliefs or ideological attitudes or religious creeds of the people of foreign white stock among whom we are promoting investment in War Bonds.

You know as well as I do the importance of these people of recent foreign extraction at this time. You are working with them very intimately and directly, helping them with their economic problems and with their social readjustments. You also are concerned as we are, and as every other agency of the Government should be, in their education in Americanism. It seems to me that you probably understand these people of recent foreign extraction better than most of us. You appreciate that their understanding of us older Americans, as well as our understanding of them, are vitally important to the world of the future in which we Americans are deeply concerned.

.   .   .

Now, the great majority of these good Americans of foreign white stock belong to local branches of national organizations which stem back to their countries of origin and their nationalistic traditions and culture. Those who were foreign born usually prefer to read papers in their own language and to listen to radio programs in their native tongue. That is quite natural. And, if we are consistent in our naming of freedom of speech as one of our essential freedoms for which we fight, we must not object if Mrs. Schiminski yearns and weeps for the land where she was born when she hears of the destruction of Polish towns and cities and the decimation of the populace, or that Mamma Cavolifiore has trouble making herself understood away from the Italian grocery on the corner, or that Mr. Schmidt still thinks in German and talks German in his own home. This thing of blood is one of the almost insuperables—perhaps rightly so—and you and I know that it takes more than a single generation for Americans of foreign extraction to get over their European rootage. If they could be plucked lightly from the soil where their seed was first planted, and if they could be transplanted to another soil very easily, would they not be belittling their ancient heritage?

Most of these people of recent foreign extraction want to be good Americans and most of them are intensely loyal to our cause today. What we have to understand is that many of them need a special approach to integrate them more securely in the national effort, and unless they are approached differently and in a way that appeals to their heartstrings as well as to their pursestrings, the ultimate result will not be accomplished. In our work with foreign extraction groups we have certainly learned that you can't talk to a Czech or a Pole as you would to an Italian or a German.

In our presentation of the Treasury's program to these people we have appealed to both their personal interests and to their Americanism, and we have also paid tribute to their contribution to our Americanism. So that when we have sold them War Bonds we have also been selling them America, and have been giving them new appreciation of their citizenship. We have been aided in this by their national organizations working through their branches all over the country, who are endeavoring to persuade every individual member to invest and to continue to invest all possible funds in War Bonds, thereby demonstrating their loyalty toward the country of their choice in its present emergency. That work has been successful and I believe you will find that as these people invest in stamps and bonds, your work among them will be easier.

All of us in this League of Nations known as the United States of America want to build a better world for the future—whatever our foreign origin may have been. People of recent foreign extraction are often more ardent in their Americanism than those of us who came over in the Mayflower or discovered California with Cabrillo. And these people are more concerned about the future and tomorrow's peace and how to establish not just a richer world for the few but a righter world for the many, where the best of us must be willing to share with the worst of us, so that the least of us may stand in the sun with the rest of us.

PART VII

The Dawn of the New Pluralism: Alienation and Group Consciousness in Ethnic America, 1960–73

INTRODUCTION*

In spite of their large numbers, working-class ethnics became the "forgotten people" of the 1960s. Ignored in the years since World War II, millions of these low-wage-earning families suddenly became threatened with the collapse of their unique life-styles. Traditional lines of communication via local elected leaders with the Establishment and with the institutions of our society no longer worked for them. Moreover, they came to believe that their city, state and federal elected representatives were concerned with the protection of the rich and the plight of the poor. No one seemed concerned with *their* needs.

Since the start of the new immigration in the 1880s, these people, in their struggle to enter the mainstream of American life, adopted the standards set forth by the institutions of Americanization. Among these were: hard work, obedience to law and order, respect for authority, family loyalty, self-reliance and patriotism. Learning that they would "make it in America" through the melting pot, most adhered persistently to these traditional values.

* This essay is based upon an interview with Nancy Seifer, Director of Community Relations, National Project on Ethnic America: A Depolarization Program of The American Jewish Committee, drawn from her experiences in municipal government from 1969–72.

In the mid-1960s they discovered that the rules of the game through which they would supposedly gain entry into American society were suddenly changed: welfare for some had become an acceptable way of life, demonstrators who openly violated the law often were not punished, police officers were labeled "pigs," draft evasion became "stylish," flag burnings were condoned by some and threats of rebellion were rewarded with ransom.

Nevertheless, most ethnics remained loyal to the traditional American values as well as their own cultural ones. Yet within their communities, anxiety was aroused by this rapid change in American attitudes exaggerated even further by the media. Coupled with their economic insecurity and their loss of political representation, this change caused the average white ethnic blue-collar American to become an "unhappy American."

According to Nancy Seifer of the National Project on Ethnic America, foremost among the causes of ethnic alienation was the economic squeeze which hit most working-class Americans hardest in the late 1960s. Many a male breadwinner held several jobs to meet the family budget—often, his wife worked as well in order to make ends meet. Ironically, he became infuriated at being called poor.

In addition, while inflation had made it impossible for him to save, his earning peak was attained long before his children reached college age and/or the need to provide nursing care for an aged parent arose. Moreover, his salary went directly toward paying bills or credit installments on his color TV, his car or other needed appliances which were considered symbols of independence and mobility.

His family may have not gone out to dinner or to a movie for a year, and often he was afraid to walk in his neighborhood after dark. Having guests to his home was often too expensive and the thought of a "vacation" was anxiety-ridden, in cases where he could not afford to take his family away. He may, in fact, never have left the city.

Seifer also reports that for decades, ethnic groups have served as mediators between the individual and the impersonal institutions of society. The melting pot, cultural pluralism and Americanization notwithstanding, the ethnic neighborhood had always served to provide stability, a sense of identity and psychological comfort to immigrants and generations of their offsprings. This stability was being threatened in most urban areas of the United States, and was giving way to frustration and chaos. The threat of the bulldozer hung overhead, with the fear of being totally uprooted and left with none of the familiar elements of life.

Perhaps worst of all, according to Seifer, they saw their values, way of life and ethnic characteristics being consistently ridiculed by the media and the liberal intellectual Establishment. Often, when they were mentioned at all they were characterized as the "silent majority," hardhats, racist pigs, honkies and bigots. Thus relegated to this verbal junk heap, they were no longer allowed any sense of importance in American society.

With the substitution of the "new politics" for "machine politics," white ethnic groups found themselves almost totally impotent politically. According to their spokesmen, middle-class liberals shifted their allegiance from those workers which existed during the days of the New Deal coalitions and beyond to the welfare poor, and their own ethnic political bosses cut off from the sources of power, were no longer able to solve their problems.

Moreover, of the 20 per cent who belong to organized labor, many felt they were not accurately represented by their leadership. No longer having a spokesman to articulate their needs, problems and aspirations, these people saw their traditional areas of employment—which they struggled as individuals to obtain—being invaded by groups worse off than they, i.e., blacks and Puerto Ricans. Furthermore, most asserted that it was more likely for a black child to be awarded a scholarship or receive a summer job than for their own children. Many felt they were unfairly ridiculed in Polish, Irish, and other ethnic jokes while black power and African culture were celebrated by the media. While they deprived themselves and their families of many benefits and comforts to pay their taxes, those same tax dollars were benefiting blacks in the form of housing, job training and education, which they needed almost as badly.

Most important psychologically, concludes Seifer, while blacks in the 1960s could look forward to further change in the system to accommodate them, the experience in America of white ethnics left them with no hope that any change would benefit them. Thus they held fast to the status quo.

A. ALIENATION IN THE ETHNIC COMMUNITY

"In the Land of the New Racists"

In an autobiographical essay, "Last Stop on the D Train," Leonard Kriegel, a second-generation American from a working-class background, analyzed the alienation existing in a Bronx, New York, neighborhood which he called home for twenty-five years. The author, a respected member of New York's academic community, placed blame for the alienation on those intellectual and Establishment elitists who had dismissed the fear and frustration of the white working class as racism. Because of this lack of concern, Kriegel asserted that those residents of his former community "are beginning to stiffen with the helpless self-defensive anguish of the victim suddenly being accused of being a victimizer."

SOURCE: Leonard Kriegel, **"Last Stop on the D Train: In the Land of the New Racists,"** *The American Scholar* (Spring 1970), pp. 272–88. Reprinted by permission.

Home is not so much a place as it is an idea of a place, a geography of the mind in which strangers and natives alike find refuge when thrust against the landscape of the familiar. The territory of the street is your own, the way you first knew the shape of summer's freedom. And now every scrawny bush, every crack in the sidewalk, every tree cut down to make way for progress infuses your own past with a reality almost Platonic. The problem is to remember it as it actually was, to stay clear of sentiment, to be able to say "This was my world" without inundating the here and now. The difficulty is that you, if a true city boy, measure even the here and now against the blistered reality still clinging to your mind, the way the images first coalesced, when you were ten or eleven, and the ideal of neighborhood burst from your own dreams. City boy still: for to belong is to love, even when it is also to reject.

And so, no matter where you are—Chelsea, The Hague, London, Rome—home remains what the past opposes to the place at which you are staying. Try as you may, ridicule yourself as you may (the voice that whispers, "Who wants to remain a Bronx initiate all his life? Let memories of Poe Park Becky die!"), home remains "the neighborhood," which you have come to think of as your parents think of Galicia, *der haym,* their memories studded with drunken peasants, and filled with the sharp smells of the living burying the dead, but soothed by order, an understandable, natural order. For even when you believed that the neighborhood was challenging your prospects—there are brokers in the most vital of imaginations—it possessed an understandable, a natural, order. Events, things, people, even time, all fell into place. The neighborhood absorbed.

It ran from Mosholu Parkway (pronounced Moshoolah by those who never knew it as home) on the east to Webster Avenue on the south, Gun Hill Road on the west, Jerome Avenue on the north. The boundaries are arbitrary. Why not include that part of Bronx Park on the other side of the police precinct house, French Charlie's, the first baseball field you ever played on? There is no answer, except that the red Victorian gingerbread of the police station loomed above the Webster Avenue El tracks, and the giant clock on its tower signaled not time but boundary. Definition was a necessity. Arbitrary . . . but also real, the way it was.

It was not the worst place in the world in which to come of age, that corner of the Bronx with its children of immigrant Jews waiting for the socialist millennium, its Italian construction workers, its Irish bus drivers. Even then a working and lower-middle class neighborhood, the ambitions of its inhabitants were reflected in the uneven line of house against sky. There were trees on the street, there was the Parkway, and there was Bronx Park for the times you wanted to risk the unknown, still wild enough then so that you might, on occasion, stub your toe on a gnarled root and come up with an arrowhead: there was Van Cortlandt Park, the name synonymous not merely with the foreign (all the names fitted that category) but also with the expectation of wealth and the promise of a Technicolor movie: there was the Oval, once a reservoir, then filled in by the W.P.A. during the Depression to house playgrounds and ball fields and a quarter-mile dirt track for running or bike riding: and there was P.S. 80 with its three large yards urging you to test your skill for fifteen minutes every day after lunch. (Memory encrusts the pride: you were the only fifth grader to hit a baseball on the fly from home plate to the cyclone fence at the other end.) Above all, there was the street scarred by the movement of seasonal games: chestnut season, scully season, marble season, skating season, baseball, football, stickball, punchball, boxball, all of them blending in memory into a single clear October day.

Across the street from the Oval, a few yards of weed-strewn lawn off Bainbridge Avenue, there was an old stone house in which Washington was said to have slept. The house has been moved next to the Oval now. It is some kind of museum or public monument, but its function, no matter how public, will not change the anachronism. Where it used to stand, there is a new apartment building, as nondescript as the old apartment buildings, blending in with them, except for the air-conditioning sleeves, a pretense at affluence. You knew that the stone house was inhabited, for rumor said it was, but you had never seen people going in and out as they did in other houses. It served as the neighborhood's ghost house, stranded there, a fact from history, a line to the past that you were told was yours in P.S. 80. Among all these four and five-story apartment buildings, a colonial stone house. And sometimes, after school, you would find yourself walking past it, repeating the names of the streets, an incantation meant to drive you, too, back into that mythical time: Hull Avenue, Perry, De Kalb, Rochambeau, Bainbridge, Gun Hill Road. Life and death mingled: time and desire and belonging and the need to prove yourself an American.

I left the neighborhood in 1957. I had left it before, but this time it was for good. I was twenty-four years old, just married, in pursuit of something I could not label but that I knew was not to be found on these streets. I moved to Chelsea in Manhattan, a distance of some sixteen miles on the West Side Drive or some eighteen or nineteen stops on the I.N.D. Line's D Train. But only if one measures space. In time, it was easily as great as the distance that separates a corn-fed Kansan provincial and a Greenwich Village hipster. The axiom is accurate; the boy from the true provinces comes to Manhattan armed with the wariness of his ignorance, while those of us who came from the Bronx had to pretend to a sophistication we simply did not possess. Weren't we, too, New Yorkers by right of birth? Had not we, too, traveled the subways to the Museum of Natural History? (Twice: the first time when I was eight years old and ran away from home with another boy and got off the train, quite accidentally, at 81st Street; another time with my fifth-grade class under the aegis of Miss Burgi, who passionately desired to expose us to what she called "your beautiful world.") The truth was that I was terrified of "downtown," for I was not at all certain what the sophistication that I was expected to possess was. But in a few weeks that sophistication could be assumed and the fear dissipated itself in the satisfaction of living in the "real" New York. The memory of my hesitant, cursory excursions downtown was now simply brushed aside.

Occasionally, I would return to visit my family. Like me, most of my friends had departed from the neighborhood. With the few who remained, I had little to share other than the memories of childhood and adolescence. In time, I stopped looking for them and went directly from the subway to my parents' apartment. In getting out, I had made it; in staying, they hadn't. I was exploring different directions now. The neighborhood embarrassed me.

It was a predominantly Jewish neighborhood, but the street on which I lived, and on which my parents live today, was Irish Catholic. There were, of course, a number of other Jewish families, some Italians, and even a scattering of those whose roots in America went back far enough so that they were able to think of themselves simply as Americans. In the middle of the street, there was a Lutheran church, but I did not know anybody who was a Lutheran. The church seemed misplaced and alien. The Christians I knew, lived among and fought, attended St. Brendan's, the Catholic church around the corner, and those of my friends who did not go to P.S. 80 attended the parochial school attached to the church. St. Brendan's was a rather nondescript red church; it looked as if it had been left over from a Paddy Chayefsky film. A few years ago it was torn down, and the New St. Brendan's is an ultra-modern church built in the form of a ship.

I grew up with a peculiar relationship to the Irish. The films I saw and the books I read told me that the Irish were a rugged, romantic people, but the people around me in the neighborhood seemed dry and withered, aged before their time. Even their children lacked youth. When they grew older they drank too much and made love too little. I remember the priest at St. Brendan's as always eating ice cream and walking down the street with the *Journal-American* tucked beneath his arm, his face fleshy and almost as florid as Hearst's headlines. When I saw my first O'Casey play, I was stunned when I realized that the people about whom he was writing were the grandparents of my Irish friends. For in the neighborhood the Irish were not like the Jews and not like the Italians. They were tight, they moved suspiciously, they seemed uncomfortable with their bodies, and they lacked imagination.

And yet, I liked them. They redeemed the absence of romance, redeemed even the absence of imagination, through a certain concern with proprieties. Soon after I became ill with polio in 1944, the candles were lit and prayers offered at St. Brendan's. The people were narrow and, even for our neighborhood, provincial, but they tried to behave decently, which is, I have discovered, the greatest virtue of the working-class Irish. The idea that they could demand anything from life had not really penetrated among them. Despite their churchgoing, they had little potential for sainthood, even less for the demonic. They were common people, in all that the term suggests, living out lives that can best be described as commonplace. In the fifties they were told by a large number of politicians and a small number of bad writers that they were the salt of the earth. This did not help them, for they rarely believed politicians and they never read writers, good or bad. Money, fame, fortune—they listened and shrugged. Accidents were not to be questioned, and money was an accident, as were fame and fortune. And not to be envied either. Their sons might ultimately rebel, might try to swallow the world whole as they became true Americans. The older people were too busy trying to live in it.

Whenever I have been away from the neighborhood for a long time, I am suspicious of my emotions when I return. When I drove up to the neighborhood on a hot Sunday afternoon last September, I had to force perspective on my world. I was coming home after a sabbatical year in Europe. For a year, I had been a spectator of America's anguish. From the sanctuary of a family hotel in the *Hoge Veluwe,* where I had gone to see the Van Gogh collection in the Kröller-Müller Museum, I had watched Aronow Auditorium burn, as white and black confronted a similarity greater than they knew on the ragged campus of City College. Somehow, it had not seemed altogether real. But it had been real. Just as Mosholu Parkway, down which I was now driving, was real. I found myself surprised at how the geography had remained more or less as I remembered it, just as City College, to which I had returned a few days earlier, had seemed as attractively raunchy as when I had left, the boarded-up windows of Aronow's simply absorbed into the general seediness of the grounds. I had expected some fundamental change in the neighborhood, the ground leveled by bulldozers maybe. But what my eyes saw was the sharp familiarity, the boundaries of childhood stretching out before me like some half-forgotten painting caught once again on the piercing sweep of line that brings not only the frame but the entire picture into focus once again. Shape and memory. The few changes—new saplings in the center of the Parkway every ten yards or so, where once there had been thick solid trees —merely sharpened the focus.

And yet, the Parkway *was* different. For, as I drove, I became increasingly aware of a dinginess, a mean and squalid old age hovering just above the line of buildings and open sky. There were still adolescents slicing the air with their footballs. It was between seasons now and a softball game was in progress on the grass across from P.S. 80. The grass seemed scrawny, as if it were looking forward to the death of summer. Perhaps it had never been anything but scrawny.

A number of people, perhaps twenty in all, were sitting on aluminum chairs on the sidewalk bordering the eastern side of the Parkway, their faces raised to the sun. Most of them were old, retired, waiting for death. When I was a child, the old people sat on wooden crates instead of aluminum chairs: otherwise, the scene was familiar. The houses on the other side of the Parkway were still a mixture of Bronx Tudor and Thirties Modern, one of them a building that had collapsed while it was being built during the Depression. A number of the laborers had died, an event that formed, according to a friend of mine, the basis for Pietro Di Donato's *Christ in Concrete*. It did not matter whether it was true. And I never bothered to check. The neighborhood always struggled for meaning. To be even the possible suggestion for a book was bound to be welcome.

I parked the car, got out, and began to walk parallel to the Parkway. At first, I did not realize why the scene depressed me so. Then I realized that I had come full circle. For these people were the new enemy, people whom I, along with most other radical and liberal intellectuals in New York, had dismissed as "white racists." These were the men and women whom my more "militant" students sneer at with a withering contempt. (*Militant:* the word brings to mind a hand blading the air with its rhetorical courage as the coin spins away, either heads or tails and who *cares?* In this kind of game, the only losers are people. The currency of commitment is to be spent at all costs.) My more militant students are themselves the sons and grandsons of these despised, children of the jailers. Radical professors, student activists, the fancy prose stylists of the *Village Voice,* the whole of what Harold Rosenberg once labeled the "herd of independent minds," on whom else could they grind their knives? Swinger and Weatherman alike, hippie and yippie, for all these the enemy has become clearly identifiable. Jewish cab drivers, Italian bricklayers, Irish bartenders, the *white racists,* gray, washed out in the bright colors of the approaching revolution. And here they were, lining the sidewalk in front of me. I was standing in the land of the faceless, the millennium snorting down my neck, cataloguing all these lives against the blank border into which they were destined to disappear.

I walked over to Bainbridge Avenue and then I walked to where the Fordham Road bus stopped on 206th Street. For a moment, my mind was back in those summer nights, and I was standing on this corner, fear spurring me on to exercise my wit in game after game of *the dozens,* verbal lashings edged with the dry hysteria of some Bronx warrior reaching for it all but not yet able to give in to his desires as he mothered the irrational in himself. An old woman holding a white umbrella stood by the bus stop, waiting. The sky was cloudless blue. She gripped the umbrella tightly. No one else was around.

During my time on the corner, simply to hold your own had been enough. In the forties and fifties, you copped your manhood by demonstrating skill with language. Language was power. Before that, it had been skill with your hands. But by my time, it was just a case of having to be smarter, more cutting, to dip your mind in salt or brine before you edged out of your apartment at night. Corner boy: which meant that you had to be nasty enough and brave enough to pass the test of the corner.

The old woman got on her bus. No one got off. The corner was deserted except for me. There were no more people and so there were no more gamblers. It was here that Pete the Bookie (not Runyonese, it was simply a neighborhood in which you were known by the job you did) used to hold court while the people inveighed against the drabness of the neighborhood's fate, its slender huskings and slim pickings. Gambling was the great social passion, as if one could stave off decay and mortality with two dollars on the right horse. Everybody gambled. "For pleasure!" I once heard a cab driver's wife scream at her husband when he accused her of gambling his salary away. "What else do you give me?" In the neighborhood, gambling, like socialism for some, was a form of therapy. It was fitting that what I knew about gambling had been taught me by my uncle the furrier, who, when he wasn't telling me of how the world had to be refashioned by and for the working class, would teach me the art of handicapping horses.

I half expected to see Little Howie on the corner. But Howie was dead, a neighborhood suicide. If I looked up, I could see the roof from which he had jumped. One would have expected something neater of Howie, who had lived by slide rules and wood carving. He was one of the few craftsmen in a neighborhood of pieceworkers. When I was nine, he taught me how to play shortstop, patiently forcing me to keep my glove down and get a jump on the ball. That was just after he had been rejected by the army for the second time. All through the war, Howie tried to enlist, but he was one half-inch too short and he wound up a flight mechanic at La Guardia. And then he just quit: he stopped working and became the Mayor of the Corner. He held court in front of the candy store, arbiter, adjudicator, legislator, offering his fund of statistics and information (much of it culled from the World Almanac) to all comers. And for what? Well, for one thing, for free. And also for love, for hunger, for fear, for loneliness. Judge and jury alike. In the coffin at the funeral parlor he already seemed unreal, skinnier than I remembered him, like some overpriced doll that stares down at you wide-eyed from the windows of F. A. O. Schwarz on Fifth Avenue.

Ours was the last stop on the line and drunks would periodically stumble out of the subway. Drunks were not unusual, nor did we pay very much attention to them. They didn't travel with the Yonkers-bound men and women who take them home for dinner. Not as a rule anyway. But, occasionally, the rush-hour crowd would clear a path for an emerging drunk, the distaste visible in their faces and stiffening spines. "So I'm drunk. But look at them, running from their own goddamn souls." I was standing with my friend Jack on the corner, leaning against the subway exit, watching the press on the buses as the late August evening approached. The drunk put a hand on my shoulder, tried to steady himself, then lurched forward until Jack caught him and jammed him, as gently as possible, against the side of the candy store. The two of us held him erect until he regained his balance. He laughed. Then he began to talk. He talked about Glasgow, about how he had shipped over while still in his teens, about making his way out West. We wound up in Larry Campbell's bar and for the next three hours he talked; he was all language and memory, and we listened. The voice was authentic as it told us of Big Bill Haywood, of the Memorial Day Massacre in Chicago, of Debs and the I.W.W. and John L. Lewis (whom he called "the buustid"), strikes, deaths, battles, a line of meaningful violence stretched clear across the country. I still needed heroes then and I quickly adopted him. For it was Big Bill Haywood, as well as Debs and Joe Hill, who had married the world of Eastern European Jews—with its pogroms, its Russian priests, its sour-breathed Cossacks, its terror and disease and massacres and, above all, its dream of the Socialist-Coming—to that America whose streets were paved with gold and which, I had been taught, needed little more than a redistribution of that gold to match the dream. "Never mind what they do to you," he advised us as we escorted him back into the subway, old and fragile and very drunk. "Just stick to your own. Never forget who you are."

But I have not stuck to my own. Instead, I have chosen to rub against the grain of this America, this *goldena medina,* and have learned to pigeonhole present and past, everything and everybody in the proper niche. American intellectuals today rather desperately strive to keep in fashion, a temptation I have not been particularly successful at resisting. I have accepted categories thrust upon the world I live in by legions of reformers who see only the kind of suffering that intellectual fashion tells them is current. And when I ask myself who these working-class racists about whom we speak so glibly are, I find that they are the people in my neighborhood, Jews, Italians and Irishmen, whose very lives are now being bleached into invisibility. And by their own grandchildren, as well as by those for whom they were never visible in the flesh but existed only in a sentimentalized myth called the working class.

They do not earn enough money to partake of the affluence they are told so scornfully is theirs; they are confused by and hostile to intellectuals for whom they have become an abstraction; they struggle to keep themselves afloat in a sea of indifference. Unlike so many radical intellectuals, they never laid claim to Gatsby's orgiastic future—and one wonders whether it is this, rather than their "racism," that has earned them such contempt. And now that future has been thrust before them, like strawberry shortcake, but they are told it is not theirs to consume. No participatory democracy for them, for *they* (a peculiar inversion, that) would not know what to do with it.

To believe that these workers are "middle class" is to construct a reality in which the foul rag and bone shop of the heart that Yeats wrote about has been absorbed, by the very people who should know better, into methodological convenience. For to insist that their "racism" is what plagues America is to define both them and racism out of meaningful existence. The truth is far simpler than that. And far more elementary and complex, too. For the people in my neighborhood feel themselves victims of a world that increasingly treats their problems with smug indifference or outright contempt. They know that they suffer, but they feel that few are interested in their suffering. Their air, too, is polluted, their schools overcrowded. The bureaucracy that measures their lives out in statistics is incompetent when it is not helpless; the tax structure is unjust. They fear retirement and personal obsolescence, and, above all, they smolder with resentment of a society for which they have been made the propitiatory sacrifice, as it reaches for every gimmick, every comprehensive cure-all, like a pickpocket turned loose in a carnival sideshow. They did not create this America, regardless of what their descendants and LeRoi Jones believe, nor have they benefited so greatly from it, regardless of what Fire Island radicals tell themselves over cocktails. My neighborhood is not belching with either affluence or indifference, and its streets are not cluttered with $13,000-a-year electricians or $15,000-a-year bricklayers.

And so I discovered that Ellison's Invisible Man has a new brother, the Irish-Jewish-Italian worker. He has been pinned to the wall and labeled: *the racist.* And here they were, these people clinging to the passing summer by the broken railings of Mosholu Parkway. Some of them were grandfathers of the revolution that never came, and now they sit and sun themselves and number among their kind a few, a very few by now, who can rattle off party congresses and five-year plans and who, if you make the mistake of listening, can tell you exactly how Stalin outmaneuvered Trotsky, how Malenkov followed Stalin, how Khrushchev followed Malenkov, and how the revolution had moved from Faust to the latest clerks in the attic, Kosygin and Brezhnev. "Did you ever read, with your education you must have read, did you ever read . . . ?" The voice trails off, dies, strangles in its own anguish. Hungary. Czechoslovakia. Anti-Semitism on the Left. The way you die on Rochambeau Avenue. This is not the way they had conceived it. "In America, they kill you with candy," my grandmother (no socialist, she) used to say. Whenever she said it, my uncle the furrier would choke on his coffee. Perhaps it is only in memory that true faith is invested. I remember two Italian anarchists who repaired my shoes (Jews own candystores, Italians own shoe repair shops, Irishmen own bars; a Bronx syllogism), who stood all day long, mannequins with leathery faces, and worked on shoes. When I came home from the hospital at thirteen, they taught me the words to *Avanti Popolo.* Tacked on the wall, staring down at them as they worked, an old picture of Franklin Delano Roosevelt, his country squire's face cut from the *Daily News* rotogravure (a minor irony that) and faded with time and dust and so many heels nailed, soles glued, hats blocked, so much leather polished. Roosevelt, they insisted, was a working-class saint. When I went to college, I would try to argue with them. But it did no good. They insisted that Roosevelt had been a great *sooshalista* trying to break the power of the oppressor, to bring down all the banks and churches and corporations. The evidence: "Dey kiola heem. For why?"

The shoe repair shop is gone, but there is a new one a few doors down. It was closed. Perhaps the two Italian anarchists are there now. I do not know. The barber shop next door, where I used to get my hair cut, has disappeared. The Mosholu Jewish Center Hebrew School, which my father forced me to attend, socialist millennium or no, used to have more than two hundred students; it has about forty now. Bainbridge Avenue is no longer very interesting. It is dominated by a large new supermarket and a very modern bank. My father, now on social security (Roosevelt, that *sooshalista,* at least gave him that, although my father would not understand were I to explain that part of the credit should be reserved for Huey Long and Dr. Townsend), supplements his income when the store is occasionally shorthanded and he is called to help out for a few hours. The bank was established after the war, prospered, soon outgrew its accommodations, and has built newer, safer, colder, better-for-depositors quarters next to the supermarket. The lot behind the bank, where I used to play touch football, has been leveled and tarred over: it is a parking lot for the bank's employees now. Bainbridge Avenue is drab and almost sedate, for the drabness is modern and indiscriminate. The corner is dead. And not only on Sundays in September. The young people do not use it any more. Drugs have killed street life in New York for the young. Drugs in Greenwich Village. Or maybe 42nd Street. A syringe, pot, the hunger of adolescents for something larger than the neighborhood—in any case, the streets are over. The corner bores the young people, and the old pass it by.

And I wonder whether what I am feeling is a different guilt now. I will not flagellate myself with this guilt, if for no other reason than that I have had enough of intellectuals who flail away at themselves in public. It is useless and distasteful and the *mea culpa* has been recited by too many of late. But I have done my share, at least as a teacher, of accommodating myself to the questionable rhetoric that has gutted the real issues plaguing this America beneath the psychic flanges and hip neuroses of radical fashionability. I have heard myself in class, shoulder to the wheel and mind to the metaphor, when my rhetoric could match that of any masseur of the public conscience who speaks from the hollows of the *Village Voice.*

In any case, the problem is not to assess guilt. That, one suspects, might be easy, even for those in my neighborhood. No

Southern Bourbons, they, no, nor high-powered industrialists ped-dling their power in smoke-filled rooms: the images are from the thirties, but grant me, at least, a purpose. For the real problem with which we are faced is the question of price. Who pays to bail out this country? And how much must be paid? There we have the heart of the matter.

For the truth is, there is nothing I can now say to the people in my neighborhood. Certainly not to these disillusioned park-bench socialists waiting for the end, for they never construed the radical vision to mean what my students think it means. Even when their politics are radical, working-class people are basically con-servative. They would not understand what rock festivals have to do with changing the lot of the poor (which does not, I hasten to add, make the music or its audience any less attractive). The vo-cabulary is different, even if the words are the same. How do you explain *life-style* to a man who still wonders how different it might have been if Trotsky . . . ? Do you tell him about Marcuse? Or Ken Kesey? Or Timothy Leary? Do you offer him his pick of quo-tations from the new Buddha's *Little Red Book?*

I tried on that hot September afternoon. I went back to the Park-way and collared one of those old men. Racism, I offered. "So," he said, "nobody here created it. You think it's new?"

This kind was new enough. Anyway, it wasn't a question of new or old. It had to be changed. "The system creates it," he answered. "When people aren't permitted to be people, that's how it gets cre-ated. So what do you want? To be Robin Hood with my life?"

He had to understand. Nothing to do with him personally. Things had to be made different. "For you, they're already differ-ent," he said. "When I was your age, radical meant you fought for the poor. You think you discovered racism? You think we didn't know? And who's going to pay? Park Avenue?" He waved his hand indicating the houses lining the west side of the Parkway. "From us you're going to take, right? That's your socialism."

It wasn't quite that way, I explained. A simple question of pri-orities. "You're a fool," he said. "You don't even know that you think we should pay. But we have nothing to pay for and nothing to pay with. Radicals." He snorted. "Clothing salesmen is what you are, Radicals!"

I quit then. Not because I thought he was altogether correct but because at this point the words stood in our way. It all came back to a question of prices. He was wary of a passion for the rights of black men that wished, in the name of social justice, to make black into white and white into black. He was bitter that the bill for reparations was to be presented to those least able to afford it. They are still Marxists in their blood, these people. My uncle, for instance, although he is no longer a nattily dressed radical gambler but instead a man who is unemployed and worried and trying to accept the fact that mink is no longer selling and that, at sixty, the few jobs around are going to younger men who can sew mink faster, that the fur trade is dying, that the union—no longer an independent radical union but reduced to a local of the butchers' union—cannot even help him find work, and that he is going to be lucky merely to make ends meet in the future, my uncle said to me in a moment of extreme bitterness recently, "For Christ's sake, poor is poor! Can't you understand?"

Not only, then, have I not stuck on my own, I have not remained loyal to an older conception of the poor that had nothing to do with color and to an idea of socialism that insisted that the brotherhood was not of the skin but rather of the passion, that it united us in a quest for social justice. Which meant that the paying had to be done by those who had too much rather than by those who barely had enough for themselves. And here lies whatever the guilt is, not in the fact that I do not glorify or mythicize these people (the first would be difficult, the second impossible). To have been bought and sold so cheaply, to have accepted without resistance the super-salesmen who peddle me everything from pop art to *kitsch* socialism, to nod passively when the "real" enemy is identified as the middle-class housewife, notoriously Jewish, in Queens—there is guilt enough here. There is even enough guilt here to be understood by "radicals" who spin their summer passions out on the beaches of Fire Island while they squeeze the soul from those who are themselves confused and frightened and beginning to suspect (perhaps with good reason) that they are defenseless.

For such "radicals" distort beyond recognition the dream of socialist humanism, while they create of radicalism a new kind of intellectual fashionability to be sold to one another, like super-market offbrands, for bargain prices. The radical as hustler, the radical "doing his thing"—the words, unfortunately, fit like a glove.

Skin-tight. *We* professors, *we* journalists, *we* know that the white working class is indelibly reactionary, and *we* are united by our passion for equality and our eagerness to give away a patrimony that never belonged to us. For we have decided that poor is not poor unless skin is skin. How else can one explain a Left, a "new" Left, if you will, that cries for a world in which all flesh is equal but some flesh is more equal than other flesh.

The neighborhood is not yet a slum. It may become one, although one suspects that its days are numbered. Nor is it a place where politics is taken as seriously as it once was. Even among the grandfathers of the revolution that never came who wait for death on the sidewalks of Mosholu Parkway, there is little talk of politics. History, we have been told, has many strange twists. Can anyone blame these old people if they do not understand life-style radicalism as what they had in mind when they launched their own struggles? When I talk to their grandchildren at City College, I frequently find myself thinking that they are right to have cashed in socialism for sun on a park bench. In any case, they do not believe that they have any choice.

For they have been forgotten—by their children, who never bothered to ask who or what they were, by the Left, by New York, by time itself. Perhaps that last is the greatest of all betrayals, for when time robs you of your dignity then memory itself becomes treacherous. And they are now the enemy, inhabitants of the country of the faceless. They are not willing to pay the price because they insist that the fault is not theirs. And they insist, in however inarticulate a fashion, that we radicals look at ourselves as we really are, nothing extenuated. The guilt, they claim, is not theirs, although they are once again being made the scapegoats of a society unwilling to face up to the dictates of its fears or its conscience and pay from where the larder really is overstuffed.

"Give a damn!" one reads on the buses of New York. "It's still 1930 in the ghettos." This is real enough, despite one's knowledge that, to the man who wrote it, 1930 means *Bonnie and Clyde,* a dreamy Technicolor landscape filmed through the haze. But it is not merely in the ghettos that 1930 is still alive. For 1930 is, as much as anything else, a particular consciousness of history. And we have forgotten how real 1930 is to people such as those in my neighborhood. For the neighborhood suffers from a sense of impending poverty, a feeling that the wind has once again shifted and that events are out of control, that time and power and calculation are rallying against them, that there is no one to listen to them, no one to speak for them, nothing against which they can protest. And so their world is to be forfeit, their reality to be surrendered, while they themselves will be cast aside, dry bones and dry souls, for one or another slogan that is simply a distortion of the truth they once viewed as elementary. Men suffer and men die. *All* men. No, they do not have to be told that it is still 1930 in the ghettos, for it has never been anything but 1930 in the neighborhood. They were not born to rule; they would settle now merely to be told that they were not born to suffer excessively either.

No place, apparently, has been reserved for them in the apocalyptic future. What they need is an Orwell whose honesty has thrust up from their own midst. What they have gotten are the barbs of swingers and the friendship of such as Mario Procaccino, and while the one may be a testimony to their virtue the other is an indication that fate, too, has settled for a quick laugh at their expense. "With friends like you," the old saying has it, "I don't need enemies."

But the truth remains, and the truth is that they are not the racists, not at least if that term has any meaning beyond that of being the most available pejorative whip for anyone in the radical circus eager to try his luck as ringmaster. For the rhetoric of radical and liberal righteousness is being created at their expense. They have been lashed by the tongues, minds and pens of their Fire Island betters—and they are now beginning to stiffen with the helpless self-defensive anguish of the victim suddenly accused of being a victimizer. And can those of us who have created our virtue at the expense of their reality escape the whispers that tell us that they, too, are suffering, that their terror and fear, like the terror and fear of the black dispossessed, are something against which, in our shame, we should protest? For my uncle is right. Poor is poor. And the brotherhood, ultimately, is not of the skin.

White Ethnic Neighborhoods: Ripe for the Bulldozer

Working-class ethnics constituted the largest single white population within America's northeastern and midwestern cities. According to Richard J. Krickus, an urban affairs specialist, these groups "are being pulled and pushed to the suburbs" because their communities have "mistakenly been identified as marginal areas doomed to become slums." As a result of this "forced" migration, the cities have been drained of a valuable source of capital, manpower and skills.

Krickus, a Lithuanian-American who was reared in an ethnic neighborhood of Newark, New Jersey, placed the blame for the working-class ethnic exodus on city planners who "have given little thought to the role of the white working class in the restoration of our older urban centers." Estranged from their city government leaders because they felt "ignored by the agencies of social change," these groups were convinced that their elected officials were determined not to allow them to preserve the integrity of their communities.

In an essay entitled *White Ethnic Neighborhoods: Ripe for the Bulldozer?*, Krickus recounted the plight of these people. More important, he presented recommendations which he felt "will give impetus to an agenda for action to reduce white ethnic alienation."

SOURCE: Richard J. Krickus, **White Ethnic Neighborhoods: Ripe for the Bulldozer?** (N.Y.: The American Jewish Committee, National Project on Ethnic America, n.d.), pp. 3–5, 14–19. Reprinted by permission.

The white ethnic communities are a social commodity our cities cannot afford to lose. Because they are, by and large, healthy social systems in an environment of social disorganization, they are a major source of stability. Nevertheless, white ethnic neighborhoods have been neglected because their housing inventory is old, densities are high, and mixed land uses are prevalent. The result is that they have mistakenly been identified as marginal areas doomed to become slums. Moreover, with a new level of self-awareness on the part of the white ethnics many observers fear heightened discord. On the contrary, assuming that the proper resources and aid are provided, such awareness may very well be utilized to promote more harmonious relations between the races.

The reasons for the white ethnics' growing alienation which is forcing them to flee the center city need to be identified: they are estranged from government, lack economic resources, have been ignored by the agencies of social change, and feel they cannot possibly preserve the integrity of their neighborhoods.

Under discussion here are some recommendations which, it is hoped, will give impetus to an agenda for action to reduce white ethnic alienation and also to provide pathways for convergence with their black neighbors, thus inducing them to remain in the cities where they presently live in large numbers. This twofold goal must be achieved if the white exodus from our older urban centers is to be checked, and if working class whites and non-white minorities are ever to cooperate in an effective coalition for change.

The White Ethnic Community

It has been a popular notion for some time that the disparate ethnic groups which came to the United States from Europe have become assimilated into mainstream American society. Scholars who have recently re-examined the "melting pot" myth point out that while the ethnics have become acculturated—that is, have adopted many mainstream cultural tastes in music, clothes, entertainment, "American materialism," and so forth—they have not been assimilated into the mainstream social system. Michael Parenti has written that the ethnics maintain "a social substructure encompassing primary and secondary group relations composed essentially of fellow ethnics." They still do business with, socialize with, and by and large marry within their own ethnic group.

Although the disparate ethnic groups may be at different stages of the assimilative process, it is clear that in our cities and suburbs they share a common "ethnic group" outlook toward social change. Even if we accept the proposition that their working class status explains their behavior better than their "ethnicity," it is proper to deal with them as distinct social units in the cities where they reside in large numbers. For they are, to all intents and purposes, the white working class in Gary, Newark, and our older industrial cities.

(The author does not accept as empirically accurate the proposition that their working class status explains their behavior better than their ethnicity. The communities most *resistant* to the forces pushing whites out of the center city are usually the more homogeneous ethnic ones in our industrial urban centers. There is some question, however, how relevant one's ethnic group status is to the younger generation and to those persons who live in "mixed neighborhoods.")

. . .

A. URBAN RENEWAL

Working class neighborhoods are likely places to redevelop, tear down for public housing, or dissect with highways, because they are, according to local redevelopment agencies' criteria, marginal communities. Dwellings are often old and rather dilapidated on the outside and, even if they do conform to housing codes, are located in high density areas where mixed land uses prevail. Authorities guided by orthodox planning principles are prone to designate these communities Urban Renewal Areas: in many cases, they really believe they are doing the people a service.

Taking a different perspective, it is obvious that in the destruction of low-rent blue-collar housing, stable social systems are being destroyed. Since the people who are moved out of these communities receive only meager relocation assistance from the city, their social loss is exacerbated by economic loss when they cannot find comparable, inexpensive living space where they relocate. It is especially galling to them when they are removed to make way for upper-middle class high-rise apartments and chic townhouse complexes. Nor can they understand why their neighborhoods should be deemed the only feasible locations for low-cost housing projects. They do not accept the "practical" explanation that the city bulldozes their communities and not middle class neighborhoods because the land on which they live is less expensive.

Proponents and opponents of urban renewal both agree that renewal is most often "shaped by the demands or the contemplated demands of the developer and the sources of investment capital." Redevelopment authorities may receive their funds from Washington, but they are highly sensitive to the "needs" of the developers and lending institutions who make programs work. On the other hand, the uprooted residents who must find new housing are often ignored. Indeed, since they are not adequately compensated for their property, they and the Federal government are subsidizing the developers who make very tidy profits by constructing apartments for upper-middle class persons who can afford expensive housing.

Another demonstration of the power which developers and bankers wield in renewal programs was evident in the West End of Boston where, in the initial stage of redevelopment, some streets were excluded because they were deemed not blighted. Nonetheless, the bankers argued that these should be torn down too because it would be difficult to sell cleared land "surrounded by aging if well-kept tenements."

Harold Kaplan, who has commented favorably on Newark's urban renewal program, succinctly summed up the power of the developers and bankers when he wrote: "The big question about any redevelopment site was whether a private firm could make a profit on middle-income housing in that area. If the answer was negative, no redeveloper would buy the site, and no FHA official would agree to insure mortgages for construction there."

The literature is replete with accounts of how shabbily people in Urban Renewal Areas have been treated. In recent years the Federal government has taken steps to minimize such injustices, but as long as working class whites lack the political resources to participate in planning schemes which affect them, their needs will be neglected. To quote Kaplan again, one of the reasons the Newark program was so successful was the permissive political environment that prevailed in the city; that is, "if those affected by clearance were consulted at every stage of planning and the plan (failed) to meet their demands, renewal projects would never get off the ground."

B. BLACKLISTING

Working class neighborhoods which escape city renewal projects are often victims of lending institutions' blacklists. As Jane Jacobs has said, blacklisting is a self-fulfilling prophecy. Applying the orthodox criteria of the planners—mixed land use, aging dwellings, and high density—banks, savings and loans corporations, and so forth, often blacklist "marginal communities," with the result that home owners cannot obtain the money they need for the upkeep of their homes. Landlords are reluctant to refurbish their buildings when they fear the community is doomed to be cleared. In these circumstances, housing in blacklisted neighborhoods declines, becoming progressively more unsightly; even the more tenacious residents are ultimately forced to move, and the inventory of unrented apartments grows. Eventually the neighborhood takes on the physical characteristics of a slum and the bankers' prophecy comes true.

C. BLOCKBUSTING

Real estate speculators are inclined to zero in on lower-middle class white communities for the purpose of blockbusting—buying cheap from white residents and selling dear to blacks who cannot purchase elsewhere. Unlike the so-called "marginal" housing discussed above, white neighborhoods involved in blockbusting often have better quality housing. Well-kept homes, single or multifamily, with lawns and large yards on tree-lined streets, are the objectives of the real estate speculators. For the potential buyers are middle-income blacks and not poor people.

Living in close proximity to black ghettos, blue-collar residents fear black penetration of their communities. Their anxiety is largely rooted in fact and fancy about the relationship between black neighbors and declining property values. Sometimes speculators set the community up for blockbusting by inducing one home owner to sell at an attractive price and then citing the presence of a black family to his neighbors as evidence that a black invasion of the community is imminent.

The essential elements in this piece are the fearfulness and insecurity of the white community. The tactic is less likely to work where the residents are middle class whites and active participants in community affairs and the local political system. The estrangement from local government of lower-middle class whites, their inability to work effectively within the complex administrative system, and their meager economic resources all conspire to make them susceptible to blockbusting.

Urban renewal, blacklisting, and blockbusting are just a few of the forces "pushing" whites from the inner city. Fear of crime, racial strife, exorbitant land costs and high taxes, plus the decline of the school system—all factors dealt with at length in the literature—are also contributing to the exodus.

At the same time there are forces "pulling" the whites to the suburbs, although the current economic picture has decreased their intensity. The FHA mortgage insurance program, the VA's mortgage guarantee program, and the new highway systems have expedited white out-migration. The availability of relatively inexpensive homes which can be purchased with small down payments and long-term mortgages and the popular belief that the suburbs are nice places to live have contributed to the decline of white communities in the inner city. These "pull" factors are, for the most part, incentives which the Federal government has provided and which have induced whites to move to the suburbs. The time has come to provide incentives to reverse this trend. It may be that the decline in housing construction and the rise in interest rates offer us the opportunity to "save" communities which until recently were in the process of dissolving.

B. REFLECTIONS OF THE "DISLOCATED WHITE ETHNIC"

"The Stepchildren of Our Time"

In the 1960s and '70s, white working-class ethnics found themselves characterized by politically liberal spokesmen as "flag-waving hardhats," "pigs" who "supported their local police" and "racists" who opposed equal opportunities for blacks. In efforts to repair the damage done by these stereotypes, ethnic leaders began to answer the charges made by these "liberal elitists" with counterclaims of their own.

The first selection which follows was written by Barbara Milulski, a Polish-American councilwoman from Baltimore. In "Who Speaks for Ethnic America?," she detailed why the white working class was "infuriated at being used and abused by the media, government and business." In the second selection, "Ozone Park Revisited," Giulio E. Miranda, an Italo-American, described conditions in his former New York City community. Miranda asserted that because this working-class district did not have "the exotic appeal of the [black] ghetto," political strategists and social scientists had unwittingly written it off "as Archie Bunker country."

SOURCE: New York *Times*, September 29, 1970. **Who Speaks for Ethnic America?** Reprinted by permission.

The Ethnic American is forgotten and forlorn. He is infuriated at being used and abused by the media, government and business. Pejorative epithets such as "pigs" and "racists" or slick, patronizing labels like the "silent majority" or "hard hats" are graphic examples of the lack of respect, understanding and appreciation of him and his way of life.

The Ethnic Americans are 40 million working class Americans who live primarily in 58 major industrial cities like Baltimore and Chicago. Our roots are in Central and Southern Europe. We have been in this country for one, two or three generations. We have made a maximum contribution to the U.S.A., yet received minimal recognition.

The ethnics came to America from the turn of the century through the twenties, until we were restricted by prejudicial immigration quotas—65,000 Anglo-Saxons to 300 Greeks. We came looking for political freedom and economic opportunity. Many fled from countries where there had been political, religious and cultural oppression for 1,000 years.

It was this working class which built the Great Cities—constructed the sky-scrapers, operated the railroads, worked on the docks, factories, steel mills and in the mines. Though our labor was in demand, we were not accepted. Our names, language, food and cultural customs were the subject of ridicule. We were discriminated against by banks, institutions of higher learning and other organizations controlled by the Yankee Patricians. There were no protective mechanisms for safety, wages and tenure. We called ourselves Americans. We were called "wop," "polack" and "hunky."

For our own protection, we formed our own institutions and organizations and clung together in our new neighborhoods. We created communities like "Little Italy" and "Polish Hill." The ethnic parish church and the fraternal organizations like the Polish Women's Alliance and the Sons of Italy became the focal points of our culture.

These neighborhoods were genuine "urban villages." Warmth, charm and zesty communal spirit were their characteristics. People knew each other. This was true not only of relatives and friends but of the grocer, politician and priest. The people were proud, industrious and ambitious. All they wanted was a chance to "make it" in America.

Here we are in the 1970's, earning from $5,000 to $10,000 per year. We are "near poor" economically. No one listens to our problems. The President's staff responds to our problems by patronizingly patting us on the head and putting pictures of construction workers on postage stamps. The media stereotype us as gangsters or dumb clods in dirty sweat-shirts. The status of manual labor has been denigrated to the point where men are often embarrassed to say they are plumbers or tugboat operators. This robs men of their pride in their work and themselves.

The Ethnic American is losing ground economically. He is the victim of both inflation and anti-inflation measures. Though wages have increased by 20 per cent since the mid sixties, true purchasing power has remained the same. He is hurt by layoffs due to cutbacks in production and construction. Tight money policies strangle him with high interest rates for installment buying and mortgages. He is the man who at 40 is told by the factory bosses that he is too old to be promoted. The old job is often threatened by automation. At the same time, his expenses are at their peak. He is paying on his home and car, probably trying to put at least one child through college.

In pursuing his dream of home ownership, he finds that it becomes a millstone rather than a milestone in his life. Since FHA loans are primarily restricted to "new" housing, he cannot buy a house in the old neighborhood. He has no silk-stocking lawyers or fancy lobbyists getting him tax breaks.

He believes in the espoused norms of American manhood like "a son should take care of his mother" and "a father should give his children every opportunity." Yet he is torn between putting out $60 a month for his mother's arthritis medication or paying for his daughter's college tuition.

When the ethnic worker looks for some modest help, he is told that his income is too high. He's "too rich" to get help when his dad goes into a nursing home. Colleges make practically no effort to provide scholarships to kids named Colstiani, Slukowski or Klima.

The one place where he felt the master of his fate and had status was in his own neighborhood. Now even that security is being threatened. He wants new schools for his children and recreation facilities for the entire family—not just the token wading pool for pre-schoolers or the occasional dance for teen-agers. He wants his street fixed and his garbage collected. He finds that the only things being planned for his area are housing projects, expressways and fertilizer factories. When he goes to City Hall to make his problems known, he is either put off, put down or put out.

Liberals scapegoat us as racists. Yet there was no racial prejudice in our hearts when we came. There were very few black people in Poland or Lithuania. The elitists who now smugly call us racists are the ones who taught us the meaning of the word: their bigotry extended to those of a different class or national origin.

Government is further polarizing people by the creation of myths that black needs are being met. Thus the ethnic worker is fooled into thinking that the blacks are getting everything.

Old prejudices and new fears are ignited. The two groups end up fighting each other for the same jobs and competing so that the new schools and recreation centers will be built in their respective communities. What results is angry confrontation for tokens, when there should be an alliance for a whole new Agenda for America. This Agenda would be created if black and white organized separately in their own communities for their own needs and came together to form an alliance based on mutual issues, interdependence and respect. This alliance would develop new strategies for community organization and political restructuring. From this, the new Agenda for America would be generated. It could include such items as "new towns in town," innovative concepts of work and creative structures for community control.

What is necessary is to get rid of the guilt of phony liberals, control by economic elitists and manipulation by selfish politicians.

Then, let us get on with creating the democratic and pluralistic society that we say we are.

source: Giulio E. Miranda, **"Ozone Park Revisited,"** 1973. Written for this volume. Printed by permission.

Ozone Park is an Italian province in Middle America. It is situated due south of Forest Hills and Kew Gardens, a pocket of white ethnic working-class people with vowel-ending names. To the west is the angry decay of East New York and to the east, South Jamaica, a rapidly spreading ghetto. It is the kind of place political strategists don't study because they have already written it off as Archie Bunker country. It has none of the exotic appeal of the ghetto to attract the social scientists. And the educators don't innovate here, because the reading scores have always been low and there's no kicks in struggling with a chunky kid named Anthony.

Here is another place where McGovern and the liberals blew it. This was labeled the turf of Minutemen and the politically irredeemable, unteachable in politics as their young were unteachable in the classroom. Ozone Park rarely makes the media, except on occasions like last month when two men (not Italos, but typical of the area) incurred the wrath of the moral leadership by living out the fantasy of 101st Avenue and going after a busload of wise-ass kids who didn't happen to be their own kind.

Ozone Park is not Mulberry Street, nor yet suburbia. It is, for the Italian-Americans who live there, a holding area for the American dream. At least that is what it was until the sixties. Now it is a last-ditch place, like Canarsie and similar outposts. There is no place left to go, and the inelegant but well-kept frame houses are bastions against incomprehensible and unacceptable change.

The journalistic drop-ins have not written well of places like this. They have pictured them as decaying and dejected, peopled by the surly and the hopeless. But to have lived in Ozone Park is to have known its strengths and joys, rooted in the persisting mores of South Italy. It nourishes and enjoys the family, neighborhood and a Catholicism happily unaltered by Father Berrigan and the dissident clergy. The Latin of the old Mass was another dialect of

Italian and elderly ladies still address saints directly, holding them strictly accountable for the consideration involved in the contracts of votive offerings.

Christmas means a baroque cascading of multi-colored lights, lumpy reindeer and a gathering of families. Old men named Pop sit in dour possession of doorways surveying fading memories, nubile granddaughters and the prospects of an undiminished patriarchy till the end of their days. So their ancestors awaited the inexorable in ancient hill towns leavening their certainties with the joys of the small tyrannies permitted the old.

In these neighborhoods the ethnic is work and the reward is family. Even those who move in more sinister patterns throughout this society know that certain rules are ancient and inviolable. Everyone knows everybody and the burden of survival is carried with a quiet joy uncelebrated by a hostile outside world. Ancient folkways still govern even the long-haired youth, unrecognized but present like the pristine color and exuberant shapes of the breads and pastries, ivory ricotta creams and green sprinklings of pistachio in the terra-cotta swirls of the cannoli, the rich *rinascimento* design in the jars of *olive condite*. The faces are archaeology come alive, Attic or Carthaginian, Roman, Norman, Saracen and Hellenic. Like the names on the door, bells and signs. Polimeni—Aragona—Greco—Romanelli. The plaster saints are *lares* and *penates,* and in the flickering candles lighted to the Madonna in the bedrooms of the old are represented the victories and failures of the encounter between paganism and early Christianity.

The McGovernites blew it here, as they did in other Italian neighborhoods which still register Democratic and now regularly produce a solid Republican vote. In part this is because too many of them have become elitists who could see no strengths in Ozone Park and who could spare no notice for the residents' legitimate fears and aspirations.

Nixon saw them as no better, but he knew with the sure instinct of the old politician how to trade upon their hungers and fears. Three generations of WASP brainwashing had prepared the ground for his purposes. These were the "poor and huddling masses," the "refuse" of Europe who had been taught in America that the way to acceptance was to forswear the old ways, forget the old language—Americanize in the image of bland blond slimness.

The sixties paved the road to the rich harvest of their vote. Labeled racists and pigs, these were the people who were pointed out by the absentee landlords of liberalism as the enemies of all good causes. Mired by their problems, under the barrage of the urban encounter, their rage accelerated surely and swiftly against a Democratic Party which they had once seen as the repository of the hopes of the underdog.

Whom were they to vote for? Would it be a party whose "ethnic quotas" excluded them in the same breath in which it labeled them ethnics? Would it be for the successful children of other immigrants who were so visible in McGovern's ranks, and whose children they felt had eluded the draft by college attendance and expatriation? Would fathers whose children had gone to war in Vietnam now vote for amnesty for sons who had escaped? Would workers weary with backbreaking jobs in ugly factories and at dangerous construction sites opt for the candidate of Ivy League campus protesters?

With a sure sense of where they hurt, Nixon offered the placebo of flattery:

"Let me tell you what I know about you," he told them in Maryland, at the Statue of Liberty—everywhere, ". . . when you run into an Italian-American community you will find that there is a strong sense of patriotism . . ." He praised the courage of a people who for a quarter of a century had been ridiculed for failing to do the bidding of Hitler and Mussolini. ". . . in our armed services, there is no group in this country that has a finer record of volunteering and serving courageously." Their religion, their value system, the work ethic . . . "Those of Italian background are builders . . . they believe in hard work, they believe in earning what they get . . ."

It is a fact that everything he said is true of Italian-Americans. It is also a fact he neither had nor offered solutions to the problems that beset them and the rest of the lower middle class. His administration produced no appropriation for the Ethnic Heritage Studies bill which would have provided some funds so that schoolchildren of white ethnic background could have learned something to counter what the media were telling them about their fathers and grandfathers.

But they bought him, because they had been taught that the

flag was sacred and they could not tolerate protesters who spit upon it. They feared the spread of the black ghetto and crime in the streets and no one had explained to them that there could be any remedy but repression. The liberals had talked at them and their spokesmen had engaged in the kind of racial politics that Clark Whelton nailed in his revelations about what really did happen in that bus incident. They were told that their ethnic group had produced organized crime, stamped indelibly "Made in Italy" —and they heard no one in Lindsay's crowd (which to them was McGovern's crowd) say he was horrified and appalled by the crime which made their wives afraid to attend evening services.

To be American, they had been taught by alien schoolteachers and equally alien Irish nuns, was to be superpatriotic. How many of them had fought in Italy, invading in "liberating" armies the towns where their grandparents still lived. Why should anyone blame them if they opted for Super-WASP Richard Nixon and his lovely blond daughter and proper wife?

Had the other side ever offered them programs and platforms to fit their needs other than in packages—all or nothing—which contained more to threaten than to solace them?

Increased Social Security benefits, elementary school sex education, human rights and abortion, programs for the aged, school busing, withdrawal from Vietnam, narcotics programs and the legalization of marijuana. You buy it all, or get none of it—and if you are opposed to any part, you are a pig, a honky—an ethnic. Safer to stand up for the flag—let your heart soar, and in the cynical South Italian saying, "A friend who hurts you is worse than an enemy who lets you alone . . ." Four more years!

But the fact is that if Italian-Americans should not have voted for Richard Nixon, perhaps they should not have voted for McGovern either. What hope was there for them in a party which had strayed so far from its base of support? Why Philadelphia Plans with no explicit solution for the whites who might lose their jobs? Where were the Italian studies to match the black studies? What legal aid for the subaffluent to pick up a tab they could no more handle than the blacks and Puerto Ricans America's racism condemned to perpetual poverty? Where was their ethnic representation in either Arthur Goldberg's or George McGovern's ticket? With teachers opposing ethnic quotas in their profession and middle-class Jews fighting low-cost housing in Forest Hills, were they to be the only altruists?

It is by now a platitude that the Democratic Party is going to have to do something very drastic to put itself together after the debacle of November 7. It will have to re-establish old alliances with working-class ethnics, among others with whom it must seek rapprochement. But this will never happen unless it fires its full complement of non-performing ethnic specialists and goes into those communities with a fair share of the patronage and a fair share of respect for what they will hear. Whatever language of racism and insensitivity, it will not be so different from what the political leaders whisper to their wives.

There are strengths from which to rebuild. If the Italian vote went 65 per cent for Nixon, the Catholic percentage was 75 per cent. This suggests a residuum of Democratic fidelity, some of which derives from the old politics (which seems to have worked better) but some from a carry-over of the conviction that this is still the party of the working class. There are needs which can gain support from Italian voters, if they are separated from those which are perceived as threatening to the life-style. It is something with which to make a beginning.

Other opportunities lie in the peculiar strengths of Italian America. The tenacity in clinging to the old neighborhoods, partly sentimental, but also derivative from the extended family pattern, can act as a glue to hold the cities from becoming racial ghettos. The Italians have shown a readiness to live in neighborhoods adjacent to those of blacks and Puerto Ricans and fight it out for the turf. This is more promising than the discreet avoidance practiced by the groups who deplore the rumbling and name-calling of black-Italian confrontation. The resistance to change is an index of inner strength. The essential tolerance of Mediterraneans has made it possible for them to live in peace with ethnic Jews, and indeed, Jews are now seeking shelter under the umbrella of Italian neighborhoods.

How to approach and develop these strengths?

At the beginning, this will be a problem for solution by Italian-Americans who have worked out their own identity problem and can serve as a bridge for their own people. There is no small measure of self-ignorance and self-hatred among us. We have suffered greatly at the hands of our exploiters, including those we have produced from our own ranks. One rarely meets an urban Italian-American who does not have problems of identity. To many, America at large is still terra incognita, a dangerous land run by a "they" who have never liked us—who moved out as we moved in—who use the media to scapegoat us for the sins of a fragmenting society and use "Mafia" and "Cosa Nostra" as new catchwords for "wop" and "guinea."

We will have to reverse a one-hundred-year-old propaganda to deculturate ourselves, that to be American is to melt as quickly as possible into the Yankee engine block. We must learn to see our parents and grandparents as the culture heroes they should have become—pioneers as surely as any others who tamed a hostile environment. When we can accept the economic poverty of our origins, we will cease our flight from ourselves and develop the empathies which can be a lens for understanding the strivings of others. Our "style" must be legitimized so that we are no longer afraid to speak out.

When some of this has come about, we will be able to demand our part and make our contribution to what must be done to move forward in a land which has never felt the full impact of the talents with which we have dazzled the world for twenty centuries.

This is for us to do. But it is for others to be ready to hear us. We cannot survive—without destructive anger—the idiot ridicule of the ethnic joke, the stereotyping and exploitation of the media, the superior smiles of those we sought and who have betrayed us as friends. We will not die of your incomprehension, but our despair may well involve your destruction.

Ozone Park is an Italian province in Middle America. It is a last-ditch place—and when it is gone, the cities are done. I go back there often, to touch my earth—to soak in its operatic sounds, to regenerate in its movement and majolica colors. For me, as for all Italos, it is sometimes necessary to go home.

Ozone Park will not always be as it is—perhaps it can be better. This is the pattern of neighborhoods it has been our genius to convert from slums and shantytowns into places to live.

When I go back, I look for Pop, who sits in front of his doorway, and I think of what he knows. I ask him, in Italian, how he is.

"Eh . . ." He gestures vaguely toward the cemetery which is

west and north at Woodhaven and Metropolitan Avenue. "By and
by, St. John's. For now, this is mine . . ." Behind him is a store-
front house, shingled gray, that would only be beautiful if you
loved it. Pop, of course, it occurs to me (perhaps because I am
still so Italo), has found something out in the long years since
Sicily and Ellis Island, or brought it with him in a battered suitcase
tied with a rope. Perhaps it was how to mix the glue that holds
life together.

"It's More Than a Dislike of Long Hair"

In 1970, New York City was sorely polarized. The school strike
of 1968, which pitted blacks against Jews, had left tremendous
scars. Old civil rights alliances were crumbling and the middle class
was leaving the city. White ethnic working-class communities
which made their anger toward the "liberalism" of the Lindsay
administration felt at the polls in 1969 were becoming increasingly
more dissatisfied and vocal. And finally, one day in May of 1970,
hardhats and college students came to blows over the Vietnam
War, a few yards from City Hall.

The hardhat stereotype became solidified in the minds of many
liberals, and in the eyes of the Lindsay administration, the "hardhat mentality" was part of the problem.

For six months prior to that organized confrontation of pro- and
anti-war demonstrations, Nancy Seifer, who had spent two years
in West Africa as a member of the Peace Corps and then organized
a leadership training program for African women, sponsored by
the Women's Africa Committee of the African-American Institute, had been directing the City Hall Neighborhood Press
Office. It was the mandate of her office to communicate with the
150 or so neighborhood as well as ethnic and foreign-language
weeklies in the city, to provide them with local news items which
emanated from all branches of city government and which the large
daily newspapers would not find of broad enough interest to
print; and to bring the problems and concerns of their neighborhoods to the attention of city agencies for prompt action.

Through interviews with the editors of these newspapers, she
became acquainted with a whole world with which the mayor's immediate staff had little contact. In familiarizing herself with the

large numbers of ethnic enclaves throughout the city, she saw that they were virtually cut off from city government. Their newspapers were more likely to print news of the "old country" or of prominent countrymen in California or Texas than they were to print news of New York City. Those neighborhoods were geographically a part of the city, but in reality more closely resembled isolated villages or small towns.

The May 1970 demonstrations had a deep impact on her. She reported that it "became clear that for grown men to use their brawn against college kids, there had to be more than just a disagreement about the war or dislike of long hair." The hostility which eventually led to violence, she asserted, "was an expression of deep-seated anger and frustration relating to a broad spectrum of concerns."

She began at that point to look more closely at the problems of white ethnic working-class communities around the city, in an attempt to document the need for City Hall and the municipal agencies to pay closer attention to them. Much of the material she gathered was derived from interviews with community leaders conducted by her staff, a small number of articles which began to appear in the press and a collection of materials made available by the National Project on Ethnic America, whose director, Irving Levine, she considers "one of the most farsighted thinkers in the country on the problems of the white working class."

While continuing to direct the City Hall Neighborhood Press Office, Seifer became increasingly interested and involved in ethnic and working-class issues and problems. In May of 1971, when that office was closed due to a retrenchment of public relations staff in all city agencies, she remained at City Hall under an agreement in which she was able to establish a small experimental Office of Ethnic Affairs, which would begin to develop links between ethnic communities and city government.

The documents which follow are a compendium of memorandums (1970–71) which Nancy Seifer, who is presently Director of Community Relations at the National Project on Ethnic America, wrote and submitted to various officials in the Lindsay administration. They contain an excellent analysis of the economic, social and political problems faced by the white ethnic minorities, and her recommendations for programs to deal with some of these problems.

SOURCE: New York City, Mayor's Press Office. **Memorandum from Nancy Seifer,** August 1970. Reprinted by permission.

The attached includes an analysis of the economic, social and political problems faced by white ethnic minorities in New York City, resulting racial polarization, and recommendations for programs to begin to deal with some of these problems.

Statements made on the following pages are based on: meetings with over 20 editors of New York City-based ethnic newspapers, and ethnic civic and religious leaders; discussions with writers and the staff of private non-profit foundations which have done work in this field; readings of much of the literature in this field (most of which has been written since the 1968 elections); and general observations.

. . .

RECOMMENDATIONS

It is the recommendation of this report that a special unit be set up within the Mayor's Office to advocate the need of lower middle class white ethnic communities in the following ways:

1. Increasing and improving city services and programs for these communities;
2. Providing them with a voice in City government by bridging the existing gap between them and the City's officials (the Mayor, in particular) and institutions;
3. Creating new programs to recognize ethnic diversity, and to stress the importance of cultural heritage and the contributions each group has made to our country and our city;
4. Working with the Mayor's Washington and Albany offices to promote and support bills which would benefit this group as well as poorer communities, and to research possibilities for funding new programs from already existing legislation.

Increasing and Improving City Programs and Services

Included here are examples of ways in which some city agencies might address themselves programmatically to certain immediate needs of this segment of the population. It is apparent that improved and increased services are in demand. (Many of HRA's programs, for which they do not meet financial qualifications, parallel programs which they need as well.)

1. Economic Development Administration—It is essential to develop job retraining opportunities for the young unskilled blue collar worker who cannot bear the thought of sweeping subway platforms or working on an assembly line for the next 50 years. Since there are no government funds available at this time, EDA might explore the possibility of setting up apprenticeship-type programs in cooperation with private industry, for family heads in the $5–10,000 income bracket. A summer job program is also of great need, to train future workers. (Nationally, statistics show that 30–40% of this group does not complete high school.)

2. Human Resources Administration—Women in this income group who want to work cannot afford to pay baby-sitting fees. They desperately need day care centers. In planning for construction of new ones, locations of working class neighborhoods must be kept in mind.

It has been suggested that an agency like the Department of Social Services might experiment with a job-linked day care center, taking the lead for private industry to follow.

Head Start-type programs are also in great demand in these neighborhoods. Nursery schools are financially out of the question.

3. Parks, Recreation and Cultural Affairs—

a) More vest pocket parks and improved recreational facilities are cited as particular needs in working class neighborhoods all over the city.

b) Every ethnic group in New York City boasts performing troupes, with traditional native costumes, which would be honored to perform at the city's request. The Department of Cultural Affairs should begin to sponsor Polka Festivals and Irish Jig Festivals, just as it is presently sponsoring African plays and Latin music concerts.

4. City Planning Commission—Urban Renewal projects can be cruelly devastating. The sense of alienation and loss which results from physical displacement is sometimes irreparable. A new type of city-community advisory council might be established to try to preserve the "sense of neighborhood" in renewal areas, and to

assure the location of new housing in the area. (Studies done on the relationship of alienation to crime emphasize the urgent need to conserve the neighborhood to some extent.)

5. Human Rights Commission—Job and housing discrimination against Poles and Hungarians, to cite two current examples, is rampant in certain areas of the city. The Commission might step up its efforts to bring to light discrimination problems faced by white ethnics, as well as those faced by other minority groups.

A Voice in City Government

This group (which represents 20% of the country's voting population and perhaps as much as 45% of the city's) is so desperately searching for a leader who will speak to and for their needs, hopes and aspirations that for the first time in decades they are questioning their political affiliation to the Democratic Party. In a survey taken in Chicago, the vast majority would have voted for Bobby Kennedy, but many switched to George Wallace. While Wallace may have appealed to their lesser instincts, he did address himself to *their* problems and offered some sort of protection. Nixon's "confidential report" on the problems of the blue collar workers was a preliminary step to a strategy for cashing in on their changing political affiliations. Neither party as presently constituted represents their needs as they are economically liberal and socially conservative.

An expert in "ethnic affairs" in New York City said recently: "They are looking for a hero. They would have loved to have loved John Lindsay, because he represents everything they would like to be, but he disappointed them. They feel he doesn't know they exist." New York City religious and civic leaders concur that despite outward signs of hostility, blue collar white ethnic residents want very much to be recognized by the Mayor.

By articulating the needs of this group, showing compassion for them and responding to their needs, the Mayor could do a great deal to lessen their hostility. He stands only to gain from such efforts. Additionally, his influence on the media and the "liberal intellectual establishment" would have a multiplier effect on reducing the escalating polarization by creating a widespread sympathetic understanding of the problems they face. (Blacks and Puerto Ricans in the city still have the most serious problems, yes, but these people are also in deep trouble.)

In order to accomplish this, the Mayor will first have to establish some credibility with white ethnic groups. Below are some suggestions.

1. Seeking out and meeting with (or sending representatives to meet with) neighborhood leaders—not the few who have "made it" in the establishment, but the guy on the block to whom everyone turns for help and advice.

2. Making a greater attempt to include them in the Urban Action Task Force structure, especially as the new neighborhood government plan becomes a reality. While they are more apt to be active in church-sponsored and ethnic-group activities, many would become involved in civic activities if city officials reached out to them.

3. Proving that John Lindsay is really Mayor of *all* the people by providing these groups with more representation at City Hall and in upper-echelon agency jobs, and dispelling the image that he only cares about and for Jews, Blacks and Puerto Ricans.

4. Attending annual functions of great importance to each of these groups without showing favoritism.

5. Utilizing speeches, interviews and press statements to let everyone know that he is aware of them and of their needs.

6. Utilizing the ethnic press (for which the American Council on Nationality Services will translate into 23 languages) in a major way. A recommended first step would involve meeting with members of the ethnic press, and inviting them to begin working with him through their newspapers to reduce racial polarization and hostility. Drug addiction, crime, housing shortages, etc., are problems to all.

7. Coordinating and expanding city-based services for veterans. (This group sends more boys to Vietnam than any other income group in the nation.)

Stressing the Importance of Cultural Heritage

Understanding the need for the existence of strong ethnic orientation and stressing the positive aspect of it is important for reasons mentioned earlier.

Moreover, an awareness of various cultural and historical ethnic traits is essential to analyzing and solving many problems. Greek "ethnos" for example, dictates independence and self-reliance. Many affluent Greek restaurateurs and landlords started out in this country as push-cart vendors, to avoid working *for* anyone else. As a result, Greeks are economically stable and less threatened by Blacks, as are Poles or Italians who fear losing their jobs through their competition with minorities.

Many observers attribute the strong law and order tendencies of most Catholics to the strict discipline inherent in a Catholic upbringing. Moreover, the fear of Communism common amongst religious Catholics can be attributed to the atheism impelled by Communism.

Another element which contributes to the intense patriotism which exists in this group, is the fact that millions of Eastern Europeans in particular came here to escape Communist domination. Most feel that no matter how bad things get here, they are still better off than they would have been in the "old country".

To promote this type of understanding and mutual awareness, the Mayor might create a Cultural Heritage Council of the City of New York, made up of representatives of the Armenian, Black-American, Chinese, Cuban, German, Greek, Haitian, Hungarian, Irish, Italian, Japanese, Jewish, Lebanese, Lithuanian, Polish, Puerto Rican, Russian, Scandinavian, Ukranian, et al. communities in New York City. The functions of such a Council might include:

1. Providing information on attitudes and values, and the impact which ethnicity in New York City has upon the society as a whole;
2. Working with the Board of Education to promote the study of their history and contributions of each immigrant group to New York City;
3. Advising the Mayor on how to handle certain inter-cultural or inter-racial problems, (to avoid situations like the 1968 school strike);
4. Promoting pride in ethnic identification by officially recognizing, on behalf of the Mayor, all major holidays and cultural events of each group;
5. Helping to serve the needs of immigrants and refugees in New York City by providing up-to-date information on available city services to the ethnic organizations which welcome new arrivals.

Federal and State Legislation

Virtually no assistance has been provided for this group by either the State or the Federal government. Such needed proposals as raising the individual income tax exemption to $1,000 or $1,200 per dependent, providing deductions for daily transportation, an educational voucher or semester-grant system, and raising public housing subsidies have been discussed in Congress for years with little or no action taken. "Invisible Americans" is a phrase which has been aptly used to describe them.

A State Youth Facilities Act was passed recently in Albany, which supposedly provides funds for building day care centers, and might prove to be of great value to working class neighborhoods.

Three types of bills affecting the income group in question are presently pending in various Congressional committees. The Mayor's vocal support for such bills would no doubt be somewhat helpful in having them passed. 1) the Community College Act, which would provide free access to 2-year colleges for all high school graduates (early statistics on Open Enrollment in New York City have shown that white ethnics have benefitted the most, being able to go from paying for evening sessions, to matriculating as fulltime day students); 2) the Ethnic Heritage Studies Act, the purpose of which is to promote cultural heritage studies in the public schools; and 3) three different plans for comprehensive and universal health insurance, the last of which was sponsored by Senator Kennedy.

SOURCE: New York City, Mayor's Press Office. **Memorandum from Nancy Seifer,** June 17, 1971. Reprinted by permission.

A quiet revolution is taking place in white working class communities of northeastern and midwestern Urban America. It is a revolution of consciousness sparked by an untenable economic situation and by indignation at having been alternately ignored and castigated by the American Establishment. It is a revolution of self-assertion which will utilize the techniques of community organization and legislative action to make its power felt at the polls.

The new revolution aims to create a "new pluralism" which will enable the poor to form coalitions, allowing what will become a majority of the nation's population to decide its own future. Its hope is to create racial harmony in the cities. Its ultimate goal is the redistribution of power and wealth in this country.

.   .   .

The growth of our cities is largely the result of foreign-born immigration. Estimates of the total number of working class White ethnic males and their families range from 30–40% of the American population. Along with Blacks and Spanish-speaking minorities (and occasional pockets of upper middle class Whites), they still form the core of our cities.

The complexity and enormity of their problems, and their powerlessness to solve them, should have, according to the rules of sociology, led to total social disorganization:

1. Inflation has made it next to impossible for them to buy homes, a traditional source of security and pride. (5 years ago, according to Romney, the national median housing price was within reach of 40% of American families. It is now, at $27,000, within the reach of 20%.) Moreover, the FHA has been refusing low-cost home improvement loans to inner city residents.

2. They cannot afford proper health care.

3. The elderly can barely survive on pensions, social security, and meagre savings.

4. The parochial schools to which they generally send their children are going bankrupt.

5. Crime is ever increasing.

6. A minority of their youngsters go to college. Most have difficulty finding jobs in the unskilled market. They neither identify with America's middle class youth culture nor with the experience of their parents. They see what lives spent in factories did to their fathers, yet have little choice. Drugs are becoming an increasing threat. The generation gap is widening.

7. Entertainment and travel are out of their reach.

8. Taxes are exorbitant.

Yet, White ethnic enclaves in our cities have retained their strength. Moreover, for the first time, they are beginning to demand recognition of their needs and of their worth. Until now, whatever they ended up with here was better than what they left in the old country. It is no longer good enough.

SOURCE: New York City, Mayor's Press Office. **Memorandum from Nancy Seifer,** February 17, 1972. Reprinted by permission.

An increasing amount of organizational activity has been taking place in lower middle class and poor white ethnic communities throughout the city. These new organizations differ entirely in substance and structure from any that previously existed in ethnic communities. They are dedicated to community development and to obtaining decent social services.

The people in these areas have long felt powerless, alienated and frustrated, while watching their neighborhoods slowly deteriorate. They feel that their elected officials have "sold them out", and that the Church, still the focal point in most communities, has not begun to meet their needs.

In the past, problems were viewed as personal. Help was sought from the local priest or politician in getting a job for a brother or a pension for a mother. Now, in a time when expressways destroy communities, factory expansion takes homes, street crime continually increases, and elderly people stay locked up inside all day, problems have become communal. Working people are seeing that they have to organize in order to protect their communities.

The new organizations which I have been concentrating on, have been formed in the heart of ethnic communities. Although most residents in these neighborhoods never took part in civic associations per se, they are responding to requests from their own leaders to come out to meetings and to work on projects. They are beginning to feel that they can make a difference. What is unique is that for the first time, these people are seeing that programs and services can be for THEM, too. It is always made clear, however, that while a particular group may sponsor a program or facility, the doors will be open to all residents who wish to take part. (There are several great examples of inter-ethnic group co-operation.) In general organizational terms, the needs of newly forming groups are as follows:

1) On-going communication channels with city agencies for general information. Even the more sophisticated of the community leaders don't begin to know the range of programs and services available to their communities. Day care and senior citizens centers are prime examples—people in white ethnic neighborhoods had no idea, until recently, that these programs were available to them as well.

2) Technical assistance in the fundamentals of obtaining program sponsorship, improved or increased services, etc. Help is particularly needed in putting together proposals and following them through. The faceless bureaucracy, with all of its rules, and regulations and agencies and names and wrong telephone numbers and endless busy signals seems overwhelming to the uninitiated.

3) Legal assistance to incorporate the organization and establish by-laws. Once incorporated, public grants and private donations can be sought.

4) Public relations. Local newspapers, newsletters, flyers, posters can all be utilized to reach as many people as possible if the know-how and equipment are available.

5) Permanent structure. This is essential if the organizational efforts are ever to make any real changes in these communities. Many of the newly formed groups are now meeting one or two evenings a month and counting on volunteers to carry out various assignments. This is unrealistic in the long run. It doesn't build housing or day care centers. *Local storefronts or other office space and paid staff must somehow, eventually, be made possible.*

The Call for Ethnic Studies

The demands for the introduction of "ethnic studies" emanated largely from blacks. Faced with the possibility of demonstrations from black-power advocates and militant students, school systems hurriedly "threw together" courses of study which included everything from black history to black theater. Witnessing the relative success of the "politics of confrontation," white ethnics began to make similar demands. At first, their suggestions to introduce ethnic history, e.g., Italian studies, were interpreted as a reactionary backlash to blacks. However, the persistence of these groups soon persuaded a number of Boards of Education to offer subjects which included the white ethnic experience in America.

The selection which follows is from the *Hearings Before the United States Senate on the Proposed Ethnic Heritage Studies Center Bill* (1971). This testimony contained the written and verbal comments of a cross section of American ethnics. The bill sought to establish multi-ethnic study centers in universities and colleges throughout the nation. It was lauded as an attempt to bring into focus one of the "most educationally neglected aspects of American life."

SOURCE: U. S. Congress, Senate, **Committee on Labor and Public Welfare,** before a Subcommittee on Education, Senate, on S. 659, 92nd Cong., 1st sess., 1971, pp. 977–80, 1065–66, 1072–76, 1129.

STATEMENT OF MONSIGNOR GENO C. BARONI
DIRECTOR, CENTER FOR URBAN ETHNIC AFFAIRS
702 LAWRENCE STREET, N. E.
WASHINGTON, D.C. 20017

Senator Pell, members of the committee, I am Monsignor Geno C. Baroni, director of the Center for Urban Ethnic Affairs. It is my pleasure to appear before you and testify on behalf of S-23, the Ethnic Heritage Studies Center Bill.

Public and private agencies devoted to the restoration of urban America have largely ignored working class whites in designing programs to eliminate poverty, substandard housing, racial discord, declining schools, and physical decay. It is difficult to rationalize the neglect of these residents given their size and strategic location in our Northern metropolitan areas. The most prominent segment of this group are the first, second, and third generation Americans of European ancestry.

While the sons and grandsons of European immigrants can be found in various social-economic strata, a large number of them are blue-collar workers. They are the backbone of the labor force in most of our industrial cities, mining towns, and manufacturing centers. They still reside in older, mixed-ethnic neighborhoods or have relocated in predominantly blue-collar suburbs. The needs, frustrations, and problems of this metropolitan population are urgent and varied.

We reject the accusation that these people are the citadel of racism in our society, although we do not deny that racism exists. We find that race relations in America's big cities have come to mean increasingly the relations between the blacks and white ethnic working class people. This has happened because, increasingly, business and institutional leadership no longer lives in the city. The upper middle class has either fled or is fleeing. It is therefore obvious that if there is to be a resolution of the racial crisis which grips our society, a critical role will be played by white working class communities.

Since the end of World War II, scholars, journalists, and social reformers have devoted little attention to the white ethnic community. It was assumed that the offspring of European immigrants had lost their identity in the "melting pot," that they were well entrenched in the middle class, and that the plight of the new urban immigrant, the non-white minority, deserved priority attention. Recent probes show that many elderly white-ethnics are poor, that most working-class families do not earn "middle class" incomes, while white blue-collar youth must grapple with the same kind of problems that have produced alienation among affluent college youth.

As a consequence of two decades of neglect, we know little about the white ethnics, their precise numbers, the composition of their communities in terms of age, occupations, income, and education; the importance of their cultural heritage in understanding their behavior. However, the academic community, mass media, the foundations, and a growing number of people in Washington have rediscovered the "white ethnic." This renewed interest is based on the realization that to ignore their valid needs is to jeopardize those efforts which are designed to restore urban America and to reduce social discord which is rooted in economic insecurity and racial misunderstanding.

What, then, is the importance of an Ethnic Heritage Studies Center Bill? The importance is basic and I specify only a few of a plethora of reasons that support this bill.

First, utilizing the accepted metaphor of melting-pot, what really has melted in this famous pot? We don't really know because the decades of neglect has robbed us of the determining data.

Second, is America—perhaps the most culturally and ethnically diverse nation in the world—really a melting pot? Perhaps, as so many of us working the field more and more realize, the uniqueness of America and its source of strength consists precisely in its multi-diversity. Again, our decades of neglect has robbed us of the determining data.

Third, at a time—our time, right now—that our society appears to be searching again for its identity (so it may know better its true purpose) the passage of S-23 will provide to so many, many Americans of Eastern and Southern European origins a prospective of their origins, their heritage and traditions, their customs and languages, their life-force! To assist in discovering a people's origin (and fortunately for the American of European ancestry this is possible) is to assist an American to answer what always remains a basic question—who am I?

Fourth, the urban turmoils of American cities today is rooted in one basic question: Is America today yet able to provide a "pursuit of happiness" for the totality of Americans that make this nation the most culturally and ethnically diverse nation in the world? As various groups see and think they see other groups receiving more of our government's attention, its time, its money; then, that group sees itself as a foster child at best; as alien at worst.

To show that America is a nation of peoples—each fully free, each fully alive, each fully developing, each fully interdependent in brotherhood, then America in its "pursuit of happiness" for all its peoples can truly show "all men are brothers."

Thank you.

STATEMENT OF JOHN RADZYMINSKI, PITTSBURGH COMMITTEE FOR ETHNIC HERITAGE STUDIES CENTER, PITTSBURGH, PA., COMPOSING A PANEL

Senator Schweiker. I call on Mr. Radzyminski.

Mr. Radzyminski. Thank you, Senator. I just want to say that I worked with the United Steel Workers for some 30 years, and I am also president of Council 38 of the Polish National Alliance, the Pan-Slavic Alliance of Pennsylvania, and I am chairman of the Pittsburgh Ethnic Heritage Study Center Committee, and am vice president of the recently established National Heritage Association.

I am here today to support the Senate bill 23 calling for here the establishment of ethnic heritage studies centers in this Nation and to tell you why I hope this bill is passed soon and why one of these centers ought to be in Pittsburgh.

Every American has his own cultural heritage and tradition. But it has been more difficult for some of us to get equal respect and recognition for our heritage.

I am Polish American and my parents came to this country from Poland. My daughter is a student at the University of Pittsburgh where she is studying linguistics.

She has heard Polish since she was little and studied it at Alliance College in Cambridge Springs, Pa.; but there is only one professor at Pittsburgh that teaches Polish.

And in only a few secondary schools can a young person learn Polish. Usually if they are interested, a family member can teach them the language or give them a sense of their heritage. But many parents don't have time or don't know enough of the language, to even teach our children.

There are more than 200,000 Polish Americans living in and around Pittsburgh who are interested in knowing more about their heritage. I am not speaking just for Poles. I now know Italians, Serbians, Ukranians, and members of many other groups who think the same way I do. Many of us still have close ties with our heritage, but the younger people seem to know less about it and be less proud of it.

I don't know if the school system is to blame or if parents are to blame or what is to blame. I only know that something should be done to allow young people to take pride in who they are, and what they are, and where they came from. I think if young people knew these things, they would be much better off.

Last year Secretary Rostow, in the Department of Labor, wrote a report about the situation of workers. A lot of these people are union members. They work hard and their labor and taxes go a long way in supporting the Government. Yet, few if any Government programs are aimed at the workers' problems.

People in the newspapers call us the forgotten Americans, the silent majority, and white racists, but we came to this country later than a lot of other immigrant groups and we do have problems in the schools, and in our neighborhoods, and even in our unions, and we work hard to preserve what we have.

I am not denying that the civil rights movement is important. I can walk into any bookstore and find lots of books on the black culture, but it is almost impossible to find anything on the Slavic groups.

Yet these two groups are comparable in size and have similar needs. The Government and the foundations are spending thousands of dollars to study blacks, Puerto Ricans, and Mexican Americans, but who's spending money studying other groups?

This country could not have been a great industrial power without our help. I wonder how many people realize that the Poles established the first factory in America in Jamestown in 1609.

You never read about it. You also never read about the fact that the Polish people had the first strike in America, when the King of England extended the right to vote to the colonists in Jamestown, and did not include the Poles.

The Polish workers laid down their tools and struck because that privilege was not extended to them. They won that strike. This was in 1619. One year before the Pilgrims came to Plymouth Rock. But you don't read about those things.

As a public relations man for the Steelworkers Union I talk to people all over the country, and I believe the economic situation is a big problem, but as someone said, "man cannot live by bread alone." Whoever said that was right. We want for ourselves and our children to be able to learn about our heritage and be proud of it just like the English, Germans, and Irish have learned to be proud about theirs.

Our homelands, Poland, Yugoslavia, Hungary, and others have fallen under the domination of communism. But this surely does not mean that the cultures that were there before that time are any less worthy of learning about.

We are loyal Americans too, and we believe that each American has a right to know about his heritage.

Knowing about our heritage will make us better able to understand other peoples'. After all, the United States is a multi-ethnic society; the more we learn and know about each other and the more we understand each other, the more respect there will be.

America can only gain by ethnic studies. This legislation if enacted can go a long way to accomplishing this goal. I want to urge its early passage.

PREPARED STATEMENT OF CHARLES KOVAL, SECRETARY-
TREASURER OF THE PITTSBURGH ETHNIC HERITAGE
STUDY CENTER COMMITTEE

I am Charles Koval from Pittsburgh, Pennsylvania. I am Secretary-Treasurer of the Pittsburgh Ethnic Heritage Study Center Committee, Advisor-Director to the Scholarship Committee of Pan-Slavic Alliance, a member of the Croatian Fraternal Union, the National Heritage Association, and various other fraternals.

I was born the son of a former coal miner. I grew up in a small residential town in Pennsylvania south of Pittsburgh, and like many small towns in that area, we were surrounded by mines and steel mill towns composed of different ethnic groups. Some people used to look down on us because we were so called "hunkies" and because we were Catholics. Therefore, I always figured I had to work 10% harder than other guys to get ahead. I can understand some of the problems the Negro has had and because of color, he must work 20% harder. People burned crosses on our lawns too because we were foreign, had different ways, and thoughts, and perhaps actions, and because we supposedly posed an economic threat. They had a lack of understanding and prejudice toward us because of it.

I worked my way through college, spent five years in the Marine Corps as an aviator and six years ago started my own business, Allegheny Planned Income, Incorporated, a brokerage firm. Although I am third generation, I inherited my interest in fraternal societies and other ethnic organizations from my parents and grandparents and have gotten a lot of satisfaction out of helping other young people whose background is similar to mine. Fraternal societies that I belong to have really done a lot to help young people get ahead and get an education. They have also instilled pride, love of country and helped foster a greater understanding of other peoples.

Fraternalism is a word familiar to most of us. It means brotherhood, peace and goodwill. This grew out of the need of various immigrant groups to deal with their problems—when they came to this country. Fraternal associations formed to establish ethnic parishes. They were also mutual aid societies that helped individuals and their families to solve such problems as paying for medical aid and death benefits when a breadwinner was taken from the family. You must remember that in the early days around the turn of the century there were no government agencies like Health, Education and Welfare or insurance companies like Blue Cross and Blue Shield to provide financial help in time of need. Since most of the men who worked in the steel mills and the mines were not citizens at first, whatever minimal benefits that companies provided its employees were not available to them. Fraternal societies were also organizations that made it possible for people of similar backgrounds to get together after work to hear and talk their own native language, and to perpetuate traditions they brought with them from their homeland.

As an example, the Croatian Fraternal Union organized in 1894, like other fraternals, still celebrates these traditions. The Croatian Fraternal Union has a cultural federation that continues to encourage folk art and folk lore, and organizes Tamburitzan groups among children throughout the country fostering in them a love for Croatian songs and music. We have held four National Tamburitzan Festivals that have attracted as many as 700 boys and girls age 8–18. Through our scholarship foundation we have distributed over $200,000.00 in grants to needy and deserving young people for their college educations. Through both organizations that I advise we gave over $25,000.00 last year.

At the present time in America, we need a new awareness of fraternalism, a new sense of brotherhood; not just for members of one ethnic group or fraternal society but for members of all groups whatever their ethnic or racial background. We must achieve this new awareness as American citizens in order to solve the many basic problems facing us.

One of the best ways I know to develop this new sense of brotherhood and to begin to solve some of these problems is through the Ethnic Heritage Study Center Act of 1971, and I urge that it be passed as soon as possible.

Now some people think that ethnic studies might cause problems, that ethnic studies might increase prejudice rather than diminish it. I don't believe this. Most of the people I know who are proud of their heritage are also more tolerant of other people. It's those who don't have pride about who they are and where they came from who are the most prejudiced. Also we are considerably better educated than our forefathers. This helps to break down suspicion, distrust and we also have more leisure time to contemplate the consequences of divisibleness on our nation.

After all isn't ignorance the main ingredient of prejudice? If people could learn more about themselves through ethnic studies programs, the new leadership which America needs might be developed.

The future leaders of America are certainly not going to be those undisciplined young radicals who have rejected the past, and along with it all the good things which America has stood for. What has made America great and will continue its ideals as a nation are those well proved virtues of discipline, hard work, respect for society and its laws, and respect for parents who care about what their children become. All societies who have "made it" have had traditions of strong family ties, religion, respect for law and order, and feeling for the best of the past. If America wants to realize the most from its people, it must begin to be honest about ethnic diversity; and it must begin to provide an equal start for its children as they move through the American school system and into the mainstream of American life.

I believe that the school and the educational system is probably the best place for developing a sense of ethnic pride and at the same time for developing responsible American citizens. First of all, our hope for a better world lies with our children. They aren't born with prejudice but we help give it to them. Young people spend a lot of time in school from the time they are 3, 4 or 5 years old to the time they graduate. Unfortunately some school systems don't really "educate". Kids complain that classes aren't relevant. What could be more "relevant" than ethnic studies, which, properly taught, can develop a sense of ethnic pride, foster greater mutual understanding among different groups, and turn out young people who have an ability to feel and act as well as to think responsibly. Furthermore, I can't help but think that such instruction would develop a renewed sense of America, its ideals and goals as a Nation. Second, how, after all, can we be critical of oppression abroad if we don't have our own house in order. The United States has a great opportunity to come forth with and develop a new sense and awareness of brotherhood. The Ethnic Heritage Study Center Act of 1971 is right on target. It would begin to put us on the right track in achieving this. We are not subscribing to the theory that this Bill would be a panacea to all of our social ills. However, we feel it would certainly help toward eventual goals of total brotherhood.

AFL-CIO STATEMENT ON ETHNIC
HERITAGE STUDIES CENTERS ACT S-23

The AFL-CIO is pleased to express its support for S-23, the Ethnic Heritage Studies Centers Act.

For generations, textbooks and other curriculum materials were preoccupied with middle-class, white America. American history was written as the story of the white man in America, predominantly the story of the Anglo-Saxon Protestant white man, with occasional reference to the French and Spanish explorers, passing mention of European immigration in the nineteenth century, and condescending, brief accounts of the slaves.

Largely as a result of efforts by civil rights groups, considerable steps have been taken to change this curriculum image of America by introducing, as a corrective measure, textbooks, courses, and teaching materials dealing with black history and black culture. The result, unfortunately, still remains a distorted picture of the American nation. This nation has been a vital amalgam of the cultures of a multitude of ethnic groups. No one is in a better position to know this than the American labor movement which includes in its ranks workers who have descended from virtually every ethnic background in the world. The labor solidarity which we have achieved has been welded from the greatest conceivable diversity.

The melting of diverse ethnic cultures into a single nation is in fact the central story of America and it is a story in which the labor movement has played a major role.

We, therefore, welcome the Ethnic Heritage Studies Centers Act which has been introduced by Senator Schweiker. It would help to bring into focus one of the most important, but most educationally neglected aspects of American life.

C. GROUP CONSCIOUSNESS AND THE "NEW PLURALISM"

Group Conflict, Group Identity and Intergroup Relations

The National Project on Ethnic America is a depolarization program of the American Jewish Committee. Created in 1968 in response to the black-white conflict, the Project has worked toward raising America's consciousness of its white ethnic groups. Presently, the program is being financed by the Ford Foundation, and has been responsible for stimulating the "rediscovery" of a large segment of dissatisfied and neglected citizens.

The Project has as its over-all aim the enhancing of a "new pluralism," a pluralism growing out of "intergroup relationships which realistically appreciate group interests and group conflict but which neither degenerate into mere numerical power struggles nor ignore the legal centrality of the individual." Moreover, those responsible for the administration of the program assert that the depolarization and subsequent unity of the nation "will not result from ignoring difference—it can only come through an intelligent response by more universalist institutions to group life needs."

The document which follows is a transcript of an interview with the staff of the AJC's depolarization program: Irving M. Levine, Urban Projects Director; Judith Herman, Ethnic Groups Director; and Nancy Seifer, Director of Community Relations. Herein are contained their thoughts on and experiences with group conflict, group identity and intergroup relations.

SOURCE: **Irving M. Levine, Judith Herman and Nancy Seifer, Interview Held at Offices of the National Project on Ethnic America,** February 1973. Printed by permission.

QUESTION: What is the aim of the National Project on Ethnic America?

I.L.: The aim of the project is to depolarize tensions between whites and blacks. The aim of the project is to build bridges between blacks and whites. The aim of the project is to have white ethnics assert a legitimate agenda in terms of their own development, both socially and economically, and also in terms of their own identity needs. The secondary aim that has also been developed out of the project is to see whether we can bring a closer relationship between students and workers, which is sort of another compartmentalization of the problem. A third aim, and this grows in importance as we go deeper into the project, is to deal creatively with the differences and growing tensions between the elite forces in American life and the populist forces, those we call the "alienated constituents." How do you close the gap between the elite liberal, the people who are in the positions of liberal influence in society, and people who used to be their constituency but who are now alienated from their leadership.

QUESTION: What is the conceptual base of the project?

I.L.: The conceptual base was a depolarization conception—that was the essential one as the goal. The other was one of creating a sense of self-pride in ethnic consciousness on the part of many ethnic groups that have lost that sense. In a way the project is attempting to offer materials, study patterns, and structures to help the schools do more and better work concerning ethnicity and ethnic studies. So we are very, very involved in how to rationalize ethnic studies; how to diminish conflict from the variety of ethnic groups that are seeking a better representation. How is this done? The mechanics of how you do it is important.

I would say that the project started out on a depolarization basis, moved rapidly to developing consciousness of a white working class agenda for social change that did not clash with the black agenda, but could be expressed in parallel efforts even when coalitions were not ready to be built yet, and has now moved more and more to the question of what is the role of ethnicity in society even when it is not a polarizing force—when it is just an identity force.

The project has worked on two levels. It has worked on a class level—white working class—and the project has worked on an ethnicity model. Why?—because it is my feeling there is a bias in the thinking in America—a neo-Marxist bias—that wants to interpret everything from a classic class approach which is not as true of America as elsewhere. We are willing to work along with class determinists as well as the ethnic determinists because we think they both have a piece of the truth. In talking about the new pluralism, we are also trying very hard to develop a better language which will more adequately reflect American reality. We have not been adequately reflecting this reality. We don't have a precise language for, say, ethnic succession in American life. We don't have an adequate understanding of it. We don't have an adequate historical sense of what happened *vis-à-vis* the various "people systems" in our urban centers. Essentially our conventional American thinking has been rural and small town or structural regarding problems in terms of housing, employment, transportation, etc. So we really cannot effectively or without embarrassment talk about the kinds of power struggles that took place and make them legitimate power struggles. Although you can talk legitimately about a class power struggle, can't you? It's more difficult to be honest about ethnic power struggles or it was, until the black revolt.

QUESTION: You have talked about the "new pluralism." What

do you mean by the "new pluralism," and how is it different from the theory of "cultural pluralism" so popular in the first quarter of the 20th century?

I.L.: The assumption is that cultural pluralism meant that individuals ought to be able to maintain their identity and their group pride. That they would grow both as Americans who adopted a common culture and as individuals who identified with their own group. The new pluralism says that it accepts cultural pluralism. That it takes it one step further. It says that there are such things as group interests, group power, group conflict, group status, and group identity. And that it's played out on the political scene, the social scene, and not just in terms of individual identity, but also in terms of the way in which groups position themselves in society. That individuals have a right to use their group as a power vehicle even though they have no right to believe that their particular group ought to dominate all other groups. In a sense, we are saying that the group is a factor. Our particular analysis of the new pluralism is all things to the individual including legal rights, all attention to the group excluding legal rights.

QUESTION: What are the implications of the new pluralism in regard to politics, economics, education, and race relations?

I.L.: In terms of the establishment of group rights, some people view the new pluralism as the need for the establishment of group rights in law. If it moves in that direction, and we think that's a negative way, it will create a percentage society, a quota society, boundaries, and everything else which we are against. But, a new pluralism which accepts the flux and the dialectic between a wide variety of identities in which an individual can have his own private acceptance or denial of his group identity, is a more positive way of looking at it. I think that this debate is beginning to become a serious one in this country. The question is whether fair share will be implanted in law and in administrative procedure. Our opinion is that the minute you get to the question of reparations, fair share, percentages, and so on, you are establishing a society where every group has a right based upon whatever they define as the boundaries of their existence to ask for fair share. In a society where group fragmentation is potentially so great, this is a prescription for disaster and ends up organizing opposition even more fiercely to legitimate needs of minorities, such as American blacks.

J.H.: The old cultural pluralism was more of a slogan than a reality—it has not been real for a lot of people. But when you start talking about the new issues—how do you balance off the needs of the individual with the needs of his group or the needs of society as a whole? For instance, you have ethnic neighborhoods struggling to preserve themselves. They want to maintain their particular life-styles. That's legitimate. Now, if they got legal power to run their own neighborhoods, which some people are saying in terms of neighborhood government—maybe that's even legitimate, but what can't they do?

I.L.: If the legal power were based on race, religion, or ethnicity, it would be a denial of the individual right to not be engulfed in and ruled by those kinds of categories.

QUESTION: Don't you see a danger in this?

I.L.: Sure there's a danger in it. There are some things that nobody should deny an individual or to a group. And there are some things that nobody should deny to the nation as a whole. In other words, how do you work out this balance? An individual's right to economic advancement, education, life, liberty, and the pursuit of happiness cannot be limited by membership in his ethnic group or by non-membership. You shouldn't be rejected or accepted for anything because of what group you happen to be born in. On the other hand, the group that wants to stay together, to be cohesive, should not be restricted from doing that. How do you work out these relationships? What happens when legitimate group interests come into conflict? Who works it out? Presently, we don't have the right mechanisms in this society to do the job. What we are saying, is that a lot more people have to start asking new questions about the future of American political democracy. I would not want to give official legal power to Jews, blacks, Italians, Mormons, any more than to some kids who create a commune. On the other hand, I would recognize informal systems, organizational realities, legitimate group interests and political influences that sometimes lead to what some inaccurately term as the establishment of "turf."

QUESTION: How would the new pluralism deal with the present demands for ethnic and racial quotas in hiring?

J.H.: There's always been succession of one ethnic group by another and ethnic clustering. But, you don't establish the succession in law, even though laws and administrative procedure are legitimately changed to ease the transition of previously deprived groups.

QUESTION: I understand and accept that, but, how do you take 60,000 frightened school teachers, or policemen, or firemen who work for municipal government and tell them that they cannot be promoted anymore?

I.L.: You don't say that. You create new opportunities for them that have something to do with their professional skills in which they can willingly move into if the social pressure and the social tensions of their daily existence is such that it drives them "batty." They'd like relief from it. Providing you are tough minded about defending individual rights, due process, and legitimate merit systems, you must still recognize that ethnic pressures will lead to decline of the influence in a particular part of the economy of previously entrenched ethnic groups. We need well thought out transition programs that even encompass legislation for the benefit of displaced middle class professionals. This can be done in much the same way that a lower class black community can introduce a poverty program. It takes a little social imagination to find out which program will do it.

QUESTION: How do you answer someone who has studied for years and in the middle of his career the rules are changed?

I.L.: He has a right to be protected and helped just as blacks have a right to entry and advancement.

QUESTION: The rules have been changed.

I.L.: I know, but we should struggle not to allow it to happen in quite the destructive way it has happened. We're talking about two things. We're talking about increasing affirmative action for blacks and other minorities, but we are also for an idea called alternative action, which is a concept the National Project on Ethnic America developed which is designed to protect the people in the system and to give them alternatives to their present existence, if they are being pressured, and on a basis that is comparable to what they now have. How can you do it? It surely isn't easy. Many say it is impossible. I disagree, we have to work out the mechanics.

J.H.: It also means that the people who are moving in can move into those alternatives too. Right now people are fighting to move in at the bottom, thus you move people at the top up. All you do is perpetuate group status distinctions. People have to be able to move in at all levels. This kind of change should be seen as something normal and natural in the process of American ethnic succession. If we look at what happened in other cities, and in other times, you see that the only way this thing was resolved was by creating expansion or by raising the consciousness of people who were being pushed out—that there were other places to go.

I.L.: It could be devised. It's people who stand with their foot at the door or those who walk in and say, "I don't care what happens to you, my time has come," who create backlash. Our concern is that we devise other models, additional models. We are talking about a strategy, for example, of taking winnable areas such as the expansion of medical education in places where it's proven there is a shortage. There's a national statistical proof that the doctor shortage has been maintained by the A.M.A. for a long time. We think that we can build a multi-ethnic coalition —black, white ethnic, Jewish, around the increase in medical school places. How do we know? It was done in Indiana recently, and a lot more money was easily appropriated by the Indiana legislature because of widespread popular support. Something like thirty percent more students are being turned out. We think that we can take a five year period or so, and turn out one hundred percent more medical students with a very different use of facilities, a very different kind of training, and a very different kind of financing pattern. That one hundred percent increase could take up the slack in all the different ethnic groups competing for places. All would do better under the system we're talking about than under the present system. Can you do it? If you don't fight for it, you don't know. You can't achieve such a complex task by sitting around knocking each other off, but by creating the coalition, naming the amount of years, getting the piece of legislation, and forcing it rapidly into public consciousness. Otherwise, you'll never get it. That's why I think we're a little different in this agency. Our position is that there are two postures in this quota system. You can be protectionist, you can be protective. We'd rather be protective. Protective means alternative action as well as affirmative action. Protectionist means that anything that hurts us in terms of the present situation is bad.

QUESTION: I want you to discuss the various ethnic pressure groups which have emerged. Do you welcome them?

I.L.: You have to. It's not a question of welcoming the individual organization. There's going to be problems. All of these organizations are rooted in such a wide variety of different traditions—different group histories—that to expect the organizations that have emerged to be coherent, smooth, professional, and ethical, is nonsense. They were meeting a need. They may have been demagogic—the wrong forms—they may turn Fascistic, they may be racist. Our role is to see that they don't become that way. A major role of the project has been to organize white ethnics who have reached a point where they might be mainstream leaders, to understand a bit more about their own backgrounds and communities. We have a network throughout the country of large numbers of young Italians, young Poles, young Ukranians, people who are modern man. I would say, who are professionals—teachers, social workers, and everything else. Who are liberals, who are progressives, who have found themselves on the peace marches, the civil rights marches, who denied their own heritage and moved into the black movement. We've said hold on to your social idealism, but recognize the importance of your own roots as well as the drama of the commitment to peace and justice. We've given them a rationale. We've helped establish them as legitimate leaders of their own people. We can cite you twenty-five who are in positions of influence at this particular time as a result of attaching themselves to our project, and we can cite you organizations that they now head. Many are still involved in internecine warfare for control of funds, which is always the early stage. But, out of the internecine warfare, out of the positioning, you are going to get a number of statesmen. People who are going to move into the ranks of real leadership. And they will have a rootedness in their own people, which is something they didn't have before. There's two types of leadership. There's the old European oriented, nationalist-chauvinist kinds of ethnic leaders, and there's a new group coming who are "bridge people type"—coalitionists. We prefer the latter.

QUESTION: Just to conclude, may I have a prognosis from each of you. Which way are we going and what do you foresee?

J.H.: I have a feeling that people are not going to settle for lives that are fairly dull and uninteresting. Some of the energy the ethnics expend will be in an anti-change direction. Nevertheless, I think that people like us are going to be successful in helping others understand how change can benefit people in their own life-styles. It's not going to be an easy thing to do because pressure against change is so easy to succumb to. And, many people want to "hide under the bed." It's going to be a very delicate kind of thing. Some people will come from under the bed and relate to each other.

N.S.: I think that it depends upon the government that is in power at the time. Also on the social factors and on the economy. There's a tremendous relationship between identity and economic need. In addition, we must not discount the future role of women in these communities. As they become more involved in jobs of their own, in community activities, and explore their different options, they will contribute significantly to the impending change.

I.L.: I think that there's going to be a big struggle in the next five years between the advocates of a progressive center and a conservative center. And that the nature of the progressive center, in order to win, is going to root itself in the life-styles of the very poor, near poor, the lower middle class, and in the new professional and technical advocate types who make up a change oriented middle and upper class.

The Ethnic Neighborhood and Group Identity

Those who advocate the concept of neighborhood government charge that city administrations have disregarded community interests, particularly in areas which were made up of varied ethnic groups with conspicuous subcultures. According to Donna E. Shalala, Professor of Political Science at the City University of New York, the "ethnic characteristics of various urban neighborhoods lead to differences in the kinds of government services desired; however, the public service bureaucracy tends to promote sameness from community to community."

In order to correct this situation, Professor Shalala suggested the establishment of a "neighborhood government system" supported by community "veto groups." She asserted that this innovation "would provide opportunities for neighborhood participation in the planning and policy-making process, as well as in the provision of services."*

In the selection which follows, "The Ethnic Neighborhood: Leave Room for a Boccie Ball," Barbara Mikulski discussed the problem as it affects America's ethnic communities. In her enlightening essay, she reported that due to the lack of an effective political voice, these neighborhoods were being "demolished by politicians, planners, and public policy makers."

SOURCE: Barbara Mikulski, "The Ethnic Neighborhood: Leave Room for a Boccie Ball," in *Pieces of a Dream: the Ethnic Worker's Crisis with America,* ed. by Michael Wenk, S. M. Tomasi and Gene Baroni (New York: Center for Migration Studies, 1972), pp. 55–61.

America's ethnic neighborhoods are alternately romanticized or demolished by politicians, planners, and public policy makers. In the first place we don't appreciate what we have when we have it. We have traditionally slaughtered or destroyed that which we later consider to be valuable. For example, we slaughtered the buffalo, we slaughtered the eagle and then we build reservations and say, "Oh, wasn't it a shame", and then we build cities. We tear down and destroy things and then we have a thing called the Smithsonian Institute. Only there is no Smithsonian Institute; there is no collector's item for neighborhoods like Little Italy or Polish Hill. Though these neighborhoods are romanticized, they are not necessarily appreciated. They represent small towns in the middle of big cities, and this is the real valuable part of those cities.

It's nice to come into Little Italy and groove on the garlic, but there is a lot about the German Towns or the Little Italy's of America that represent its unseen heart. The family structure, the ethnic organizations, political clubs, the relationship between school, church, and lending institutions form the community. It is not bricks, mortar, or European recipes, but how people live with each

* Donna E. Shalala, *Neighborhood Governance: Issues and Proposals* (New York: The American Jewish Committee, 1971), pp. 4–5.

other and the institutions they create that form the neighborhood. The Commuter Romantics relish the surface but don't perceive the substance.

In my neighborhood the parish church formed the nucleus of the community; linked to it were men's organizations called the Holy Name Society, the Ladies Sodality, Boy Scout troups, Girl Scout troups, Catholic Youth Organizations, Drum and Bugle Corps, the whole community of Highlandtown was involved in either that Church or the others like it. They look at St. Leo's, love the stained glass, and are esthetically excited about the Bell Tower. But to the people of Little Italy, history is not the buildings but what happened in those buildings—the Inauguration Party of the first Italian Mayor, the Farewell Party for the first to go to West Point, the christening of the fourth great-grandchild of the local grocer, the funeral of one of the early immigrant women. These are the events of life commemorated and lived with all the feelings and emotions that constitute an authentic community.

One of the problems of the cities is the lack of emotion. The only kind of emotion that is being played out, particularly by the media, is the emotion of violence; not the emotion of pride, integrity, or honor. And yet these are in our neighborhoods too. But, they are not perceived by the audiences that come by on little field trips or planning expeditions.

One of the problems with ethnic neighborhoods is that they have always been considered the other side of the tracks.

Being "put down" had an effect on lots of us. It eroded our spirit. It battered our sense of security. So, many split to the suburbs where they could join the homogenized melting pot. The exodus started after World War II, accelerated by FHA financing which made it possible to live in a house that had three cubic inches of grass and assured status. If you moved to suburbia, you would finally find the recognition and acceptance from the larger America that the people in the old neighborhood had always wanted.

The GI Bill gave many of our men the economic ladder to go up and the FHA gave them the money to get out. Meanwhile, back in the old neighborhood there was no FHA financing available. So those who wanted to buy houses couldn't get an FHA or VA loan. The only loan that you can get is through the building and loans that the ethnics themselves created and that necessitated a one third down payment. So, that if a guy who came back from Vietnam and wanted to buy a $12,000 house in my neighborhood and was 21 years old, didn't have $4,000 for a down payment, he couldn't get a mortgage. So here he is. He has risked his life for his country, he wants to live in the old neighborhood, he wants to be part of the city scene, and there is no kind of encouragement; there is no kind of mechanism to do that. There is target area funding for housing and redevelopment but that rarely, if ever, touches the blue collar neighborhoods. Compounding the problem is the fact that banking institutions refuse to lend money to the middle cities' communities because they call us "gray areas," "transitional areas" or whatever. So the only people who can then buy those houses when the elderly die are speculators and the block buster. There are lots of ways that these housing problems can be met. One would be for the public sector to do away with target area funding and make that money available generally across the board.

Now, these invisible bureaucrats have several strikes against them. First, they think they have all the answers; that they are enlightened and we are the reactionary. It's my feeling that the people in the middle cities have the vitality, have the concepts, and vision to make the cities work. Why? Because they know what's going on there. Very often the people who plan the programs are people who have had no culture base and by that I mean culture in the sociological sense. They know about symphonies, and they know about Bach and Beethoven, and stuff like that, but by culture, I mean where it is rooted into the traditions, values, and social practices of a people. Because their own lives have been so sterile, they tend to plan sterile programs. They're so hung up in their organizations charts, they forget that they're organizing for people, people who live within a family and a family that lives within a community. They forget that you have to plan recreation that's not all team, field, male oriented. When you plan recreation for a neighborhood, you've got to plan it with the family orientation, places where little kids can roller skate, both boys and girls. You have to plan things that senior citizens can do, not a golf course where you have to buy fancy equipment, maybe miniature golf and leave room for boccie ball. Now those guys wouldn't even know what a boccie ball is. They probably think it's a new rock band.

Now, who's going to sensitize them? The same people who play boccie ball.

One of the bright hopes of this country is the new public interest groups being formed. A public interest group is a fancy term to mean a block club . . . an improvement association . . . a coalition to fight the expressway . . . a welfare rights group. It means all of these local citizens' groups that are organized either around a neighborhood issue or community or their own way of life. It's these groups that are really the new sources of power within neighborhoods. It's not the old political machine; they have gotten out of touch with their community. But, now local public interest organizations are being formed, and these local organizations are forming coalitions with other groups. They're forming coalitions, not because they love one another, but they're coming together out of mutual need and mutual dependency because they feel it is necessary for their survival. And that kind of coalition creates a sense of respect and commitment that I've never seen before.

These are the groups that Ralph Nader talks about. The people who are in those groups are a new breed. They are what Nader calls the "citizen advocate". The ethnic "citizen advocate" represents a new way for Americans to obtain their identity. In the past, Americans have gained their identity and sense of meaning from the work that they did. But, the "citizen advocate" now gets his own identity from participation in his own community and enjoying his own ethnicity.

We were organized in the '30's. Those organizations centered around two things: preserving our own identity which came through church, school, fraternal organizations, Polish day nurseries, and creating our own economy. The Pulaski Building and Loan Association lent us money and the Polish National Alliance gave insurance. We organized these institutions for our own survival. The downtown banks wouldn't lend money to people named Konarski. We also organized in our factories and wherever we worked because we saw that we were not being protected. Our wages were low and we were suffering from all the abuses that came with the so-called great industrial revolution.

Then came the '50's. When I was growing up in the '50's, I used to go to Interfaith Baseball Nights. That's how we were going to create brotherhood. Somehow or other, if we all sat around and watched somebody sock a home run on that one hot night in July, we were all going to love one another the other 364 days out of the year.

Then, we got more sophisticated and along came the '60's. We got into sensitivity sessions and we held hands, and we learned to sing hymns, and we hugged and kissed each other.

Now we are in 1972, and we're still a very polarized society, because we always talked about "us" and "them". What do "they" want? How can we help "them" today? What can "we" do for "you"?

But when you've got an issue and you say I've got a problem and who else has the problem, and you get together because you need each other, that makes it a whole different ball game.

And, all of a sudden the average working class citizen looked around in his old neighborhood . . . he looked around at his job . . . and he knew that he had had it, and that he wasn't making it and that nobody cared about him, and he became very angry. Like so many of us, he felt that the Republicans ignored him and the Democrats took him for granted. He said that he was upset and concerned because he had fought in the Korean War, he had fought at Pork Chop Hill, and now the very country that he fought to defend, that very same government was forcing him to organize in his own neighborhood; organize to protect himself against an unwanted freeway, organize to protect himself from truck traffic that runs through residential streets. He had to organize against the very government that he fought to defend.

Sometimes people ask if you organize around the issue of ethnicity. I think that's a possibility; however, I think that the real thing to organize around are issues related to very concrete things like a person's neighborhood and the problems faced in the neighborhoods. The problems people face because of their job or economic position. I think you organize around economic, political, and social issues. And those issues are the same whether we're talking about a working class black community or a working class white community or the barrio for the Chicano, or whatever. And it's those kinds of issues that can bring us together and cross racial lines. For example, the whole issue of drugs is eating every community up whether it's the Italian community, the Polish community, the Chicano community, Puerto Rican community, or black community. But, once we win the issues, drugs, pollution, freeways, transportation, all of the things that are always listed in the latest issue of the *New Republic* or *Nation* or *Transaction* or any urban crisis textbook. Once we win those issues, we still are going to have to live, we still are going to have to have traditions for births and values for when people move from adolescence to adulthood. That's one of the things that is so sterile about America. It's my belief that the community organizations and the organizing around issues will get people the resources to live and it will be ethnicity and its rituals and traditions that will help people determine how they should live. I'll be glad when I stop the expressway. But, on Christmas Eve I won't be worried about transportation. I want to celebrate with the Wigilia and Opatek and all the things that have been in my family for a thousand years, whether there was an expressway, or Czar, or whatever was the enemy of the time.

The reason I maintain the orientation to organize around social, political, and economic issues is that they form a common basis. If you organize around ethnicity, you then constantly have to worry about the differences among people. You have to worry about ethnic pride, ethnic consciousness, and ethnocentricism. Ethnic pride and ethnic consciousness could provide a richness to this America that we really don't have now. But, ethnocentricism will sow the seeds of our own defeat and our own divisiveness.

However, I think there should be ethnic organizations. I think there should be things to raise the consciousnesses of people based on their ethnicity. I wanted to know the story of what the Poles contributed to America and I'd like to share that with other people. I want to have organizations that commemorate certain historical occasions and I think it's important to have these types of organizations. But, they're not the ones that are going to bring about political change. They're going to be the ones that provide a certain kind of way that will enrich our lifestyle.

The old neighborhood isn't the way it was when I was a kid. When I was growing up, you had a lot of activity that centered around the church. There is no other institution in America outside the family that's under greater attack than the church. And, the concepts of family, church, and community are the three things that are under the most discussion in America right now and quite frankly the ethnic people find all of this horrifying. They are horrified because their whole life was centered around these two major institutions. The Catholic School which formed such a keystone to the community is under financial distress. These are just a few examples of what's happening to the old neighborhood. Some of the other problems that are being faced by the old neighborhood are those issues confronting the local entrepreneur. My father has been in the grocery business for thirty-six years on the same corner. He works seventy hours a week in that grocery store. He provided food for that neighborhood when people didn't even have refrigeration but kept their food on ice. The store used to be open at 5:00 A.M. so women could come and buy fresh meat for their husbands to carry to lunch down at the steel mill. My father's whole business is oriented to that community. He gives credit when people need it. If the steel mill goes on strike, my father carries families on the books until that strike is over. His whole business is characterized by a high degree of personalism. However, with the new kinds of prices and the competition from supermarkets, he's being pushed out of business. So are many small businessmen like him. If we want them to survive, we have to come up with a new way for them to operate.

I feel the city's being abandoned. There was an article in *Public Interest* that I felt described what's happening in the city very well. It says in some ways the federal government is treating the city like a sandbox. Do you know what that means? They give us a few toys, and they let us fight over them like kids do in a sandbox. They give us a toy called the Community Action Program, or they give us a toy called Model Cities, and then we fight over who's going to get the Iron Enriched Milk Program, when in fact we need many other kinds of things. But one of the things that's happening because of this is that coalitions are forming . . . new kinds of organizations that would never have been formed before.

Now, what has happened is that we have come together, and we have organized to get the resources that we need for our local communities, for those decentralized areas. But we have found that the resources are not there to meet our needs. For all of the power that we've tried to develop, for all of the coalitions that we've tried to develop, those resources are not in the City of Baltimore today. Everywhere we go, we're told that there's no money.

What are we going to do? Where is the money? The Mayor

tells us he doesn't have it. The Governor tells us he doesn't have it. Well, I'm not sure where the money is, and I'm not sure how we're going to get it. We have the coalitions. We have the will. We have a different kind of spirit—it's a much more populist spirit. But where is it all going to go?

The question is not who speaks for us because we speak for ourselves. That fact is we don't need incentives to get started, we need help to keep going.

There are a lot of programs that are just very basic. When you talk about police protection, police are police. He's the guy on the beat. You can put him on a bike, you can put him in a car, you can put him on a team. You can call it the Soul Squad, you can call it anything, but you need that cop on the beat and where is the money. A cop on the beat whether he is part of a Soul Squad, Bike Squad, Tree Squad, Narco Squad, or whatever squad still gets paid $10,000 a year and where are we going to get the money. And it's those kind of issues, the nuts and bolts, that we need help with. But help means money. How do we get that money and put it back in the cities? Neighborhoods are as much of a resource as are water and electricity. But for some reason America is willing to put millions into nuclear power plants and nothing into neighborhoods.

The spirit of the people is going to change this. There is a bigger movement going on now than we realize. It is happening in the ethnic communities of this nation. It will be both the agony and the hope of the country as we move into the 21st century.

Index